ADOBE®
Acrobat® 5
MASTER CLASS
Interactivity and Multimedia for PDF

PATTIE BELLE HASTINGS, BJØRN AKSELSEN, & SANDEE COHEN

Adobe Acrobat 5 Master Class:
Interactivity and Multimedia for PDF

Pattie Belle Hastings, Bjørn Akselsen, and Sandee Cohen

This Adobe Press book is published by Peachpit Press.
Peachpit Press
1249 Eighth Street
Berkeley, CA 94710
tel 510.524-2178
fax 510.524-2221
www.peachpit.com

Peachpit Press is a division of Pearson Education

For the latest on Adobe Press books, go to
www.adobe.com/adobepress

Book Design: Bjørn Akselsen, Pattie Belle Hastings
Cover Design: Bjørn Akselsen, Pattie Belle Hastings
Technical Editor: Max Wyss
Editor: Cary Norsworthy
Copy Editors: Mindi R. Englart, Janet Reed
WebDAV Administrator: Adam Z Lein
Production Coordinator: David Van Ness
Index: Karin Arrigoni

ISBN 0-201-74883-5
9 8 7 6 5 4 3 2 1

Printed and bound in the United States of America

For August Layne, whose curiosity and zest for life inspires us in so many ways.
For Cosimo, Viola, and Pixel because life would be so dull without the love and company of pets.

Contents

Preface

As designers, we frequently become frustrated with the demands the computer revolution imposes on us in order to stay current. The learning curve on some of the software is so steep that we can't become current on one version before we are asked again to upgrade! In the beginning, there were simply marker pens, the T-square, and Letraset press type. The playing field was level. There's something we miss about the immediacy, spontaneity, and tactileness of those stone-age tools. Now, we have all retooled to become system analysts, cross-platform specialists, business executives, and so forth. Yes, we love all the new applications that give us the ability to set type and print out proofs from our desktop. But when you add everything a designer needs to know in terms of interactivity and multimedia, our life has not become easier, but more complex.

We've traded in the mystique of the creative process with something that is almost predictably programmable. The only problem is that we don't have time to program. Who hasn't opened manuals for software, such as Macromedia Director, with a perennial optimism: "I'm going to learn this software by reading a little every day before I go to bed."? Dream on.

Our bookshelf is filled with good intentions—evidence of our unfulfilled fantasies of software proficiency. This only adds to the insecurity that "perhaps we will become dinosaurs." But, now and then, something comes along that really seems too good to be true. Adobe Acrobat is one of those things. In its inception, it was simply considered a quick cross-platform document distribution program. It's now become a tool that brings together many of the software capabilities we have labored to learn.

Acrobat not only provides a quick way to send documents from a PC to a Macintosh, it is now a full-fledged multimedia, web-integrated program. Acrobat makes it simple for content providers to distribute their creations without needing to be experts on multiple software programs. From our desktop, we can now create files that incorporate sound, movies, interactive buttons, forms that calculate, and so forth—in just a few simple steps.

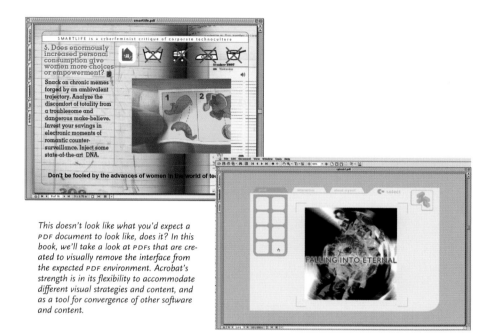

This doesn't look like what you'd expect a PDF document to look like, does it? In this book, we'll take a look at PDFs that are created to visually remove the interface from the expected PDF environment. Acrobat's strength is in its flexibility to accommodate different visual strategies and content, and as a tool for convergence of other software and content.

Pattie Belle and Bjørn became involved with Acrobat after they decided to use the program for some experimental work. They instantly realized that they could do the same sort of work that everyone else was doing—but without the steep learning curve that other applications required. Sandee started teaching Acrobat when the Acrobat instructor at her school moved out of town. It didn't take long for all of us to fall in love with the interactive and multimedia features in Acrobat. Without too much effort, we were able to create buttons, play movies, and design presentations.

If there is one thing we're disappointed with regarding Acrobat, it's how few people know the about the multimedia powers and features of the program. That's why we wrote this book. We're convinced that after you see how easy it is to create sophisticated projects like the ones featured here, you will want to create your own presentations using Acrobat. We are convinced that Acrobat has a bright future, due to its appeal to people like us; those who want to have access to interactivity and multimedia without having to switch careers.

Acknowledgments

From Pattie Belle and Bjørn:

Over the course of a year or so, we have labored intensely to make this book happen. As designers we have grown accustomed to handling large projects and page-intensive publications, but nothing really compares to the mental juggling that must happen to manifest the writing and design of an entire book.

Writing isn't the only thing we do. So, the fact that this book did happen is no little feat. We managed to carve out hours here and there from an already overextended schedule filled with family duties, design practice, teaching, and the myriad activities of daily life. We often desired to avoid the challenging for the mundane or routine, in order to get through the day. We now know that plodding along, day by day, in the face of an overwhelming task, was a worthwhile strategy.

In appreciating what we have accomplished, we're panicked by the idea that we might forget to thank someone for the immense support and help that we have received.

The biggest thanks go to our co-author Sandee Cohen, who took the ball and ran with it. We could not have finished this book without her. Sandee came into this project with an enthusiasm about Acrobat that equaled our own. Her excitement and energy propelled the project to completion and we are so incredibly, enormously grateful to her.

We've been so fortunate to have a wide-ranging, global network of PDF authorities take interest in the book and offer their suggestions. Thank you all. Special thanks to Max Wyss in Switzerland, Ted Padova, author of the PDF Bible (among other titles), Kurt Foss and Karl de Abrew of Planet PDF, and all the forum members of Planet PDF. Huge thanks also go to Adam Z Lein, our intrepid webDAV administrator.

The list is not complete without the mention of the wonderful people at Peachpit Press, all of whom have helped the bits and pieces come together. Thanks to all of you in general, and to Cary Norsworthy in particular, for her unwavering support.

We don't want this list to be too long, but we want to mention the enormous bond we feel with our daughter. In many ways, she may be the one who has had to sacrifice most, in that our evenings and weekends have been a series of tag-team events. She's had to endure many an absentminded nod, and a "perhaps later, dear." We cannot help feeling that whatever the price was, we as a family have come out of it stronger.

Of course, family, colleagues, and friends have all pitched in and offered emotional support. Next year we'll be home for Thanksgiving!

From Sandee:

My thanks go to all the members of the team mentioned above. In addition, I would like to thank Pattie Belle and Bjørn for asking me to join them in the project. If it was difficult to adjust to a new member of the team coming in mid-way, they never showed it. This has been one of the best collaborative experiences in my career.

I also would like to thank Nancy Ruenzel of Peachpit Press for giving me the time to take on this project—time that should have been spent on other work.

A big thank you goes to the staff of Photospin.com who have graciously allowed me to use photos from their collection in my books. Not only have I been able to use their print images, but their collection of movies has been excellent. I can't think of a better source for stock photography and multimedia content.

Special thanks also go to Dov Isaacs of Adobe Systems who took time out of his schedule to explain the differences between how Acrobat Distiller creates PDF files and how InDesign exports PDF files.

Finally, I would like to thank Michael Randazzo and the staff of the New School Computer Instruction Center for giving me the time to write, in addition to my teaching assignments.

1

Introduction

As this book goes to press there have been more than 400 million copies of Adobe

Acrobat Reader distributed worldwide. While the majority of PDF files are still

created with the end result of printing in mind, we will concentrate on the cre-

ation of completely digital and interactive documents. We like to think of Adobe

Acrobat 5 as the point at which all the other tools we use converge. It is the place

that Adobe InDesign meets Adobe AfterEffects, or Adobe Photoshop meets audio,

or at times where all the applications we use meet at once. So, rather than jump

into the middle of Acrobat 5, we thought we'd start at the beginning and take

you through the entire process. In this chapter we'll look at basic concepts, the

changes and improvements to Acrobat 5, tools, menus, and the interface, to

bring the beginner up to speed.

1.1   About This Book

How do you define a program like Adobe Acrobat? In this book, you'll learn that it's a stage for print, movies, animations, interactive elements, and sounds. It's tempting to get lost in the details trying to cover every possible facet of the program. However, we have focused on providing an easy recipe-style book to help you create interactive and screen-based PDF documents.

So, then, let's take a moment to tell you what this book is not. Most important, this book is not a comprehensive guide to creating PDF documents for printing, prepress, or even distribution based on printing work flows. Prepress is a totally different area of the PDF world. There are other books that cover using PDF for prepress and commercial printing.

We don't try to detail every nuance and option for working with the tools or commands. We also expect you to have a certain familiarity with beginner-level tasks, such as opening menus, choosing tools, and selecting objects. Of course, we'll give you enough steps to get familiar with Acrobat. But we believe that the best way to learn is to play and experiment.

OUR GOALS

So, who is the book for? (We're glad you asked.) This book is for anyone who suspects there's more to Acrobat than initially meets the eye. Sandee remembers many years ago when she opened a CD-ROM that had a series of interactive files demonstrating new features in Adobe Photoshop. There were movies, sounds, screen shots, and links to background material. She got even more excited when she found out the presentation materials were assembled in Adobe Acrobat. Perhaps you've viewed a presentation with enhanced custom-navigational tools and wondered how it was put together.

Most likely, you are already familiar with Acrobat. (It's hard to find anyone with a computer who has never received a PDF file—even if it was just to read the installation instructions for a software application.) Perhaps you converted a spreadsheet file into a PDF so that your client could read the information. You may have been one of the millions of American taxpayers who downloaded a PDF version of various Internal Revenue Service documents. You may have heard that Acrobat is the major growth software for Adobe Systems Inc., and you'd like to know what all the fuss is about. It could also be that you hadn't given any previous consideration to the opportunities of PDF until you picked up this book. Personally, we think PDF (and Acrobat) will conquer the world.

MORE THAN JUST PDF

However, this book is far more than just click-and-drag exercises for learning how to create Acrobat files. We've tried to do something a little different from the usual computer how-to books—that is, to look at the philosophy and design theories behind successful interactive PDF presentations.

For example, it's not enough just to give you the steps to create a navigation button that moves the user from page to page. You also need to think about what types of documents need their own navigational elements

> **ⓘ INFORMATION TIPS**
>
> *Look for these yellow sidebars throughout the book. They contain references to websites and other resources you can go to for more information. They may contain special tips and techniques or give information regarding special files you can find on the CD-ROM that comes with this book.*

or when you can use the built-in navigation buttons in Acrobat. However, as soon as we start those types of discussions we enter a world where there are no hard and fast rules. So don't be surprised if there are sections of the book that ask questions without providing all the answers.

ⓘ MAC OS 9 RAM

We recommend an Acrobat RAM allotment of 64 megabytes minimum for Mac OS 9 users. If you have never changed the memory of an application before, select the application icon (it can't be running) and go to File>Get Info>Memory. Change the Minimum Size to the Preferred Size recommendation. Then change the Preferred Size to 64,000 K (or more if you can spare it). This is not a problem for Mac OS X or Windows users.

HOW THE BOOK WORKS

We assume that you have already installed Acrobat 5 as instructed by Adobe. In addition to the Acrobat Master Class CD, you may want to have the Acrobat 5 application CD handy. It contains many helpful documents and samples, some of which we refer to throughout the book.

We expect that our readers will have very different levels of familiarity with the various Acrobat products. So we have designed most of the book to be relatively freestanding—you can easily skip around among the chapters or reverse the order in which you attack them.

This book features QuickStep exercises that help you learn how to work with Acrobat's tools and commands. There are two parts to these QuickSteps: numbered exercises within the body of the pages and visual step-by-step illustrations at the bottom of the pages. This gives you a variety of options in how to use the exercises.

You will also see feature pages that show how the tools and techniques in each chapter are combined to create groundbreaking Acrobat documents. We are grateful to the many designers who have allowed us to feature their work in the book, and given us permission to include their documents on the CD. This means you can dissect the documents by opening them up and looking at how all the elements have been assembled.

Finally, there are many Acrobat designers who have become quite famous in the world of PDF. The showcase sections of the book give you a chance to see how some of these experts work. What kinds of problems do they have to deal with? What tools do they use? What are their backgrounds and training? These showcases will give you an understanding of the process that professional Acrobat creators use.

Once you feel confident with the tools and Acrobat work environment, you may be ready to start using some of the many keyboard shortcuts. In the back of the book we have included a QuickGuide to Tools and Shortcuts that covers the main functions of the application.

CROSS PLATFORM ISSUES

We admit that we all got our start working with Macintosh computers. However, we recognize that one of the attractions of working with PDF documents is that the same file can be displayed on many different platforms. So we recognize that many designers work with either Macintosh or Windows operating systems (and others...) creating Acrobat documents.

For the most part, there is very little difference between Acrobat features on Windows or Macintosh. However, there are times, especially for keyboard shortcuts, where there are differences between the two platforms. We have labeled those differences with (w) for Windows and (m) for Macintosh. We've also shown two sets of illustrations where there is a significant difference between the two platforms.

WHAT'S ON THE CD-ROM

Due to their generosity and spirit of sharing information and ideas, many of our expert Acrobat contributors have allowed us to include their work on the accompanying CD-ROM. We have also included PDF documents that have been created by the coauthors—some in the course of writing this book.

How-to books and step-by-step descriptions are great, but nothing compares to working with and examining the actual documents that are being described. With these documents, you can experience all the special interactive elements in the PDF file. In fact, we believe that the CD that accompanies this book is as valuable as the book itself.

Even better, most of the PDFs on the CD are unprotected, so you may examine them using Acrobat's tools and properties to see how they were designed and created. A few of the documents contain proprietary knowledge, so you'll be able to view the PDF files, but they will be secured from editing and copying. We have also included a special PDF with links to all the resources mentioned in the book. So instead of having to copy and type in URL addresses, you can use the PDF document as a set of links.

> **MAC VS. WINDOWS**
>
> *Don't be alarmed! Our method of indicating keyboard commands might be slightly different from what you've seen before. Throughout the text, we use (w) for Windows and (m) for Macintosh.*

Finally, we have included a few goodies on the CD, including some custom stamps and navigation buttons to use in your own files. Be sure to look for the Goodies folder on the Acrobat 5 Master Class CD!

QUICKSTEPS

You can follow the Quick-Step exercises three different ways.

Read the numbered steps within the main body of the text. These steps give you detailed instructions as to which commands to choose and which buttons to click. The text also gives you insights about why to choose the options. We recommend this method for those who are familiar with Acrobat and understand the interface.

Look through the numbered illustrations in the brown area at the bottom of the pages. This is a visual crash course in how to do the exercise. We recommend this method for those who have already read through the body text and need a quick refresher.

Use both the numbered exercises and the illustrations. This is the most complete technique. We recommend it for beginning students who need to understand the concepts behind the technique as well as make sure they have clicked the right buttons.

FEATURES

Features give guided tours of PDF documents we think will be of particular interest to you. You can find some of the featured PDF documents on the CD-ROM. This gives you an excellent opportunity to play with the finished PDF document. It also lets you go on your own expedition to explore all the settings for the various Acrobat forms, links, comments, and other elements.

Some of these featured pages may seem far beyond your current abilities. Don't let that intimidate you. We hope you will find these features inspiring examples of what you can do with Acrobat.

SHOWCASES

Showcases are special sections within the chapters that feature leading experts working with Acrobat.

Think of these showcases as guest lecturers to our Master Class. Instead of step-by-step exercises, you get a chance to understand how the experts work, what kind of clients they work with, and what other tools they use.

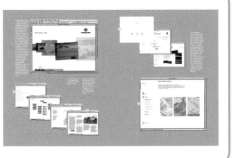

1.2 | What's New in Acrobat 5

In this section we'll outline some of the differences between Acrobat 4 and Acrobat 5. If you are still using Acrobat 4, this information should help you decide to upgrade to version 5. Acrobat 5 has improvements and new tools in virtually all areas of its interactive and multimedia features, whether it's sharing comments through your web browser, security updates, or JavaScript implementation.

WORK ENVIRONMENT

As soon as you open Acrobat 5, you'll see many changes in the document windows and work environment.

User Interface/Work Area

If you have just upgraded from version 4, the Acrobat 5 screen will look very different. The Tool bar on the left side of the screen has moved under the menu bar, so it resembles the tool bars in Microsoft Office applications. The tools can be rearranged or detached into free-floating palettes.

Navigation Pane Enhancements

Bookmarks, Comments, and Signatures can be accessed from the navigation pane, where you can click on the tabs to expose these features and additional options. New palettes include the Info palette and the Fields palette, which displays all the form fields in a document. The Tags palette allows you to tag the content structure information, used for reflow. You can move the palettes around freely or dock them in the Palette Tab area.

SECURITY FEATURES

Acrobat 5 comes with an option for 128-bit security in addition to the 40-bit encryption of Acrobat 4, enabling you to choose between the two levels. The new security features provide much more flexibility in allowing permissions for printing, copying, and access. The 128-bit encryption level is not backward compatible—meaning those with Acrobat Reader 4 will not be able to view the document.

DIGITAL SIGNATURES

Digital Signatures have been in Acrobat since version 4, but are now better embedded and include certificate-based Self-Sign-Security. Acrobat 5 allows third-party digital signatures to plug into Acrobat files. Acrobat also comes with a Public-Private key option that allows workgroups to authenticate documents without requiring a third-party certification. You can also request and exchange security certificates from within Acrobat via e-mail.

ENHANCED BATCH PROCESSING

Acrobat 5 has powerful Batch Processing controls that let you string together a sequence of commands as one super-command. The Batch Processing command can process a selection of files automatically. Once you have created a batch processing command, you can store and reuse it. You can also write your own commands using JavaScript. Acrobat 5 comes with several preset batch processing commands.

ENHANCED DISABILITY ACCESS

Some new features make it easier for those with disabilities to access PDF files. For instance, the high-contrast settings make it easier for those with limited vision to read pages. Acrobat 5 lets you create documents that can be converted from printed text into speech using screen readers (currently Windows only). Version 5 also adds a wide variety of keyboard shortcuts that make it easier for those with disabilities to use all the features in Acrobat.

IMAGE AND TEXT EXTRACTION

With the new Extract Image As command, you may export a PDF as an image in the following formats: TIFF, JPEG, and PNG. You can also use the Save As command to convert the text in an Acrobat document to RTF (rich text format) files. There's a new XML export plug-in as well.

From the Save As command, you can export your PDF files as EPS, PostScript, TIFF, JPEG, or PNG files. Each page in a document is saved individually as a separate image file and some of the formats have settings that can be customized.

SPELL-CHECK

The new spell-check feature lets you check the spelling in the document, and form fields and comments using the dictionaries for 16 languages, including several English varieties. You can also add to words and edit the dictionaries.

ENHANCED ONLINE WORK FLOW

With Acrobat 5 you can use a network or the Internet to edit, proof, and approve documents. For instance, multiple users can access the same PDF document and add comments that all members of the group can read.

NEW PRINT OPTIONS

Advanced options in the Print dialog box let you choose to print odd or even pages; rotate and center pages; and control the overlap of pages. The new tiling options let you print oversized documents onto several smaller sheets of paper. Acrobat 5 also prints transparent elements created in Adobe applications such as Illustrator 10, InDesign 2, or Photoshop.

PDF CONSULTANT

The PDF Consultant is a new Tools menu item that allows you to analyze a document for space usage and perform limited optimization functions, such as the removal of all form fields.

WEB CAPTURE

The Open Web Page command allows for the retrieval and conversion of websites to PDF files. Improvements to this feature include links between pages as well as to outside documents and the ability to include cascading style sheets and JavaScript commands.

MICROSOFT OFFICE INTEGRATION

Acrobat automatically installs a button and menu command for the Adobe PDFMaker macro into Microsoft Office applications. Clicking the button converts Office documents to Adobe PDF files using the Acrobat Distiller. You wouldn't know it though, Distiller never shows up. This makes it very simple to create professional PDF documents from Office files.

ENHANCED COMMENTS FEATURES

The new Find Comments command lets you search for text within the comment fields. You can filter and sort comments based on author, date modified, or the type of comment tool. Moreover, you can set the transparency for how comments appear on the page, and comments can be printed as part of the page.

ENHANCED JAVASCRIPT ENGINE

The significantly enhanced JavaScript engine, based on JavaScript 1.5, allows a wide range of functionality, including one function that is absolutely necessary for batch processing, the run-time error handler with try...catch.

1.3 Acrobat Components and Work Flow

Acrobat's suite of software, PDF generation options, outside applications and plug-ins, and internal commands and tools can confuse the novice. One way to understand the process is to imagine going to a Broadway show called "Acrobat." When the curtain rises, the various performers come on stage to perform their parts. The lead character may be called "Acrobat," but he relies on help from the other characters, with different names, to complete the performance.

OVERVIEW

For those of you fairly new to the Acrobat program, the range of programs under the general Acrobat category may seem confusing, particularly between the two main programs, Acrobat and Acrobat Reader. One way to clarify the roles is to view Acrobat as the enabling tool, and Reader as the viewing tool. In addition to these two major components, Acrobat contains "sub-programs," such as Distiller, Capture, and Approval, and a host of plug-ins that add functionality to your Acrobat files. We'll discuss these in a bit.

The beauty of Acrobat is that you may approach the program and its capabilities according to your own needs. For example, you can learn very quickly how to create simple text-based PDFs from a content-creating application and distribute them without further enhancements, just as a means of getting textual information out.

Spending a bit more time, you can discover how to process a PDF and enhance the document with functions and tools, such as sounds, links, and bookmarks.

On an advanced level, you can learn how to use Acrobat not only to process existing text files into a PDF (repurposing), but also to transform otherwise static PDF material by adding functions, interactivity, and navigation to it.

On an even more advanced level, you may also use Acrobat as a stand-alone application, creating high-end documents from other sources or from within Acrobat. You may want to know how Acrobat can become a multimedia showcase—where nothing gives away the fact that you're looking at a PDF presentation.

You may want to learn how to create interactive/smart forms, which can perform tasks, like adding up values; showing mutually exclusive buttons; creating scripts that perform complicated tasks; or sending the information to a database.

Whatever your level of familiarity with the software, Acrobat offers you significant opportunities for tailoring a work flow that suits you and allows for continual expansion, adjustment, and improvement.

ACROBAT WORK FLOW

Let's look first at Acrobat, the main program that you'll use. As we mentioned, Acrobat is the stage—the place where you assemble content from other sources to create a composite presentation. The content can almost be anything: text and graphic files that have been processed (distilled) into a PDF, sounds, movies, and links to other files.

In addition, Acrobat is the place where you add functionality, interactivity, and accessi-

This chart shows the software and tools used in each step of creating, enhancing, and viewing PDF documents.

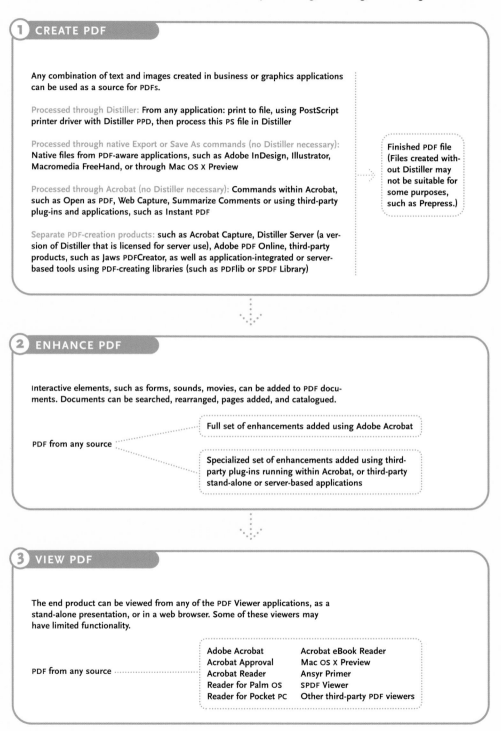

1 CREATE PDF

Any combination of text and images created in business or graphics applications can be used as a source for PDFs.

Processed through Distiller: **From any application: print to file, using PostScript printer driver with Distiller PPD, then process this PS file in Distiller**

Processed through native Export or Save As commands (no Distiller necessary): **Native files from PDF-aware applications, such as Adobe InDesign, Illustrator, Macromedia FreeHand, or through Mac OS X Preview**

Processed through Acrobat (no Distiller necessary): **Commands within Acrobat, such as Open as PDF, Web Capture, Summarize Comments or using third-party plug-ins and applications, such as Instant PDF**

Separate PDF-creation products: **such as Acrobat Capture, Distiller Server (a version of Distiller that is licensed for server use), Adobe PDF Online, third-party products, such as Jaws PDFCreator, as well as application-integrated or server-based tools using PDF-creating libraries (such as PDFlib or SPDF Library)**

Finished PDF file (Files created without Distiller may not be suitable for some purposes, such as Prepress.)

2 ENHANCE PDF

Interactive elements, such as forms, sounds, movies, can be added to PDF documents. Documents can be searched, rearranged, pages added, and catalogued.

PDF from any source

Full set of enhancements added using Adobe Acrobat

Specialized set of enhancements added using third-party plug-ins running within Acrobat, or third-party stand-alone or server-based applications

3 VIEW PDF

The end product can be viewed from any of the PDF Viewer applications, as a stand-alone presentation, or in a web browser. Some of these viewers may have limited functionality.

PDF from any source

Adobe Acrobat
Acrobat Approval
Acrobat Reader
Reader for Palm OS
Reader for Pocket PC

Acrobat eBook Reader
Mac OS X Preview
Ansyr Primer
SPDF Viewer
Other third-party PDF viewers

bility to the PDF files, such as search functions, form-fields that calculate values, and interactive buttons and links.

CREATING A PDF FILE

Unless you inherit a PDF from a long-lost relative, you must create it. For example, text and graphics files must be processed into a PDF file by creating a PostScript file, using an appropriate PostScript printer driver (PPD), with the Distiller PPD. The file is then converted into a PDF document with Acrobat Distiller, which is installed as part of the Acrobat package.

Distiller allows you to create a PDF with a very high degree of control. For instance, a PDF for prepress must be created so that it can be printed with the correct color separations, image resolutions, fonts, and printer marks. However, a PDF that will be part of a web page needs to be created with totally different settings. There are many ways of setting the Distiller options, as we'll see in the Creating PDFs chapter.

> **i BUYING DISTILLER**
>
> *Everyone installs Distiller with the full version of Adobe Acrobat. Distiller also comes with other Adobe products, such as PageMaker and FrameMaker, so it's possible to distill a document without owning Adobe Acrobat.*

If you use PDF-aware applications, such as Adobe InDesign, Adobe Illustrator, or Macromedia FreeHand, you may have used the Save As or Export commands to create PDF documents directly from those applications—without Distiller. The wisdom of doing this is hotly debated. If you want to create a PDF for commercial prepress or intend to widely distribute your documents, you will want to use the Distiller route. If you wish to create multimedia presentations, you may not need the precision that Distiller gives. Although you might expect Adobe applications, such as Illustrator or InDesign to be the same, they may not use the same imaging model or the same PDF generating codebase. We have heard complaints about both.

Try the built-in Save or Export command. If you like what you see, then keep the PDF. If not, throw out that file and create a new one using Distiller.

You can also be a magician and pull PDF documents out of thin air—using the Web Capture command with HTML pages. There are other options for creating PDFs: third-party programs, such as Jaws PDF Creator (which they say produces results acceptable for prepress), and PDF-creation libraries, such as PDFlib.

Programs such as Adobe Acrobat Capture take a scanned document and convert the text image into editable text within a PDF document. You can also send scans to the Adobe PDF Online service, which will convert scans into PDF files.

However, for simplicity, let's just say that Distiller is the application that you use to create PDFs. The PDF can then be enhanced in Acrobat or sent out to others "as is." Sadly, most are content to send out their PDF files without enhancements.

ENHANCING PDF FILES

In Acrobat, you can enhance a PDF in almost unlimited ways by using the built-in commands and tools or third-party plug-ins. This includes adding interactivity, multimedia, and advanced functionality.

One increasingly popular feature of Acrobat is the ability to create form fields that users can fill out on screen, even in Reader, and print as a hard copy. The Internal Revenue Service uses such forms for tax documents that can be downloaded from their site (www.irs.com).

However, as soon as you make any changes to a PDF file, you have to save those changes. If your audience has the full copy of Acrobat, there is no problem. However, because it is much more likely that your audience will use the free Acrobat Reader to view the file, the changes will not be saveable. Reader is not able to save those changes. Fortunately Adobe has created Acrobat Approval. This program, a less costly version of Acrobat aimed primarily at forms users, is an alternative to Adobe Acrobat that allows users to save form data.

Note that if you use the PDF as part of an editorial review/proofing cycle, you almost certainly want your audience to use the main Acrobat application. This lets others add and delete comments or annotations to the file.

VIEWING PDF FILES

As the last step in the work flow, you need an application for viewing PDF files. (Strictly speaking, you had to view the PDF if you enhanced it.) Since you can't always expect your audience to pay for the complete Acrobat package, others will most likely view your files using the free Acrobat Reader, which can be downloaded from www.adobe.com/support/downloads/main.html. (You can also distribute Acrobat Reader on CD-ROM or other media as long as you comply with the Adobe End-User License Agreement.)

You may wonder why Adobe doesn't allow you to create a presentation or projector file that incorporates both the player and the content in one file. While this approach is useful for presentation software such as Microsoft PowerPoint, it has its drawbacks. The projector file cannot be made cross-platform, so you'll need two different versions of the file. Also, the projector file will be bigger than the content file.

When you use Reader, the software just displays the product. You don't have the ability to create or enhance the files. Those in your audience who have Acrobat can open the file there and make changes, provided you have not enabled the security functions.

Acrobat Reader now also has two "sister" applications meant for the growing PDA market: Reader for Palm OS, and Reader for Pocket PC. These versions of Reader let you read PDF files on portable devices. Although Adobe arrived a little late to the ball, a superior PDF viewer for the Pocket PC and Palm OS has existed for some time. The Ansyr Primer PDF viewer for Palm OS and Pocket PC can also fill forms and supports links.

Another Adobe PDF viewer is Acrobat eBook Reader. The eBook Reader is specially designed for viewing PDF files that have been sold or distributed as eBooks. The eBook Reader has special features that enhance reading books in PDF format. For instance, you can highlight important text, write electronic margin notes, or bookmark a page to easily flip back to it later.

PLANNING YOUR WORK FLOW

At first glance, it may seem that the Acrobat work flow requires a strict linear approach: create, enhance, and view. Though linear planning and working yields the best result, there is great flexibility in adding or changing content, even after your PDF file is created and distributed.

Let's say you start with a QuarkXPress document and use Distiller to create a PDF of the file. Then you use Acrobat to enhance the file with multimedia content, form fields, interactive buttons, and so on. What happens if the PDF becomes outdated or needs revisions? Fortunately, you can replace the original PDF that came from QuarkXPress with the new PDF without losing all the enhancements you added. To do this you'll open your enhanced PDF and go to Document>Replace Pages and switch in the new PDF pages. The "background" of the page changes while your enhancements (links, fields, etc.) remain.

Another approach would be to predefine some of the interactive elements in the authoring application. Unless there are built-in capabilities in the authoring program, this will require knowledge of PostScript programming and the PDFMark operator. This is the best approach if you want an automated document creation process.

1.4 Adobe Acrobat Work Area

In this section you will get to know the Adobe Acrobat user interface and work environment. As you become more familiar with the tools and menus, we have no doubt that you will be surprised at Acrobat's versatility and range of functions. In fact, we're still surprised at the complexity of the program despite its easy-to-use appearance.

One of the benefits of Acrobat is that the work environment uses tools, commands, and palettes that should look familiar if you have used any Adobe products, such as PageMaker, Illustrator, or Photoshop. Certain tools have become unmistakingly recognizable, such as the Zoom In/Out tools, and the Hand tool.

Because many of the other tools are specific to Acrobat features, we will detail their use and specifications in the chapters to come. Here's a quick overview.

THE TOOLS

Tools can be selected by clicking the Tool bar or by invoking a keyboard shortcut (see a comprehensive list in the QuickGuide to Tools and Shortcuts section in the back of the book). If you don't know what each tool does, position the cursor over the tool and pause for a moment. A Tool Tip will appear that shows the name of the tool and its keyboard shortcut. (If you don't see the Tool Tip immediately, hold your cursor over the tool for a moment until the Tool Tip appears).

Some tools are nested under others in tool groups. You can access them by pressing the More Tools triangle ▼ to the right of the tool. You can cycle through the tools in a group by holding the Shift key and pressing the keyboard shortcut for the first tool in the group. For instance, the keyboard shortcut for the Note tool is the S key. If you press Shift+S, you will move from the Note tool to the Free Text tool to the Sound Attachment tool to the Stamp tool to the File Attachment tool and back to the Note tool.

MENUS

As in most other computer applications, the menus list the commands that are available. Many of these commands are also shown as a tool bar button, navigation pane command, or keyboard shortcut.

NAVIGATING WITH THE TOOL BAR

The Acrobat Tool bar contains buttons that let you move around documents. Look closely and you'll see that the buttons for these tools resemble the controls on many consumer electronics, web browsers, and other software.

◀ ▶ **The Next Page or Previous Page** buttons move through the PDF file consecutively, one page at a time. Each click moves one page toward the end or the beginning of the file.

◀◀ ▶▶ **The First or Last Page** buttons move you to the first or last page of the document.

◀ ➡ **The Go To Previous or Next View** buttons move through the views that you have seen. For instance, if you jumped from the first page to the tenth, then zoomed in to the screen 300% and then skipped to the last page, the Go To Previous View button will take you from the

MENU BAR
This is the menu for the application commands.

TOOL BARS
Only Acrobat contains the full range of editing and comments tools.

Acrobat Reader and Acrobat Approval contain limited sets of tools.

① 🍎 **File Edit Document Tools View Window Help**

Menu bar

② 🗀📂💾🖨📑🖨▾ 🔍🔍▾ 🔳 | ◀ ◀ ▶ ▶| | ◀ ➡ | ⊖ 70% ▾ ⊕ | 📄📑📑📄 📑▾

File

Navigation

View History

Viewing

③ 🖐🔍▾ T▾ 🔳 | 📄▾ ✏ ▾ ∠▾ 🔳🔳 | 🔳 🔖 🔱 🔲🔳 T▾

Basic

Commenting

Editing

① 🍎 **File Edit Document Tools View Window Help**

② 🗀📂💾🖨📑🖨▾ 🔍🔍▾ 🔳 | ◀ ◀ ▶ ▶| | ◀ ➡ | ⊖ 70% ▾ ⊕ | 📄📑📑📄 📑▾

③ 🖐🔍▾ T▾ 🔳 | 📄▾ ✏ ▾ ∠▾ 🔳🔳 | 🔳 🔖 🔱 🔲🔳 T▾

Creating Time

🗑 Thumbnail ▾

Bookmarks *Articles* *Destinations* **Thumbnails** *Comments* *Signatures* *Fields*

1	2
3	4
5	6
7	8
9	10

PART 1   PART 2   PART 3   ARTICLES
Exercise 1   *Exercise 3*   *Energy 101*   *Value of Time*
Exercise 2   *Exercise 4*   *Exercise 7*   *Digital vs Analog*
      Exercise 5   *Eat, Drink & be Merry*
      Exercise 6

USING THIS WORKSHOP

NAVIGATION
There are three ways of navigating through this document. You can use the navigation tools that are built into the Acrobat Reader, the navigation bar at the bottom of the pages, or the sectional navigation on the top of the pages.

EXERCISES
The exercises in this workshop have been included as interactive forms that can be filled-in and printed from the free Adobe Acrobat Reader, but be

forewarned you will not be able to save what you have filled-in unless you have the full version of Adobe Acrobat or the new Acrobat Approval. If you are using Acrobat Reader, we suggest that you print each form as you finish it to make sure you don't lose any of your writing.

Six months from now, you can go through the book again, find things you might have missed, revise your dreams and goals, or do it all over again.

◁▷ | ◀ ◀   3 of 45   ▶ ▶| | 9 x 6 in   ▢ ◫ ▦ ◀ | ▷

NAVIGATION PANE
This area is activated by clicking the Tab palette or the Navigation Pane icon in the Tool bar. What navigation elements are available depends on

what settings have been defined for how the document should appear when opened.

DOCUMENT PANE
This is the area where the document is displayed. The Document Open options control how this area first appears.

STATUS BAR
This area of the page contains controls for moving through the document and displaying pages.

File Tool Bar

Open
Open Web Page
Save
Print
E-Mail
▼ Create Adobe PDF Online
    Paper Capture Online
    Search Adobe PDF Online
Find
▼ Search
    Search Results
    Previous Highlight
    Next Highlight
Show/Hide Navigation Pane

Basic Tools Bar

Hand Tool
▼ Zoom In Tool
    Zoom Out Tool
▼ Text Select Tool
    Column Select Tool
Graphics Select Tool

Navigation Tool Bar

Previous Page/Next Page
First Page/Last Page

View History Tool Bar

Go To Previous/Next View

Commenting Tool Bar

▼ Note Tool
    Free Text Tool
    Sound Attachment Tool
    Stamp Tool
    File Attachment Tool
▼ Pencil Tool
    Square Tool
    Circle Tool
    Line Tool
▼ Highlight Tool
    Strike Out Tool
    Underline Tool
Spell Check
Digital Signature Tool

Editing Tool Bar

Movie Tool
Link Tool
Article Tool
Crop Tool
Form Tool
▼ Touch Up Text Tool
    Touch Up Object Tool
    Touch Up Order Tool

Viewing Tool Bar

Zoom Out/Zoom In
Actual Size
Fit in Window
Fit Width
Reflow
▼ Rotate View Clockwise
    Rotate View Counter Clockwise

last page back to the 300% view on page 10. The Go To Next View is only available when you have moved to a previous view. The Go To Previous or Next View buttons even jump from one PDF document to another.

The Hand tool enables you to move freely around or between pages (provided you have selected Continuous under the view settings).

The Zoom In or Zoom Out tools allow you to zoom in or out on the page. To quickly switch from Zoom Out to Zoom In and vice versa, press the Alt (w)/Option (m) key when the Zoom tool is active.

The Zoom In and Out buttons let you move in or out on the magnification. By clicking the + or – buttons on the side, you can go up or down successively, according to a list of preset magnification factors. When these buttons are attached to the Tool bar, they are surrounded by a field that lets you enter any numerical magnification value from 8.33% to 1600%. The little triangle next to the value gives you the option of selecting several different set values directly, fit to screen, and so on. In addition to these tools, you can also use the keyboard shortcuts such as Command 1, actual size (Ctrl 1 in Windows), Command 3, fit visible (Ctrl 3 in Windows). Look under the View menu for a more extensive list of options.

The Find tool lets you look through the current document for a specific word or phrase. This is similar to the Find command in a word processing program.

The Search tool works with multiple documents and provides a more powerful way to search text. Once you have used the Catalog function of Acrobat 5 to create an index of a

> **ⓘ HAND TOOL RULES**
>
> *The Hand tool is the primary tool when viewing PDF documents. Not only does it let you move around the document, but it also indicates where you can click into forms, follow articles, and prompt links.*

document or set of documents, you can search the PDF documents using specific words or phrases. You will learn more about searching and indexing later in this book.

THE NAVIGATION PANE

As you look at the document window, you may notice tabs on the left side, in the Tab palettes. These tabs open into the Navigation Pane and give you options for moving around a document. You can tear off any of the tabs from the Tab palette to make them free-standing palettes.

Open and close the Navigation Pane by clicking on a tab in the Tab palette or on the Navigation Pane tool in the Tool bar. Each tab controls a different type of navigation element. For instance, the Thumbnail tab shows small graphics of each page in the document. The Bookmarks tab shows the bookmarks, usually text hyperlinks that take you to various parts of the document or elsewhere. These links are all created in the full version of Acrobat. If the author has not enabled these functions, they will not appear in the document for the viewer.

Consider how you want to use the elements in the Navigation Pane. For instance, a PDF that asks questions and prompts viewers to choose answers shouldn't show thumbnail graphics that might give away the answers. Readers of a long, technical document might want more utilitarian bookmarks and might not appreciate the time spent on fancy navigational buttons.

When you print out a PDF, elements in the Navigation Pane, such as the bookmarks do not print.

BOOKMARKS

Bookmarks can act as hyperlinks. When you move your cursor over a bookmark, the text becomes underlined to indicate that it is the active link. When you click a bookmark, it highlights and sends you to the associated location in the document.

The Previous and Next Page tools navigate forward and backward through the document one page at the time.

The Zoom In and Zoom Out tools allow you to zoom in and out by holding down the Alt/Option key.

The Zoom bar allows you to click an icon to zoom in and out, or you can enter a numeric value for the size of the document view.

The Find and Search tools enable the user to search for words. The Find tool is easy to use, but works locally on a limited level. The Search tool requires an index.

The Hand tool allows you to move the page in any direction. It also lets you detect Link fields and areas where to enter form data.

The Go To Previous and Next View buttons let you retrace what you have seen—just as the Previous and Next buttons in a web browser. This tool works across a single or multiple PDF files.

The Page View buttons allow you to adjust the view of the page to Actual Size, Fit Window, and Fit Width.

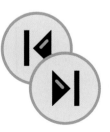

The First Page button sends you to the first page of the PDF document. The Last Page button sends you to the last page.

The Navigation Pane button allows you to open or collapse the Navigation Pane. You can also open and close the pane by clicking the tabs in the Tab palette.

Bookmarks can also trigger actions, such as the display of multimedia content (e.g., Flash animations or sounds) or a JavaScript action.

THUMBNAILS

Thumbnails are also hyperlinks that take you to the pages they represent. A rectangle within the thumbnail lets you zoom in on specific areas of the page and move around the page. If thumbnails have not been embedded in the document, they can automatically be generated by selecting the Thumbnail tab in the Navigation Pane.

Thumbnails are more than just navigational elements. You can drag the thumbnails around to change the order of pages. You can also delete a page by selecting its thumbnail and then clicking the Delete Selected Page (trash can) icon, or by dragging them onto the Trash Can icon. It is not possible to delete a page if there is only one page in the document.

DESTINATIONS *(only in Acrobat)*

At first glance Destinations may seem similar to Bookmarks, but they aren't. Destinations are targets attached to specific points in the content of a document. Bookmarks are starting points.

Because they are intended to be used by the developer of the document, Destinations are not automatically loaded into the Destination Navigation Pane when a document is opened. To load them, you need to choose Scan Document from the Destinations options or click the Scan button to see the Destinations. Once you see the Destinations, you can use them for navigation; jump to the Destination by double-clicking the icon next to the destination title.

Destinations can be sorted according to their name or their current page. They are tied to a specific page and, unlike Bookmarks, don't lose their links if you add or delete pages in the document. However, Destinations can't be made into actions, and thus can't display multimedia components as well as cross-document links.

Named Destinations are a reliable way to get to a specific place within a PDF from the "outside world," such as from a web link. In dynamically created or assembled PDFs, such as those created by server software, named Destinations are the only way to set up navigation.

Because Destinations are available only in Acrobat they are not used as often as Bookmarks. (The Acrobat Help file has an extensive set of Destinations as well as Bookmarks.)

ARTICLES

This tool lets you build contents that belong together logically, but are distributed over the document, by defining areas on a single page or multiple pages into a linked path called an Article. Once you have defined the Article, the user can click inside the active area to read a the content as one continuous segment. The pages do not have to be consecutive, and the path can include enlarged views, multimedia content, and so on.

The articles in the document are listed in the Navigation Pane. Double-click to jump to a specific Article. To follow the links of an Article, click the Hand tool inside the active area.

COMMENTS *(only in Acrobat)*

Comments creation and editing functions are only available to viewers using Acrobat and do not appear as a tab in Reader or Approval. Comments use a host of tools such as visual post-it notes, sound attachments, and pencil marks. These are helpful tools in the proofing and review process.

FIELDS *(only in Acrobat)*

When opened, the Fields tab reveals a list of the form fields in the document. When the Forms tool is activated, double-clicking a field in the list takes you to the page it is on and activates the field for editing. The Fields Navigation Pane is really a document developer tool. It is not

BOOKMARKS

Bookmarks are action triggers, such as hyperlinks. When you move the cursor over a Bookmark, the text will become highlighted. The Actions (including JavaScripts) that can be attached to Bookmarks allow you to create a versatile and powerful Navigation Pane.

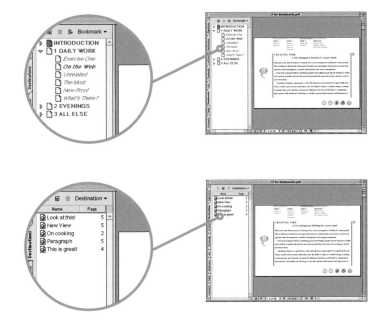

DESTINATIONS

Intended to be used by the developer of the document, Destinations are only available in Acrobat. Destinations are targets attached to a specific point/page in a document, and have several uses as well as certain limitations.

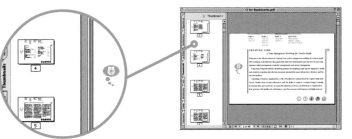

THUMBNAILS

Thumbnails are visual representations of pages and act as links to specific pages. Thumbnails can be used with the cursor to zoom in/out in view. They can also be used to rearrange pages.

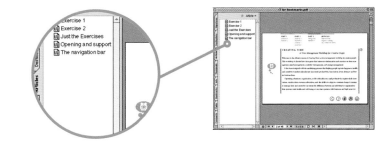

ARTICLES

Articles are strings of content that belongs logically together. The tool allows you to create viewing sequences in a logical order, independent of the location of the elements in the document.

FIELDS

Fields are interactive elements for user input and display output. The Fields Navigation Pane unveils all fields of the document. When the Forms tool is active, double-clicking a name jumps to the location of the field and makes it active for editing. The Field tab is only available in Acrobat.

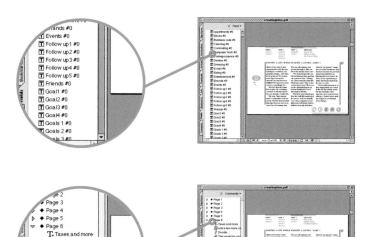

COMMENTS

Clicking on a comment entry jumps to the comment and activates it. Comments can be listed by type, page, author, and date. The Comments tab is only available in Acrobat.

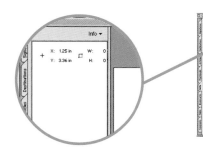

INFO

This is a basic measure/coordinate tool that gives you the exact location of your cursor as you move it in the document window.

SIGNATURES

This tab shows a list of all the digital signatures that have been attached to the document and their verification status. It also shows modifications that have been made since the document was signed.

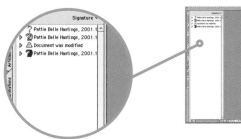

meant for the casual viewer of a document, so it is not available in Reader and Approval.

INFO *(only in Acrobat)*

This tab displays the coordinates of an object or your cursor on a page. The menu for the Info tab lets you choose the units of measurements for the document. Your choices are points, inches, or millimeters.

SIGNATURES *(only in Acrobat)*

At its most basic level, this tab displays each of the digital signatures and their verification status that have been embedded in the document. Digital signatures use encrypted elements to verify a signature and identify the person who applied it (in order to approve the document).

The Signatures tab gives you a list of all the signatures applied to the document, as well as the changes occurring to the document after the first signature has been applied. The commands in the Signatures tab let you verify signatures and compare one signed version of the document to another version. You can also revert the document back to a signed version.

USING CONTEXT MENUS

Context menus are quick ways of enabling the list of commands and tools linked to a specific area in a document. On the Macintosh, you can access the Context menus by holding the Control key and clicking anywhere on the screen. In Windows, you click the right-mouse button.

Context menus change depending on where you click. For instance, if you click in the document window, the Context menu displays commands that navigate and display pages. If you click on a form field, the Context menu shows commands that affect the field.

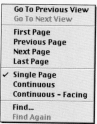

CONTEXT MENU

Contextual menus can be accessed from most anywhere in the window by a Control-click (M) or a Right-mouse-click (W). As the name suggests, the menu that is displayed depends on where the cursor is. Below is the Context menu from the Document window.

CUSTOMIZING THE TOOL BAR

The Tool bar can be customized in Acrobat according to your needs. However, the way you set up your Tool bars is specific to your computer. None of your changes will be applied when your viewers open the PDF document on their own computer screens.

Tools are separated in the Tool bar by thin gray vertical lines. These are used to rearrange or reposition the tool groups.

To make the Tool bar display the tools in a group without having to use a pull-down menu, expand the button to display all the tools horizontally instead of vertically. When you want go back to the initial vertical setting, simply click on the triangle to collapse the tools.

When you first open Reader, Approval, or Acrobat, your Tool bars are neatly arranged at the top of the document window. However, it is very easy to rearrange the Tool bars and place them anywhere on your screen.

To drag the Tool bar to a new location, simply position the mouse over the little gray separator bar and drag the Tool bar. You'll see a black outline box until you position the Tool bar and release the mouse. The bar takes on a different look and can be moved freely around the window. You can reorient it, making it vertical if it appears horizontal and vice versa, by Control-clicking (Mac) or Right-mouse-clicking (Windows) in the Tool bar. A Context menu appears that lets you select your Tool bar orientation. This context menu will also let you display or hide the Tool bars in the window.

You can even combine several different Tool bars into a super-panel that can be positioned anywhere in the document window. Use the small gray separator bar (at the top in the vertical orientation or far left in the horizontal) to drag a second Tool bar into the first. Drag the gray separator bar to separate them again.

TOOL GROUP EXPANSION

By selecting Expand This Button in an editing tools pull-down menu, the tools will expand from a menu to a group of icons and be listed horizontally as in illustration 2.

To collapse the tools back to the pull-down menu format, click the little triangle pointing left at the end of the tool group.

FLOATING TOOLS

You can position the Tool bar anywhere in the window by clicking the vertical separator bar (1) and dragging the Tool bar (2) to its desired location. If you want to position the

Tools menu back into the Tool bar, reverse the process, dragging the horizontal or vertical bar in the floating tool menu.

CUSTOM TOOL BAR

You can design the Tool bars to include as many or as few of the tool groups as you desire. Go to Window>Tool bars and select the Tool bar you want from the list. The check mark

indicates which tools are "on." As you experiment with the settings, notice how the tool groups disappear and reappear in the bar.

CUSTOMIZING THE NAVIGATION PANE

As with the Tool bars you can drag the tabs out of the Navigation palette to create floating navigation palettes. You can have as many floating palettes as you want. Since the vertical Navigation Pane some-

times can take up a lot of space, repositioning the palettes horizontally may make the work area more navigable.

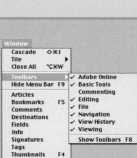

1.5 Acrobat Reader Viewing Area

Sometimes it's hard to distinguish between Acrobat and Reader because of their almost identical interfaces. Just remember that Acrobat is the software where editing and enabling tools reside. Reader is used just for viewing PDF files. As Max, our technical editor, says, "...if it could save, it would be named Saver, wouldn't it?" Most of the menus, palettes, and tools in Reader are designed strictly for navigation and interaction. The Acrobat Reader software is one of the top-twenty downloads for both Macintosh or Windows on the ZDNet Downloads pages. It is also distributed on millions of CD-ROM disks as the application that reads PDF product manuals. (The recent release of QuarkXPress 5.0 came only with an electronic PDF manual. The printed manual was an additional cost.) If you own the full version of Acrobat, you will rarely need Reader. However, if you don't own Acrobat, you must have Reader.

As you see from the comparison on the next page, Acrobat Reader is essentially Acrobat minus the Commenting and Editing Tool bars, it does not have any tools to create, edit, or enhance documents.

INTERFACE ELEMENTS

Reader's tools, buttons, and menu commands are meant for navigation and work exactly like the ones in Acrobat.

Reader's Navigation Pane contains only the Bookmarks, Articles, and Thumbnail tabs. You can control what the viewer sees in Reader by how you save the file in Acrobat. For instance, you can set the open options to completely hide the Navigation Pane when the document is opened.

Reader 5 has a Save a Copy command under the File menu. With this command, a copy of the file opened in Reader can be saved. This is essentially a shortcut to the copying file action in the operating system. It does not, however, save any changes to the document (such as filled out form fields).

DISTRIBUTION

Reader is everywhere you can imagine. If you go to a website that contains PDF documents, you will almost always find a link to the Adobe site where you can download Reader. If you receive a CD-ROM with PDF files on it, you will often find an installer for Reader. This means that if you create your own PDF documents, you can distribute them along with Reader on physical media such as CD-ROM disks. You will find the guidelines for the distribution of Reader on the Adobe website.

Although Acrobat itself is available for Windows and Macintosh operating systems only, you can download versions of Reader for Windows (95, 98, ME, NT, 2000/XP, and 3.1), Macintosh (68K, 7.5.3, 8.1–8.5, 8.6, 9.X, and OS X), Linux, Sun Solaris (X86 and PARC), SGI IRIX, IBMAIX, HP-UX, OS 2 Warp, and Digital Unix. There are also versions of Reader for the Palm OS and Pocket PC.

> **ⓘ ACROBAT APPROVAL**
>
> *If you need to save changes to PDF files, but are not willing to pay for the creation, editing, and enhancing tools of the full-blown Acrobat, you can purchase the low-cost Acrobat Approval at www.adobe.com. Because Approval is intended by Adobe to be used primarily to save form data, we cover it in the Forms chapter.*

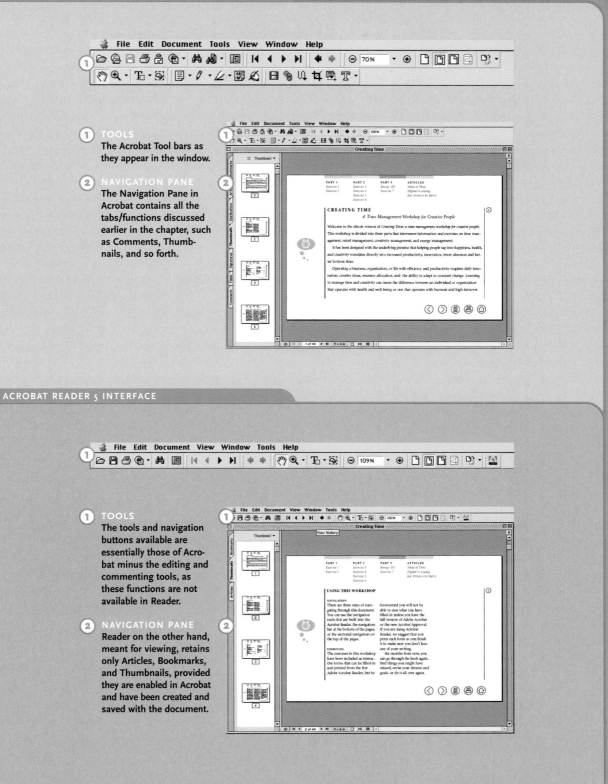

① TOOLS
The Acrobat Tool bars as they appear in the window.

② NAVIGATION PANE
The Navigation Pane in Acrobat contains all the tabs/functions discussed earlier in the chapter, such as Comments, Thumbnails, and so forth.

① TOOLS
The tools and navigation buttons available are essentially those of Acrobat minus the editing and commenting tools, as these functions are not available in Reader.

② NAVIGATION PANE
Reader on the other hand, meant for viewing, retains only Articles, Bookmarks, and Thumbnails, provided they are enabled in Acrobat and have been created and saved with the document.

Creating PDFs

A PDF is generally the final version of a document that you have designed, laid out, and proofed in an authoring program. This end format ensures the integrity of content and appearance of a document across multiple platforms. While you can make changes to the text and images within a PDF, you'll find it more effective to correct your original document in the authoring application. Then use Acrobat to add interactivity and functionality. Now, with that said, we'll talk about making a good PDF.

2.1 Creating PDFs

Creating PDF documents is very much like making spaghetti sauce. The "best" sauce is created from scratch, but some people take shortcuts and use store-bought sauce. For the most part, the best way to convert documents into PDF files is to use Acrobat Distiller. However, some applications provide their own shortcut commands to create PDF documents. This chapter takes you through the PDF creation process using several methods. In order to get the most out of this chapter, you should have Acrobat 5, along with the upgrade to version 5.0.5, properly installed. This places all the necessary files for creating PDFs in the appropriate locations. (However as every computer has a unique set-up, we cannot cover every possible variation for operating systems, software versions, and printers.)

Many of you have created PDFs from authoring applications by using the Print dialog box, which—behind the scenes—creates a PostScript file using the Acrobat Distiller, and then converts it to a PDF. However, there are times when you want to automate or fine-tune your PDF conversion process, and making PDFs the quick-and-dirty way is not always the most effective. In this chapter, we will show you how to exercise more control over the PostScript parameters that create your PDFs by going through a visible two-step process to generate your final files. Then we'll go into specific techniques for creating PDFs using some of the most popular graphics programs.

We'll also cover reasons why you may not want to use the Save As and Export As PDF commands in applications such as Adobe Illustrator and Macromedia FreeHand.

Once you have determined the best Distiller settings for your PDFs, you can make your work easier by designating "Watched Folders" in Distiller for a sort of automatic processing. We'll discuss setting up Watched Folders and the advantages of creating your PDFs this way.

Print dialog boxes vary from system to system and application to application. In fact, your print dialog boxes may not match our examples exactly, but you should get a pretty good idea of how things will work. If there is any confusion about your set-up or we haven't covered your favorite software, consult the authoring application's user manual on creating PostScript files.

USING DISTILLER 5

Creating a PDF using Distiller 5 generally takes two steps. First you use the Print dialog box to create a PostScript (PS) file from your authoring application. This is sometimes called "printing to disk" or "printing to file," because you don't actually send the print information to the printer. Rather, you capture information as an electronic file. Then, you distill the PS file to create a PDF. Print dialog settings and Distiller settings determine the final quality and size of the PDF. Although it may seem that the Print and Distiller settings should be carved in stone, you will go through a bit of trial-and-error in developing a PDF creation work flow.

CREATING POSTSCRIPT FILES

Create PostScript files with the Adobe PostScript driver and the Acrobat Distiller PPD (Postscript Printer Description) by using the print command in the authoring application.

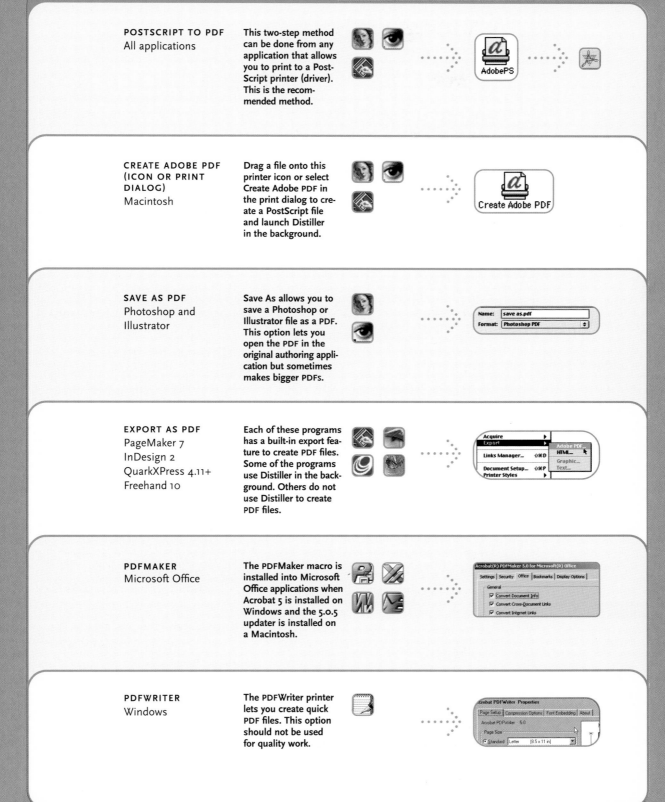

POSTSCRIPT TO PDF
All applications

This two-step method can be done from any application that allows you to print to a Post-Script printer (driver). This is the recommended method.

CREATE ADOBE PDF (ICON OR PRINT DIALOG)
Macintosh

Drag a file onto this printer icon or select Create Adobe PDF in the print dialog to create a PostScript file and launch Distiller in the background.

SAVE AS PDF
Photoshop and Illustrator

Save As allows you to save a Photoshop or Illustrator file as a PDF. This option lets you open the PDF in the original authoring application but sometimes makes bigger PDFs.

EXPORT AS PDF
PageMaker 7
InDesign 2
QuarkXPress 4.11+
Freehand 10

Each of these programs has a built-in export feature to create PDF files. Some of the programs use Distiller in the background. Others do not use Distiller to create PDF files.

PDFMAKER
Microsoft Office

The PDFMaker macro is installed into Microsoft Office applications when Acrobat 5 is installed on Windows and the 5.0.5 updater is installed on a Macintosh.

PDFWRITER
Windows

The PDFWriter printer lets you create quick PDF files. This option should not be used for quality work.

(Before you start making PostScript files, check to make sure you have the most recent Post-Script driver, which you can download from www.adobe.com.) Just as you would send the document to a printer, you send a document to a PostScript file. Distiller then converts the PostScript file and creates a PDF. Even though there are other, quicker ways to create a PDF, sophisticated users prefer this two-step process to control the parameters that go into the Post-Script file, which in turn allows them even more control over the final PDF file. This process yields the best results in terms of quality, and we advise that you get to know and love this process.

Creating a PostScript File on Windows

To create a PostScript file on a Windows system, open the document in the authoring application and choose File>Print. Select a PostScript printer or Acrobat Distiller (the default PostScript printer) from the list and Choose Print to File. Be sure that the ".ps" extension is included in the file name and choose a location for the Post-Script file. Select Properties in the Print Setup dialog box and select any options you desire, including the option to embed fonts, and click Print or OK. The PostScript file will be created and saved at the location you selected.

Creating a PostScript File on Mac

Before you print your PostScript file, make sure you have a default PostScript printer set up with the AdobePS printer driver. Open the Chooser; select the AdobePS printer driver; select a Post-Script printer; and click Setup. Then click Select PPD; select Acrobat Distiller (PPD) in the list; click Select; and click OK. Close the Chooser. To create the PostScript file, open the document in the authoring application and choose File>Print. In the Print dialog box select Save As File and Destination File from the pop-up menus, which will change the options panel in the dialog box. Choose PostScript Job from the Format pop-up menu, select PostScript Level 2 and 3, Data Format Binary, Font Inclusion All, and click Save. These are the basic settings that we recommend, but they are not carved in stone.

Using the Desktop Printer Icons on Mac

With Acrobat 5 installed, the first time you select the AdobePS icon and a printer in the chooser, you'll see two new Printer icons on your desk-top. The first is Create Adobe PDF. This short-cut lets you create PDFs in one step from any application's print dialog. This is the standard AdobePS dialog with the settings for the "Cre-ate Adobe PDF" desktop printer already selected, which lets you choose the desired Distiller Job Option. (Distiller Job Options are the group of settings you use for different types of PDF files. For instance, the job options for prepress PDF files are different from the ones for screen presentations.) You won't see a PostScript file created, nor will you see Distiller launched as

---

PRINT TO POSTSCRIPT

1 You "print" a PostScript file by setting the Printer Description to Acrobat Distiller and the Desti-nation to File. This changes the Print but-ton to a Save button. Each OS and authoring application will have print dialog box varia-tions. This screen shot shows the print dialog box from QuarkXPress 4 on Mac OS 9.

an application. However, the Create Adobe PDF icon does those steps in the background. (Pattie Belle doesn't use the Create Adobe PDF icon because she prefers to reuse the PostScript file to make other kinds of PDF files. However, Sandee loves the convenience.)

The second icon is Virtual Printer, which allows you to create PostScript files without having a PostScript printer connected to your computer. Just drag the file printer onto the icon and set the options for the PostScript file.

CONVERTING POSTSCRIPT

There are a number of ways to go about this part of the process, as well. You can convert a PostScript file by opening it in Distiller; dragging it onto the Distiller icon; dragging it into the Distiller window; or placing the PS file in a Watched Folder. If you launch Distiller in order to open a file, you can select your job options before conversion. If you drag and drop, Distiller uses the last set of job options chosen for the file conversion. Watched Folders also use the current job options unless specific Job Options have been assigned to the folder. As the file is converted, the Distiller window displays information about the job being processed. If for some reason the file can't be converted, the reason or error message will be displayed here. Distiller error messages can be rather cryptic.

Opening PostScript in Distiller

Convert your PostScript file to PDF by launching Distiller and choosing File>Open. Select the PostScript file; click Open; name the file; choose a location for the PDF file; and click Save. If you hold down the Shift key (w) or the Option key (m) while opening the PS file, Distiller will automatically name the file by changing .ps to .pdf and will save it in the same location as the PS file.

Dragging PostScript onto Distiller

Drag a PS file onto the Distiller icon to launch Distiller and convert the file to PDF with the current Job Options. This approach changes the extension on the file name to .pdf and saves it in the same location as the PS file. Dragging a file into the Distiller application window has the same result. Windows users have an added bonus with the ability to easily append a PS file to the end of an existing PDF. Simply drag the PS file into the Acrobat 5 window of the open PDF, and it will be converted and added to the end of the document.

Distiller 5 Settings

If you are not familiar with Distiller, you might think of it as a kind of PostScript printer that outputs PDF instead of toner on paper. Distiller is installed during the Acrobat 5 installation and can be found in the Acrobat 5 application folder. For handy access, make a Distiller icon alias or

---

2 *The PostScript file contains the complete package of all the information necessary to create the PDF. The same PostScript file can be used to make several different kinds of PDFs. This is a good method if you wish to make a screen version and a print version without having to print twice from the authoring application.*

3 *Choose the appropriate Distiller settings for the type of PDF you want to make; select File> Open and choose the PostScript file you wish to convert. The bottom portion of the Distiller dialog box will report the conversion progress and processing errors if there are any.*

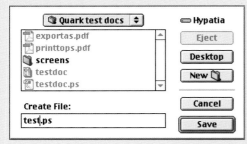

shortcut for your desktop for quick launching or making drag-and-drop file conversions.

DISTILLER'S DEFAULT JOB OPTIONS

Distiller is an extremely powerful engine with many settings that affect the resulting PDF. We suggest that you carefully read the documentation that comes with Distiller. One of the main things to remember about Distiller is that it uses the last set of Job Options you chose unless you specify otherwise, so check your Job Options before converting files. A brief description of the four "factory installed" Distiller Job Option follows.

eBook

The default setting for Distiller 5 Job Options is eBook. (There's nothing special about this setting; it's just the first in the alphabetical list.) The eBook Job Options were designed for PDF files that will be read on-screen (or projected) and in eBook form, but we find that it works well for a wide variety of content and presentations. We use eBook most often for digital documents. The file size has been balanced against image resolution to create a small file that looks good and prints easily at draft quality. Some of the Job Options settings include color space conversion to sRGB; color

and grayscale images downsampled at 150 Dots Per Inch (DPI); monochrome images at 300 DPI; document fonts (except Base 14) subset embedded; all information is compressed and Acrobat 4.0+ compatible.

Screen

Screen Job Options is designed for documents that will be viewed on screen. The Screen setting produces a very small file, optimized for byte serving on the Web or ideal for distributing as an e-mail attachment. Screen resamples images to 72 DPI resolution and applies medium compression; converts color spaces to CalRGB, Cal-Gray, or Lab; and creates documents compatible with Acrobat 3.0+. All document fonts (except Base 14) are subset embedded.

Print

The Print setting produces a PDF file that prints well on a standard 300–600 DPI office printer. File size is balanced against print quality by using very little resolution downsampling and applying a high compression. This allows the PDF to preserve the qualities of the original document. All document fonts are subset embedded and color spaces are tagged for color management.

Press

The Press Job Options are designed for high resolution imagesetting to film or plate in the commercial printing process. Size is not a factor

---

⚡ DISTILLER DETAILS

① *You can choose one of the existing Distiller Job Option settings, such as eBook, or customize your settings by clicking the tabs in the Job Options dialog box and making changes to the compatibility, compression, and color. Save them under another name.*

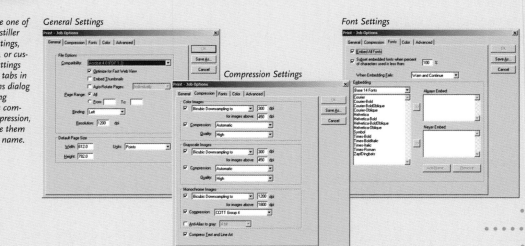

General Settings

Compression Settings

Font Settings

with this setting, and files tend to be the maximum size in order to preserve the document completely for accurate printing. All settings reflect the high resolution required of professional printing. This includes standard resolution of color images at 300 DPI and monochrome images at 1200 DPI. All document fonts are subset embedded.

MODIFYING JOB OPTIONS

Each of the factory installed Job Options can be customized and saved to a new name to create new settings that will appear in the list of choices. For instance, Sandee created a new Print Option with Acrobat 5 compatibility that maintains the transparency in InDesign documents. You may want to experiment with the Distiller Job Options to balance file size and image quality for a particular project. We recommend that you create a single PostScript file and then use various Job Options settings to create several different PDF files. Each of the Distiller settings is covered in detail in the Acrobat 5 Help document.

If you modify the settings for version compatibility, compression, fonts, color, or the advanced options in Distiller 5, you can always save your settings as a new Job Options file and add it to the list of Job Option choices. When you make changes and name your new set, it will be saved as a .joboptions file in the Distiller/Settings folder. (Don't worry about screwing up the original factory settings. Any changes you make to those settings have to be saved as a new .joboptions file.) Job Options are normal files that can be copied and distributed. This is particularly useful in the prepress environment. You should ask for the service bureau's or print shop's Job Options, which are optimized for their work flow.

You can also change some or all of the Job Option settings on the fly when converting a file in Distiller or printing from your authoring application or PDFMaker 5. In addition, you can modify Job Options in Microsoft Office applications (w) by choosing Acrobat>Change Conversion Settings and selecting Edit Conversion settings.

EMBEDDING FONTS

One of the chief benefits of working with PDF files is that you can embed (include) the fonts in the PDF file. First determine how many characters in the font you want to embed in the file. We recommend that you choose to *subset embed* the fonts that you use when creating your PDFs, unless you are creating PDFs for prepress. The Subset Embed option allows you to embed only the characters used in your document. (The more characters you embed in the file, the larger the final PDF becomes.) This ensures that the text in the document appears as designed and that it will print properly using the original fonts. If you don't embed the fonts, Acrobat

Color Settings

Advanced Settings

(2) *The Distiller Preferences control what happens when Distiller processes a PostScript file, such as creating a notification and automatically opening the new PDF in a viewer.*

45

creates an electronic substitute based on the Multiple Master (MM) serif and sans serif fonts that are installed with Acrobat 5. Acrobat impersonates the original font by stretching or condensing the MM fonts using the metrics data provided by the original font. Obviously, the success of this method is extremely limited. The more unusual the typeface—such as a script or specialty font—the less successful the result. Never ever rely on font substitution when you intend to print the documents.

The most confusing setting for subset embedding is choosing the subset percentage. Let's say you select Subset Fonts Below 35%; this means that if you use more than 35% of the font's characters, Distiller will embed all the characters in the font, thus increasing file size. Rule of thumb for file size: a fully embedded font is about 40 KB. We always Subset Embed at 100% to ensure that only the characters used in the document are embedded and to try and keep our file sizes down.

So when might you want to embed all the characters in a font? Sandee does this when she sends PDF files of her books to a print house for final output. As long as all the characters are embedded, the print house can make minor text corrections in her PDF documents. Without all the font characters in the file, it could not. (Sandee doesn't care about the file size when she sends her documents for final output.) Never subset if you intend to reuse your doc-

uments by combining them with other PDF documents. This can create problems if the names of the subsetted fonts match and possibly prevent the combining of documents. It also creates multiple occurrences of the same font within the document, which might destabilize the Acrobat viewer.

In order for Distiller to embed fonts, it must know where they are located on your computer. By default, Distiller looks in the System folder of the hard drive and the Acrobat Resource folder that is installed with Acrobat 5. If you want to add folders to the list that Distiller looks through, go to Settings>Font Locations from the main Distiller menu. Active locations appear with a small folder icon. If the connection to these folders has somehow been lost, you will see a red x through the folder icon or no icon at all. You can easily reestablish the Distiller connection to these folders with the Add and Remove buttons in the Font Locations dialog box.

Let's say someone has sent you a PDF but has forgotten to embed the font. You don't have to worry about seeing the correct font display if you have exactly the same font version on your system. But what if you want to change some of the text in the file? Since you have the font on your system, you can go to Tools>Touch-up Text>Text Attributes and check the Embed box. This embeds the entire single-byte font (which includes most roman-based faces) in

⚡ EMBEDDING FONTS

① *You need to add your fonts to the PostScript file in order to embed them in the PDF. Unless you are sticking to the Base 14 fonts, you definitely want to embed your fonts. Remember, the location of these settings will vary with application and OS.*

② *Set the Subset fonts percentage to control how much of the font characters will be embedded in the file.*

If it is set to 100%, it will only embed the characters used in the document.

the file, so it's not a size-savvy approach and should therefore be used as last resort. Multibyte fonts, such as Asian character sets, as well as TrueType fonts in general, are subset embedded when you choose Embed in the Text Attributes box.

Another way to embed or re-embed a font in an existing PDF is to save the Acrobat PDF as a PostScript File (Save As> Format>PostScript File) and then distill the PS file into a new PDF. But what happens if you have form fields, links, and other interactivity in the original document? The new PDF won't contain that enhanced content. Open the original PDF and go to Document>Replace Pages. Then choose all the pages in the newly distilled PDF. All fields, links, and interactivity in the original file remain in place; the old pages are discarded, and the new pages (along with the embedded fonts) are inserted "underneath" the enhanced elements. This same solution can be used when combining two or more PDF files that have the same font subset. Subsets of the same fonts in different documents are not combined along with the pages. This creates larger file sizes than necessary, so we advise saving the file as PS and redistilling.

In order to safely edit text in PDF files, you must have the font installed on your computer.

If you don't have the font and you try to edit the document using the Touch-up Text tool, you may receive a warning dialog box that changes will remove the embedding. You will be allowed only to make limited changes to the text, such as deleting characters or changing the color, tracking, word spacing, and justification. You will not be able to add words or characters.

FONT LICENSES AND EMBEDDING

Now that we have told you how to embed fonts and why you should, let's look at whether you are even allowed to embed your favorite typeface. Some fonts have license restrictions that are written into the code (they may be marked by a symbol in the Distiller Font dialog box) and prevent them from being embedded. If you select one of these from the font list, a description of the restriction may appear in the comments area of the Job Options dialog box. Some fonts are designed (not always purposefully...) so they cannot be embedded, resulting in a processing error message in Distiller. All font foundries have different written restrictions and end-user license agreements that cover usage in PDF documents.

If your fonts come from Adobe, you can rest assured that the license includes embedding in PDF. If your fonts come from somewhere else, you have no such assurance and you need to check the individual Licensing Agreements

③ *Can't remember if you selected Embed Fonts when you made that PDF? In Acrobat, open the Document Fonts dialog box to see which fonts are embedded in the file.*

④ *You can embed fonts "after the fact" into existing PDF files with the Text Attributes palette. Go to Tools>Touch-up Text>Text Attributes, select the Touch-up Text tool and insert the cursor into the text in question. Click the Embed box and voilà!*

for usage. However, Adobe's license permits embedding typefaces into documents for the purposes of viewing and printing only.

If anyone edits a PDF document containing embedded fonts, those fonts must be licensed to and installed on the editor's computer. Most licenses, including Adobe's, do not allow access to the embedded typefaces for use in other documents. We're not programmers or hackers and haven't a clue how to extract an embedded font for use in other documents. This doesn't seem like something that is important to your average user, but that is what the license says.

If you can't find the license for a font that you wish to use, then you must seek out the type foundry that created it. Some foundries have their Licensing Agreements posted on their web sites and others require that you call or e-mail them in order to get accurate information or a translation of the often cloudy terminology in their licenses. At the end of this section we've included a few license variations from various foundries and their web addresses.

Don't assume that if Distiller can embed your font and that if no license restrictions appear in the dialog box, that your license allows for embedding. Also, don't hesitate to call and talk to someone. In the process of examining the agreements for the fonts we own, we have had to make a few calls. In most cases the companies were solidly behind

licenses that allow embedding and were encouraging their various font designers to agree to this. The people we spoke to understood the need for designers and producers to include font data in digital documents. But this is not always the case, as you will see. We advise that you inquire before you purchase, read those licensing agreements carefully, and avoid using or buying fonts that do not allow for embedding in PDFs. Font buyer beware.

Of course, if you're like Sandee, who uses applications such as FontLab or Fontographer to make her own fonts, you will have no problems embedding those fonts in your PDF documents.

www.adobe.com/type/embedding.html
This is Adobe's "Font Embedding Notification" site, which includes general information about embedding and how to identify the foundry that created a font.

www.adobe.com/type/topics/licenseqa.html#q20
Adobe's Type Licensing FAQ uses a question-and- answer format to explain the legalities of font embedding. This FAQ says that the Agfa license allows for embedding, but as you will see shortly, this is not true if you are creating an eBook. So, we suggest that in all cases you refer to the original font license.

⚡ WATCHED FOLDERS

① *Use the Watched Folders dialog box in Distiller to set which folders are watched and the options for how they are treated.*

② *Clicking the Add button allows you to navigate to and select the folders to be watched.*

www.microsoft.com/typography/default.asp

This is Microsoft's typography site, which includes links to dozens upon dozens of font foundries in addition to lots of valuable information links about typography.

www.fontexplorer.com

In the Linotype License, the specific section regarding embedding reads as follows: "*Embedding of the Font-Software into electronic documents or Internet pages is only permitted in a secured read-only mode. Licensee must ensure that recipients of electronic documents or Internet pages cannot extract the font software from such documents or use the embedded font software for editing purposes or for the creation of new documents.*" Our super-strict legal background tells us this means we can embed Linotype fonts in documents, but those files have to be locked so nobody can do anything except read the PDF. They can't modify the file, modify the text, or save the file under a different name.

www.bitstream.com

Bitstream has been making fine digital fonts longer than Adobe has. The Bitstream license includes this sentence: "*You may also 'embed' Bitstream typefaces within PostScript-Language files, .pdf files, and .evy files for distribution, viewing, and imaging to other parties.*"

www.emigre.com/EmbeddingPDF.html

Designers have been using the unique Emigré font families for more than a decade. Here's an extract of what they want you to do in order to embed their fonts in a PDF: It must be a non-editable PDF and the fonts must be subset embedded. "*The PDF must be set to View & Print only (the PDF must be set to no editing.) There are 2 choices; per use, or flat annual fee: The per use fee of $00.10 (10¢) applies per PDF file, per font. For a flat annual fee of $150.00 a licensed user can distribute an unlimited number of subset embedded PDF files, regardless of number of fonts used, within a period of one year.*" This is of course on top of what you have paid to "own" the fonts for other uses.

http://studio.agfamonotype.com/fonts/ index.asp?c=ebookfonts.htm

Agfa also charges an additional fee but, it seems, only if you are creating an eBook. They rationalize this fee because "*The difference is that e-books are software products which, in the event that you embed fonts, include the proprietary font software within your e-book software product. To include Agfa Monotype font software in a commercial software product you require a font license that grants such distribution rights.*" Just as publishers need to obtain permission from their authors and artists to distribute their works electronically, publishers need a separate license to embed fonts into

③ *Click the Job Options button to choose which .joboptions file is applied to each Watched Folder. Any custom .joboptions files that you have created will be available.*

④ *Drop your PostScript file into the In folder of the Watched Folder. A PDF soon appears in the Out folder. If you have instructed Dis-* *tiller to save and move the PostScript file to the Out folder, you can use it again to make a different "flavor" PDF.*

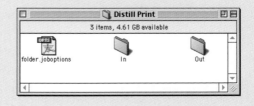

commercial eBooks. Agfa Monotype, like most other type companies, licenses fonts for in-house use on a set number of workstations (typically five).

The End-User License Agreement that is included with every font software package does not allow the redistribution of the font data, such as when fonts are embedded into eBooks. Does this mean that any PDF that is sold is considered an eBook or a "commercial software product"? You must call to find out how much this will cost you.

www.t26.com/changeyourface.htm

The popular T.26 foundry does not allow for embedding fonts, but encourages you to contact them about special licenses for specific cases and projects.

www.linguistsoftware.com/embed.htm

Linguist Software wants you to pay "*a $50 per year per font style custom font embedding license fee.*" There are lots of additional directions and restrictions including an acknowledgment in a prominent place in each PDF document containing its fonts: "*The font(s) used to publish this work is available from Linguist's Software, Inc., PO Box 580, Edmonds, WA 98020-0580 USA, tel (425) 775-1130, www.linguistsoftware.com.*" Note that the web address must function as a link to their web site if the PDF files are being distributed on the web. Yikes. There are just too many other font makers out there to bother with this one.

WATCHED FOLDERS

Pattie Belle uses Watched Folders when converting PS files to PDFs. She has three Watched Folders designated in her Distiller settings that convert files to her three favorite PDF flavors—eBook, Screen, and Print. Adobe's packaged settings perfectly suit her needs 95% of the time, so she hasn't modified any of the settings

assigned to these folders. She saves her PS files right into the Watched Folders and lets Distiller do its thing. The neat thing about this method is that she can take the same PostScript file and drop it into another Watched Folder to make another PDF with different settings. This is her favorite "think once and then forget about it" way of making PDFs. Here's how it works.

Configure Distiller to look in assigned folders for PostScript files by first creating the folders in the location you desire and naming them. Pattie Belle likes to name hers to reference the type of PDF she is creating. So the folders are named Distill eBook, Distill Print, and Distill Screen. Once you have created your folders, launch Distiller and go to Settings>Watched Folders and use the Add button to access them. If you want to use one of the Job Options saved in the Distiller>Settings folder, select Load Options and pick from the list. A copy of the .joboptions file is created in the Watched Folder with the name folder.joboptions. If you want to customize your settings, select Job Options to see Distiller's tabbed option choices. Once you have designated a Watched Folder, Distiller automatically creates an In folder and an Out folder within it. Copy, move, or save your PS files in the In folder; you will find the converted PDF files in the Out folder.

When Distiller is running, it automatically checks these folders in the time frame you have selected, and when it finds a PS file in the In folder it will automatically convert it to PDF. Set this time interval in the Watched Folders dialog box. Distiller can watch up to 100 folders at an interval of 1 second to 9999 seconds (almost 3 hours). You can even designate a drive as a Watched Folder. If you haven't assigned any options to the folder, Distiller will use the current settings. Distiller has to be running in order to process Watched Folders. When you have Watched Folders accessible via a local network, you must have a license for everyone using these folders.

CREATING ADOBE PDFs (MAC ONLY)

Sandee prefers to create quick PDF documents from word processing applications by simply dragging the icon of the file onto the Create AdobePDF printer driver. The Create AdobePDF dialog box lets you choose one of the Job Options that were created in Distiller. The only disadvantage to this method is there is no saved PostScript file to use for other PDF files. However, there is a PostScript file created in the computer's memory. And Distiller does control how the PDF is created.

PDFWRITER (WINDOWS ONLY)

The PDFWriter is a printer driver for Windows. It is not a PostScript printer driver and does not use Distiller to create PDF files. We strongly recommend against using it for any kind of prepress work. It should not be used for files with EPS (encapsulated PostScript) graphics. You can use it for text files with graphics that do not require separations.

OS X SAVE AS PDF (MAC ONLY)

Macintosh OS X uses PDF for its display engine. This makes it very easy to create PDFs in OS X. Simply choose File>Save As PDF. If you don't have that command, choose File>Print and then click the Preview button. This creates a PDF and launches the Preview application in OS X that reads PDFs. You can then save that preview document as a PDF.

CREATING PDFs FROM THE AUTHORING APPLICATION

We hold Distiller as the Gold Standard for creating the smallest and best-written PDF files. However, we sometimes use the built-in commands in various applications for creating PDF files. For instance, Macromedia FreeHand, Adobe Illustrator, and Adobe Photoshop have commands that let you create PDF files without using the Distiller application. Other programs, such as QuarkXPress, have commands within the program but require Distiller to actually create the PDF.

When you use authoring applications to create PDF files, you may find your files are much bigger than an identical PDF created through Distiller. With some vector graphics, such as those in Illustrator and FreeHand, the difference in file size may be negligible; however other graphics may create larger files from Illustrator than from Distiller. Distiller has more controls for resolution and subsetting fonts, and we've found that sometimes Distiller makes a smaller file and other times Illustrator does. And we still don't know why.

Most of the time we use Distiller. However, since Sandee uses InDesign 2.0 for almost all of her page layouts, she relies heavily on its Export command to create PDF files. She rarely finds any difference between Distiller and In-Design's built-in Export command. If you need to make a quick PDF, go ahead and use the built-in commands in the application. If the file seems too large, or the images don't look good, then use the tried-and-true Distiller method.

In the following pages we'll cover the built-in commands and controls for some of the most popular graphics programs. These are additional ways to create PDFs from PostScript to Distiller or by using the Create Adobe PDF (Macintosh) driver. If you use an application that we don't discuss here, check the manual that came with the application.

QuarkXPress 4+

QuarkXPress has a built-in Export As PDF command that makes it easy to create PDF files. This built-in command also makes it easy to convert lists and indexes into hyperlinks within the PDF. You need a copy of Distiller in order to use the Export As PDF command.

Export As PDF

In order to Export as PDF using QuarkXPress 4, you must have installed PDF Filter XTension. You can download this XTension from the Quark web site. You can set the PDF Export Preferences at print time, but we recommend that you set these in advance by selecting Edit>Preferences>PDF Export.

To create a PDF file with the Export As PDF command, open the document you want to convert to PDF and select Utilities>Export As PDF. Then in the dialog box, name the file and select a folder for storage. Choose Preferences if you want to modify the default settings.

When you are ready, click Save. Quark will create a PostScript file and send it to Distiller, which places the PDF file in the designated folder.

Printing a PDF

This is much like creating a PostScript file from any other application, except that the QuarkXPress Print dialog box is complex and sometimes confusing. The wrong setting on one of the Print dialog tabs can cause badly made PostScript and PDF files.

Open the document you want to convert to PDF and go to File>Print. Then select the Setup tab in the Print dialog box. Choose the Acrobat Distiller PPD from the Printer Description pop-up menu and specify the paper size. Always check the Preview tab to make sure you have the correct paper size. Select Printer at the bottom of the dialog box and Create AdobePDF from the Printer pop-up menu. Then choose Post-Script Settings from the Printer Options pop-up menu and PostScript job from the Format pop-up menu. Choose Binary from the Data Format pop-up menu, PostScript level 1, 2 & 3 compatible, and Select All from the Font Inclusion pop-up menu. Click OK, which returns you to the QuarkXPress Print dialog box. There are five tabs—Document, Setup, Output, Options, and Preview. The settings we cover are only for creating digital documents.

The Document Tab lets you set options for the document's title, subject, author, and keywords. The most important settings on the Setup tab are printer description (Distiller), paper size, and orientation. On the Output tab, print colors should be Composite RGB for screen documents with a resolution as low as possible for small file size. On the Options tab, output should be normal, data should be binary, and OPI (Open Prepress Interface) should include images. The Preview tab will let you know if your paper size and orientation is correct. The Bleed tab settings are only necessary for print documents.

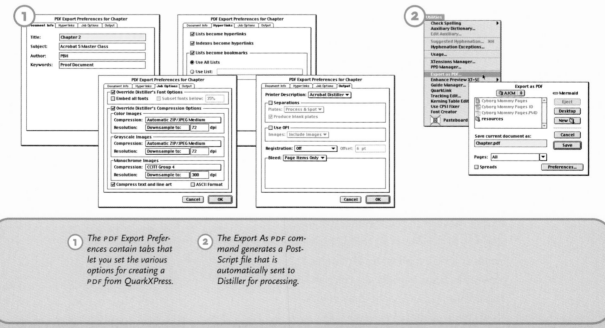

① The PDF Export Preferences contain tabs that let you set the various options for creating a PDF from QuarkXPress.

② The Export As PDF command generates a PostScript file that is automatically sent to Distiller for processing.

PageMaker 7

Adobe has added quite a few sophisticated features to PageMaker's Export> Adobe PDF command. This includes powerful PDF work flow features, such as the ability to create tagged PDFs. (We'll look at integrating some of those with Acrobat 5 later.) PageMaker 7 also has very thorough references for PDF creation in its online Help and User Guides.

Installing Distiller

Unlike its Adobe cousin, InDesign, PageMaker's Export command requires a copy of Distiller to be installed. If you have not previously installed Acrobat and Distiller, you can install the copy of Distiller 5 that is on the PageMaker 7 CD-ROM.

Export Adobe PDF

Open the document you want to convert to PDF and select File>Export>Adobe PDF. The dialog box that opens contains five panels for setting the PDF options. Click the General panel to choose the Job Options. (PageMaker automatically links to those Job Options that are defined in your copy of Distiller.) The Doc-ument Info tab lets you set the Title and other options for the file. The tabs for Hyperlinks and Articles/ Bookmarks let you auto-matically create those Acro-bat elements directly from the PageMaker document. For instance, if you have created a table of contents or index using PageMaker's commands, the references in those pages can be auto-matically turned into hyper-links. Also, if you click the Define button under the Articles section, you can choose those stories in the document that you want to string together as a single article. The Security tab lets you add passwords that control who may open the document. (Of course, you can always set the security options in Acrobat itself.) Once you have chosen your options, click Export. Select the folder where you want to save the file, name the file, and click Save. Page-Maker processes the Post-Script file, runs Distiller, and creates the PDF.

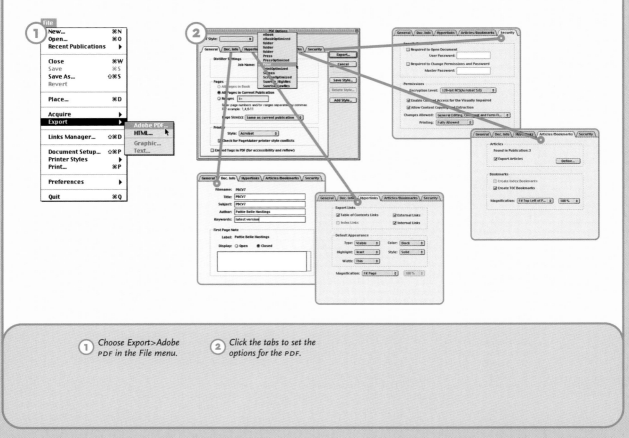

① Choose Export>Adobe PDF in the File menu.

② Click the tabs to set the options for the PDF.

InDesign 2

Adobe couldn't have made it easier to create PDF files from InDesign 2. (Unlike PageMaker, InDesign's built-in Export command does not use Distiller as part of the PDF-creation process.)

Export As PDF

Once you choose File> Export, you name the file; choose a location; and then select Adobe PDF from the Formats list. When you click the Save button, you open the Export PDF dialog box.

PDF Settings

If you have printed from InDesign 2, you will find the Export PDF dialog very similar. Simply choose a category from the list on the left, and set the options. The interface for these settings is very close to the settings in Distiller. In the General category, you can choose the pages as well as set the compatibility and the options, including hyperlinks. (The hyperlinks options are not as extensive as those in Page-Maker.) The Compression category controls how the document graphics are handled. Marks & Bleeds control prepress features. The Advanced category controls colors and fonts. The Security category lets you set security options. The Summary category shows a list of all the settings, which you can save as a text file.

PDF Styles

You can create your own PDF styles by choosing File> Define PDF Style or clicking the Save Style button in the Export PDF dialog box. The new style appears in the Style menu of the Export PDF dialog box. The big question is how good is the PDF created without Distiller. While we don't pretend to have tested every single possible type of file, Sandee is very pleased with the results. In a side-by-side test using equivalent settings, she found no significant differences between the Export command versus the two-step PostScript and Distiller method.

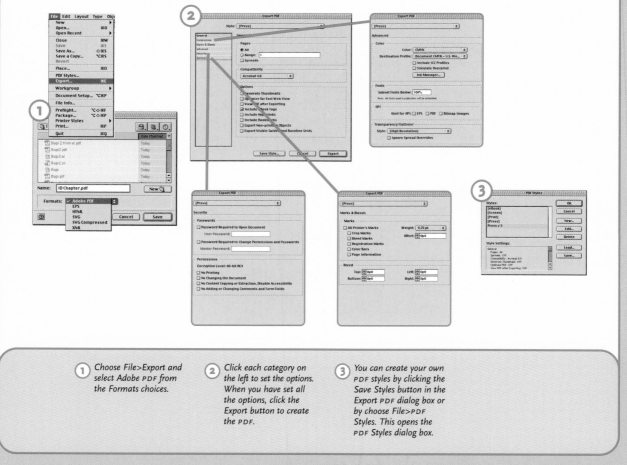

1. Choose File>Export and select Adobe PDF from the Formats choices.

2. Click each category on the left to set the options. When you have set all the options, click the Export button to create the PDF.

3. You can create your own PDF styles by clicking the Save Styles button in the Export PDF dialog box or by choose File>PDF Styles. This opens the PDF Styles dialog box.

Illustrator 9+

Starting with version 9, Adobe changed the internal file format for Illustrator files to the PDF format. However, this doesn't mean that ordinary Illustrator files are suitable for use as PDF presentations or that you should use Illustrator as a PDF editor.

Save As PDF
In order to create a PDF file, you need to choose File> Save As. Pick a location and name for the file. Select Adobe PDF from the Formats menu. When you click the Save button, the Adobe PDF Format Options dialog box appears.

Setting the PDF Options
Choose one of the two settings from the Options Set menu or set your own custom options. The General category lets you set file compatibility, font embed-ding and subsetting, and color controls and thumb-nail options. The Compression category controls how images and raster effects, such as drop shadows, are handled. If you have used transparency effects in your Illustrator document, these are only retained by select-ing Acrobat 5 compatibility.

The Default Options creates a PDF that includes all the information neces-sary to edit it in Illustrator. The Screen Optimized set creates a much smaller file that is more suitable for web-delivery presentations. Only choose Preserve Illus-trator Editing Capabilities if you need to reopen and edit the PDF in Adobe Illus-trator. What happens, though, if you add interac-tive elements such as form fields, articles, and links in Acrobat, and then need to make changes back in Illustrator? When you open the PDF in Illustrator, you won't see any of the Acro-bat elements. But when you open the PDF again in Acro-bat, the interactive elements will still be in the PDF. This round-trip editing is a spe-cial feature of Illustrator.

Setting the PDF Options
As much as Sandee enjoys the convenience of creating PDF files directly from Illus-trator, Pattie Belle is not too sure that Illustrator's options always create the smallest PDF files. For some of our tests, we found the Post-Script to Distiller route created much smaller files. For other artwork, Illustra-tor's Save As command created smaller files. We can't tell if it's due to the different types of graphics or the fact that Distiller has far more options for controlling the final PDF.

We do feel, though, that if your PDF created directly from Illustrator is too big, you should try the Post-Script to Distiller route.

Multi-page PDF Files
If you want to create multi-page documents, then use the PostScript to Distiller method. Ordinarily Illus-trator doesn't print multi-ple pages unless you choose the Tile options in the Print dialog box. Sadly, tiling pages does not create multi-page PDF documents using Illustrator's Save As com-mand. However, if you turn tiling on and then create a PostScript file, Distiller does create a multi-page PDF.

1. Select File>Save As and choose the Adobe PDF for-mat. Click the Save button.

2. Use one of the two preset Options sets or choose Custom.

3. Set the General and Com-pression options for the file. Click the OK button to cre-ate the PDF.

Photoshop 6+

The PDF controls in Photoshop 6+ are deceptively simple. You choose File> Save As and then choose Photoshop PDF from the Formats list. If you choose to save Layers, you will create a much larger PDF than if you flatten the file by merging the layers. If you do flatten the layers, preserve a layered version of the file.

When you click the Save button, you open the PDF Options dialog box. One thing you will notice is how few settings are in this dialog box compared to Distiller. For instance, there are no controls for changing resolution. However, if you think about it, you don't really need those controls. Since you're working in Photoshop, you can always downsample the resolution of the file before you create the PDF. You also don't need the controls to choose among color, grayscale, or bitmapped files. Your Photoshop document can only be one type of image mode.

If one of the settings is grayed out, that feature is not included in the file. For instance, the Include Transparency is only available if the file is on a transparent background. Vector data is only available if you have added vector shapes or fonts to the file. (Although Photoshop allows you to embed fonts, it does not provide controls for embed subsetting.)

Photoshop 7 Security
If you work with Photoshop 7, you can set the additional security options. These options are different depending on whether you choose Acrobat 4 or Acrobat 5 encryption. Even if you don't care much about the encryption process, you only get the option for Low Resolution printing if you have chosen the Acrobat 5 encryption.

Adding Annotations
One of the surprising benefits of using Photoshop to create PDF files is that you have two annotation tools to add comments or sound to the document. While we are ambivalent about the idea of Photoshop graphics making noises, Sandee likes the idea of adding comments. They make it much easier for her to communicate with the people who need to review her files. However, Bjørn warns that adding comments and notes to files going to prepress is not always a good idea.

① Select File>Save As, and then choose Photoshop PDF as format.

② Select the file type from the resulting dialog box. Click OK.

③ You can create your own PDF styles by clicking the Save Styles button in the Export PDF dialog box or by choosing File>PDF Styles. This opens the PDF Styles dialog box.

Macromedia FreeHand 10

For the longest time, this was Sandee's favorite application for making quick PDF files to use as the icons for buttons and custom stamps. (We'll cover creating icons and custom stamps later.) It fulfilled all her needs. The vector format allowed the icons to be scaled without getting pixelated. It has multi-pages, which Illustrator lacks. And the built-in export was quick. However, the lack of support for Acrobat 5 and transparency forced her to abandon FreeHand in favor of InDesign 2.

Export PDF

FreeHand creates PDF files using the Export command. Unlike QuarkXPress, which uses Distiller to create the PDF, FreeHand uses its own code. The results are excellent for documents with just vector information. But if you have raster images, you may not like how those images are compressed. We do not use FreeHand's Export as PDF command for commercial prepress.

Once you choose PDF from the Formats list, you can click the Setup button to set the specific controls for the usual PDF settings, including compression, version compatibility, color, and font embedding. You will notice that although FreeHand lets you apply compression to color and grayscale images, it has no controls for downsampling

high-resolution placed images. One way to handle this is to use FreeHand's Rasterize command, which lets you change the resolution of any placed image. So although FreeHand's PDF export command doesn't resample images, you can change the resolution of placed images before you export the file as a PDF. This can help reduce its file size.

Interactivity Links

FreeHand also lets you export the links you have applied to objects and convert them into hyperlinks in the PDF document. This includes links to outside web pages as well as links that let you move within the FreeHand document.

FreeHand also lets you convert notes you have applied to objects as PDF annotations. This lets you create simple interactive documents solely with FreeHand. The Editable Text Format option allows you to open and edit the PDF in either FreeHand or Illustrator. Choosing Editable Text Format makes for larger file sizes, just as the Preserve Illustrator Editing Capabilities setting does in Illustrator, because it includes a copy of the source file in the PDF.

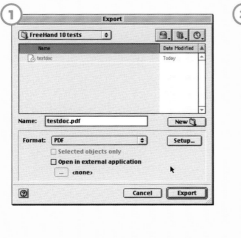

1 Select File>Export and choose the Setup button to define export settings.

2 Modify the settings for PDF in the PDF Export dialog box.

Microsoft Office

Given the market share of Microsoft Office applications, it is no surprise that Adobe would create special features especially for those applications. In the case of Acrobat, this has meant adding the special PDFMaker macro for Microsoft Office applications. (A macro is a special set of commands that help automate a series of actions in Office applications.)

The default Acrobat 5 installation (w) includes Adobe PDFMaker, and the Acrobat 5.0.5 update includes a macro with much more limited capabilities for the Macintosh version of Microsoft Office. When you install Acrobat, the installer checks for Microsoft Office. If the installer finds Microsoft Office applications, it installs the macro.

The macro consists of a PDFMaker button that is added to the Microsoft Office tool bar as well as an Acrobat menu that contains commands for creating Adobe PDF files. PDF files created with PDF-Maker 5 (Windows only) can generate tagged PDFs and preserve any hyperlinks, styles, or bookmarks that are present in the source document.

Using PDFMaker 5

In the document you want to convert to PDF, select Acrobat>Convert to Adobe PDF or click the Acrobat icon on the tool bar. Select your PDF file options from the Output, Bookmarks, and Display Options tabs then click Create. The PDF is created with Distiller launched in the background. If you've selected "Prompt for the PDF filename," you can select a location and name for the PDF.

Tagged PDF files

There is one additional benefit of the PDFMaker macro. Not only does the macro create a PDF, but it also lets you preserve links and creates Tagged PDF files (again, Windows only).

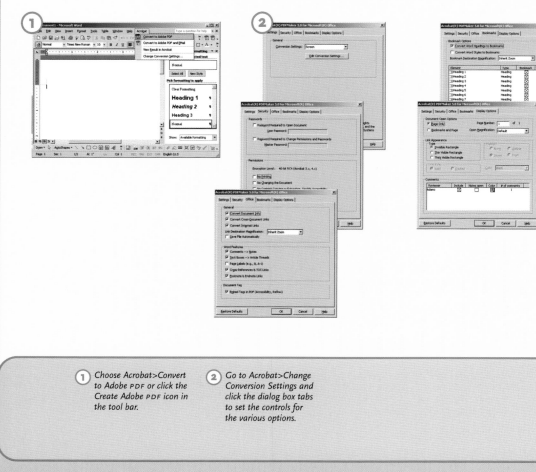

1. Choose Acrobat>Convert to Adobe PDF or click the Create Adobe PDF icon in the tool bar.

2. Go to Acrobat>Change Conversion Settings and click the dialog box tabs to set the controls for the various options.

Open as Adobe PDF & Open Web Page

Acrobat 5 can create PDF files on the fly from certain image and text files or from web pages. These files are created within Acrobat itself, without Distiller.

Open as Adobe PDF

The Open as Adobe PDF command lets you convert the following files into PDF: BMP, CompuServe® GIF, HTML, JPEG, PCX, PICT (Mac only), PNG, text, and TIFF files. Simply choose File>Open as Adobe PDF and select your file type from the Show Files menu. Then select the file or files you want to convert to PDF, choose the color and compression settings, and click Open. If you have a document open, it will ask whether you want to append the converted files to the current document or open them as a new document.

Open Web Page

This command is a slick way to capture HTML web pages and convert them to PDF files. Just choose File> Open Web Page. The Open Web Page dialog box appears, where you can enter the URL of the page you want to capture. Choose how many levels of links for the web page you want to capture. Check the options to control what links are followed. (For instance, choose the option to stay on the same server to avoid capturing ad pages.)

Click the Conversion Settings button to open that dialog box. This lets you control how images and text are converted as well as choose the page sizes. Click the Download button. Acrobat uses an existing Internet connection to find the URL and convert it to PDF. You can also convert web pages to PDF pages by clicking a web link in a PDF file. If your web Capture preferences are set to Open Web-links in Acrobat, a plus sign appears when you put the Hand tool over the link. Click to convert that Web page to PDF.

The PDF that is created from the web pages maintains the hyperlinks that were present in the original HTML pages. PDF files created by the Open Web Page method can be tagged documents.

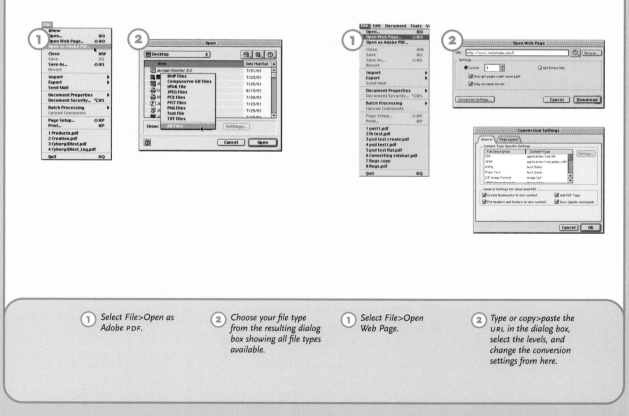

1. Select File>Open as Adobe PDF.

2. Choose your file type from the resulting dialog box showing all file types available.

1. Select File>Open Web Page.

2. Type or copy>paste the URL in the dialog box, select the levels, and change the conversion settings from here.

2.2 | Managing File Size

The main purpose of Acrobat's capabilities is to add interactive value to PDF documents. But all the cool bells and whistles you can add to your document in Acrobat come with a price—increased file size. You can keep the file size manageable, however, if you plan your document in advance.

If you've taken into consideration the uses of your document and have done your homework by creating trial PDFs from your favorite authoring applications, then you shouldn't experience many surprises in the final size of your files. Here are a few things to remember when designing your documents. (Of course if your PDF documents will be distributed via physical media, such as CD-ROM, you don't have to worry about file size.)

LESS IS MORE

Keep file size as low as possible by making sure that you are using the right Distiller settings for the kind of document you wish to produce and ensuring that the PDF is well made from the start. You can begin this process in your authoring program by placing as many repeating page elements on the document master pages as possible. When Distiller processes the PostScript, it will consolidate the repeating elements.

Graphics and Fonts

Be sure to keep in mind your end distribution as you design the document. For instance, if your goal is to send the document as an email attachment to be printed on office printers, don't waste file size with high-resolution graphics. Use the downsampling controls to lower the resolution of color and grayscale images to 72 DPI, and use vector graphics whenever possible (unless they are rather complex). Push the amount of JPEG compression as far as you

possibly can. Even high-compression is appropriate for many on-screen views.

Make sure that you subset embed your fonts—don't embed the whole font unless it is absolutely necessary. Also watch the number of fonts that you use and embed. Remember that styles such as italic and bold are considered separate fonts. So although you may think you've used only two fonts, Minion and Futura, in your document, you actually have used six fonts if you've styled the text as italic and bold. Don't design a document with ten fonts in it if your main concern is file size. In fact, consider designing your document with the Base 14 fonts and not embedding at all.

Will you have to create your file in a lower version of Acrobat, such as Acrobat 4? This can change the file size, especially if you have used transparency elements. When such files are converted to the Acrobat 4 (PDF 1.3) file format, any transparency elements will be flattened in a way that adds to the file size.

If you are concerned about file size, flatten Photoshop images and do not select the option in Illustrator to Preserve Illustrator Editing Capabilities. If you are truly obsessed with file size, make two documents—one with the built-in Save or Export commands and the other using the PostScript to Distiller method. Then compare the results. (Even a difference of 40K can matter when creating a file for the web.)

Check your default settings when creating PDFs. Avoid making ASCII PDFs by mistake. We've seen a couple of times where the default setting in the print dialog Data Format box was set to ASCII instead of Binary. It's very easy to do this, and it adds to the file size.

Enhanced Elements

Thumbnails, Bookmarks, Comments, Form Fields, JavaScript, and all the "value added" tools increase the size of a file. Take this into consideration as you plan or design the document. Tagging and structure also increase file size considerably. These are necessary for documents that are repurposable, or accessible to people with disabilities, or viewable on a PDA, but if you don't need it—why add it? What is most import for the document? Small size? Easy navigation? Form fields? Interactivity? We'll say it again in case it didn't sink in before: plan ahead.

Dead or duplicate links, buttons, and fields add to size. Some of these can be found and managed using the built-in PDF Consultant (see next section), but if you produce a large number of PDFs with lots of links, you'll want to invest in ARTS Link Checker and Link Tool plug-ins, which we cover in more depth later in the book. These two tools will allow you to save an enormous amount of time and help you manage file size.

MULTIMEDIA EFFECTS

Multimedia elements such as sound files also increase file size. If you use a button to embed sound in your files, the sound file is added to the size of your PDF file. However, you can use the Movie tool to add sound as an invisible movie. You can then set the button to play the movie instead of playing an embedded sound file. That way the sound file is not added to the PDF. What's the benefit? Well, if you use the sound file only once in your document, there is no real savings—the sound file must still be shipped with the PDF. However, if you use the sound in many buttons in your document, this method does save file size. Instead of repeatedly embedding the same sound file in the document, you use the sound-as-movie file. Of course a better way to limit file size is to use extremely small sound files or no sound at all. If you use movies in your document, then size is probably not much of a factor. You do have the option of creating .mov files from .swf files for small movie size, but we'll discuss that further in the multimedia chapter.

Finally, PDF files are not like Photoshop files. You can't crop the pages to reduce the file size. Cropped pages and items in Acrobat still retain the data, even if you can't see it. Be sure to crop pages in your authoring program, before you make the PDF.

The most important step in managing file size is to make Save As your final step in the

PDF CONSULTANT

You might be wondering if there's a way to shrink the file size of your PDF. Go to Tools> PDF Consultant and select from three options to analyze the document, optimize space, or remove unwanted elements. The Audit Space Usage option will let you know how much of the file is image, fonts, forms, and so on.

Space Audit

Results

Percentage	Bytes	Description
0.0%	0	Thumbnails
31.6%	1992262	Images
0.0%	69	Bookmarks
1.0%	63056	Content Streams
0.2%	13416	Fonts
0.0%	0	Structure Info
50.7%	3199721	Forms
15.6%	982266	Comments
0.0%	0	Named Destination
0.3%	20706	Cross Reference Ta
0.6%	39038	Unknown
100.0%	6310534	Total
	6310534	File Size in Bytes

[OK] [Remove Eleme]

Optimize Space

Bookmarks and Links
☑ Remove Bookmarks with invalid destinations
☑ Remove Link annotations with invalid destinations

Named Destinations
☑ Change Unused Named Destinations
◉ Remove unused only
○ Convert into direct links
○ Convert all into direct lin

Detect and Remove

Removing items listed here removes corresponding functionality from your PDF document.

☑ All Comments (notes, files, sounds, ...)
  ☑ File Attachments Only
  ☑ Multimedia
☑ Forms Actions (submit, reset, ...)
☑ JavaScript Actions
☑ External cross references (web links, files, ...)
☑ Image Alternates

[Remove] [Analyze]

[Close]

Warnings and Errors

Detect and Remove - Analysis completed successfully.
  1059 Comment(s) Found
  91 JavaScript Action(s) Found

[OK]

61

creation process. Save As rewrites the file so that unused items in the document are discarded. If you set your preferences for Optimize for Fast Web View, then the Save As process will also prepare the file for optimized viewing in a web browser, which may however make the file a little bit bigger.

If you have a complex form with lots of JavaScript, Acrobat might not do such a great job of "cleaning up" during a Save As. Our technical editor, Max, recommends that you work out your code in a development version of the form and then create a fresh PDF without any form fields or JavaScripts. Then copy and paste the form fields and scripts from your development version of the form into the clean version. This can reduce the file size drastically.

BATCH ANALYSIS

If you need to analyze and repair a number of documents at once, you can access and configure PDF Consultant using the Batch Processing command. See Chapter 7 for more on Batch processing.

PDF CONSULTANT

Acrobat 5 comes with a document inspection tool called PDF Consultant. This feature can analyze and remove elements from PDF documents before distribution. There are three main sections of this tool, Audit Space Usage, Detect and Remove, and Optimize Space. To access PDF Consultant from Acrobat's main menu go to Tools>PDF Consultant and choose from the three options. More thorough information about your documents can be displayed with third-party inspection/analyzing tools, as provided with PitStop, for example.

Audit Space Usage

Audit Space Usage analyzes the file and provides a dialog box report that includes the percentage of the total file size and the exact number of bytes used for document elements such as fonts, images, bookmarks, forms, destinations, and comments. To audit the space usage of your document choose, Tools>PDF

Consultant>Audit Space Usage. The length of time this audit takes depends on file size and complexity. Once you have reviewed the audit report, exit by clicking the OK button or you can go directly to the Detect and Remove option by clicking the Remove Elements button. Be careful though, "unknown space" does not necessarily designate something that can be thrown away; for example, Document Level JavaScripts appear as "unknown."

Detect and Remove

The Detect and Remove dialog box offers a selection of elements to be removed from the PDF. To access this tool, choose Tools>PDF Consultant>Detect and Remove. If you first click the Analyze button in the box, it will search the document and report the exact number of comments (form fields, buttons, annotations, etc.), JavaScript actions, image alternates, external links, and file attachments the document contains. Again, the larger and more complex the document, the longer this will take. You can then decide whether you want to remove items from the document. If so, check off the unwanted elements from the Detect and Remove list and then click the remove button.

Optimize Space

This option allows you to optimize the file size by removing bookmarks and links with invalid destinations or by converting destinations into links if it will save space. Go to Tools>PDF Consultant>Optimize Space, select the items you wish to remove or modify, and click OK. Of course if you have no invalid bookmarks, links, or destinations, you won't be able to save any space using this option.

Quite a Box of Tricks

In addition to the features within Acrobat, you may want to use Quite Software's Quite a Box of Tricks (QBT). The QBT plug-in modifies and further optimizes PDF documents for a number of purposes, including file size management and for prepress. We recommend going to the Quite web site (www.quite.com) and downloading a demo version of the plug-in. The demo is a fully functioning version of the software, which marks documents with an x until the registration code is entered.

Once you install QBT it appears under Plug-ins>

Quite a Box of Tricks. This opens the QBT tool palette, which has five sections.

Shrinking Files

Click the Shrink button to subsample and compress images without going back to the original application and redistilling. You can also find images that are above a certain resolution. (Pattie Belle uses it to make sure made-for-screen documents don't have images over 72 DPI.) Just one or two high-resolution images converted to screen resolution can bring down a file's size.

Getting Info

You can click the Info button to get information on either images or text in the document. You can cycle through each image in the document individually and shrink them separately for even more control over your final results.

Use the QBT selection cursor to select a bit of type in your file. The Info section gives you the name of the font, point size, and type of font. It also tells you if it is embedded or subset embedded.

Other Controls

Click the Fields button to flatten or remove fields and annotations. Click the Colours button to convert and manipulate process and spot colors. Use the Transform button to scale pages, rotate pages by any angle, and mirror pages for film output or for creating fabric transfers. The Transform section also lets you change the thickness of all rule lines in a document to prevent problems in printing hairline rules.

Quite a Box of Tricks is available for $210 from www.epublishstore.com.

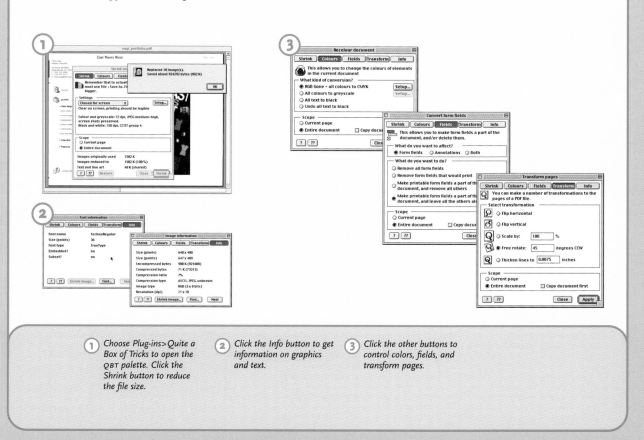

1. Choose Plug-ins>Quite a Box of Tricks to open the QBT palette. Click the Shrink button to reduce the file size.

2. Click the Info button to get information on graphics and text.

3. Click the other buttons to control colors, fields, and transform pages.

2.3 | Alternative PDF Conversion Tools

What if you have a client or colleague who needs to create a single PDF but doesn't want to purchase Acrobat to create just one file? Or you have just opened a box of paper documents that you would like to convert to a PDF file? This section looks at some of the options for creating PDF documents without Acrobat.

CAPTURE PAGES

Back in Acrobat 4, there was a plug-in called Capture Pages, based on the Acrobat Capture 2 engine, that let you open a scanned image and convert it into a PDF document with searchable, editable text. When Acrobat 5 shipped, this feature had disappeared! Adobe recommended that users upload scans to the new Create Adobe PDF Online web service for conversion. As you can imagine, the removal of functionality from the new version of Acrobat caused an outcry. A free paper capture plug-in, now based on the Capture 3 engine, was subsequently released, but for Windows only. (At the time of this writing no such provision has been made for Macintosh users.)

> **(i) PDF CREATORS**
>
> *A few other PDF creation utilities include Jaws PDF Creator, Amyuni PDF Converter, and PDF Machine, all of which can be found or purchased through Planet PDFs online ePublish Store, www.epublishstore.com.*

CREATE ADOBE PDF ONLINE

Create Adobe PDF Online is Adobe's web-based conversion service. Supported formats include Microsoft Office files, graphics formats, and many other file types. You can also submit a URL and receive a web page captured in PDF. Create Adobe PDF Online can also be used to create Tagged PDFs from submitted documents.

The Paper Capture Online service can be used to create searchable PDF files from scanned paper documents. You scan the document, and Create Adobe PDF Online does the optical character recognition (OCR) for you. You can register for a free trial or sign up for the subscription service.

ACROBAT CAPTURE

Neither Capture Pages nor the Create Adobe PDF Online service can handle large quantities of scanned images. So Adobe created a product called Acrobat Capture, which is actually three products: Version 2 works with Windows 95, 98, or NT. Version 3 Personal Edition works with Windows NT or later (2000 and XP). Both of these have a dongle that limits the product to creating 20,000 pages. You have to purchase another dongle to create more pages. Version 3 Cluster Edition lets you make an unlimited number of documents.

GOBCL

BCL Computers develops and sells a number of creation and conversion plug-ins for Adobe Acrobat including Magellan PDF to HTML conversion plug-in. Their free online PDF conversion service, goBCL, also lets you submit files for conversion through your web browser.

goBCL processes your document and in a few minutes e-mails you the finished PDF file. It accepts fewer formats than Adobe's online service, but includes rich text, simple text, Word, Excel, and PowerPoint. goBCL also performs PDF to HTML conversions. You upload a PDF and they e-mail a compressed file that includes the HTML, JPEGs, metatags, and hyperlinks.

Create Adobe PDF Online & goBCL

Create Adobe PDF Online

The Create Adobe PDF Online web service lets you upload the following file formats: Microsoft Word, Publisher, PowerPoint, Excel, Rich Text Format, Text, Illustrator, InDesign, FrameMaker, PageMaker, Photoshop, Corel WordPerfect, PostScript, Encapsulated PostScript, Windows bitmap, GIF, JPEG, PCX, PNG, RLE, and TIFF.

There is a free trial for five uploads. Uploaded files are limited to 100 MB and a processing time limit of 10 minutes. Subscribers have an expanded processing time limit of 15 minutes, priority queuing, and the ability to create Tagged PDF files.

goBCL

A free alternative to Create Adobe PDF Online is provided by BCL computers. When you go to the goBCL site (www.gobcl.com) you need to create an account. Once you have done that, you can go to the conversion page and choose between conversion to PDF or HTML. PDF conversions are limited to 5 MB documents in the following formats: Microsoft Word, Publisher, PowerPoint, Excel, Rich Text Format, and Text.

The converted file is sent back to you via e-mail.

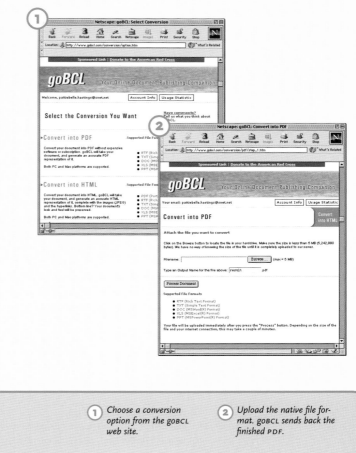

① *The Create Adobe PDF Online service lets you upload files for conversion to PDF.*

① *Choose a conversion option from the goBCL web site.*

② *Upload the native file format. goBCL sends back the finished PDF.*

3

PDF Navigation

How will your viewers get around your document? Will they need to jump from one page to another many pages away? Do you want them to see all the menu commands and Acrobat elements? Or do you want your Acrobat presentation to take over the computer screen? How much experience will they have with using a computer? Using Acrobat? Do they need a lesson to use Acrobat's features? Acrobat 5 and Reader 5 provide you with a huge arsenal of navigation tools, buttons, menu commands, and icons. This chapter examines the various navigation choices—and targets which features you should use and which ones you may not want to include.

3.1 Designing User Interface and Navigation for PDF

In addition to its built-in navigation tools, Adobe Acrobat 5 has unlimited possibilities for creating your own navigational systems and user interface. Programming for navigational interactivity can range from simple page action buttons to complex, custom JavaScript actions. Whatever direction you choose, the design of your system should be well thought out and tested in advance. Here we'll take a look at some of the issues facing the designer, such as the audience considerations, architecture, the benefits of repurposing versus redesign, and navigational systems.

To create a successful PDF conducive to viewing information, start by considering the architecture of the document as well as the navigation or "user interface."

KNOW YOUR AUDIENCE

The very beginning of this process is to consider the audience. Who will view this document? In what environment will the PDF be displayed? Will it be in a web browser, in an eBook reader, on a PDA? How familiar is the user with PDF or Reader's built-in navigation options?

For example, a catalog of window parts downloaded from a web site has a very different aim than a legal document presented to executives in an office or a multimedia presentation. The catalog needs to be designed for extremely quick loads and simple navigation that guides the user quickly from the entrance to the destination. The objective is to get the customer from one product to another with no delays. For a legal document, you need all the information conveyed in a logical sequence. A capabilities brochure may need to be a self-running presentation, where the key points display with little or no user interaction.

It may be difficult to think this way about PDF, but invariably, the decisions it generates will yield quite different results in terms of page layout, type size, navigation, and interactivity. All of these decisions will drive the user experience and determine your level of success.

ARCHITECTURE

In the same way that people experience websites or books, your audience will approach the PDF medium with a set of expectations as well as preset cognitive responses. The interface, or architecture, of the document will deeply affect whether your audience finds the environment inviting and conducive to understanding.

We can think of the relationship between document architecture and navigation as the relationship between a building and its signage. An office building, for example, is designed efficiently, with a lobby and elevators leading up to the business suites. Often service functions are located on the entrance level of the building within easy reach of the public and the business traffic going to and from the offices.

In a similar way, the signage in the lobby reflects the building's architecture. You can see which company is located on what floor, but rarely, if ever, will you see what is located within each room on a level. In a similar way it is

ⓘ **STUDY MATERIALS**

One of the best theoreticians in the field of presenting visual information is Professor Edward R. Tufte. See his books Envisioning Information, The Visual Display of Quantitative Information, *and* Visual Explanations.

This architecture is the most common linear approach to a PDF document. Typically, these documents are self-contained—with all the pages in a single PDF—without many external links or cross linked files. They often have internal links but no custom navigation design.

For lengthy or interconnected documents, documents meant for distribution on CD-ROM, or those used as a PDF archive system, the architecture might resemble a file folder system with a main document acting as the table of contents. Linking and indexing goes across PDF files.

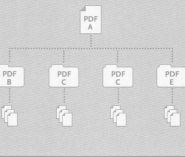

The architecture on the right is more complex, bringing in links/functions that take the user into a web browser or play a linked Flash movie. The linked media may then take the user to a new PDF, or back to the starting point. Typically, documents of this nature contain a custom interface.

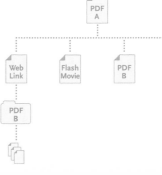

This structure takes the interconnectivity of pages and documents to the extreme, where everything is endlessly interconnected, linked, and customized. This is the next generation PDF, one that takes advantage of all the tools and commands in Acrobat. It is however the most demanding for the creator.

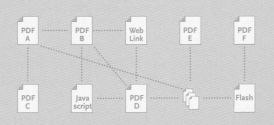

important to integrate architecture and navigation for PDF; you need to balance immediacy of content with ease of finding your way through a document.

As an example, you do not want to overwhelm viewers on the opening page, revealing all the sub-levels of content. Instead give them a clear path that logically maps out the content to the index.

REDESIGN OR REPURPOSING

PDF designers often have to decide whether to retrofit an existing document or redesign it to make it more dynamic. Too many content creators distribute PDFs that are direct translations of printed documents. They fail to consider the different experience of viewing and interacting with documents on screen and what that means to the design of the page.

A successful PDF document, depending on how it's presented/read, will almost always be a hybrid between paper document, web page, book, and slide projection. While a PDF may look like a book, it may also contain web links that will be lost if users find the document too taxing to read on-screen and print it out.

When repurposing documents, consider that they might be going from a print format to a computer screen or PDA. Generally a printed document will be portrait; that is its height will be greater than its width. However, the overwhelming majority of computer screens have a landscape orientation, where the width is greater than the height. And PDA devices vary. How can one layout meet all these orientations?

While repurposing is a challenge, decisions should be made according to each situation, which may result in a document of a different size, another font, larger type size, less text per page, more pictures, and so forth. If you have to

> **ⓘ LESS IS MORE**
>
> *This phrase is associated with Buckminster Fuller and Mies van der Rohe. But it originally came from a poem by Robert Browning. This same poem ends with the lines "Ah, but a man's reach should exceed his grasp, Or what's a heaven for?"*

publish the same contents over different media, you can do this with the same source document. You will have to make extensive use of styles. Authoring application style sheets will enable you to create output documents for each medium. Such a procedure will require serious document planning. You may even have to use a contents management system.

LESS IS MORE

PDF documents are easier on the user when simplicity guides the design. For example, if we make the assumption that the PDF will be read on-screen, we already have some cues about how to begin making decisions: Most people will find it easier to read larger type on-screen, especially in lengthy documents (see also the eBook Reader chapter). Aside from typographic choices, most PDF documents can follow a few simple guidelines to become more user-friendly.

Design your document using a grid that is consistent for most of the document. Though individual content may be presented in a different grid structure or color for emphasis, a grid that remains consistent throughout is easier to read.

A PDF for screen viewing will benefit from less and larger type per page than its printed counterpart—12- or 13-point type is often more effective for screen purposes, while printed matter may use 9- or 10-point type.

Consider reducing the number of elements per screen. While a busy layout may work for shorter documents, or for a particular audience/purpose, or for printed matter, large busy documents will overwhelm the reader.

Sadly, simplistic guidelines like these may not be right for your situation. While the advice holds true in general, there are plenty of examples where organized chaos is called for (i.e., a surfer magazine for teens or the CNN web site).

NAVIGATION AND INTERACTIVITY

To go back to our building analogy, you must decide how viewers will move from floor to floor and open office doors. Print readers have long been taught to use their fingers to turn the pages in a book. A PDF document offers a wide range of electronic choices to navigate from page to page. There are essentially three navigational possibilities, as you'll see below.

Acrobat's Built-in Features

Readers can use Acrobat's built-in navigation tools, buttons, and commands. The advantage to this method is that you, the content creator, don't have to add special navigational elements to your pages. There are several disadvantages to this. Your document must be viewed in the context of a computer application—with menus, scroll bars, the navigation pane, and tool bars cluttering your design. You have to rely on your viewers' understanding of how to use the Acrobat elements. You can't control the state of the application. This means that elements you expect the viewer to use—for example, the Next Page button—may not be visible on the screen.

> **ⓘ IMPORTANCE?**
>
> *If you question the importance of information design, just ask the residents of Palm Beach, Florida, about the infamous "butterfly" ballot.*

Custom Navigational Elements

As an alternative to Acrobat's commands, readers can use custom-designed navigation elements. The advantage to customizing is that you can design the elements precisely with your audience in mind. If your readers do not understand iconography, you can create elements with written labels: Next Page, Previous Page, Home, End, and so on. If they are not sophisticated enough to enter complex web addresses, you can create links that automatically launch a web browser and take them to a web page. You also get the benefit of complete control over the look and feel of your PDF presentation.

Your document can take over the computer screen and become its own operating environment without any distractions from the "outside world." The downside is this type of total control takes more planning and labor. You also have to test your interface thoroughly to make sure you don't send your readers down a path with no route to return.

A Mixture of Both

The final choice, a mixture of Acrobat's features and custom elements, allows you to control as much as you want with custom links within the document pages. Your viewers get to use whichever menus and buttons are most comfortable for them.

Most PDF documents created today fall into the first category. A few others use a mixture of Acrobat and custom elements. And there are a number of brave content creators who have created their own interfaces with no direct access to the Acrobat features at all.

Other Navigation Elements

A simple click on an Acrobat page may launch a web browser and send the reader to a web page. This means you do not need to integrate the Acrobat document with the web page, or with other media such as an eBook Reader or media plug-ins such as QuickTime or Flash.

3.2 Controlling the Initial View of Your Document

In the theater a hush falls on the audience as the curtains open. The initial view of the stage sets the tone for the rest of the play. In this chapter you'll see how you can set the stage for your PDF document by controlling what the user finds when the curtain rises (figuratively) on the file. Though the viewer may override many of your initial settings once the document is opened, you can control that first impression. This is very important since it gives you the ability to make an aesthetic statement and steer the user in exploring your file.

DOCUMENT OPEN OPTIONS

It's important to remember that almost any settings you specify affect only the initial view of the file. The users may override most of your settings with their own viewing preferences once they have opened the document. The consolation is that the changes they make in Reader to the viewing cannot be saved. This means that every time the document is opened, it will revert to the settings that you specified in the original PDF.

Sadly, a large number of PDFs are distributed with Acrobat 5's default Open Document Options. A few simple customized specifications in this dialog box can make a huge difference in the presentation and reception of the final document. To modify these settings go to File> Document Properties>Open Options. The Document Open Options dialog box appears.

Initial view

The three radio buttons for the Initial View let you choose to see just the page, the page and bookmarks, or the page and thumbnails. These settings are not permanent, though; the user can still use the Window menu or Navigation pane to see the bookmarks or thumbnails.

The page number option allows you to set the page number that the viewer encounters

when opening the document. Sandee has used this setting to have her presentation open to the last page, which explained the navigation controls for the document.

The Magnification menu lets you define the zoom view of the page. You may set a value anywhere between 8.33% and 1600%. (When setting view, remember that the size of your audiences' monitors may vary greatly, so select a view that makes sense for a broad range of screen sizes.) However, instead of choosing a specific magnification amount, you can choose one of the "Fit" settings: Fit in Window, Fit Width, or Fit Visible. They change the magnification relative to the size of the page and of the window the document opens in. Fit in Window changes the magnification so that the entire page is always visible. Fit Width changes the page magnification so that the width fits exactly in the document window. Fit Visible changes the page magnification so that the information on the page fits in the document window. The white space in the margins is not seen. One of the cool things about the Fit settings is that they are always on until you set an actual magnification amount. For instance, if you have set the page to Fit in Window, the magnification changes if you change the size of the document window.

As the content creator, you control how your audience encounters your file. How you define the initial view settings can produce results as different as these two examples. On top, the more traditional, and often appropriate, Reader interface and user controls.

On the bottom, an interactive document using a highly customized interface, navigation, and view to create a user experience that is very different. This document retains none of the usual and familiar Reader interface or tools. Each approach has its place and time, and your goals, knowledge of the program, and audience drives what is appropriate.

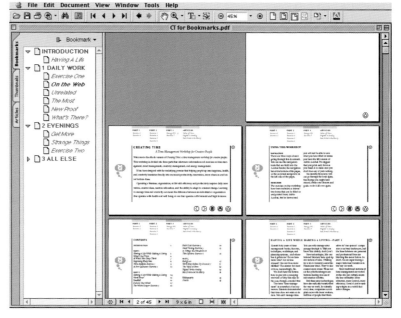

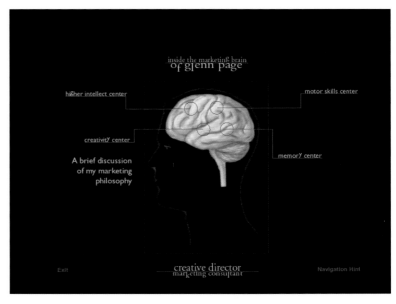

The Page layout menu allows you to specify Single Page, Continuous, or Continuous-Facing. The Single Page option displays each page of the PDF document by itself. Your readers must use a command or button to advance to the next page. The Hand tool does not let you drag from page to page. This mode is preferred for page-oriented documents, such as games or forms where you do not want the viewer to inadvertently advance to the next page. The Continuous option displays all the pages in the document as a single long window. The Hand tool lets you drag from page to page in this mode. The Continuous-Facing option displays pages as spreads of a document. (In a book, a spread is the left- and right-hand pages that face each other.) Sandee likes this option to display the spreads of her InDesign pages. The Default option opens the document to whatever setting is active on the viewer's machine.

Window Options

The check boxes listed under Window Options in the Open Document dialog box allow you to further alter the default settings. You can check more than one option here.

The option to Resize Window to Initial Page always ensures that the document window fits to the page view value defined. This means that the window fits to the edge of the page—no excess. We recommend that in general you set the page magnification to 100% and check Resize Window to Initial Page. This ensures that your document opens at its original size. The document window then sizes itself so that it fits snugly around the active area of the document. This ensures that your viewers see the pages at their actual size without extra space around the pages. We also recommend you select the option to Center Window on Screen. This automatically centers the document window in the viewing area. These specifications make for a neat and tidy presentation

of the document and will create a suitable initial view for many kinds of interactive documents.

The Display Document Title changes the information that appears in the document's Title Bar. Ordinarily the Title Bar displays the name of the document as it appears in the computer's filing system. For instance, you may have labeled a document with the utilitarian name "Sept Financial Data Presentation.pdf." Rather than display that dismal title at the top of the document window throughout your presentation, you can choose File>Document Properties>Summary. This opens the Document Summary dialog box. Use the Title field to enter a snappy title, such as "Our Financial Future," and then check Display Document Title. This makes a much more professional presentation.

We'll cover the setting for Open in Full Screen Mode later in chapter 10. This mode essentially opens the document as a "slide" presentation without any computer interface elements. While it's very handy for a presentation, you should keep in mind that the only way the user can exit Full Screen, which does not display the tool bars or menus, is by pushing the Escape key or Control/Command + L. However, it is unlikely that your average user will know these shortcuts. So if you do choose this setting, make sure to build in an obvious escape from this mode. One way to do this would be to have a button on every page that executes the Full Screen menu item. If the user presses this button while in Full Screen, it will return the view to normal and vice versa. Be sure to make this button's purpose obvious by naming it clearly and using the Button description option to explain what it will do when the user's cursor passes over it.

There are, of course, many other ways to design the exit from Full Screen mode. Some people create a button that quits Acrobat entirely, as a Full Screen or controlled view escape. Rarely do we wish to quit the application on exiting a document, so we recommend strongly against making Quit the only escape option.

User Interface Options

There are three settings for the user interface options: Hide Menu bar, Hide Tool bar, and Hide Window Controls. When Hide Menu bar is chosen, the document opens without the commands at the top of the screen visible. If you choose this command, make sure you memorize the keyboard shortcut (F9) to override the setting.

The Hide Tool bar command turns off the display of the tool bars that contain the tools and button commands. (This includes the tools attached to the top of the screen and those that appear as free-standing palettes.) Your viewers can use the keyboard shortcut (F8) to override this setting.

The Hide Window controls turn off the display of the document window elements, such as the Scroll bars, the Navigation pane, and the magnification and navigation commands at the bottom of the document window. We have always thought this setting prevented viewers from accessing the Bookmarks and Thumbnails palettes in the Navigation pane. However, Sandee recently found a loophole that negates the effects of the Hide Window Controls setting.

Sandee's Loophole

Unlike the Initial View options, the command to Hide Window Controls can't be changed by a simple menu command. This means that if you hide the window controls, the document always opens with the Navigation pane turned off. If you have also set the document security options to prevent changes, your viewer should not be able to see the Bookmarks and Thumbnails palettes—at least that's what it did in Acrobat 4 and Reader 4. In version 4 if you hid the Navigation pane, you also hid the Bookmarks and Thumbnails because they were permanently attached to the Navigation pane.

But things are different in Acrobat 5. In Acrobat 5 and Acrobat Reader 5, a viewer can drag the Bookmarks and Thumbnails from the Navigation pane. This means that if the viewer opens a document that has the Window Controls hidden, the Bookmarks and Thumbnails may still be visible as free-standing palettes. While this isn't a deadly breach of document security, it does add one more uncertainty to how your readers will see documents.

We would like to suggest to Adobe that they consider adding another item to the User Interface Options—Hide Panels. This would ensure that any free-standing panels, such as Bookmarks and Thumbnails, are always hidden.

Using Scroll Bars

When you hide the window controls, you hide the display of the document window scroll bars. This is quite handy if you want to use only internal navigational elements in your document. However, if the document consists of pages, it can be very disconcerting to your viewers. Many users ignore Acrobat's navigation tools and buttons in favor of the scroll bars. As designers, Pattie Belle and Bjørn sometimes like the cleaner look that hiding the scroll bars gives to a presentation. However, as content creators, they recognize that using the scroll bars has become extremely integral to on-screen viewing.

A user who has become accustomed to scrolling through the pages of a PDF may be mystified and frustrated to enter a document where the scroll bars have been disabled. You

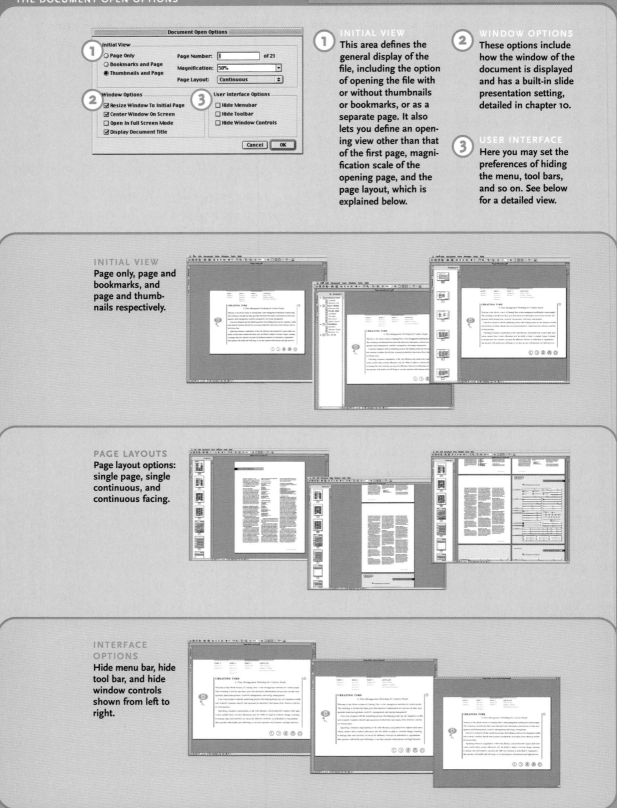

INITIAL VIEW

1 This area defines the general display of the file, including the option of opening the file with or without thumbnails or bookmarks, or as a separate page. It also lets you define an opening view other than that of the first page, magnification scale of the opening page, and the page layout, which is explained below.

WINDOW OPTIONS

2 These options include how the window of the document is displayed and has a built-in slide presentation setting, detailed in chapter 10.

USER INTERFACE

3 Here you may set the preferences of hiding the menu, tool bars, and so on. See below for a detailed view.

INITIAL VIEW
Page only, page and bookmarks, and page and thumbnails respectively.

PAGE LAYOUTS
Page layout options: single page, single continuous, and continuous facing.

INTERFACE OPTIONS
Hide menu bar, hide tool bar, and hide window controls shown from left to right.

will have removed the most obvious tool for navigation. As the viewer uses the scroll bar, the bottom left frame displays the page number, and when the viewer uses the slider in the scroll bar, a pop-up shows the page number in the middle of the window. Judge carefully if you should remove the window controls from your document. You should have a very good reason for doing it and a well-designed substitute for navigation.

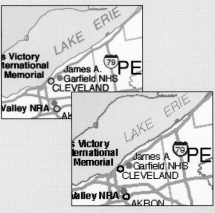

TESTING 1 2 3

Before you hide too many elements when your document opens, send it to some typical users and ask them to open it and then navigate through the pages. You may find that your audience is much more experienced in navigating through the PDF or far less experienced.

DISPLAY PREFERENCES

The Document Open Options let you control some of what the viewer sees on the screen. However, there are a set of preferences that you have very little control over—the Display Preferences. If you choose Edit>Preferences>General and then click the Display category, you will see the Smoothing options. These options control how text, vector art, and pixel images are displayed. You may want to turn on Smooth Line Art to improve how it looks on screen. Or you may want turn all the settings off to improve the screen redraw performance. Whatever settings you do choose, though, will not be the same settings that your readers have. When you change the settings, they are applied only to that specific computer. The settings don't travel with the file. (We'll discuss the CoolType Smoothing controls in the chapter on eBooks.) So as much as it may horrify you, it is very possible that your viewers will see your beautiful text, art, and images with ugly jagged edges. This is another case where you may need to educate your viewer to change display preferences, especially if you have documents with vector illustrations.

SMOOTHING OPTIONS

The Display Preferences for Smoothing control the appearance of text, line art, and images. However, these settings can be changed by the user—not by the content creator. So while you may see a presentation that looks like the top image of the map, your viewers may see the bottom display.

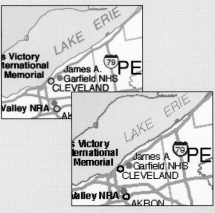

3.3 Using Bookmarks

Bookmarks function as a high-tech variety of your own physical bookmarks, dog-eared pages, and sticky flags. They help you quickly find a specific page in a document. Acrobat bookmarks have the additional benefit of letting the user quickly jump to other content, files, and multimedia components. A list of bookmarks acts a bit like the Favorites list or Bookmark menu in a web browser.

Bookmarks function similar to links in a web browser. When selecting a bookmark, it becomes highlighted and normally transports you to the associated location and view in the document. Bookmarks can be customized and linked to other content as well, such as movies and external files. As you add, erase, nest, and rearrange bookmarks, you can create a versatile navigation panel that serves in addition to, or in place of, a table of contents.

To access the Bookmarks panel, click the Bookmarks tab in the Navigation Pane. If you don't see the Bookmarks tab, you might find it in the document window as a free-standing palette. Or access it by choosing Window> Bookmarks to open the palette. (You can then drag it back into the Navigation Pane if you'd like.) With the Bookmarks palette visible, you can see whether the document contains bookmarks. As we mentioned in the previous chapter, applications such as PageMaker, InDesign, and QuarkXPress can automatically create Bookmarks from the table of contents, lists, and built-in commands. The Open Web Page creates bookmarks for each HTML page converted to PDF. You can also create your own bookmarks from scratch.

BOOKMARK PALETTE

If you have no bookmarks, the palette looks rather empty. However, notice the little icons at the top of the palette. These are buttons you can click for the most common commands to create a new bookmark, delete a selected bookmark, or expand a bookmark to see the nested elements.

The little triangle on the top right corner of the Bookmark palette opens the Bookmark menu. The menu differs slightly depending on whether you have selected an existing bookmark or are creating a new one. In the former case, you have a few more options from the menu (e.g., deleting the bookmark or renaming it).

As you work with bookmarks, remember that you select a bookmark by a single click. You can select multiple bookmarks by holding the Shift key and then clicking another bookmark. This will select all those in-between. You can select non-contiguous bookmarks by clicking them while holding the Ctrl key (w) or Command key (m).

BOOKMARK MENU COMMANDS

If you haven't looked at the Bookmark palette menu, you're missing much of the control of bookmarks. Some of the menu commands are not available unless you have a bookmark selected in the palette.

General Bookmark Commands

Most of the commands in the Bookmarks palette menu let you create and modify bookmarks. The New Bookmark command creates

CREATE NEW BOOKMARK
Clicking this icon adds a bookmark to the list in the current position. The bookmark will be untitled. Give it a name.

DELETE SELECTED BOOKMARKS
Click to delete a bookmark. You may select as many bookmarks as you wish and delete them together.

EXPAND THE CURRENT BOOKMARK
With a bookmark selected, this button expands any bookmarks that are nested.

BOOKMARKS
When expanded, bookmarks lists all the occurring bookmarks in the document. You can customize the list by giving the entries colors and styles. You can also nest the listings, as shown here.

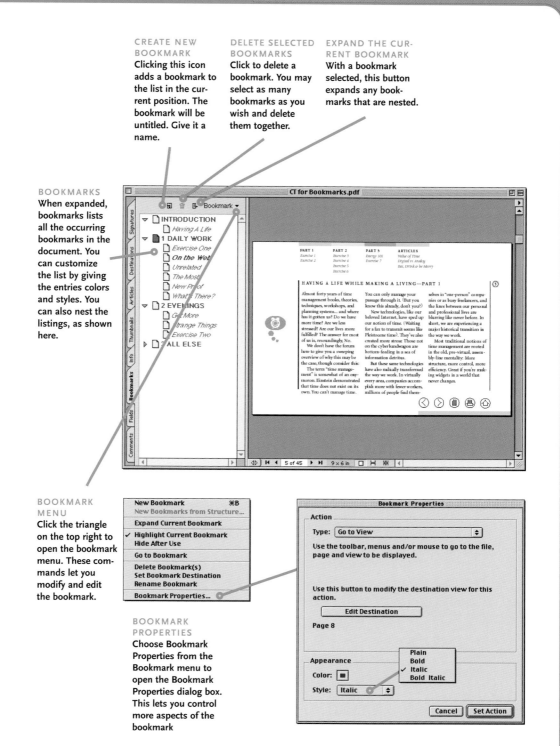

BOOKMARK MENU
Click the triangle on the top right to open the bookmark menu. These commands let you modify and edit the bookmark.

BOOKMARK PROPERTIES
Choose Bookmark Properties from the Bookmark menu to open the Bookmark Properties dialog box. This lets you control more aspects of the bookmark

a bookmark that sends your viewer to the page and view that you have selected. (We'll cover creating a bookmark in detail shortly.) Press the keyboard shortcut Cmd+B or click the New Bookmark icon.

If you have a Tagged PDF document, you can use the Bookmark from Structure command to generate bookmarks automatically from the tagged elements in the document. Choose the command and the Structure Elements dialog box appears. Select those tags you want to turn into bookmarks, and then click OK. The tagged bookmarks appear in the Bookmarks palette. The icons for tagged bookmarks display lines that indicate they were generated from tags.

The Delete Bookmark(s) command is straightforward. Select one or more bookmarks. Then choose the Delete Bookmark(s) command. You can also delete selected bookmarks by pressing the Delete key on your keyboard.

The Highlight Current Bookmark command highlights the icon next to the bookmark after it has been selected. This is very useful to help you remember which bookmark you last clicked—somewhat like a bookmark's bookmark.

When you select the Hide After Use command, the Bookmarks palette along with the Navigation Pane collapses once you select a bookmark. However, this command does not hide a free-standing Bookmarks palette.

The Go to Bookmark command seems like more trouble than it's worth. Ordinarily, a single click on a bookmark sends you to the destination. However, if you hold the Shift key and click on a bookmark, you will select the bookmark without moving to its destination. You can then choose the Go to Bookmark command to invoke the destination. The Go to Bookmark command is important if you work with Bookmarks programmatically.

The Set Bookmark Destination command should probably be renamed "Reset Bookmark Destination." This command lets you apply any current view as the new destination for a bookmark.

Nested Bookmarks

To make a possibly growing list of bookmarks more user friendly, you can nest bookmarks as lower-level elements in other bookmarks. The Expand Bookmark command opens a top-level bookmark to display the next-level bookmark. You can also use the Expand Bookmark icon at the top panel. Use the plus sign (w) or triangle (m) next to a nested bookmark to expand it one level at a time. (Hold the Alt key [w] or Option key [m] to expand all the levels of a bookmark.) Also, when your bookmarks panel is active, you can use the right and left arrow keys to expand and collapse bookmarks

🔆 MAKING A BOOKMARK

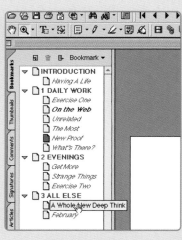

① The first thing to do is to set the page and document window view that you want to display once the bookmark is selected. Then use the pull-down menu and select New Bookmark (this could also be done by using the New Bookmark icon at the far left in the bookmarks palette).

② Once the bookmark is defined, it will be listed in the Navigation Pane as "Untitled." The cursor is in the title field, and the next step is to name the bookmark.

Bookmark Names and Properties

If you want to alter the name of a bookmark you may do so with this option. You can also rename the bookmark by double-clicking on its name in the Bookmarks panel. This will activate the bookmark, but also change the cursor to an I-beam in the text box.

Bookmarks come with a range of interesting properties that can enhance the on-screen display of your file. The Properties dialog box lets you change the bookmark from a simple Go to View command to other types of commands. For example, you can set the bookmark to open an external file, go to a web site, resize the view, display multimedia content (e.g., Flash animations, sound, or movies), or invoke a JavaScript action. This allows you to use a combination of bookmarks in very effective ways. For instance, a PDF catalogue for a record company might have a bookmark for each CD the catalogue. Nested inside those bookmarks could be one bookmark that plays a sound sample from the CD and another that takes users to the website where they can purchase the CD.

The default action attached to a bookmark is "Go to View," but this is only one action among many available. It's important to understand that the bookmarks work differently when Actions are attached. They substitute the selected action for Go to View. For example, if you attach a sound to a bookmark, it will not transport you anywhere but will merely play the sound.

Acrobat 5 added the option of setting font/color properties for bookmarks. This means that you can create a customized list that acts much like a navigation menu and/or TOC. This very useful tool allows you to create a much more hierarchical and user-friendly list by applying colors and font styles to the entries in the list. It is possible to use Unicode coded characters, such as Asian fonts, for Bookmark names, if the system-provided font supports those characters.

MAKING BOOKMARKS

Here we'll make a very basic Go to View Bookmark. First, open the bookmarks panel by clicking its tab in the Navigation Pane.

Step ① Set the View

First display your page and view as you want it to appear when the user clicks the bookmark. Navigate to the correct page and set the view using any of the tools.

Step ② Create the Bookmark

When you're satisfied with the view in the document window, go to the New Bookmark tool or the pull-down menu to make a bookmark. Once the bookmark is listed "Untitled," enter a proper name for the bookmark in the Navigation Pane. It is now ready for use.

---

⑤ SOUND BOOKMARK

① We wanted to add a bookmark that incorporated a welcome audio file. Since adding an action to a bookmark removes the link to a specific page and plays wherever in the document it is accessed, we did nothing to the view. From the pull-down menu we selected New Bookmark and named it.

② After naming the bookmark, we selected it and accessed Properties from the pull-down menu. In Type, we selected Sound. We then chose our sound file from the Select Sound button and clicked Set Action. The sound is now ready to play anywhere in the file by clicking this bookmark.

One of Sandee's favorite techniques is to select text with the Text Select tool and then create a bookmark. The selected text is automatically used as the name of the bookmark.

The Navigation Pane lists the bookmarks in the order they are created, independent of page numbers. You can, however, organize them to become a more user-friendly list or TOC by customizing the bookmark names, using colors (as previously discussed), and nesting.

Nesting is indicated by a plus sign (W) or a triangle (M) to the left of the bookmark icon. You create a nested bookmark by dragging the selected bookmark (or bookmarks) under the title of the bookmark that you want to contain the nest. A small black line indicates that you can move the items into the nest. You can nest bookmarks as many levels deep as you want.

You can reposition a bookmark in a similar way; instead of positioning the bookmark under the bookmark title as you would for nesting, place it under the Page icon on the left side. The black line indicates where the bookmark will be positioned. If you move or delete a parent bookmark, all the nested bookmarks follow the parent.

MAKING A SOUND BOOKMARK

As mentioned, you can attach actions other than Go to View to a bookmark. Instead of acting as a hotlink to a page destination, the bookmark triggers the action, e.g., plays a movie or sound. Sadly, a bookmark can only have one purpose in life—so it can't play a sound and take you to a destination, unless you program a series of actions in JavaScript and have that Bookmark run the JavaScript. It remains a single-action Bookmark, but the JavaScript enables it to activate more than one action.

Step ① Create the Bookmark

Since we don't care about the destination, simply click the New Bookmark icon and name the bookmark.

Step ② Select the Action

With the bookmark selected, choose Bookmark Properties from the Palette menu. Use the Type menu to choose the Sound command. Then click the button below to select the sound you want to attach to the bookmark. When done, click Set Action.

WHEN TO USE BOOKMARKS

The question that ultimately comes up is when to use bookmarks. If you have a table of contents in your document with dynamic links, why would you need bookmarks? One reason is that the Bookmarks palette can always be visible. As soon as you select a table of contents link, the page disappears.

Nested bookmarks can be very helpful for long documents or groups of documents with many links. Instead of scrolling down page after page of links, nested bookmarks take up very little space for many levels. (The Acrobat Help document is a good example of this type of compact bookmarking.) Bookmarks are not limited to "their" document; they can be used for sets of documents, such as chapters in a book, and give full access to the complete book.

Bookmarks also let you name destinations in ways that might not be appropriate in a table of contents. For instance, you can create a set of bookmarks with labels for specific readers: Notes for Sandee, Pattie Belle's Chapters, Bjørn's Work. These aren't labels you would want in the document, but they do help the people working with the document. Of course, you have to consider whether your audience will understand how to use bookmarks.

This interactive map of Nanaimo shows how bookmarks can be used in creative and user-friendly ways. The cartographer, Angus Weller, created a bookmark list that works like an extended map legend. Each bookmark is hotlinked to a spot on the map. Viewers use the legend to find a street, school, or other location. They click the bookmark to go to an enlarged view with the location displayed in the middle of the screen.

As anyone who has used a map has found, legends can be difficult to use. This one is a dream. The map also contain links in strategic areas, like the ferry company. In this example, the link takes you to the BC Ferries website, where you'll find schedules and so forth. This interactive map adds real value to the content of the map. Note: As sophisticated as this legend is, the steps to create it are quite simple. Define each bookmark and then nest them as desired.

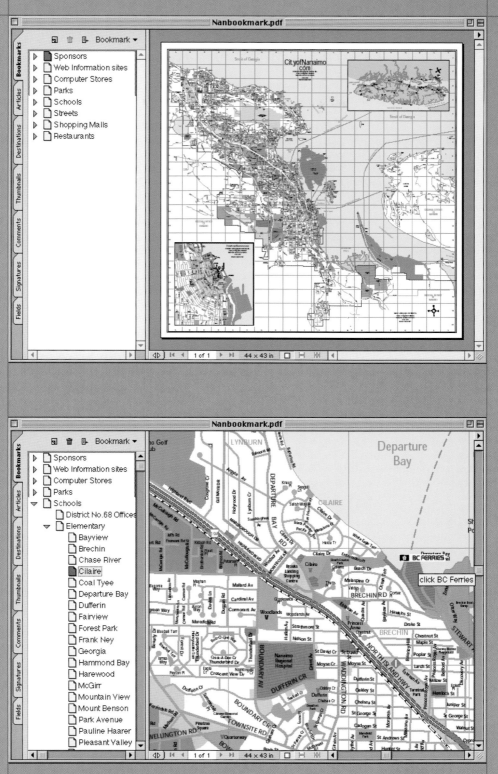

3.4 | Using Thumbnails

A Thumbnail is a small representation or preview of a page. Thumbnails are generated automatically (unless specified) and function as hyperlinks, enhancing navigation. The thumbnail view and tool can also be used as an editing tool (in Acrobat) as you can reorganize and move the thumbnails (and thus the pages in a document) around like cards in a deck.

EMBEDDING THUMBNAILS

In Acrobat 4, you had to execute a command to create thumbnails for the pages in a document. You then needed to save the document in order to keep the thumbnails. You could also execute a command to delete all the thumbnails in a document to reduce the size of the file. (Each thumbnail adds about 3 K to a file so a hundred-page document would have an additional 300 K.) However, if someone with Reader 4 opened the file without thumbnails, they would not be able to see any thumbnails.

All that has changed in version 5. In Acrobat 5 and Reader 5, you don't have to save the thumbnails with the document. They are generated automatically as soon as the user opens the Thumbnails palette. In addition, there are commands in the Thumbnails palette menu that allow you to embed or remove embedded thumbnails in the document. Why would you want to embed thumbnails in a document when they are generated automatically? You might want to do so if you expect your document to be viewed using Reader 4.

NAVIGATING WITH THUMBNAILS

Thumbnails act as hyperlinks. You simply click the thumbnail to move to that page. However, thumbnails can also be used as a zoom tool that lets you change the magnification of the selected page.

When you select the thumbnail for a page, you see a bounding box around the thumbnail. If you position the cursor over the bottom-right corner of the box, the cursor changes to a two-headed arrow. Drag this arrow to resize the bounding box. As you change the size of the box you change the area of the page that is displayed. The smaller the outline box, the higher the magnification setting for the page. Once you have zoomed in on the page, you can also position the outline box to move around the page. Position the cursor on the edge of the box and drag with the Hand cursor. The view in the document window changes as you move the box.

WHEN TO USE THUMBNAILS

You have the option of opening a document with the Page and Bookmarks palette visible or the Page and Thumbnails palette displayed. The question is which should you present to your viewers first? If you don't have the time or inclination to create bookmarks, then thumbnails are more valuable—especially since they are automatically generated in the palette. However, before you set the file to open with the Thumbnail palette visible, consider carefully what the thumbnails in your document look like. One rule of thumb (no pun intended) is to not open the Thumbnails palette if all the thumbnails look identical. For instance, if all the pages of the document are filled with text,

DELETE PAGES
You may select as many thumbnails as you wish and delete them simultaneously.

MENU
Click the thumbnail pull-down menu to reveal a host of page-editing features, as well as display options.

LARGE VS. SMALL
You may choose between two thumbnail display sizes in the menu: large and small.

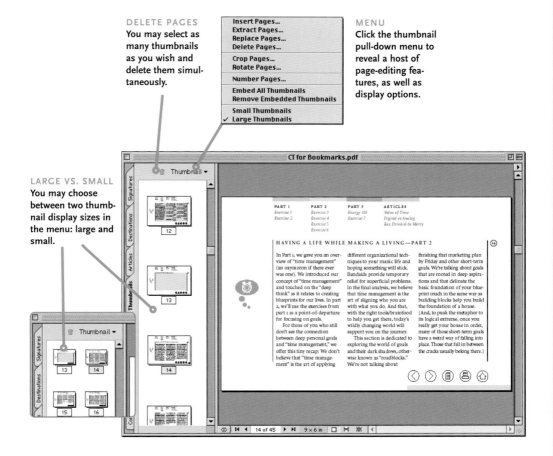

VIEW AREA
Using the page view outline, you can select the area of the full-sized document that you want to view.

the user will have few visual cues for choosing a specific page.

Of course even the most varied thumbnails aren't worth a dime if users don't know what to do with them. So you need to judge how familiar your viewers are with Acrobat and Reader. Remember that you can use the Thumbnail palette menu to name each page. This gives thumbnails the added benefit of descriptive titles.

THUMBNAILS MENU COMMANDS

The Thumbnails palette menu is on the top of the Thumbnails palette. You have a choice of viewing small or large thumbnails. This command is the only option that is available from the Thumbnails palette menu in Reader or in a web browser. The rest of the commands are available in Acrobat and are used for editing the document pages.

Page Management Commands

The page management commands let you add, delete, and extract pages from the document. The Insert Pages command lets you select pages from another PDF document to add to the current file. (The Insert Pages command is also available from the Document menu.) However, you can also insert pages visually by dragging thumbnails from one file into the Thumbnails palette of another. Don't forget you can insert pages that are of different sizes from your original document.

The Extract Pages command copies pages from the current document and opens them as a new PDF file. You also have the option of deleting the pages that you extract as part of the extraction.

The Replace Pages command lets you choose pages from one document to swap for pages in the current file. When you choose this command from within a document, you are asked to open another file as a source for the

new page. Once you click on the file that you want to use, a dialog box prompts you to define the range of pages you want to substitute. As we mentioned in Chapter 2, the Replace Pages command replaces only the graphics and text elements on the page. Enhanced content—such as form fields, comments, and links—from the original page is kept on the new pages. This makes it easy to make changes to a document without losing custom navigations and elements.

A single click on a thumbnail navigates to the page as well as selects that thumbnail. You can select additional thumbnails by holding the Shift key and clicking another thumbnail. This selects all the pages between the two. You can select non-contiguous pages by holding the Control key (w) or Command key (m) and clicking each individual page. After selecting pages, you can delete them by choosing the Delete Pages menu command or by clicking the Delete Pages icon at the top of the Thumbnails palette. (If your fingers are near the keyboard, just press the Delete key.)

Perhaps the most versatile and intuitive feature of the Thumbnail palette is the ability it gives the user to move pages around. You can select thumbnails, individually or in groups, and rearrange them within the palette. When you move a thumbnail, you also move the associated page. You don't have to worry about the links, as they are all preserved and follow the page wherever it goes.

One command you may feel is missing from the Thumbnails palette menu is one to duplicate pages. Do not fear, you can easily duplicate pages by holding the Alt key (w) or Option key (m) as you drag the selected thumbnails to a new location. A highlight bar indicates where the new pages will be positioned. When you release the mouse, the copied thumbnail appears with all enhanced elements.

To copy a thumbnail and place it in a different PDF document, open both the file you want to copy from and the one you want to copy to. Then drag the thumbnail from one page to another. Watch for the highlight to position the page, then release the mouse button.

LIGHT BOX

If you pull the Thumbnails palette out of the Navigation Pane you can expand it to cover your entire computer screen. If you choose the Large Thumbnail option in the palette, you can view your pages as an electronic light box.

Modifying Page Commands

When you use the Crop Pages command, the Crop Pages dialog box opens with numerical controls for the top, bottom, left, and right margins. The Crop Pages dialog box gives you the option to crop all the pages in the document, just the selected pages, or a range of pages.

An important option for the Crop Page dialog box is Remove White Margins. This automatically trims the pages to just the live area of the page. Those who want to crop visually can also use the Crop tool to outline the area you want keep.

The Rotate Pages command rotates pages 90-degrees clockwise, 90-degrees counter clockwise, or 180-degrees. Ordinarily you would choose the proper rotation in your authoring application. However, you may need to change the orientation of the pages inserted from other documents. One of the most clever features of the Rotate Pages dialog box is the ability it offers to rotate all the portrait pages or all the landscape pages. (Portrait pages are those where the height is greater than the width. Landscape pages are those where the width is greater than the height.) This is extremely helpful if you have inserted many pages from a document with a different orientation.

Numbering Pages

At first glance the Number Pages dialog box looks like an ordinary feature that simply adds numbers to pages, restarts the page numbers from a certain number, and customizes the style of numbers from Arabic to Roman. But hidden in the Prefix field is the ability to name the thumbnails with labels.

Let's say your document is a high-school history book with different chapters and student exercises. Instead of consecutive numbers for all the pages, you can use the Prefix option to apply a label to a group of pages. For instance, select the pages for a group of student exercises and apply the prefix "Class Exercise." The thumbnails for those pages are then labeled "Class Exercises 1," "Class Exercises 2," and so on.

Even better, if you change the Style of the page to None, the label appears with no numbers at all. This gives your readers the freedom to move to any page in the document without feeling they are reading pages out of order. Watch out if someone turns off the Preference setting in the Options category for "Use Logical Page Numbers." With that setting turned off, your custom labels will not display.

3.5 Making Destinations for Acrobat

Destinations are navigational "targets" that work within a single open document. These targets are used for creating navigational systems called Named Destinations and are only available in Reader through bookmarks. It is also only through Bookmarks that destinations are accessible across documents. Destinations have no properties or editing features; they are mainly a tool for developers.

WHEN TO USE DESTINATIONS

The strength of a destination is that it sorts the target (a kind of link) by name and/or page number, and retains the link to the page rather than the content. This means that if you move a page, or delete it, the link stays activated for the page number, not the moved page/content. Destinations are meant as authoring tools, not end-user tools. However, they can be used as very useful targets for bookmarks. For example, Framemaker creates all its PDF navigation using Named Destinations.

USING DESTINATIONS

At first Destinations may seem similar to bookmarks, but they are quite different. First, when opening a document's destinations palette tab, you have to scan the document to see if destinations exist by clicking the destination scan icon at the top left of the Destinations palette. If scanning returns results, the destinations are listed in the Navigation Pane.

Second, unlike bookmarks, you invoke the destination link by double-clicking the icon to the left of the destination title in the Navigation Pane. This sends you to a page and a view specified by the document author.

> **LINK DESTINATIONS**
>
> *Destinations cannot target from one document to another. However, you can set a link in one document to a destination in another. Use the Link tool in the source file and specify link action (Goto View), then select the destination in the destination list in the next document. When the link is invoked in the first file, it transports you to the destination defined.*

Third, unlike bookmarks, there are no properties associated with Destinations because they are targets. You cannot further enhance the link with colors, actions, or multimedia content. Nor is there any real reason to, because the appearance of a target is irrelevant.

Finally, unlike thumbnails, you can't move destinations around or use them to modify a document, but you can sort the Destinations according to page number and name from the bar immediately above the Destinations list. One thing that's important to remember when using destinations is that the page numbering system (numbering, prefix, etc.) that you define in the Bookmarks properties, will also be used by the Destinations. For example, if you decide that you want to give all your pages a "Document A" prefix, that is what will be displayed in the destinations palette.

MAKING DESTINATIONS

Destinations are created much like bookmarks. When you are on a page and have defined a view, click the New Destination icon or select it from the pull-down menu. The destination appears with its name highlighted. Simply type a new name for it. Give the destination a descriptive title.

SCANNING
To display a list of destinations in the Navigation Pane, you must first scan the document using this icon or the destination pull-down menu.

CREATE NEW DESTINATION
Create a new destination by clicking this icon or selecting the New destination option in the destination pull-down menu. Sort destinations in the list by page or name by clicking the titles in the panel.

DELETE
Delete destinations by selecting them and clicking the Trash Can icon.

DESTINATION MENU
The destination menu contains just two options: New destination and Scan Document.

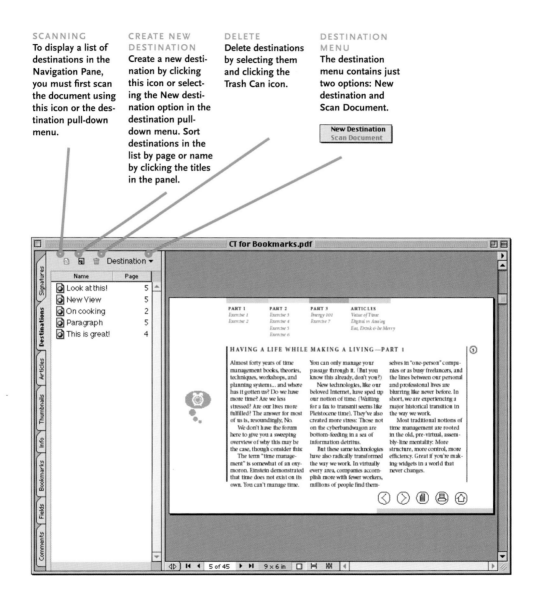

3.6 | Defining and Reading Articles

Acrobat's articles are the electronic equivalent of articles in newspapers and magazines. However, unlike their print counterparts, Acrobat's articles can be set for more than just text. They also help your readers quickly navigate to follow a selected story. Using articles, your readers can jump pages in a single bound and zoom in and out of a document.

WHEN TO USE ARTICLES

Articles can be extremely helpful for navigating through complex documents. Consider the situation where a user needs to read only certain parts of a long, complex document (e.g., a Visa application). In this case, the user would have to wade through the introductory information, perhaps information pertinent only to certain countries, then fill out a form (or several forms) and submit it. With articles, you may specify users and create user-specific strings of text in the introduction to the document. To follow our Visa example, a list of nationalities (or other values), could start the user on an Article path that guides them through instructions, qualifying information, lists, and ultimately the customized forms based on his or her unique circumstances.

Keep in mind that articles are more complex and less intuitive than bookmarks or thumbnails. You may need to give your audience some extra explanation to use articles effectively.

CREATING ARTICLES

Create articles by dragging the Article tool to define the area that you want inside the Article thread. The most obvious area to select is a column of text, but you can also define the area around any portion of the document window that you want to string together. For instance, you can define all the images in a document as an article. This lets viewers quickly click through all the images in the document.

Once you have defined an article, it is listed in the Article palette in the Navigation Pane and you can modify its properties in the Article palette. To create an article, follow the steps below.

Step ① Draw the Initial Articles

The Article tool ⬙ is located in the tool bar. Once selected, the tool shows up as a crosshair. Draw a box around the content you want to include. Keep in mind that the area within the box will be displayed across the width of the document window. This means that the maximum width of the box will be displayed, eliminating the rest of the document from view.

An article can only define content within a single page, not across pages. That's where the link between article segments is necessary. Once you draw the first article segment, a rectangle appears in outline with black resizing boxes. On the top, you will see a dashed number (a-b), where "a" indicates the article number, and "b" indicates the segment created in that string. For example, 2–5 indicates that you're working on the second article's fifth

---

ⓘ INSTANT ARTICLES

One of the supreme advantages of using PageMaker is that you can automatically create articles from stories. We would greatly appreciate such a feature in QuarkXPress and InDesign.

DELETE ARTICLE

Selecting an article and clicking the trash can will remove an entire article.

ARTICLE MENU

Clicking this accesses the menu items and the article properties.

Hide After Use
Read Article
Clear
Rename
Properties..

Article Properties
Title: Exercise 1
Subject: Time Analysis
Author: Pattie Belle
Keywords:
Cancel OK

ARTICLE RECTANGLE

Articles are created by selecting the Article tool in the tool bar and dragging the tool to enclose an area that you want the viewer to see. Once you release the rectangle, it becomes a selection that can be modified by using the square modifier handles. The article tool then lets you define the next article segment. The box in the upper middle defines the article number, and segment within the article. The + sign at the bottom right indicates that there are more segments to the article.

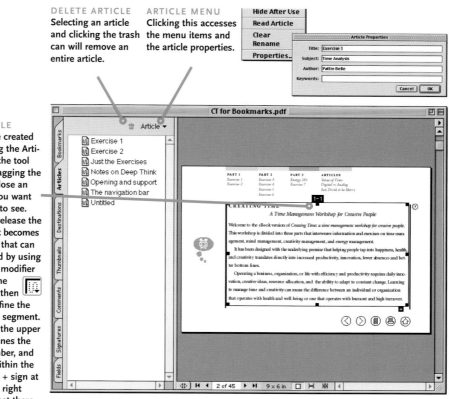

ARTICLE VIEWS

The Article tool crops the page according to the rectangle you define. This means that you can crop out any irrelevant con-tent to guide the viewer through a nar-row path. If you want a consistent frame of view, simply make the rectangle the same width.

CURSOR VIEWS

As you move the cur-sor over an article segment, it changes and become a hand with certain proper-ties indicating the specifics of that seg-ment.

Hand tool

Next View

Previous View

At Beginning of Article or Jump to Beginning/ End of Article

At End of Article

Enter into an Article

segment. In the lower right corner, you will also see a +, revealing that more article segments can be added.

Step ② Draw the Next Article Segment

You can now draw the next rectangle, either on the same page or somewhere else. (Use any of the navigation commands or buttons to move to each area of the article.) Note how the article tool has changed ⬚ to indicate that new segments can be added. As you add new segments, note how the article numbers change.

Step ③ End and Name the Article

When you have entered all the different components to the path, you must instruct Acrobat that the article is ending. You do this by pressing Return/Enter on the keyboard or switching to another tool, such as the Hand tool. The Article Properties dialog box appears prompting you to enter a title for the document, subject, author name, and keywords. What you name the article is important—this will appear in the Article palette.

Modifying Articles

Once you have created an article, you can use the Article tool to move or modify the segments. You can add segments to the article by selecting the article tool and clicking on the + link at the bottom. You can then draw a new segment. As you add new segments, the numbering automatically updates.

You can also remove segments by selecting them with the article tool and using delete on your keyboard. A dialog box pops up, prompting you to choose whether you want to remove the whole article thread or just the selected segment.

ARTICLE MENU OPTIONS

The Article palette menu contains additional commands for working with articles.

Article Management Commands

With the Hide After Use command selected, the Navigation Pane collapses once you have double-clicked one of the articles in the list. This feature can be desirable since the Navigation Pane takes up space in the document window.

The Read Article command performs the same function as double-clicking the article entry in the palette.

The Clear command deletes the article from the list and clears all article segments on the page. You can also click the Delete Article icon at the top of the Article palette.

Rename

Use the Rename command to highlight the name of the article in the palette. Use the Properties command to open the Article Properties dialog box, where you can change the name, subject, author name, and keywords. The items in the Properties dialog box are just to provide

---

⊕ DEFINING ARTICLES

① We wanted to make an article that took the viewer directly from a reading segment to a fill-out "Notes" section. First we opened the Article tab. Selecting the Article tool, ⬆ we drew a rectangle around the text that we wanted. The rectangle defines the viewing area.

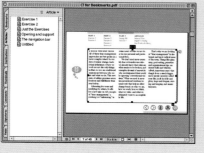

② Next we move four pages ahead to the Notes box where we wanted to viewer to go after clicking the first article area. Then we drew the second article segment with the Article tool. Note how the article tool changes its appearance after the first segment. ⬚

③ We then pressed Return/Enter on the keyboard. This let Acrobat know that was the end of the article. This opened the Article properties dialog box, which prompted us to enter the article's name, subject, author, and keywords. After we entered the information, we clicked OK. The article appears in the Article palette.

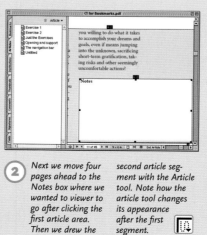

more information about the article. Acrobat does not use them as part of the Find or Search commands.

READING/VIEWING ARTICLES

Unless your readers have a little background on using articles, they may not get much out of the feature. Analyze your audience and decide whether you need to have an introductory explanation about working with articles.

Step ① Double-Click the Article Icon

Double-clicking or selecting Read Article from the pull-down menu takes you to the first segment in the article thread. The magnification is automatically set so that the entire width of the article fits inside the viewing area of the window.

You can also enter an article by positioning the Hand tool anywhere in the article segments on the page. The Hand tool displays a down arrow with a bar. Click to enter the article.

Step ② Move Through the Article

Move the cursor over the article. This displays the Article Hand tool with a down arrow visible which indicates that there is more in the article. Click to move to the next segment of the article.

Moving Through the Article

When you click with the Article Hand tool, the cursor usually displays a down arrow indicating that the next click will move to a new segment. However, if you hold down the modifier keys, you can change where the article takes you.

Hold the Shift key to change the Article Hand tool cursor to the up arrow. This indicates that the next click brings you to the previous view.

Hold the Alt (w) or Option (m) key to jump to the beginning of the article. Hold the Control + Shift (w) or Option + Shift (m) keys to jump to the end of the article. The cursor is the same for both of these jumps: an up arrow with a bar across the top.

When you have reached the end of the article, the cursor displays a down arrow with a bar across the bottom. Press the Return key or click to go back to the view from which you began reading the article.

You can also press the Return/Enter key to move forward through the article or Shift + Return/Enter to move backward through the article.

⚡ READING ARTICLES

① To read the article we defined, we selected the Hand tool. In the Article palette, we double-clicked the name of the article we defined previously. This displays the first segment of the article. We could also have double-clicked on the page inside the article area.

② Moving the cursor over the text in the article reveals the hand with an arrow pointing downward. This indicates that each click moves to the next view in the article string. As you see below, this view is larger, focusing on the fill-out section for the user.

3.7 | Traveling through Maps

Angus Weller is a cartographer who lives and works near Vancouver, B.C. Several years ago, he decided to abandon traditional map publishing for digital map production on the Internet. He has a growing library of more than 300 PDF maps on his website that are available for free with security encryptions. These maps can also be purchased as editable Illustrator and Acrobat documents.

Acrobat PDF documents have always had a good integration with vector graphics. Starting with Adobe Illustrator 9 that integration has become even better. Angus uses Illustrator to create the original artwork for his maps. (He has been using Illustrator since its second version, called Illustrator 88.) Since Illustrator's native file format is now PDF-related, he can use the Save As command to turn his files into PDFs.

Angus just used the basic features of Acrobat in most of his early maps. He felt the built-in features of the program were powerful enough and he didn't need button rollovers or custom links. In the last year he has become more creative, adding links to off-site databases and embedded HTML locations. For instance, his map of the United States contains an HTML link to the official website for each state.

One of the benefits of working with Illustrator and Acrobat is the ability to easily move documents back and forth between Illustrator and Acrobat without losing enhanced Acrobat content. Angus can save an Illustrator file as a PDF including the editable Illustrator file. He can use Acrobat to add links, buttons, or bookmarks to the file. However, if he has to make changes to the basic map information, he can use Illustrator to re-open the file. He won't see the Acrobat elements in Illustrator, but they remain when he opens the file in Acrobat. This round-trip editing is an important advantage.

Angus is currently working on a project that he feels is "too large"—this is an interactive Atlas of Greater Vancouver, which is located at: (http://www.mapmatrix.com/tmhtm/htmgvrd/gvrdkey.html). Angus says the final project "would have paper, Internet, and disk products." This allows him to merge traditional map making with electronic PDF presentations.

With the Nanaimo map, he was trying to create a "micro-website" that has bookmarks, rollovers that display generic graphics or company logos, links to community websites, and data on issues like "Emergency Preparedness," local history, educational and leisure catalogs, and current affairs. The map is currently nearing completion. It took about a month to research the information and build in Illustrator. Angus' next stage is to go out and sell the concept to the local business community.

Angus enjoys both aspects of his electronic map making. Creating the front-end graphics in Illustrator appeals to his artistic and design background. Adding the interactive PDF elements lets him take the informational aspects of cartography to new levels.

○ ON THE CD

Samples of Angus Weller's PDF maps can be found on the Acrobat Master Class CD. *You can find out more information and see more of his work at www.mapmatrix.com.*

If only printed maps were as versatile as this electronic version from Angus Weller. In addition to the navigational bookmarks, he has added electronic links to places of interest. When the reader clicks the link, Acrobat launches the web browser and takes the viewer to the website for that attraction.

This United States PDF road map contains some special electronic features. Readers can use Acrobat's Zoom tools to see the entire map or enlarge the view on specific areas. Each state on the map is hyperlinked to the official state website. What a great way to learn about the United States!

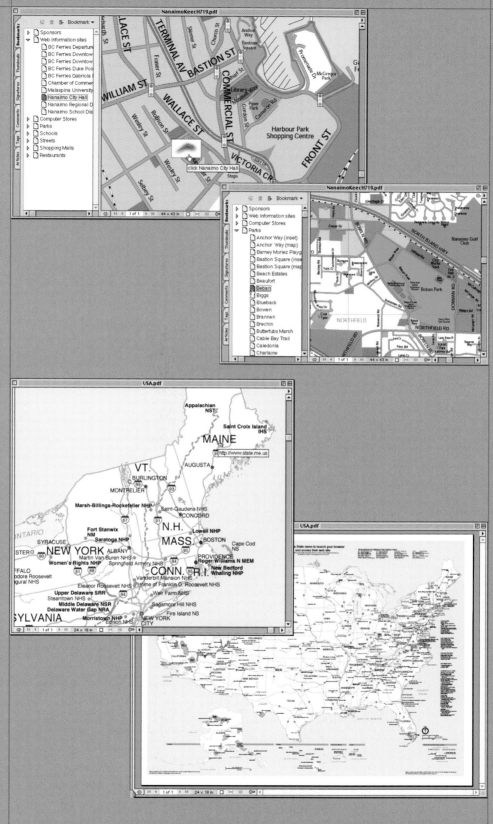

3.8 | eBook Navigation

Ted Padova, Acrobat expert extraordinaire and author of the Acrobat PDF Bible, *not only knows his subject, but he also puts it to excellent use. His Acrobat Tip Sampler eBooks are great examples of many of the subjects we discuss in this book. Ted uses custom navigation in these eBooks, but also gives the user the option of having all the familiar Acrobat navigation tools available. He also uses a beginning page of the book to explain the navigation and design of the document.*

If anyone could ring all the navigational bells and blow all the interactive whistles in Acrobat it would have to be Ted Padova. Since Ted uses so many custom-made navigation elements, he can't rely on his Reader users (especially beginning Acrobat students) to be acquainted with all the features in his documents. So, as soon as readers move past the title page and a Welcome page, they discover a Legend that provides a detailed, interactive explanation of his custom navigation elements, followed by a Table of Contents with interactive navigational links.

Ted does the design and layout in Quark-Xpress using master page backgrounds and grids. He places the normal state (also called the Up state) of the navigation button on these pages. He creates separate PDF documents that contain the rollover states (also called the Over state) for these buttons. He uses Acrobat's button dialog box to integrate the Up and Over states. (See the next chapter for details on how to create button states.)

One of the more sophisticated decisions Ted made was to use Adobe Photoshop instead of Adobe Illustrator to create the graphics for his buttons. Most designers have been taught to favor vector graphics, especially in documents that can be magnified on-screen. This is because vector graphics (called line art in Acrobat) maintain their appearance as the viewer enlarges the page. Bitmapped images can become jagged as the viewer enlarges the page.

Ted has good reasons for using Photoshop graphics. He knows that the default setting for the Display options is to turn on smoothing for text and bitmapped images, but not for line art such as the graphics created by Illustrator, Adobe InDesign, or Macromedia FreeHand. By creating the graphics in Photoshop he made sure that the graphics would look good for the huge majority of readers who never bother to change their default settings.

As you can see from the pages shown here, the eBook opens with the Navigation Pane, document window elements, and menu bars visible. The document window is small enough that the entire page is visible, even when the file is opened on smaller monitors. Although there are no bookmarks in the document, all the pages are visually different from each other. This makes the built-in document thumbnails very useful as navigation elements.

◉ ON THE CD

Ted Padova's Acrobat Tip Sampler *eBooks can be found on the* Acrobat Master Class CD. *With no security options at all, you can completely dissect the elements to see how they were put together. You also get great additional Acrobat tips in the process! We are very grateful for Ted's generosity in supplying the sampler.*

Ted tells you how to use his book right up front. He covers not only how to navigate through the book, but also how to use the interactive buttons (on the right side of the page) that he has incorporated to add more content to the tip pages.

His legend page explains each navigation button as you roll over it, in addition to having descriptive tool tips assigned to each button. He also demonstrates the use of comment notes to provide copy and paste JavaScript for the tips.

The page design of these eBooks uses the same grid and background throughout. They have been beautifully designed for screen use, as well as print.

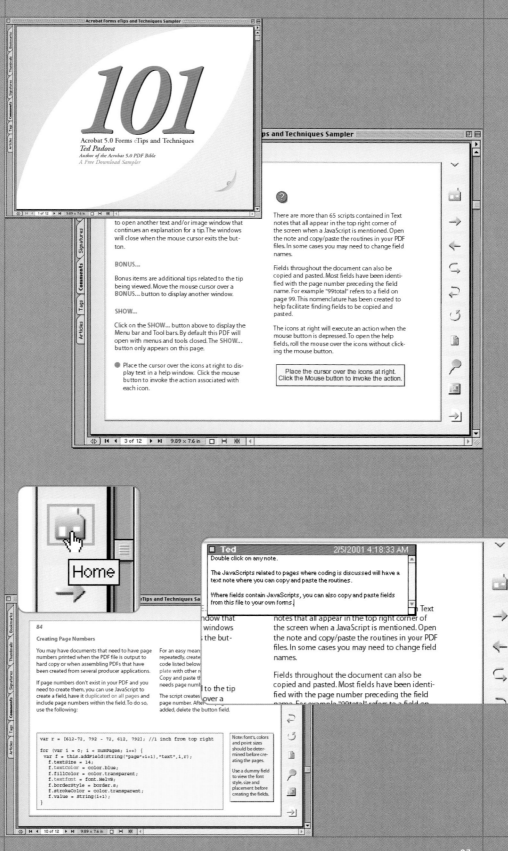

Interactive PDF

One of the most interesting aspects of Acrobat lies in its ability to provide on-screen user experiences, whether it's an interactive form or a multimedia presentation using QuickTime VR or interactive Flash movies. Although PDF has long been known as a cross-platform page display and publishing format, more people are now becoming aware of the program's powerful interactive opportunities. Whether you wish to add high-level customized interaction, or merely want to utilize the many built-in interactive features, Acrobat makes it easy to create the interface. As with all other interactive design projects (websites, CD-ROMs, stand-alone applications, etc.), you must start with a plan and a structure. This chapter will take you through the steps of creating a unique PDF document.

4.1 Designing Interactivity

If you come to interactive PDF from a web or multimedia design background, then you probably have experience and knowledge that you can immediately apply to PDF design. If your background is primarily designing print documents, you'll have to learn some of the basic tenets of producing interactive documents/experiences.

Let's start by explaining what we mean by an interactive PDF. The minimum requirement for a document to be considered interactive is that it contain internal links that the user clicks to move from one page to another. These links may have been created automatically in an application such as PageMaker or InDesign, or they may have been added using Acrobat's Link tool.

From the minimum requirement above, the level of interactivity increases to include links to external PDF documents, websites, and other files created in other applications. Continuing along this road, you can incorporate a variety of rollover effects, calculations, JavaScripts, and video and audio files. The possibilities are endless.

The first thing to consider when creating your interactive PDF is the flow and hierarchy of information—as you would when designing for the printed page. Next, consider the type of interactivity you will include in the document. Should the interactive elements help in document navigation? Should they display special icons or graphics? Should they control sound and animation? Last, consider what tools you should use to make your PDF come to life. Acrobat provides two primary tools for creating links and buttons. To add

ON THE CD

We have provided you with many of the interactive documents mentioned in this chapter. You can take these files, open them, select the links or buttons, and examine all the settings. This is a great way to see how the experts assemble their documents.

hyperlinks to your PDF, use the Link tool. To add graphic elements to your page and use them as buttons or rollovers, use the Form tool. Both tools offer options that are as versatile as their web counterparts. You'll learn about these tools and their properties in this chapter.

Remember that testing PDF files is as important as testing website design. Just as software companies have to beta test their products to discover where the code doesn't work correctly, so PDF content creators should test their presentations. For instance, you may open and navigate through your document on your large-screen monitors with no problem. But you may discover that you cannot move around the file when you open it on a friend's notebook screen.

Try to find a wide variety of levels of users—experts, novices, and anyone in your target audience—as testers. You'd be surprised how quickly users will do the one thing you never expected anyone to try. Don't wait until your presentation is close to a final form. It's very possible your testers will find bugs that require a major rethinking of the document.

Once you've got everything working just the way it should, the software might get upgraded to a new version—and you'll have to test and debug all over again!

In this chapter, we'll start with creating and working with the easiest interactive element of all—a basic link.

Some of the interactive elements may not be obvious to the casual viewer. Since Pattie Belle is presenting the work, she doesn't need to explain where the triggers are for the interactive elements.

Button

Comment (closed)

Pattie Belle's lectures on art and technology cram in everything she can think of—movies, sound, links, rollovers, comments, and more. She figures that if she's going to be standing there talking, she better give the audience something fun to look at.

Sound Comment

Comment (open)

Movie

Rollover

4.2 | The Link Tool

In addition to Acrobat's built-in navigation tools, there are unlimited possibilities for adding your own interactive elements. These elements can take the form of links and buttons that move the viewer to new destinations, page actions that play movies or sounds, or custom JavaScript commands. Whatever elements you choose, your system should be well thought out and tested.

Hyperlinking is one of the primary interactive features of the web. Similarly, Acrobat allows you to add hyperlinks to PDF documents. You use Acrobat's Link tool 🔗 to define a "hotspot," which is the active area for a command or link. Similarly to what happens inside a web browser, when the viewer moves the cursor inside the link area, the open hand cursor changes to a pointing finger. This indicates that the viewer can click to trigger the link. Unlike the buttons created with the Form tool, the hotspots created by the Link tool can only be triggered by a click. There are no Rollover states and no access from the keyboard.

Create a link by selecting the Link tool. Then drag to create a rectangle of the desired size. When you release the mouse button, the Link Properties dialog box automatically opens. After you define the link properties, the hotspot, which frames the link area, displays an outline box with four handles. Use the handles to resize the active link area. You can also reposition the link by dragging the outline box to a new location.

The Link Properties can be opened again later by selecting the Link tool and double-clicking inside the link outline box. You can also choose Edit>Properties or use the context-sensitive menu (Right-click for Windows or Ctrl-click for the Mac). When you choose the Link tool, all links on the page display with their outline boxes visible. You can double-click any existing link to modify its properties.

Remove links by selecting them and pressing the Delete key on your keyboard or by choosing Edit>Clear.

LINK APPEARANCE OPTIONS

The Link Properties dialog box controls two qualities of the Link hotspot area. First, it controls the appearance. Second, it controls the action—what happens when the mouse is clicked inside the hotspot area.

In the Appearance area, your first choice is to decide whether to make the hotspot rectangle visible or invisible. Which one you choose depends entirely on the circumstance, but as a rule of thumb, unless the link has a cue that lets the audience know it's a hyperlink, you'll need to create visual hotspots. For instance, if you have previously applied a special color or typeface to your linked text, you can use an invisible link over that area. The special text treatment serves as an indication that a link exists. However, if you want to add a link over an empty area of the page or over text that does not have special treatment, you will most likely want to create a visible rectangle.

> **ⓘ WHO'S ON TOP?**
>
> *One little bit of information that we like to keep in mind is that the Link plane is always above the plane that holds comments and fields. This means that a link is always available even if a form field has been applied in the same spot.*

TYPE
This option controls whether the link displays an outline box or not. If you select Visible, you'll have further options to the right—Width, Color, and Style.

HIGHLIGHT
This option lets you select what happens once the user clicks on the link. The examples on the right show Inverse, Outline, and Inset, respectively.

OUTLINE WIDTH
This option is available if you choose Visible Rectangle. The examples on the right show the three widths.

Invisible Rectangle
✓ Visible Rectangle

✓ None
Invert
Outline
Inset

✓ Thin
Medium
Thick

Link Properties

Appearance

Type: Visible Rectangle ⬍   Width: Thin ⬍

Highlight: None ⬍   Color: ■

Style: Solid ⬍

✓ Solid
Dashed

Action

Type: Execute Menu Item ⬍

Execute a menu item in Acrobat.

✓ Execute Menu Item
Go to View
Import Form Data
JavaScript
Movie
Open File
Read Article
Reset Form
Show/Hide Field
Sound
Submit Form
World Wide Web Link
None

Use this button to set the menu item to execute.

Edit Menu Item...

Execute: None

Cancel   Set Link

COLOR
Click to open and set the color of a visible rectangle.

OUTLINE STYLE
Style gives you the option of a solid or dashed outline rectangle.

ACTION TYPE
This list gives you access to an extensive collection of features that add functions to a link, such as Open File, which displays another file once you click the link, and Submit Form.

Menu Item

Please select the menu item you want to execute from the menu bar.

Cancel   OK

EDIT MENU ITEM
This is where you specify the settings for your particular Action Type above. Some of the Actions have a large collection of editing capabilities, others very few.

Once you choose the option for a visible rectangle, you can style the appearance of the rectangle as follows.

Width: This option lets you control the thickness of the border. Your choices are thin, medium, and thick. These settings are not actual width sizes for the border. Rather, they are dynamic widths that display the same width regardless of the magnification of the page. So the thin setting stays thin even if you zoom in on the hotspot.

Color: This lets you set a color for the border. When you click the small square, the color settings dialog box for the operating system opens. You can then choose the color.

Style: This lets you choose between a solid line or a dashed border. Although the dashed line could be useful for coupons, we much prefer a solid border. In addition to the options for a visible rectangle, you have options for how the link area appears when the viewer clicks the link. This is called the Highlight.

None: This option results in no highlight when the link is invoked.

Invert: This option reverses the color of the graphics or text inside the hotspot. These reverses are based on RGB screen values. So a yellow area becomes blue, red becomes green, and black becomes white.

Outline: This option inverts the appearance of the hotspot's outline. If you have a red border for the hotspot, the outline highlight turns it green.

Inset: This setting shifts the appearance of artwork within the hotspot area. It also adds black lines to the top and left sides of the hotspot. This creates the illusion that a button is being pressed into the page.

SETTING LINK ACTIONS

Link Actions are a list of commands that can be executed when the viewer clicks inside a hotspot area. At the very least, the Link Actions let you apply a hyperlink to move from one page to another. However, the opportunities for interesting pop-ups, content activation, and other effects are virtually limitless with these actions.

Execute Menu Item: When you assign this action to a link hotspot, you have the option of letting the user perform any of Acrobat's menu commands with the click of a link. For example, you can create a hotspot that changes the display of the PDF from single page to continuous pages, or rotates the window when you click the hotspot area.

The implications of the Execute Menu Item action are quite sophisticated. If you want, you could use the Execute Menu Item action to recreate the entire set of Acrobat's menu commands as custom link actions.

So if you set the document's open options to hide the menu bar, you can still provide access to the menu commands through your own custom links. There is a slight difference between operating systems in how you choose the menu commands. Windows users choose the items in a special Menu Items selection box.

⊛ CREATING LINKS

1 In this example we wanted to create links from the table of contents to the pages. We selected the Link tool and drew a rectangle around the "Introduction" entry and released the mouse.

2 As the mouse was released, the Link Properties dialog box appeared. From the Type options, we selected Go to View. We then chose Invert from the Highlight menu. This creates a reversed box when the link is clicked. Next, we set the link in the Action menu by selecting Go to View.

Mac users choose the items directly from the menus in the menu bar.

Of course the menu commands available to users depends on which version of Acrobat or Reader they have. If you enable a menu action containing a tool that is not available in a user's version of Reader, it renders the link useless. Also note that the menu item commands are not available when you view the document in a web browser. This is a very severe limitation if you are intending to make your document available via the web.

Go to View: This lets you navigate to a view on the same page, a different page, or in a different document. When you choose this option in the Link Properties, you will then use the navigation commands or tools to move to the view—even though the Link Properties dialog box is still visible.

One of the things you should be aware of is the Options preference to open cross-document links in the same window. This setting is turned on by default. If you create a link action to open a new document, that new document will open in the current document window. However, if you have changed your preference, you will have new documents open in a new window. You can't rely on your viewers having the same preference setting.

Note: If you work with Acrobat 4, you will see a Go to View action listed for buttons created with the Form tool. Although the com-mand looks the same, it does not allow you to navigate to set a specific destination or view. Adobe must have felt the limited command was confusing, because the action is no longer available for button actions in Acrobat 5. So unless you use a custom JavaScript, the Go to View action is available only as a link.

Import Form Data: This action triggers the command to import the information in an FDF (Forms Data Format file). This information can be used as part of e-commerce information or editorial markup.

JavaScript: The JavaScript action allows you to attach JavaScript commands to the document. You can even script a few commands into a single supercommand.

Movie: This action plays a movie file (placed using the Movie tool). As described earlier, Acrobat can play either a movie or sound file with this command.

Open File: This action lets you choose another file to open. This can be another PDF file (however, it is highly recommended to use the Go to View command for opening another PDF document) or one from a different application. For example, if you want to show your viewers an Excel document, you can use this action to open that file. The file must be where the Acrobat file can find it. The best location is the same directory as the PDF document. Note that when clicking on such a link, a warning message pops up that asks for permission to open another program. This is a security measure and can't be disabled (it is essentially an Emergency Stop function).

Even though the Link Properties dialog box is still active, we can navigate through the document to set the page we wanted the link to take us to. We then clicked the Set Link button to set the action for the link.

Testing the link, we see that when the hand cursor moves over the hotspot, the hand changes to the pointing *finger. This indicates an active link. When clicked, the black on white type becomes reversed.*

Read Article: This command lets you assign a hotspot to open the first view of an Article. This is very helpful if you don't expect your viewers to be familiar with how the Hand tool can trigger Articles.

Reset Form: This action resets form fields to the default values.

Show/Hide Field: This option lets you display or hide form fields. Although you can do this with a Link Action, you have far more choices with the Form tool (covered later in this chapter).

Sound: This action plays a sound when the hotspot is activated.

Submit Form: This option lets you submit the information in a form to a web server.

World Wide Web Link: This action lets you enter a URL to go to a specific web page. When a viewer clicks the link they can view the page in a web browser or convert the page into a PDF.

None: The None setting does nothing.

CREATING INSTANT WEB LINKS

To create web links, you may not have to manually create all your links. Simply choose Tools> Locate Web Addresses>Create Web Links from URLs in text. Acrobat then draws a link over any web addresses that it finds in the document.

Most of the time this command works well, but it doesn't recognize abbreviated web links, such as www.vectorbabe.com. The command only converts a full address such as http://www.vectorbabe.com (Sandee's web page). It also won't create the correct link if the address breaks across two lines.

If you use this command, check carefully to make sure none of your web links have been truncated into incorrect addresses.

LINKS FROM OTHER APPLICATIONS

You can also create Go to View links automatically when you create PDF documents from InDesign, PageMaker, QuarkXPress, and FreeHand. These programs will automatically create web links as well as internal hyperlinks.

InDesign, Framemaker, and InDesign let you choose to create links from the table of contents generated from the Table of Contents command, the index created from the Index command, and links created using the Hyperlinks palette. PageMaker gives you a little more control over which links are actually exported. PageMaker also lets you choose the settings for the appearance of the links. Framemaker converts all Framemaker-generated links into PDF links (Table of Contents, Indexes, Cross references, etc.).

QuarkXPress lets you convert its own lists and indexes into Acrobat links. However, you don't get to choose the link appearance. If you create many complex documents in Quark-XPress that require a lot of linking, you may want to consider the XTension PDF Design Pro from Techno Design. This extension lets you map internal and web links to character styles applied to text. You can also choose the appearance of the links before you create the PDF document.

FreeHand automatically converts its internal links, which navigate between pages as well as external links, which can open web pages.

ARTS Link Suite

If you have spent any time working with Acrobat's built-in Link tool, you will have noticed a few functional deficiencies, such as the inability to copy and paste a link or to check for and change "dead" links. This can become an overwhelming and time-consuming task if you have a heavy PDF link work flow.

ARTS Link Suite consists of ARTS Link Checker and ARTS Link tool. These two Acrobat plug-ins fall in to our category of "can't live without" items.

The Link Checker does just what it says—checks for bad and broken links. (Bad links are links that send the viewer to biker bars. Broken links are links that send the viewer to the edge of the earth where they fall off.)

You can have it take you to the page the bad link is on, create a report of pages with bad links, flash the bad links on the page, count the links in a document, and more.

ARTS Link tool adds the flexibility to copy a link and then paste it in the same position on all the other pages. This is something that Acrobat itself lets you do with buttons created with the Form tool but not with Links—hence the need for the Link tool.

The Batch button allows you to paste links throughout an entire group of documents. This makes creating a global link navigation system fast and easy.

The Link tool also lets you globally change appearance properties, such as the border color and the highlight effect.

You can also use it to set the base URL for links in a document or a batch of documents. ARTS Link Tool is available for $299 and ARTS Link Checker for $99. Or you can purchase them together as ARTS Link Suite for $349 from www.epublishstore.com. Demo versions are also available.

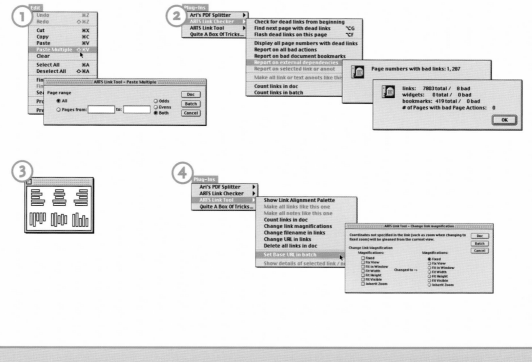

① ARTS Link tool adds the Paste Multiple command to the Edit menu. This allows you to copy and paste links on another page or an entire range of pages.

② ARTS Link Checker adds a menu item to the Plug-ins menu with a slew of commands that report on the links in a document.

③ With the ARTS Link tool you can Shift-click to select multiple links. Then, you can use the Link Alignment palette to move the links to align their tops, bottoms, edges, or centers.

④ Use the Batch Processing features to change properties such as the magnifications and URL destinations.

Initially Michael King of King Design in Norway was disappointed that this report on environmental issues by the Norwegian Railroad Commission would only be made available in PDF format. So Michael used the opportunity to create a document purely for on-screen viewing. This meant formatting a simple yet elegant navigational structure (which disappears when printed), as well as creating an architecture that lends itself to non-linear viewing, including web links. The navigation bar consists of 3 upper levels (1); Contents (Innhold), Print (Utskrift), and Summary (Sammendrag). Though the buttons don't change properties when clicked, they contribute to the overall intuitive user interface.

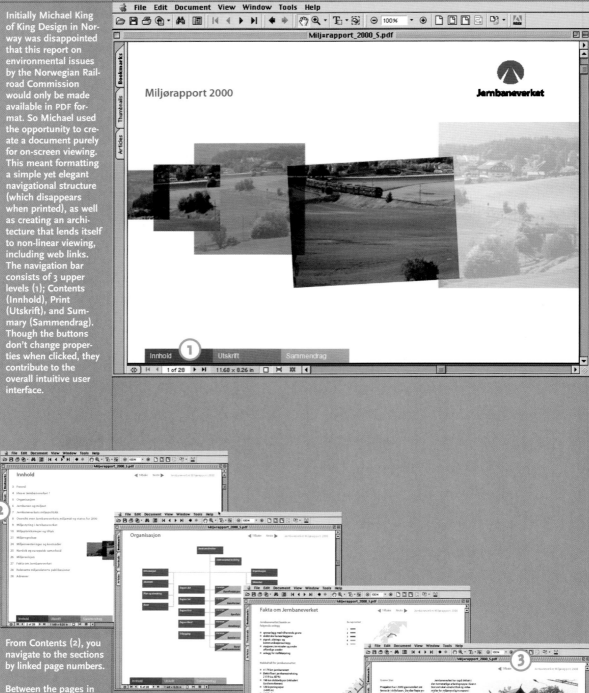

From Contents (2), you navigate to the sections by linked page numbers.

Between the pages in the document, King used Previous Page and Next Page buttons (3), functions that most users have been conditioned to use from web browsers and consumer electronics.

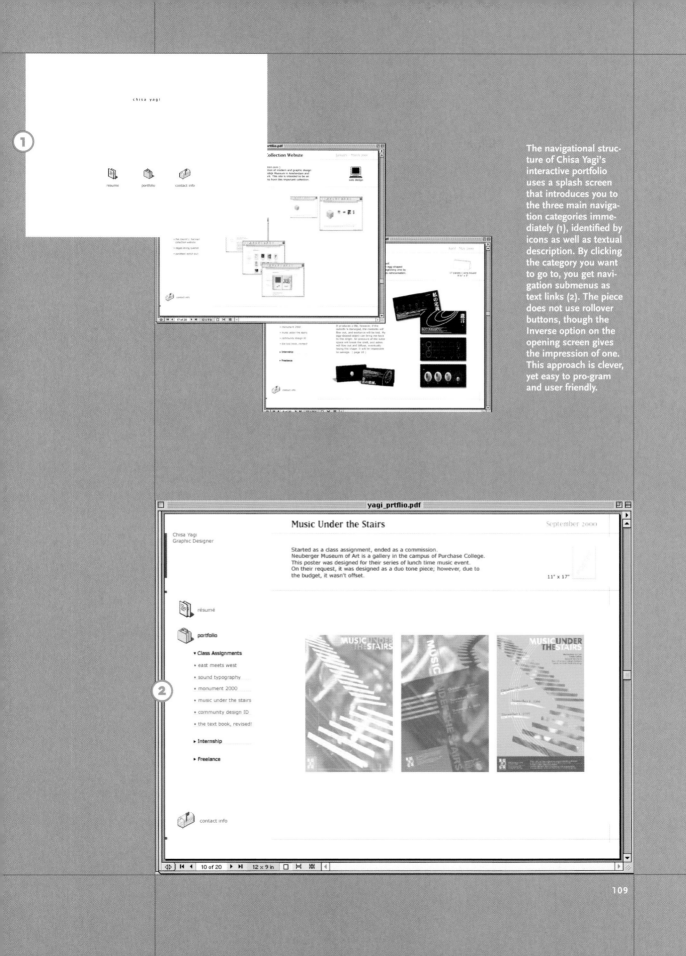

The navigational structure of Chisa Yagi's interactive portfolio uses a splash screen that introduces you to the three main navigation categories immediately (1), identified by icons as well as textual description. By clicking the category you want to go to, you get navigation submenus as text links (2). The piece does not use rollover buttons, though the Inverse option on the opening screen gives the impression of one. This approach is clever, yet easy to pro-gram and user friendly.

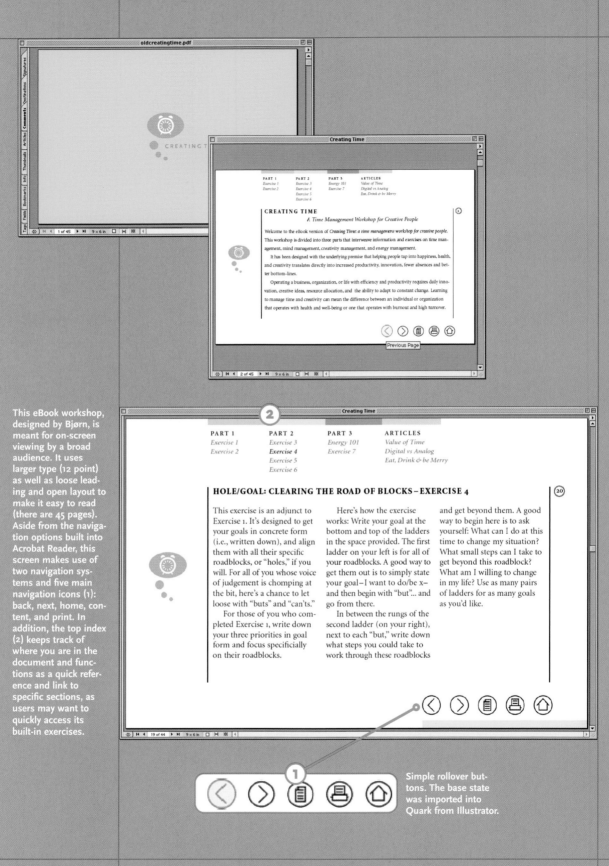

This eBook workshop, designed by Bjørn, is meant for on-screen viewing by a broad audience. It uses larger type (12 point) as well as loose leading and open layout to make it easy to read (there are 45 pages). Aside from the navigation options built into Acrobat Reader, this screen makes use of two navigation systems and five main navigation icons (1): back, next, home, content, and print. In addition, the top index (2) keeps track of where you are in the document and functions as a quick reference and link to specific sections, as users may want to quickly access its built-in exercises.

PART 1
Exercise 1
Exercise 2

PART 2
Exercise 3
Exercise 4
Exercise 5
Exercise 6

PART 3
Energy 101
Exercise 7

ARTICLES
Value of Time
Digital vs Analog
Eat, Drink & be Merry

HOLE/GOAL: CLEARING THE ROAD OF BLOCKS – EXERCISE 4

This exercise is an adjunct to Exercise 1. It's designed to get your goals in concrete form (i.e., written down), and align them with all their specific roadblocks, or "holes," if you will. For all of you whose voice of judgement is chomping at the bit, here's a chance to let loose with "buts" and "can'ts."

For those of you who completed Exercise 1, write down your three priorities in goal form and focus specifically on their roadblocks.

Here's how the exercise works: Write your goal at the bottom and top of the ladders in the space provided. The first ladder on your left is for all of your roadblocks. A good way to get them out is to simply state your goal–I want to do/be x–and then begin with "but"... and go from there.

In between the rungs of the second ladder (on your right), next to each "but," write down what steps you could take to work through these roadblocks

and get beyond them. A good way to begin here is to ask yourself: What can I do at this time to change my situation? What small steps can I take to get beyond this roadblock? What am I willing to change in my life? Use as many pairs of ladders for as many goals as you'd like.

Simple rollover buttons. The base state was imported into Quark from Illustrator.

110

This remarkable self-promotion piece is an example of taking the PDF format to its limits. Glenn Page used the brain as metaphor for the design of the navigation. When users position the mouse over these categories, descriptive text explaining the category pops up in a different location (1). The presentation is further enhanced by using the full-screen mode and an audio introduction.

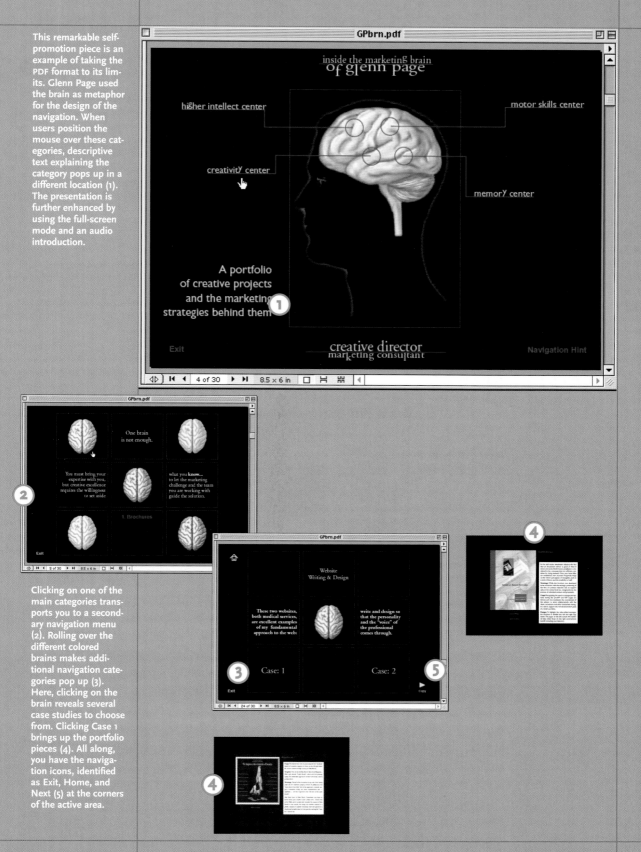

Clicking on one of the main categories transports you to a secondary navigation menu (2). Rolling over the different colored brains makes additional navigation categories pop up (3). Here, clicking on the brain reveals several case studies to choose from. Clicking Case 1 brings up the portfolio pieces (4). All along, you have the navigation icons, identified as Exit, Home, and Next (5) at the corners of the active area.

4.3 Managing Links with Adobe GoLive

If you own GoLive 5 or 6, you already have a powerful PDF link editor in your possession. We first came across mention of this method in the Planet PDF forum and tracked down the source to Deborah Shadovitz, author of the GoLive 5 Bible. She filled us in on the details and gave us permission to pass her wisdom on to you. It just so happens that Pattie Belle had slapped together a PDF website that was rife with "dead links" or "empty references," so we're using it here to show you how easy it is to check your links and fix them with GoLive.

If your presentations consist of single PDF documents, you've probably never run into missing or broken links. However, some elaborate PDF presentations can contain hundreds of individual PDF files that all contain links to open other documents in the presentation.

Fortunately, the links in a PDF document use the same basic structure as the links in HTML web pages. So it is no wonder that the powerful link management features in Adobe GoLive can also be used to check the links in PDF documents.

You don't need to prepare your PDF files any special way—just add your PDF files to a folder. If a PDF contains links to other files or web destinations, you can use GoLive to reassign their destinations.

Note: GoLive will correct the reference within the link object. However, GoLive does not correct any text that might have been underneath the electronic link. This means it is possible for a link to take the viewer to one destination while the visible text displays something else.

FIXING PDF TO PDF REFERENCES

Step (1) **Create a PDF site**

There are at least a couple of methods for editing links in GoLive. We'll take you through the method that Deborah Shadovitz taught us. The first thing you have to do is make the PDF documents part of a website. Fortunately, it is quite easy to create a website with GoLive.

When you start GoLive 6 it asks you if you want to open and work on an existing website or if you want to create a new site. You want to create a new site. You can do this quite easily by using using GoLive's Site Wizard.

In the Options for Local Sites dialog box, you have a choice of where to get the pages for your site. If this were an ordinary website, you might start with a blank page, but in this case you want to choose Import from Folder. You then click the Next button to go to the next step in the Site Wizard.

The Site Wizard asks you to select the folder that contains the PDF documents that you want to check. You also need to select a home page for the site. Since the site doesn't have a home page, you can instruct the Site Wizard to create a generic home page.

As the next step the Site Wizard asks you to select a folder that will become the directory for the site. This is not a big deal—Pattie Belle

First you set up a "site" using your folder of PDFs. You can create a generic home page for GoLive to reference and choose the PDF folder to save the GoLive site data. The GoLive Site Wizard will walk you through this simple process.

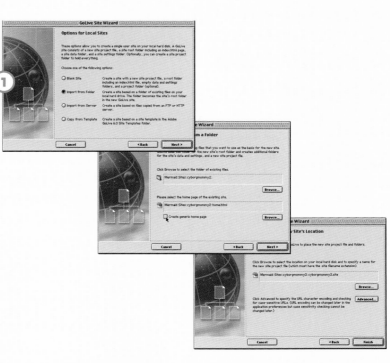

After you have gone through Site Wizard, your folder of files will appear in the site window. Look at all those pretty green bugs! Select a PDF, open the In & Out Links window, and just point and shoot. Better than a backyard bug zapper.

If you select the empty reference icon and then point and shoot, you can fix a whole mess of PDFs at once.

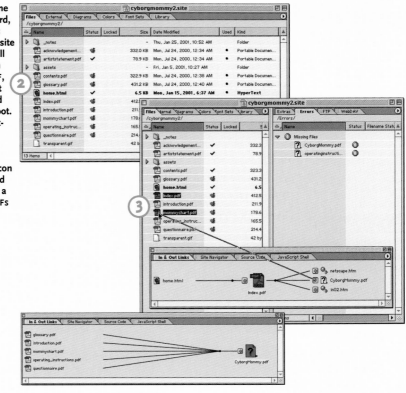

uses the same folder that contains the PDF documents that she is checking. You can now click the Finish button to leave the Site Wizard.

GoLive then presents a Site window that shows the files that are part of the local site. These are the PDF documents that you want to have checked.

If you wish to add PDF documents that are not already in the Site window, just drag them into the site folder. GoLive updates the links as it copies the file into the Site window. This changes all the URL links from relative links to absolute in the process.

Step ② Identifying Bad Links

Website designers use GoLive's Site window to see a list of all the pages and assets in a website. In this case there is only a single HTML page for the site, but there are many PDF documents for the site. Fortunately GoLive doesn't differentiate between checking HTML pages and checking PDF files.

Notice all those little green ladybugs beside the PDFs in the File tab of the site window. Those indicate the broken links in the site. If you work with GoLive 6, the Errors section of the Site Window shows the name of each missing link. GoLive 5 users don't have this list.

If you're wondering how missing links can be created, it might be because the link refers to a file that no longer exists or has had its name changed. In the example of these PDF

documents Pattie Belle had broken up two large PDF documents into a bunch of smaller ones. This created the bad links—references to files that no longer existed.

Step ③ Fixing Bad Link References

Fortunately GoLive not only identifies the broken links for you, it also lets you relink the bad references. Start by selecting a problem PDF from the Errors list or the Site Window. Then open the In and Out Links window. You'll see a mini diagram of the links to and from the file.

To reassign a new PDF destination for a broken link, click the link icon next to the question mark and drag it to the file you wish to reference in the site window. That's it. You can clean up a mess of PDF documents in a matter of minutes.

You can also work backward, so to speak. Click the icon for the the empty reference in the In & Out Links window. The view changes to show all the files that reference that broken link. All you have to do is point and shoot to a new PDF file. This automatically fixes the all the broken references pertaining to that file.

FIXING EXTERNAL REFERENCES

Step ① Fixing External URL References

After you have finished fixing the references between the PDF files, you need to check and clean up the references for any external references in the documents. For instance, you

① GoLive reports all of the URLs referenced in the PDF in the Site window. With the Inspector open, select a URL from the list and click the Edit button to change the destination.

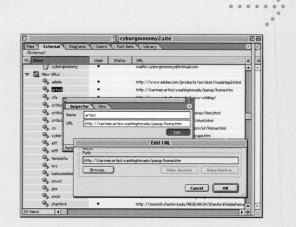

may have referenced a website as being http://www.anyoldsite.com/page.html and then you have discovered that page.html needs to be changed to mypage.html. Obviously you need to fix that reference.

Click the External tab in the Site window. You should see a list of the external URL links used in the site. If you don't see the list, choose Site>Get References Used. This command searches the entire site for all link destinations —URLs and e-mail addresses.

Open the Inspector window and select a URL from the list in the External tab of the Site Window. The URL appears in the Inspector window. You can then click the Edit button and correct the URL.

Step ② Point and Shoot URL References

You can also use the same point and shoot method to fix URL links that we've used on the PDF references. However, this method only works if you already have the URL you want to use in your Site window. Make sure that the In & Out Links window is open. Select the URL you wish to change from the list in the Site window. This causes the URL to appear in the In & Out Links window, where you can click the link button and drag to another URL in the Site window to change the destination.

Globally Changing References

You may have designed your PDF document with multiple references to the same URL destination. Rather than point and shoot to fix each reference, you can globally change all the references to that URL destination. Simple choose Site>Change References. The Change References dialog box appears. Type the new URL destination and then click the OK button. You can also do this by selecting the URL from the External tab of the Site window and go to Site>Change References.

Using the Corrected PDF documents

Don't be afraid of working with GoLive's Site window to change your PDF documents. For instance, just because the PDF files have been defined as part of a website doesn't mean they have to stay in the site folder. Once you have fixed the links, you can move the PDF files anywhere you want. However, you may find it helpful to keep them in the site folder for future checks.

② You can also use the point and shoot method from the In & Out Links palette into the Site window. Of course, this only works if you already have the desired URL in the list.

Change URL destinations globally by selecting one URL from the Site window and going to Site>Change References, where you can type in the new destination.

4.4 Creating Custom Navigation for PDF

In addition to Acrobat's built-in navigation tools, you'll find unlimited possibilities for adding your own navigational systems. In this section, you'll learn how to define the role of custom navigation architecture and how to build it. Programming navigational interactivity can range from simple linked buttons to complex actions attached to buttons and custom JavaScripts. Whatever direction you choose, the design of your system should be tested in advance.

CREATING INTERFACE/NAVIGATION

Before setting out to create a navigation system, consider the following issues of interface and interactive functionality.

First, carefully consider whether a custom user interface will add to the user experience. (It's always better to reconsider this point than creating a product that systemically malfunctions). Custom interface can interfere with function, even though the intentions are good. We've seen plenty of cases where an audience has been conditioned to expect a certain interface, and renovations were not helpful—even though the design looked great.

For example, consider an auto dealership that receives a monthly PDF describing new auto parts. There are Bookmarks that act as a table of contents within the PDF that direct the reader to the various auto parts. Now assume that the architecture is redesigned, so viewers use custom buttons in place of a Bookmarked table of contents. The custom navigation elements may look better, but the user functionality may be compromised. The old adage "Form follows function" may not be as important as "If it ain't broke, don't fix it."

RESOURCE

If you are interested in more background on interface design, we recommend About Face, The Essentials of User Interface Design *by Alan Cooper. He stresses that instead of adding features to software, it is more useful to consider the user's goals.*

Second, decide whether you will use the built-in navigation tools and commands in addition to custom ones, or will you disable the built-in navigational features? This is a complex question. You can choose to avoid the time and effort it takes to create Bookmarks; however, the viewer may miss the functionality that Bookmarks provided. You may choose to hide the initial display of tool bars and navigation elements, but remember that the user can override your specifications, and keyboard shortcuts will always work. Depending on your unique situation, it may be best to include a core of built-in functions as an option for the user.

Last, three main areas are important to keep in mind: Cognition, Consistency, and Communication.

Cognition

Consider how well the audience will understand, learn, and remember the "set of instructions" that a navigation system inherently includes. When designing a navigation panel, for example, you should anticipate the users' familiarity with the tools you create. Consider the age range of your audience, their familiarity with on-screen interactivity, and how they might respond to certain verbal and visual cues.

This fun and interactive document made by Chisa Yagi makes use of the folder tabs convention as a navigational tool (similar to Acrobat's own Navigation Pane). The tabs are integrated into the rest of the presentation as part of the notebook graphic. This creates a cohesive presentation. This unconventional approach works well despite the fact that the author "violates" normal conventions for navigation, such as using a navigation bar that reads vertically and is positioned on the right of the page. This is an example where breaking the rules produces a great design solution.

The inside pages contain an impressive collection of rollover buttons and animations. At the bottom is a rollover history timeline. Positioning the mouse over a rice cooker picture yields a pop-up field and explanation/history.

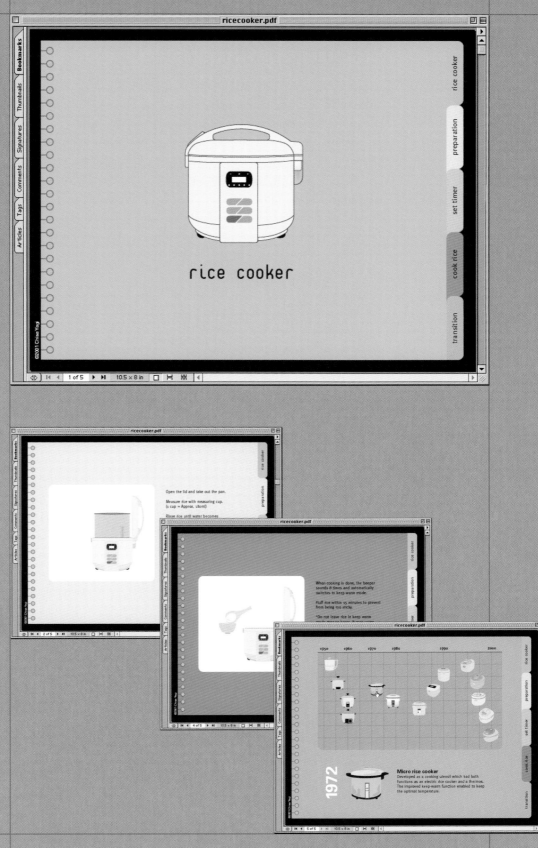

Written cues are important and often overlooked. Consider how and what words are used, as well as their context, vernacular, and conventions for naming navigation items and locations. Make sure your viewers understand your naming and labeling systems, and be consistent with the meaning of words. Make sure your categories follow a logical structure. Choose clear and concise labels and text for categories and buttons. For example, "Home" and "Welcome" should typically precede other navigation elements.

You should also make sure that the syntax and meaning of your labels correspond to audiences expectations. Brevity and clarity are virtues—for example, the word "Contents" is a perfectly good substitute for "Table of Contents." Avoid long explanations when a few simple words will do the trick.

At the same time, instructions (i.e., buttons) should be specific and clear. For example, "catalog" and "products" may confuse an audience as to what is where.

Use a voice that fits the audience and situation (technical, promotional, friendly, etc.). Avoid vernacular, unless it is appropriate for a particular audience. Don't use compounds and acronyms, unless they carry meaning for your audience. For instance, you may be quite familiar with the term FAQ, but your audience might need to have the term defined.

This is not only increasingly important when dealing with a cross-cultural and international audience, but many of us forget that even a homogeneous audience may have a different understanding of basic words. A younger audience may respond well to a description of product displays as "goodies," while an older audience may respond better to "products."

Navigation categories must be practical for the user. This mean that there may be a trade-off between immediacy of information and clarity. We have found that giving the viewer four to six main navigation choices works best.

This makes for quick cognition, without forcing the user to scan each category or sub-category.

Physical cues, such as layout, design, and positioning are of critical importance to usability. Consider your choice of labeling, as well as spatial organization, general appearance, and the positioning of the navigation bar. (Although no drinks are served, a navigation bar is the general term used to describe the arrangement of a collection of hyperlinks that send viewers to different locations.)

The overall design of a page dictates where a navigation bar makes sense. Although there is no convincing research we know of that supports positioning navigation in a particular area, most designers place their navigation controls at the top or left side of the page. Few designers devise right-hand side or bottom navigation. There are some people who claim that right-side navigation is a better place for Roman language readers. They believe that a right-side navigation panel is lest likely to intrude on someone reading a page from left to right. However, as more people have become accustomed to web pages that position navigation elements on the top or left side of the page, familiarity has made those positions a more logical choice. Throughout this book, we will show you some examples of successful PDFs that go against the grain.

Another issue is the use of icons and symbols for navigation. Easily recognizable icons can help you overcome language barriers when working with an international client base. When deciding to use graphic symbols to represent an idea, make sure the symbols will be clear to your audience. For example, seasoned web users will likely recognize a small house as the graphic for the Home Page, but novices may not.

It's always a good idea to label buttons with a clear name. The name used for a button appears as a tool tip that becomes visible when a user holds the cursor over a button. While labels such as "First Button," "Second

Button," and so on may make sense to you, they provide little help for your audience.

Consistency

Perhaps the most important decisions you can make concern navigation consistency across your document. A viewer may forgive imperfect labeling, links that do not work, and perhaps even confusing design, but a document that has unclear or inconsistent navigation will surely lose viewers.

Navigation buttons should therefore appear in the same order, color scheme, size, and spatial arrangement and position on the screen throughout the document.

Communication

The last general navigation issue to consider is the function of communication. Interaction is based on the idea that certain instructions produce results when carried out by the user. A powerful feature of the PDF format is that navigation can be triggered by a variety of events.

The simplest form of communication is the interaction a user gets from a button, whether it is a plain link or a rollover. Communication also involves certain functions that may be triggered by user input through Actions (i.e., the execution of a string of commands). Here we'll cover the construction of a navigation bar/system, button links that use the link tool as an enabler, and rollover buttons which use the Form tool.

CREATING A NAVIGATION BAR

The simplest way to create a navigation bar is to make hyperlink areas using the Link tool. Unlike more sophisticated buttons created with the Form tool (covered later in this section), the hyperlinks created with the Link tool display only the most minimal graphics and user feedback. You can choose to outline the link area with a visible rectangle and apply an elec-

tronic highlight that appears when the link is clicked. Create more elaborate graphic elements for link areas in the authoring application.

The advantage of using the Link tool instead of the Form tool is that you can quickly get a functional navigation system (with a host of Actions attached if needed) with a minimum of effort. Another advantage is that links add little to the final file size, particularly if they are on every page of a long document, unlike the buttons created with the Form tool. A huge disadvantage is that the core Acrobat program contains very few features that most graphic artists would expect to use with links. For instance, there are no commands to align links, paste them throughout the document, or automatically change their actions. This may not matter if you're creating just one or two links in a document. However, if you expect to do a lot of work with links, then we recommend the ARTS Link tool by A Round Table Solution.

You can create a very simple button with Up and Down states by creating a link that has an Inverse option applied. This creates a link area that shows a graphic in the Up state and a negative image of the graphic when the button is clicked (the Down state). Below is a procedure for creating a simple link button to use as part of a navigation bar.

Step ① Create Navigation Bar Links

If you want a navigation bar that uses special graphics as well as text, you should create the visuals in an authoring application such as InDesign or QuarkXPress. If the graphics are very elaborate, Bjørn uses Adobe Illustrator to create visuals and icons for the entire bar. He then imports the Illustrator EPS file into a page layout program, such as QuarkXPress. After the document is approved, he processes the PDF file with Acrobat Distiller.

Step ② Create Link Hotspots

Open the PDF in Acrobat. Here you can create the links for each element in the navigation bar—one link at the time. Select the Link tool and drag a rectangle that covers the area you want to be the hotspot for the link.

Step ③ Setting the Link Properties

Once you release the mouse, the Link Properties dialog box opens. Set the options as discussed in the previous section on Links.

Repeat this procedure for the other buttons in the navigation bar and the document. If your document has a lot of buttons, you can use the ARTS Link tool plug-in to copy and distribute the links through the document.

CREATING ROLLOVER BUTTONS

A rollover button is similar to a link hotspot except that rollover buttons shows one graphic when the mouse is away from the button and a different graphic when the mouse moves over the button and/or when the button is pressed.

Designers use different methods to create graphics for rollover buttons. Bjørn and Pattie Belle like to create the base graphics in an authoring application. This allows them to preview the overall look of the page with the Up graphics in place. An Up graphic shows how the button looks in the normal (or base) state when the cursor is not over the button.

Sandee is more likely to leave the space for the rollover graphics empty and create all the graphic states in a separate document.

Pattie Belle, Bjørn, and Sandee all create separate graphics for the Over and Down button states. The Over state is the appearance when the mouse moves over the button. The Down state is the appearance when the mouse presses the button. In Acrobat 4 and earlier versions, these graphics had to be saved as PDF files. Before Acrobat 5, Bjørn and Pattie Belle used a combination of Adobe Illustrator and Photoshop to save the files in PDF format. Sandee used InDesign. However, with version 5, Adobe added new file formats: TIFF, PNG, Compuserve GIF, JPEG, BMP, PCX, and PICT. While we appreciate the fact that we can use the new formats, we are unsure of how compression is applied to these graphics. So we all continue to save our graphics in the PDF format, which is also the only one that is properly scalable, as long as the artwork is vector or text-based. All other formats are raster images, which do not scale well.

With the release of Illustrator 9, we have another choice for button icons. The native format for Illustrator 9 files is actually PDF. This means that native Illustrator files appear when you go to import button graphics.

Rollover buttons are created using the Form tool (not the Links tool). When you draw a box with the Forms tool to define your button

⚡ CREATING GRAPHIC LINKS

① Although link hotspots don't contain their own graphics, you can use graphics that are already on the page to indicate a link. For the Creating Time interactive book, we designed graphic icons for a navigation bar in Adobe Illustrator. We then imported the navigation strip into QuarkXPress and processed the QuarkXPress file as a PDF document.

② We opened the file in Acrobat and gave all the navigation buttons a link by individually drawing a rectangle around the graphic after selecting the Link tool. Releasing the mouse brings up the Link Properties, where we defined the link destination.

area, you'll open the Field Properties dialog box. This box contains options that allow you to choose how your different button states look and act. Follow the steps below to create a rollover button.

Step ① Create the File and Up Graphics

Prepare a file with rollover buttons as you would one with links. Bjørn and Pattie Belle often use Adobe Illustrator to create visuals and icons. They then import the graphics for the Up state into a QuarkXPress file, where they add the rest of the text and graphics. After the document is approved, they convert the file into a PDF file using Distiller.

Step ② Create the Additional Graphic States

Before you work on the PDF file, you need to create separate graphics for the Down and Rollover states. Remember that the Down state is the appearance of the button when the mouse is pressed down. The Rollover state is the appearance when the mouse passes over the button. Save each state as its own separate PDF file, or as a page in a multiple-page PDF.

Pattie Belle and Bjørn often create button graphics in Illustrator and then use Photoshop to convert them into individual PDF files. Photoshop makes it easy to trim the file to the exact size of the graphic, but the scalability of the icons is lost.

Sandee uses Illustrator to create her graphics and then pastes them into InDesign. Each page in InDesign holds one button state. She makes sure the page size is the same size as her button graphics. She then saves the file as a multi-page PDF.

Step ③ Create the Button

You can now open the PDF in Acrobat. All of the Up states will be visible. Now use the Form tool to create the button. Click the Form tool and drag a rectangle to create the hotspot area for the button. This creates an outline box with resizing handles. When you release the mouse button, the Field Properties dialog box appears.

Strictly speaking, you have created a form field. This is the same type of element that is used to enter data, to create check boxes, and to create radio buttons. Since you want the field to be a button, use the Type menu to choose Button. Next, choose a name for the field. The name is the identity that you (as designer) will use within Acrobat to choose this field from the others in the document. You should also enter a description for the field in the Short Description area. This is the information that appears to your viewers as a tool tip for the field.

The dialog box has tabs for Appearance, Options, and Actions. Although you may not need to set all the features in the tabs, you should click each one to make sure you don't overlook an important setting.

③ In Link Properties, we chose Invisible Rectangle for Type and Invert in the Highlight option. Then, under the Action pull down menu, we selected Menu Item. We then clicked the Edit Menu Item button. This let us use the Menu bar to select the menu item that we wanted the link to prompt. We chose Previous Page for the graphic that points to the left.

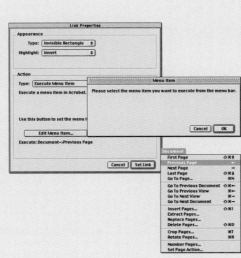

As we clicked to check the link, the inverse highlight appeared. In order to create the rest of the link hotspots, we repeated the process for all the links in the file. We used the ARTS Link tool plug-in, which automated the process.

Setting the Appearance Controls

The Appearance tab lets you set the look of a button. In addition to the graphics you create for a button, you can set your own Border and Background colors. Remember, if you choose a background color, you will not be able to see through to any graphics behind the button. If you choose a border color, you can set the width and style. Border width choices are the same as the Link tool width choices. The Style choices have the same Solid and Dashed borders as the Link tool. You'll also find more elaborate settings for Beveled, Inset, and Underlined borders. These settings help to make your buttons look more three-dimensional.

Text options let you set the color, font, and point size for text labels that you can have Acrobat automatically apply to the button. If you want to assign a label to the button, you do so under the Options tab.

The Read Only check box should not be selected. The Read Only setting creates a form field that the viewer can't activate. This might be a good idea if you want to prevent someone from changing the amount in a sales tax form, but it is not a good idea for a button that should be clicked.

The menu for the Form field lets you control what the viewer sees and whether the button appears when printed. The Hidden settings make it impossible for someone to know the button is there. The Visible settings are much more useful. Depending on the nature of the files, you might find that the majority of the users are printing the file out and reading the prints. If you don't want the buttons and navigational elements cluttering the printed document, choose Visible But Doesn't Print. (This is one of the reasons why Sandee leaves the area under the buttons empty. The only graphics come from the button itself.)

Button Options

The Highlight menu lets you specify the appearance a user will see when a button is pressed. This is an electronic effect that changes the appearance of the Up state to the chosen highlight when a button is pressed. Select Push (under the option tab) to choose options when you create rollovers. The Push highlight is the only setting that contains the option to create a rollover. Do not use the Invert and Outline options, as they only work in the Up state.

When you choose the Push highlight, you'll see three settings for the Button Face When area. Here, you can choose the button's appearance for the three Push button states. The Up state is the appearance when the mouse is not over the button area. The Down state is the appearance when the mouse presses the button. The Rollover state is the appearance when the mouse moves over the button but does not press it. Because Bjørn and Pattie Belle place their Up

---

❸ CREATING ROLLOVERS

(1) *We wanted to create rollover buttons for our 45-page Creating Time interactive book. We created the document, including the navigation bar in Quark-XPress. (The navigation bar itself was designed in Adobe Illustrator.) We created all the normal state buttons and saved them as EPS files before we imported the whole navigation strip into Quark. Next, we processed the Quark file as a PDF.*

(2) *We prepared the Over graphics in Adobe Illustrator and saved them as individual PDF files.*

graphics on the original page layout, they only need to create the Down and Rollover states for their buttons. However, because Sandee leaves that area empty before she exports her layout into PDF, she needs to create the graphics for all three button states.

In the Layout section, you can choose to have a text label, an icon graphic, or both in various arrangements. If you choose the text label, enter text in the Text field in Define Face Attributes. (The font, size, and color of the text is controlled by the Text setting under the Appearance tab.)

<table>
<tr><td>ⓘ USING PLUG-INS</td></tr>
</table>

We usually hesitate to recommend purchasing software plug-ins. We feel that plug-ins should be for highly specialized tasks or for fun enhancements. Acrobat plug-ins are a different story. There are plug-ins you must have to successfully use Acrobat for prepress. Similarly there are plug-ins that are very useful for enhancing interactive documents.

Most of the time, we don't choose the text option. We'd rather create our own graphics and incorporate the text labels into the graphics file.

The Icon setting only allows you to import a graphic to be used inside the button. As mentioned earlier, previous versions of Acrobat only imported PDF graphics. Today there is a much longer list of file formats that are supported. In the Layout, select Icon Only. Then click the Select Icon button. This opens a dialog box where you can navigate to find the PDF files created for the Up and Rollover states. Bjørn and Pattie Belle create their button graphics in Illustrator or Photoshop.

Because Sandee uses InDesign, she has multiple pages to choose from for the PDF icons. She likes to assemble all the icons for all the buttons into one document. That way she can browse through a single file to view all her button icons.

Once you choose an icon for the Up state, you then need to set the icon for the Down and the Rollover states. Click the menu for Down and repeat the process of choosing the icon. Then do the same for the Rollover state.

When you import icons into a button, they are automatically scaled to fit inside the button area. If you change the size of the button, the icon scales to fit the new size. If you click the Advanced Layout button, you can control how the imported graphics are scaled and specifiy their position in the button.

Step ④ Attach an Action/Link

In the Actions tab, you can set actions or commands that are invoked for each mouse event such as a click down, release up, enter, exit, and so on. For a simple rollover button, you can set a menu command such as Go to Next Page to be the action. When you choose Mouse Up from the When This Happens area, the menu command will be invoked when the mouse button is released.

To add an action, click the Add button. The Add an Action dialog box appears. Select Execute Menu Item from the Type pull down

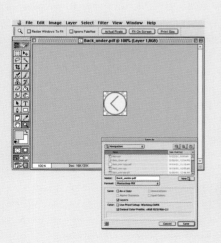

③ We then went on to create the rollover itself. We opened the PDF document made in step 1, then selected the Form tool and drew a box around the "Back" button in the navigation bar. We used the same steps to create the other buttons. As we let up the mouse button, the Field Properties dialog box opened. We named it "back" and selected "Button" under Type. In the Appearance section, we made sure that no border or background color was selected. Under Common Properties, we chose Visible But Doesn't Print, which speeds up printing for the user.

menu. Then use the Edit Menu Item button to select the Acrobat menu item. In our example, we chose the Previous Page command from the Document menu.

For a simple rollover button with a menu command, select Mouse Up from the When This Happens area. This means that the button will show the Rollover effect as the mouse moves over the button. The viewer then clicks inside the button. When the mouse button is pressed down, the button shows the Down state of the rollover. When the mouse button is released, this is considered the Up state. The menu item is then executed as part of the Up State. (Don't worry about the Focus and Blur states for a normal mouse click. These actions are used for more advanced button actions.)

When working with the Field properties dialog box, don't confuse the button appearance states in the Options tab with the mouse events in the Actions tab.

Step ⑤ Duplicating the Buttons

Setting a button for one or two pages is hardly a problem. But what if you want the same button to appear on every page of a hundred-page document? The thought of having to go through each of these steps on every page can be overwhelming.

Once you have created all the navigation buttons on your first page, Acrobat provides a way to easily replicate them throughout the doc-

ument. Choose the Form tool and Shift+click to select all the navigation buttons on a page. With the buttons selected, go to Tools>Forms> Fields>Duplicate. This opens the Duplicate Field dialog box, which lets you define the pages where you want the buttons duplicated.

Not only does the command duplicate the buttons onto the new pages, it also places them into the same position. Before you duplicate the buttons throughout the document, make sure that all your buttons work the way you intend. Unfortunately, there is no way to have one button act as the master for the other buttons placed from the Duplicate command. For instance, if you change the action or icon for one of the buttons, the behavior of the others does not automatically change. You also can't move the buttons on one page and have all the others follow suit.

What happens if you need to change a button? Fortunately, you can delete all the buttons with the same name. Select the button and then press the Delete key on your keyboard. If this button has been duplicated on other pages, an alert box appears and asks if you want to delete the other buttons. You can then remake the a corrected button and duplicate it on all the other pages.

Step ⑥ Testing

Knowing that "things" do happen in electronic documents, we always advocate testing the

⚡ CREATING ROLLOVERS

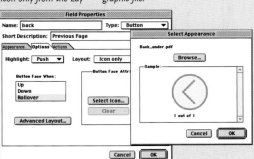

We clicked the Options tab to add the rollover graphic. We chose Push in Highlight and rollover from the Button Face When area. We chose Icon only from the Lay-out menu and clicked the Select Icon button to open the Select Appearance dialog box. We then clicked the Browse button to navigate and select our graphic file.

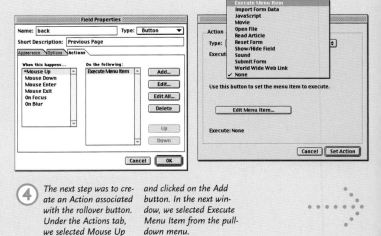

④ *The next step was to create an Action associated with the rollover button. Under the Actions tab, we selected Mouse Up and clicked on the Add button. In the next window, we selected Execute Menu Item from the pull-down menu.*

files—especially interactive documents—in a variety of settings. Test files in Acrobat as well as Reader. If you can, test in both the Windows and Macintosh platforms. You should also test the file in previous versions of Acrobat and Reader. If there are differences, you may want to alert your viewers that they need the latest version of the software.

CHOOSING LINKS OR BUTTONS

At this point you might wonder which one is better: links or buttons? Although they both let you jump from one place to another, and they share many actions, there are distinct differences between them.

A link uses about 200 bytes less than a simple button. That difference adds up for a link repeated on every page in a 200-page document.

Link actions include the Go to View command. Buttons do not have Go to View. This makes it much more difficult to use buttons to jump to a specific point on a page.

Links can apply only one action on a mouse click. Buttons can apply multiple actions on different types of mouse events. (We'll cover more of this in the next section on More Interactive Ideas.)

Buttons have more options for their appearances. Not only will you find options for background color and beveled edges, but buttons let you import images to use as icons.

Acrobat gives you commands to manage buttons. You can use the Tools>Forms>Fields>Duplicate command to place the same button throughout the document. You can select several buttons and use the Align, Center, Distribute, and Size commands under the Fields menu to modify the buttons on a page. (Of course if you have the ARTS Link tool you have almost the same control over links.)

We then clicked the Edit Menu Item button in the Acrobat window to select the menu item and chose Previous Page. Then we clicked Set Action and closed out of the Field Properties. We repeated these steps for the other actions.

⑤ *We checked that all the rollovers were working. Now we wanted to get all the navigation elements onto all the pages without going these steps for each page and but-*

ton. We selected all the button Form Fields using Shift click and used the Duplicate Field under Tools>Forms>Fields. We entered the page range and clicked ok.

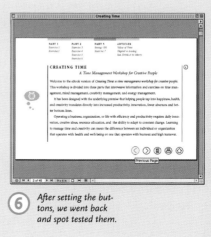

⑥ *After setting the buttons, we went back and spot tested them.*

4·5 Moving Beyond Simple Actions

We find it interesting that some designers, who spend hours creating elaborate JavaScript buttons and links for a website, are satisfied to send out a PDF document with just a few destination links. We're the first to admit that even we haven't had time to fully explore Acrobat's seemingly endless interactive features, but we can shed some light and point the way for you.

Acrobat buttons allow for a variety of interactive actions that add functionality and boost visual appeal. A button can trigger multiple actions. Instead of just moving to a page, a button action can move to a page while playing a sound along the way. Multiple button actions can also be triggered during each mouse event.

Instead of an action happening on the mouse click, a series of events can occur: one button action can happen when the mouse moves over the button; another action can happen when the mouse is clicked; and a final action can happen when the mouse moves away from the button. This makes for a much more powerful set of interactive choices.

ACTIONS

Think of actions as special effects for PDF documents. There are five different ways to invoke actions in PDF files.

In addition to navigating to different locations in a document, you can use actions to play movies and sound clips, and execute menu items and JavaScript, among many other actions.

Link actions: The viewer clicks a link element to trigger an action. Choose an action from the Actions menu in the Link Properties dialog box. Only one action can be assigned to each link.

Bookmark actions: The viewer clicks one of the Bookmarks to trigger a Bookmark action. Choose an action type from the Type menu in the Bookmark Properties dialog box. Only one action can be assigned to each Bookmark.

Button/Form Field actions: The viewer can click or move the cursor over a form field (usually a button) to trigger the action. Choose an action type from the Type menu in the Add an Action dialog box. (Access the Add an Action dialog box through the Field Properties dialog box.) Multiple field actions can be applied from the same mouse event.

Page actions: The viewer does not have to do anything to trigger a page action. As soon as the page opens or closes the action is triggered. You create a page action by choosing Document>Set Page Action>Page Open>Add. Multiple actions can be applied to the same page. Page actions play in the order, from top to bottom, that they appear in the Add Action dialog box.

Document actions: The viewer doesn't have to do anything to trigger a document action. As soon as the document opens, the action is triggered. Besides the Document Opens action (the document level scripts), there are five additional actions: willPrint, didPrint, willSave, didSave, and willClose. Document actions consist only of the actions written in the JavaScript language. Learning JavaScript is beyond the scope of this book. However, we'll go over some of the basics of working with JavaScript actions in the next section.

MORE ON PAGE ACTIONS

The connection between an action and clicking a Bookmark, link, or button is obvious—the viewer clicks and the action happens. Page

Acrobat buttons are created using the Form tool. Buttons can combine text, graphics, and Roll-over tool tips to enhance the design and functionality of a page and to lead the viewer through interactive choices. Although it is possible to create amazing levels of button action complexity, Adobe recommends that you not exceed ten actions per mouse event.

APPEARANCE

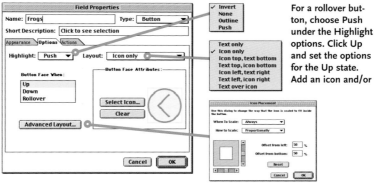

The Border appearance controls the look of your custom icon. Text color is applied only if you choose one of the Text options for Layout under the Options tab. The Form Field option lets you control whether objects are visible and whether they will print.

OPTIONS

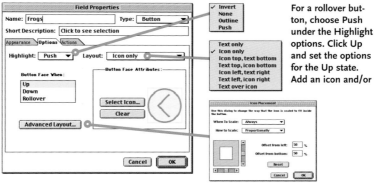

For a rollover button, choose Push under the Highlight options. Click Up and set the options for the Up state. Add an icon and/or text to the button using the Layout menu. Click the Select Icon button to choose the icon graphic. Then click on Advanced Layout to control whether and how the icon is scaled within the button. Repeat for the Down and Rollover states.

ACTIONS

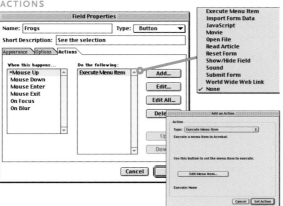

Use the Actions tab to define the actions for different mouse events. Choose the action from the pull down menu in the Add an Action dialog box. Then click the Add button to define the action associated with that mouse event. Here you have a virtually limitless list of options for adding actions and functionality to your button.

actions are different. When the page opens or closes, things happen without the viewer doing anything. We mainly use page actions to play movies or sound, or to execute JavaScript, which is just a fraction of what is possible.

Our colleague, Michael King, uses the Go to Next Page Action to quickly simulate an animation for client approval before creating the actual SWF in Flash. He starts by creating a PDF document in which each page displays a frame for the animation. Each page of the PDF document has a page action applied to it that goes to the next page. So all he has to do is to click the button to go to the first page and the rest of the pages are displayed. It's not a real animation, and he can't control the timing (unless he uses a special JavaScript command), but it makes a good comp for a client.

Glenn Page uses a page action set to Next Page to beautifully orchestrate the delivery of a stand-alone PDF presentation. The how-to is simple. First, navigate to the page on which you wish to add or edit a page action. Choose Document>Set Page Action and select Page Open. Click Add and choose an action. To move to the next page, choose Execute Menu Item and then choose the Document>Next Page command. You can add additional actions to Page Open or Page Close and they will occur in the order of the list. To delete a page action, select it on the Do the Following Things list and click Delete.

There is a bit of a conundrum in working with Page actions. If you choose the Next Page as the page action, how can you edit the action later? As soon as you move to that page the action will be invoked and you'll no longer be on that page. Fortunately, Adobe has thought of this problem. First choose View>Continuous-Facing Pages. Then move to the page. The page actions won't be invoked in that View setting.

SHOW/HIDE FIELDS

You can design page elements to be invisible until you trigger their appearance with the mouse. This action is called "Show/Hide Fields." Show/Hide Field is a type of Rollover effect that consists of two separate elements. The first element is the form field that contains the information that is shown and hidden. The form field can be set to be a button that displays graphics or a text field that displays written text.

The second element is the item that triggers the action. If a link triggers the action, it happens only on the mouse click. If a button triggers the action, it can happen on a mouse click or when the mouse moves in or out of the button area. You can also apply Show/Hide actions to Bookmarks and page actions. Some web designers call these actions disjointed Rollovers—the mouse action in one area triggers an effect somewhere else.

⚡ SHOW/HIDE FIELD

① Use the Form tool to draw the rectangle that will contain the graphic or text that is shown or hidden. Use the Select Icon button in the Field Properties dialog box to add the previously-created graphic. Turn off all the options under the Appearance tab.

1972

Micro rice cooker
Developed as a cooking utensil which had both functions as an electric rice cooker and a thermos. The improved keep-warm function enabled to keep the optimal temperature.

Field Properties

Name: description 14   Type: Button

Short Description:

Appearance Options Actions

Highlight: None   Layout: Icon only

Button Face When:
Up

Button Face Attributes:

Select Icon...
Clear

Advanced Layout...

Cancel   OK

Since buttons can apply actions on different mouse events, we find it best to use buttons as the trigger elements. For example, when you move a cursor over a button that contains the name of a product, a picture of the product or pricing information appears nearby. As the cursor moves away from the button, the detail disappears.

Here are the steps to create a button that triggers a Show/Hide effect in a graphic field.

Step ① Create the Show and Hide Field
The order here is important; you can't show or hide an object that doesn't exist. First you need to create the image or text field that will be shown and hidden. Select the Form tool and drag a box to define the area of the hidden field. Since you can't use numerical controls to set the size of this area, try creating a box on your original layout to define how big the field should be. When you release the mouse button, the Field Properties dialog box opens. Give the field a name that will make it clear that this is a field to be shown or hidden. Choose Button from the Type menu. The Button field lets you apply a graphic to be shown and hidden. If you want to reveal text, set the type of field to Text and enter the text in the Default area of the Options tab.

To add a graphic to the button, choose Icon Only from the Options tab. Click the Add Icon button and then click the Browse button to navigate to your prepared icon graphic. Click OK.

Under the Appearance tab, there is no need for a highlight. So you can set that option to None. Most likely you won't need a border or background color for the field.

Step ② Create the Trigger Button
You now need to create the button that contains the action that that shows or hides the graphic. This button can either be invisible in the document, or have its own rollover appearance. Either way, the button triggers the action.

Use the Form tool to create the button. In the Field Properties dialog box, choose Button as the Type and name the field. Pattie Belle usually adds the word Show to help her sort the fields that trigger the actions from the ones that are being triggered. For example, if the hidden field is called Robot, then the trigger button would be called Show Robot.

Step ③ Set the Trigger Action
You can find the controls that apply actions for the trigger under the Actions tab. The first step of the disjointed rollover is to create the action for what happens when the mouse rolls into the button area. In the list for When This Happens, click the event called Mouse Enter. Then click the Add button to choose the Show/Hide action from the Type menu. Now click the Edit button. This opens the Show/Hide Field dialog box. This box lists all the fields in the document. Scroll through the list to find the field that con-

② Use the Form tool to create a second button that will trigger the event.

③ You now need to set the actions for the button. Under the Actions tab, click the Mouse Enter mouse event. Then use the Add button to apply the Show/Hide Field for the type of action. Click the Edit button to open the Show/Hide Field dialog box. Choose the field and set the radio button to Show. Repeat the same step for the Mouse Exit event, except in this case set the Show/Hide Field to Hide.

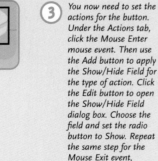

129

tains the graphic you want to show. (This long list shows why it's important to name your fields in a manner that makes it easy to understand which fields are for the buttons and which ones are for the graphics.) Click the Set Action button. You now see the field you wish to Show/Hide listed under the Do the Following area.

Repeat the process to apply an action for the events that happen when the mouse leaves the button area. Click the listing for Mouse Exit and apply the Show/Hide action. This time, choose Hide for the action. You can test the disjointed rollover by switching to the Hand tool and moving the cursor across the hotspot area. You may have to do this one time before the original field hides itself, but from then on it should work as desired.

MULTI-SHOW/HIDE FIELD EFFECTS

The Show/Hide effect doesn't have to happen only during the Mouse Enter and Mouse Exit events. The actions to show or hide a field can be applied using different buttons. Sandee teaches a technique she calls a Multi-Show/Hide effect that uses a mouse click on one button to show a field, and a rollover on a second button to hide the field. The benefit of this technique is that the viewer can click on a field and then move the mouse off the button without losing the display of the field. Here's how she creates a Multi-Show/Hide effect.

Step ① Create the Buttons and Fields

As explained previously, use the Form tool to create the fields that contain the graphics to be shown or hidden. Then create the trigger buttons that will show and hide the graphics. In this example, the three fields that contain the graphics are stacked above each other in the same position. Ordinarily, you might want to create the trigger buttons and graphic fields in pairs. Each time you create a graphic field, you immediately create the trigger button and set all its options. However, with Multi-Show/Hide fields, you'll need to have all the graphic fields finished before you start setting the trigger button actions.

If you are used to working in graphic applications such as QuarkXPress or Adobe Illustrator, you may feel a little frustrated working with Acrobat's fields. If one field is above another, there are no Move to Front or Send to Back commands to help you change the order of the object. This can make it difficult to work with multiple fields—especially if they need to be on top of each other.

Fortunately, Acrobat has a set of powerful commands under the Tools>Forms>Fields menu. The Size>Both commands let you select multiple fields and resize them so they are all the same size. The first field selected (outlined in red) is used as reference, and all other selected fields (outlined in blue) auto-

⚡ MULTIPLE SHOW/HIDE

① Create the trigger buttons and the fields containing the icons.

② Select one of the trigger buttons. Choose the Mouse Up event and then click the Add button. This lets you apply the Show/Hide Field action to Show the field graphic.

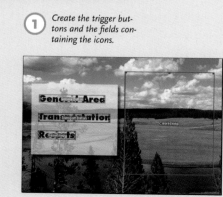

maticaly adjust to it. The Align commands let you stack the fields in the same position.

Step ② Set the Button to Show the Field

You can now select the first button that you'd like to act as a trigger to show a field. Double-click the button with the Form tool to open the Field Properties dialog box. Under the Actions tab, click the Mouse Up event. Then click the Add button and choose Show/Hide Field and select the field that contains the graphic.

Step ③ Set the Button to Hide Other Fields

If the three fields occupy the same area, you'll want to make sure that the graphics in the other fields are not visible, or they could hide the graphic that this button triggers. Therefore, you'll need to make the same button hide any other fields that might be visible. Use the Mouse Enter event to automatically hide the field when the viewer moves the cursor inside the button.

Click the Mouse Enter event. Then click the Add button and choose the Show/Hide field action. Instead of hiding the field you chose in the previous step, set the action to hide one of the other fields on the page. In this example, there are two other fields in the same area. So there should be two Mouse Enter events to hide those fields.

You should now select another trigger button and repeat steps 2 and 3 so that the trigger shows one field on the Mouse Down event and hides the other two fields on the Mouse Enter event. Continue until you have set all the trigger buttons on the page.

Step ④ Test the Buttons

Your final step is to test all your trigger buttons. Move the mouse over a trigger button. You shouldn't see anything happen until you click the button. The graphic should appear in the field area. Now move the mouse off the button. The graphic should still be visible. Now move the mouse over a different trigger button. The graphic that was visible disappears. Then, when you click that trigger button, a new graphic appears.

③ Set the actions for the Mouse Enter to Hide the other fields on the page. Repeat steps 2 and 3 for the other trigger buttons on the page.

④ Click OK to test the trigger buttons. When you click one trigger button, the graphic in the field appears. As you move over a different trigger button, the graphic disappears.

Jamie Costa used this interesting approach to a portfolio presentation while at SUNY, Purchase (State University of New York). The portfolio begins with a white index card. A small spinning animation plays and repeats.

As the viewer moves the mouse to the rollover spot on the screen, a door appears with the invitation to "enter."

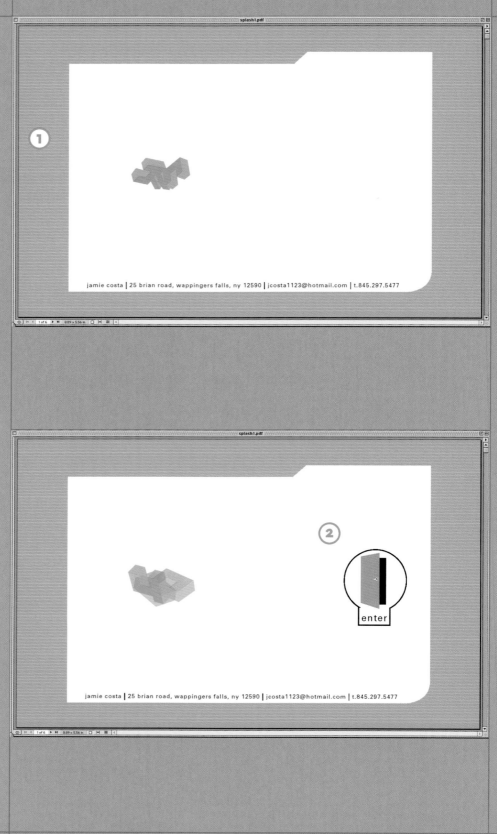

A click on the door takes the viewer to the main area (3). In the main area there are three tabs for each of the library cards (3).

The file tabs are the main navigation structure. By clicking on a tab, the tab becomes active, revealing a grid field that includes 6–8 cells (4). These are Rollover buttons. The cells have no textual or iconic explanation other than the portfolio pieces that immediately load in the frame (5). The piece is full of visual surprises.

This works because it is visually exciting. In a situation where the design and navigation could have been predictable, this is a refreshing approach.

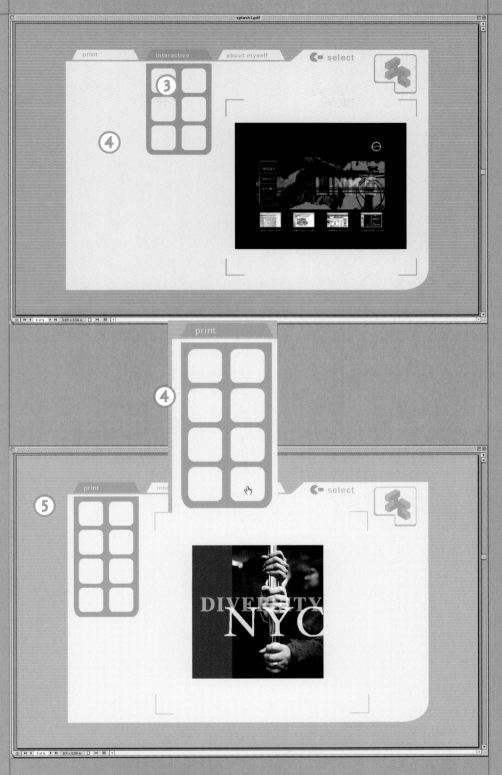

4.6 | Acrobat JavaScript Basics

JavaScript programming adds amazing levels of functionality and interactive possibilities to PDFs. There are already a few wizards out there performing JavaScript magic on a scale that brings ooohhs and aahhhs from the crowd, but as of this writing there is no definitive guidebook. You will find extensive coverage of its implementation in the Acrobat JavaScript Object Specification (menu>Help>Acrobat JavaScript Guide), but most of this 295-page document has been written for programmers by programmers. Although some sections provide useful hints for the beginner, the document assumes that the reader has some programming familiarity. We count ourselves among the novices, but we'll try to pass along what we have thus far learned from the wizards.

Acrobat JavaScript is built on top of Netscape's core JavaScript, so it includes the features you also find in browser-based languages, such as Math, String, Date, Array, and Regular Expression Objects. You can use JavaScript to execute menu commands, change the appearance of form fields, call page transitions, and much, much more.

WHERE TO PUT YOUR SCRIPTS

The obvious place to add JavaScript is in a JavaScript action. As you have seen in the previous section, there are JavaScript actions for Bookmarks, form fields, links, page Actions, and document level actions. With all the field-related actions, you have about a dozen events to choose from. Deciding where to place your code is usually a simple matter, but may require some serious considerations: Code should be linked as closely as possible to the action or form field it is designed to control. Therefore, if you want a button to trigger a (JavaScript) command, you would add the JavaScript action as part of the mouse events for the button.

You will, however, often find that some of the same kinds of operations need to be performed in many different places. For example, you may have a recurring need to calculate the average of a group of numbers. Rather than write the same number-averaging code over and over, it makes more sense to write one function that does this task and put that function at the document level. There, it can be accessed by any JavaScript action in your document.

INTERNAL JAVASCRIPTS

As we mentioned in the previous section, there are several ways of adding JavaScript actions within a PDF document.

You can choose to add JavaScript to Bookmarks, links, or button fields. JavaScripts for buttons can be associated with mouse events such as Up, Down, Enter, Exit, Focus, and Blur. In data entry fields, such as Text fields, you have additional events where you can attach JavaScripts: the Keystroke, Validate, Calculate, and Format events. This high number of events makes it important that you understand how to use them as well as their sequence. Assigning a script to the wrong event can affect the performance of the form. Putting inappropriate code in the Validation event can cause endless loops, which will crash Acrobat (and perhaps the whole system) eventually.

JavaScripts can be assigned to Page Actions. These scripts are executed when a page of the

JavaScript Navigation Button

Here is a very easy way to add a JavaScript action to a document. If you are creating a navigation bar for a PDF, you may find that you want to allow your viewer to easily jump back to the table of contents. If the contents page is not on the first or last page of the document, you won't be able to do this with a Menu Item action. Fortunately, there is a very short and sweet line of JavaScript that will do this for you.

Step 1 Make a Button
Make your form button in the desired location on the page and with its appearance defined. Remember, you must name it and add a description (Contents) so it will appear when the user's mouse enters the field.

Step 2 Add JavaScript to a Mouse Event
In the Actions Tab of the Field Properties dialog box, select Mouse Up and click the Add button. Select JavaScript from the list and click the Edit button. This will open the JavaScript edit box where you can type in the following line of code:

```
this.pageNum=3;
```

The number indicates the page in the PDF document, so you'll want to make sure that you have the right number there. In Acrobat, the page numbering system begins with the first page as zero, so if your TOC is on what you call page 4, Acrobat sees it as being on a page with the number 3.

After you have typed in your code, click OK and then set action. Close the dialog box and your button is ready to go. If, for some reason, you have set it for the wrong page, you can easily go back into the field properties and edit your script.

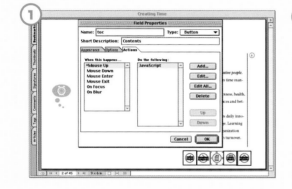

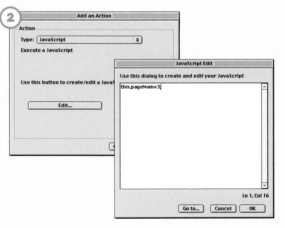

① Create a button and set the Mouse Event to Mouse Up. Then click the Add button.

② Choose JavaScript for the Action Type. Enter the JavaScript code in the JavaScript Edit dialog box.

document opens or closes. When executed on the first page of an opening document, the Page Open event can be used to trigger scripts that are executed when the document opens.

You can also set JavaScripts to run when the document opens. These are called Document-level scripts (Tools>JavaScript>Document JavaScripts). Here, you define functions and variables, which become available for any JavaScript action in the document.

JavaScripts can also be assigned to document actions. This is done through the Tools>JavaScript>Set Document Actions. These document JavaScripts can be added for the following events: Document Will Close (when a document closes), Document Will Save (right before a document is saved), Document Did Save (right after a document is saved), Document Will Print (right before a document is printed), and Document Did Print (right after a document is printed).

EXTERNAL JAVASCRIPTS

There are three ways to execute external JavaScripts that are not contained within the PDF document.

Folder Level JavaScripts

Also called Application Level JavaScripts, these are text files that contain the JavaScript commands. The files are saved with a .js extension and placed in the JavaScripts folder in either the Acrobat or Reader application folder, or the user's Acrobat User Data folder. When Acrobat or Reader is launched, it scans these folders and executes any JavaScript files it finds. (Pattie Belle has a .js file in her folder that creates a menu item for numbering pages in a PDF.)

Console JavaScripts

These are typed into the Acrobat Console and executed manually from there. This is primarily a testing feature of Acrobat, but can come

in very handy as you'll see in the presentation chapter of this book.

Batch JavaScripts

These are called from batch sequences. This allows you to apply a JavaScript to each of the selected files. There is a document explaining this application on the Acrobat 5 application CD. Look for it in the Batch folder.

PDF JAVASCRIPT RESTRICTIONS

If you have created JavaScript commands for HTML applications, you must keep in mind that JavaScript in Acrobat is not the same as it is for browsers. JavaScript for PDF runs inside Acrobat or Acrobat Reader. Some objects you may have worked with in a browser environment don't exist in the PDF JavaScript implementation. On the other hand, you'll find many objects unknown in web browser implementations.

In fact, many of the objects and methods you have used in HTML-based JavaScript are really part of client-side or server-side extensions to the core language. The methods available for Acrobat JavaScript differ from HTML and server-based JavaScript. For example, HTML JavaScript cannot look within a PDF document and PDF JavaScript can't look inside an HTML page, but both kinds of code can communicate with a server.

ADDING JAVASCRIPT ACTIONS

A JavaScript action allows you to invoke a JavaScript from a form field, a link, a Bookmark, a document, or a page action, but it does require some familiarity with JavaScript.

Field level script

Inserting JavaScript at field level makes that script available for that specific field only. Neither functions nor variables defined on the field level are accessible from other scripts.

Document-level script

Inserting JavaScript at the document level makes the functions and variables available to all JavaScripts in the document.

Application-level script

Inserting a function as an Application-level script makes the function available to all JavaScripts in the application. Application-level scripts are contained in files with a .js extension. In Acrobat 4, these scripts are located within the Plug-ins folder in the JavaScripts sub folder of the Acrobat installation. In Acrobat 5, they are in the JavaScripts folder that is installed along with Acrobat.

JAVASCRIPT ACTIONS

To create a JavaScript action, start by making or selecting a form field, link, Bookmark, or page action. In the properties dialog box, select JavaScript as the action. Click Edit and type the script in the text box (or copy and paste it). Click OK and then click Set Action or Set Link.

DOCUMENT JAVASCRIPTS

To create a Document Level JavaScript, first create and edit the JavaScript in a programmer's text editor, such as BBEdit or Note Pad, and copy and paste the code in Tools>JavaScript> Document Javascripts. You can also edit all your document-level JavaScripts at once, after they have been created, by going to Tools> Javascript>Edit All JavaScripts.

APPLICATION LEVEL JAVASCRIPT

To create an application-level JavaScript, create a text file (in a text editor such as BBEdit) containing the JavaScript code. Name and save the file with a .js extension and place the text file into the JavaScript directory inside the Acrobat folder, or into the JavaScript folder in the Adobe folder in the Users Document folder.

WHERE TO GO FROM HERE?

If you are not familiar with JavaScript, you can find many excellent sources and tutorials for learning the core language on the Internet. There are also many books in print on Java-Script, but none (yet) specifically on Acrobat JavaScript, except one chapter in the "PostScript und PDF-Bibel" by Thomas Merz—a good incentive to learn German, as the newest edition has not yet been translated into English. There are a couple of eBooks available by Kas Thomas (one of the wizards we referred to earlier) that can be found in the ePublish Store on PlanetPDF: *Acrobat JavaScript from Square Zero* and *Advanced Acrobat JavaScript*.

Or maybe you dove right into Acrobat JavaScript and you're having trouble with your code—the PlanetPDF JavaScript Forum (www.planetpdf.com) is an excellent place to have an expert look over your code and advise you.

4.7 Scholarly Pursuits

Spring Semester 2001: Pattie Belle began teaching Acrobat as a core application in her introductory course in Interactive Design. There's usually a wide range of experience among the students in this class. Some have taken a web design course, some have not; some know a little Flash, some do not. None have ever used Acrobat beyond opening a PDF in Reader. By the time they get to this class, they are all familiar with Photoshop, Illustrator, QuarkXpress, and/or Indesign. The reaction to Acrobat is always the same, "I didn't know you could do that!" and "This is so easy! Why hasn't anyone taught us this before?"

Since Pattie Belle's students have no real history with the application, they bring no expectations and no baggage about what a PDF is supposed to (or not supposed to) look like. The result is almost always amazing. Good design shows through without being encumbered by the limitations of HTML or a student's lack of knowledge about Flash Actionscript. Acrobat allows Pattie Belle to focus on the fundamentals of creating an interactive experience when students are pressed for time, yet it doesn't involve the high learning curve of some other interactive applications.

Most of the work generated is image- or design-dependent, so the students generally work between Photoshop, Illustrator, and InDesign for the authoring applications. Pattie Belle usually uses the Save as PDF method in class, because size is not a factor for these documents.

When students are designing navigation schemes and interactivity, they are encouraged to create as little work or button-pushing as possible for the viewer. The group acts as testers for each other's documents to discover what works and what doesn't. Some solutions are more successful than others—judge for yourself when examining the student samples on the CD.

Without the constraints of client feedback and strict deadlines, students have the freedom to push the boundaries of what is possible. This also means that they frequently brush up against the limitations of the software.

In our laboratory, we discovered the use of PDF for CD-based and e-mail portfolios. PDF is the perfect vehicle for design samples, motion graphics, and resumes. PDF also allows students to show off their ability to create cool interactive experiences. Using PDF makes creating a portfolio fast and easy.

The group of former students who have work included in this book include Chisa Yagi, Melinda Van Vliet, Jamie Costa, Melissa Olsen, and Chris Von Achen.

ON THE CD

Many of the documents that you see throughout this book were created by Pattie Belle's students at SUNY Purchase College in the Spring of 2001. You'll find these documents in the Student Work folder on the Master Class CD.

Because PDF traverses a fine line between print and web, it can incorporate the best of both worlds. Pattie Belle's students seem to have an intuitive grasp on this aspect of PDF, as they fluidly combine aspects of web design with forms common to print design. It's all in the detail. Here are a few buttons, rollovers and show/hide fields from a selection of student work.

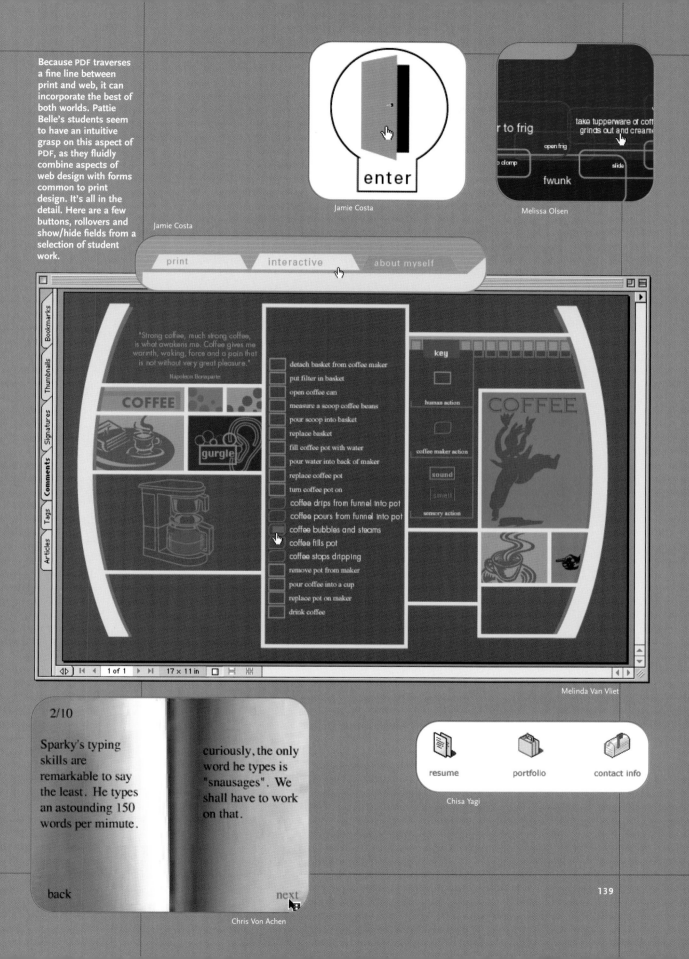

enter

Jamie Costa

take tupperware of coff grinds out and cream

fwunk

Melissa Olsen

Jamie Costa

print   interactive   about myself

"Strong coffee, much strong coffee, is what awakens me. Coffee gives me warmth, waking, force and a pain that is not without very great pleasure."

Napoleon Bonaparte

COFFEE

gurgle

detach basket from coffee maker
put filter in basket
open coffee can
measure a scoop coffee beans
pour scoop into basket
replace basket
fill coffee pot with water
pour water into back of maker
replace coffee pot
turn coffee pot on
coffee drips from funnel into pot
coffee pours from funnel into pot
coffee bubbles and steams
coffee fills pot
coffee stops dripping
remove pot from maker
pour coffee into a cup
replace pot on maker
drink coffee

key

human action

coffee maker action

sound

smell

sensory action

COFFEE

Bookmarks · Thumbnails · Signatures · Comments · Tags · Articles

1 of 1   17 x 11 in

Melinda Van Vliet

2/10

Sparky's typing skills are remarkable to say the least. He types an astounding 150 words per mimute.

curiously, the only word he types is "snausages". We shall have to work on that.

back   next

Chris Von Achen

resume   portfolio   contact info

Chisa Yagi

5

Interactive Forms

Conventional wisdom says that it is easier to use HTML as the basis for web-based forms. However, after Pattie Belle and Bjørn analyzed the costs and benefits of redesigning a printed form for the Web, they know firsthand what is involved in designing a database-integrated form as HTML. After exploring the form possibilities in Acrobat, they became firm believers in the benefits of PDF documents. The simple interface and ease with which you can publish forms online is groundbreaking. There is no need for a separate and redesigned website. You can easily retain the look of the original form, and the creation process is fairly quick and simple. And with the addition of JavaScript, the PDF form can be as dynamic as any HTML document. This chapter will take you through a variety of exercises that can help you create sophisticated form documents.

5.1 | Introduction to Forms

Forms can be filled in and printed from any application in the Acrobat software suite and from inside a web browser with the Reader plug-in. The PDF format preserves the appearance of a document, which is especially beneficial when an enormous amount of time and thought have gone into the design of a complex form. To understand how this process works, imagine that the Form tool adds an invisible layer on top of the document, giving you an almost unlimited set of preset or custom tools, such as fill-in text boxes, check boxes, and buttons. The finished PDF forms can be distributed via the web, e-mail, disk, or CD-ROM, depending on the use of the form. Once you have created your form in Acrobat 5, it can easily be enhanced. With custom scripting and databases, the form data can be submitted by the user from the web to server-side applications.

ABOUT PDF FORMS

As mentioned, a major benefit of Acrobat forms is that you can use an existing form designed for print, convert it into a PDF, enhance it with form fields in Acrobat, and then publish it on the web. Filling out a PDF form is similar to filling out online web forms, with one important difference. HTML form documents do not always look the same as their printed counterparts. With Acrobat forms, the original printed version of the document can be used as the primary image of the file. When the form fields are added, they create electronic entry points where a user can input the form data.

Designers who create printed forms use a variety of input conventions, such as fields to enter text, check boxes, and option lists. Designers working with Acrobat's form fields have a similar set of electronic tools: data fields, scroll down menus, radio buttons, and so on. As you'll discover, Acrobat forms aren't simply a direct translation of their print counterparts. Forms also contain special capabilities to create interactive experiences, such as rollover buttons, buttons that trigger actions, as well as other creative, interactive options.

To make forms, you will use Acrobat (full version). To fill out forms, you can use Acrobat (full version), Acrobat Reader, or Acrobat Approval.

USABILITY ISSUES

There are some crucial issues about usability to consider when making a form available for onscreen use. First, you'll need to make sure that the forms are user-friendly. We assume such considerations have already been made for the form's printed counterpart. If not, it might be necessary to redesign the form. Second, and more importantly, you'll need to make sure that the user knows how to fill in the form online. Many people are used to websites that contain electronic input data conventions. However, your form may be targeted at an audience that is unfamiliar with web forms. For example if you have created a form with some complexity for an audience not yet used to electronic forms, you may have to add instructions on how to use this electronic version. Third, try to predict user behavior. You can opt to have the user simply fill out the form and print it from their desktop. Or, you may decide to add

TEXT FIELDS
are fill-in form fields that can accommodate text as well as numbers. This allows you to create areas in which users can enter text or numerical data.

RADIO BUTTONS
are used for situations in which the user must select one choice from a set of choices by pressing one button. There are a variety of appearance options available.

SIGNATURE
fields allow for the digital signing of documents for identification and authentication of the user, and for confirming the contents of the form at that time.

Text fields can contain numeric data. In this example, the final field uses a calculation to create an average of the values in the previous fields.

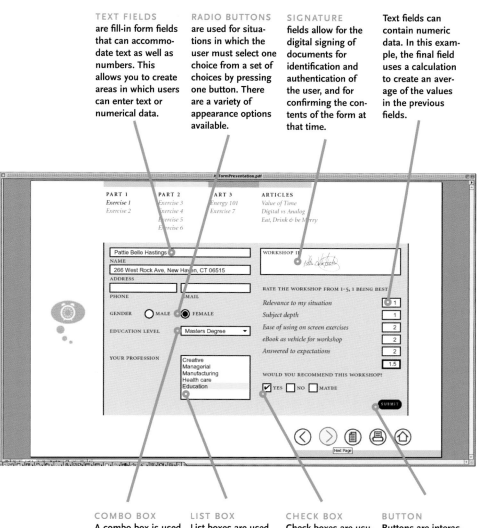

COMBO BOX
A combo box is used for a list in which you can select and see only one entry at the time. The list is presented as a drop down menu, accessed by clicking the little downward facing triangle.

LIST BOX
List boxes are used for a list in which you can select one or more entries. The list is presented as a scrolling menu, as opposed to combo boxes, where the entire list is visible.

CHECK BOX
Check boxes are usually used for a list in which you select or deselect a choice. There are a number of options available for appearance.

BUTTON
Buttons are interactive elements in the form. They are used to trigger actions, such as playing sounds, printing, submitting data, or initiating a custom script. They can appear as rollovers or "plain" buttons.

a button that submits the form data (for example, as FDF) to a server that can send you information as e-mail or put information into a database.

FIELD TYPES

It's important to understand that the fields created with the Form tool are not merely data-entry spaces, but can take on a variety of appearances and functions. You've already seen in Chapter 4 how the Form tool can create button fields with custom icons that respond to Rollover effects. There are other types of fields that can be created with the Form tool. Here's a brief rundown of the different types of form fields.

> ### ⓘ SAMPLE FORMS
>
> *The Acrobat 5 CD ROM contains a wealth of sample forms and form-creation tutorials. Use the CD ROM to begin your research when starting out with an Acrobat forms implementation. Look in the folder labeled Forms on the main level of the Acrobat CD.*

Button fields: These are very versatile in that they are the interactive elements of the form. Button fields can have actions attached, such as opening the print dialog box, playing sound/video, or any custom function defined in a script. They can also be set up as rollover buttons (buttons that change appearance when the mouse moves over them). Buttons are covered in detail in Chapter 4.

Text fields: These are the fields in which the user can enter either text or numerical data, or where data can be displayed and formatted as a result of a particular calculation.

Check Box fields: These are basic boxes that can be designated as on or off. A click inside the check box reveals (or hides) a designated character such as a check, circle, cross, diamond, square, or star. Check boxes allow the user to select or deselect an item, such as a single item in a shopping list.

Radio Button fields: A radio button field is like a check box in that it can be clicked on. Radio buttons are designed so that only one button in a set can be in the on position. For instance, you would use a radio button to have the user indicate their age group or income level. Radio buttons have the same appearance options as check boxes: check, circle, cross, diamond, square, or star.

Combo box fields: Combo boxes are similar to drop-down menus that appear in computer applications. The user clicks an onscreen element that displays the list of entries in the combo box. The user can then choose one of the items listed in the menu. Use a combo box field when you don't want a form to appear cluttered with items. A combo box also makes it possible to make sure that a selection is correctly spelled or input by the user. For instance, a combo box is very useful for displaying the special two-letter codes for the individual U.S. states.

List Box fields: List box fields are similar to combo boxes in that they allow you to chose from a list of entries. However, instead of a long menu display, a list box contains scroll bars that allow the viewer to move through various items. List boxes also continue to show the other entries in the list even after the selection has been made, because the viewer has the option to select more than one item in the list.

Signature fields: Signature fields allow a user to sign a document. The document is then saved with information in the signature field that provides verification that the document had been seen and signed by the viewer.

FIELD SETTINGS

There are three settings at the top of the Field Properties dialog box that are common to all types of fields.

Name: All fields must have their own individual name. Certain naming conventions help you use the data in forms more efficiently, so this is not a trivial issue. See the next section, Naming Form Fields, for more details on how to use naming conventions.

Type: This is where you choose the type of form field, such as buttons, text, and combo boxes, as discussed earlier.

Short Description: While the field name is required, the Short Description for a field is not. However, the short description provides a tool tip that is displayed when the viewer pauses the mouse cursor over the field. This feature lets you add simple, short instructions for filling in forms.

APPEARANCE TAB SETTINGS

The Appearance tab defines the visual aspects of a field and is fairly consistent, regardless of Type selected above. (See Chapter 4 for more details on setting the Appearance tab options.)

Border and Background controls: The Border area lets you define border color and background color in the form field. Leave these settings unchecked if you don't want the field to interfere with your design. However, note that the border width is still taken into consideration for displaying the field's contents.

Text controls: The Text options for color, font, and type size control the appearance of text displayed in a field. For example, you can specify that all text input be set in red. For fonts, you should use one of the Base-14 fonts, as these fonts are available for most users. For text we use sans serif fonts, since they tend to be more legible on-screen. If you select the Auto from the type size option, it will size the text to fit into the field. The minimum size it scales down to is 4 points.

Common Properties: In the Common Properties, leave the Read Only option unchecked, unless you don't want the user to be able to interact with the field (enter values, click a button). The Read Only property may be used for a field that contains the result of a calculation with the values in other fields. You wouldn't want the user to be able to modify data in this kind of field. The Required option makes sure that this field has a value when the form data is submitted to a web server. You can also choose whether the field is Visible, Hidden, Visible But Doesn't Print, or Hidden But Printable. The Visible option is the most commonly used option.

OPTIONS TAB SETTINGS

The settings in the Options tab change depending on which type of form field has been selected. For example, the signature field doesn't have an Options tab.

Text field options

Default: This option allows you to create text that appears in a form once the form is reset. This option comes in handy, as it gives you an opportunity to add additional information that will help users fill out the form.

Alignment: This control defines how text is aligned in a field. You can choose left aligned, right aligned, or center aligned.

Multi-line: This feature allows you to have a form field consisting of several text lines. Once the user enters more text than fits in the width of a field, a new line is added.

Do not scroll: This refers to scrolling through multi-line fields. This option limits the amount of text to only that which can be displayed in a field.

Limit of x characters: You can control how many characters the user can enter in a text box. This feature may be useful when the forms data is submitted to a fixed-field-length database.

Password: When this option is selected, text entered in the particular field being displayed shows as asterisks (*). This is useful whenever a password entry is required. This option provides a measure of privacy, but does not replace security features.

Field is used for file selection: When this option is set, the field contains a path name to a file whose contents will be submitted as the field's value.

Do not spell-check: Acrobat allows you to check the spelling for form fields and comments. Turn this option off if you don't want the contents of the form field spell-checked. Turn this option on if you do want the contents of the form field spell-checked.

Check Boxes and Radio Buttons Options

Check style: This gives you a selection of six different characters to insert in a field: Check, Circle, Cross, Diamond, Square, or Star.

Export value: The export value is the value assigned to a field. This value will be sent when the form is submitted to a web server, and is also used as the field value in JavaScript.

Default is checked: This field will be checked when the form is reset. Note that "deselect" is only available when using a check box, or when multiple instances of the field are present and one of them is selected.

APPEARANCE

Common Properties
Read Only pertains to fields that the user can't interact with. Required means that the field must contain data in order to submit the final form. Form Fields can be Visible, Hidden, Non-Printable, and Printable But Not Displayed.

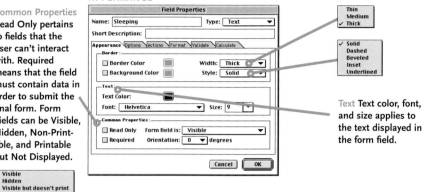

Text Text color, font, and size applies to the text displayed in the form field.

OPTIONS

The options tab is dependent on which form type is selected.
Text Gives you a range of options to control the entry and display of text.
Check Boxes/Radio Buttons Here you select a style and define the export value for the checked state.
List Boxes/Combo Boxes Here you enter the items to be displayed and control the order in which they are displayed.
Buttons Here you define the appearance of the button.

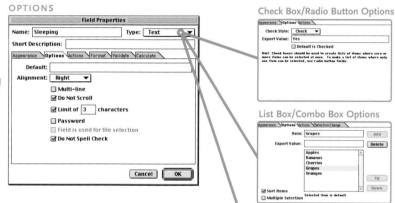

Check Box/Radio Button Options

List Box/Combo Box Options

Button Options

ACTIONS

Actions can be attached to a form field, using one of these six events. For a more comprehensive explanation, see chapter 4.

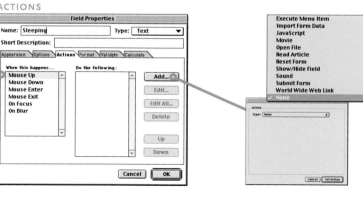

FORMAT

The format options are important because they control how form data is entered and presented. The Format tab only appears for Text and combo box fields.

Field Properties

Name: Total   Type: Text

Short Description:

Appearance | Options | Actions | **Format** | Validate | Calculate

Category:
None
Custom
Number
Percentage
Date
Time
Special

Category Options:
Currency symbol: None
Decimal and 1000s style: 1234.56
Negative number style:
● –1234
○ 1234
○ (1234)   Decimal places: 0
○ (1234)

The number format is used for the display of numbers, including currency.

Cancel | OK

None No specific formatting applied. Default.

Custom Here you enter custom scripts that you want attached to the Keystroke and Format events.

Number This gives you a host of selection for number display, including decimals, currency symbols and so on.

Percentage Sets the display of percentages, and the number of decimals.

Date Lists available date formats.

Time Lists available time formats.

Special Sets special formatting, such as the U.S. way to format zip codes or phone numbers.

VALIDATE

The Validation properties allow you to control the Validate event for the field. You determine the range of valid entries, mainly via custom scripts. The Validate tab is only available for Text and combo box fields.

Field Properties

Name: Sleeping   Type: Text

Short Description:

Appearance | Options | Actions | Format | **Validate** | Calculate

● Value is not validated.

○ Custom validation script:
Edit...

Cancel | OK

CALCULATE

In this tab, which is only displayed when the Format of the field has been set to Number, you can choose from predefined calculations, such as summing up or averaging a selection of field values.

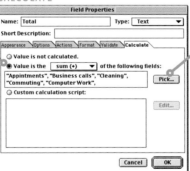

✓ sum (+)
product (*)
average
minimum
maximum

Field Properties

Name: Total   Type: Text

Short Description:

Appearance | Options | Actions | Format | Validate | **Calculate**

○ Value is not calculated.
● Value is the [sum (+)] of the following fields:
"Appintments", "Business calls", "Cleaning",
"Commuting", "Computer Work",   Pick...
○ Custom calculation script:
Edit...

Cancel | OK

The Pick button provides a list of form fields you can choose to include in the predefined calculation. The Calculate tab is only available for Text and combo box fields.

Select a Field

Select a field in the document to be calculation.

Print
Reading
Research
Sat
Self
Sep
Shopping
Sleeping
Spirit
Sun
TV

SIGNATURES

The signed tab (only available if signature is selected in type), allows control over the behavior of the form after a digital signature has been applied.

Field Properties

Name: Sleeping   Type: Signature

Short Description:

Appearance | Actions | **Signed**

○ Nothing happens when the signature field is signed.
● Mark as read-only   ✓ all fields
                         just these fields
                         all fields except these   Pick...

○ This script executes when the signature is signed:
Edit...

Cancel | OK

List or Combo Box Options

Item: Here you type in a name for list items, one at a time.

Export value: Here you specify the value for a field to be submitted to a server, or to be used in JavaScript.

Add: When you click this button, your item is added to the list; all selections will appear on the list.

Delete, Up, or Down: These options all relate to a list of items. You may delete, or change the order of, list entries by selecting an entry and clicking these buttons.

Sort items: Selecting this option will sort your entries in alphanumerical order.

Combo Box Options

Editable: This option makes it possible for the user to enter her own value in a combo Box field.

Do not spell check: This option turns off the spell-check options for the field.

List Box Options

Multiple selection: This option enables the user to select more than one item from a list of entries. You may want to give the user instructions on how to select multiple items: Hold the Shift key and click to select contiguous items. Hold the Cmd key (M) or the Ctrl key (W) to select non-contiguous items.

Button Options

The button options are directed toward creating interactive buttons and/or executing actions. For more information on setting these options, see Chapter 4.

ACTIONS TAB SETTINGS

You may specify an action with the form field. From the menu of mouse actions, you can define the event that will cause the associated action(s) to occur. For more extensive explanations of different types of actions, go to chapter 4.

Mouse up: Actions assigned occur when the mouse button is released.

Mouse down: Actions assigned occur when the mouse button is pressed.

Mouse enter: Actions assigned occur when the mouse cursor moves over a field.

Mouse exit: Actions assigned occur when the mouse cursor moves out of a field.

On focus: Actions assigned occur when a form field gets activated (gets the focus).

On blur: Actions assigned occur when the form field gets deactivated (loses the focus).

FORMAT TAB SETTINGS

This tab is only available for combo box fields and Text fields. It lists seven categories that control the style of the form data. For instance, if you want the form to show a price in dollars, you can set the format to automatically show the dollar symbol.

None: This is the Acrobat default. It applies no action to the Format (and Keystroke) events.

Number: This sets the field value to be a number. It limits data entry to numerical data only. With this option, you can then choose one of ten currency symbols, such as dollar, yen, and Euro. You can also define the number of decimals and how negative numbers are displayed.

Percentage: This style controls the display of percentages.

Date and Time: These two options set the style of the data to show either a date, a time, or both. If the user enters a date in another format (such as Jan 2, 1954) the field is automatically corrected to display the desired format (such as 1/2/54).

Special: This category lets you select the format for United States social security numbers, Zip codes, and telephone numbers. These special configurations prohibit the user from entering the wrong number of digits in a field.

Custom: This category allows you to add any JavaScript to the Keystroke and Format events. Normally, it would be a script for formatting the field value, but other functions can be initiated as well.

VALIDATE TAB SETTINGS

This tab is only available for combo box fields and Text fields. Here you can set validation controls to check entered data for validity or plausibility. If the format of a field is set to a number, the validation tab contains a setting to specify a minimum and maximum number for the data. This allows you to prevent a user from ordering less than a certain number of items or more than would be reasonable. The setting for Custom Validation Script is always available and lets you execute any kind of Java-Script in the Validate event. This would normally be a validating script, but any other action can be initiated as well.

CALCULATE TAB SETTINGS

This tab is only available for combo box fields and Text fields. It controls the actions in a Format event. If the format is a number, the Calculate tab displays the controls that allow you to use predefined calculations (Sum, Product, Average, Maximum, and Minimum). Except for Format selection, any JavaScript can be assigned to the Calculate event.

Click the Pick button to define the values of fields to which you'd like to apply the predefined calculations. (This button is only available if the field format has been set to Number.) The Select a Field dialog box will appear. This box displays a list of all the fields in your document. Scroll through the list and choose the fields that you want to use as part of the calculation. When you have selected all the fields, click Done. Be sure to set the type of calculation from the pull-down menu. The field automatically calculates the values based on the data entered in the designated fields.

SELECTION CHANGE TAB SETTINGS

This option is only available for list boxes. It allows you to apply a JavaScript to the Selection Change event of the list box field. For

instance, if the user selects the color red, the JavaScript can limit choices in other areas to only those products available in red.

SIGNED TAB SETTINGS

This tab is only available for Signature fields. (For more about digital signatures, see the security section in chapter 8.) You have the following options:

Make nothing happen when the signature field is signed: No action is triggered when the field is signed.

Mark as read-only: If the digital signature is applied, selecting this option gives you the choice of making all fields, or only certain fields, Read Only. This is an excellent way to prevent any further changes to the form field values.

The script executes when the signature is signed: This option allows you to designate a JavaScript to be added once the signature is added. For instance, the JavaScript can send an e-mail notification or initiate a next step in the work flow.

EDITING FIELDS

Once you have created a field, you can edit it at any time by choosing Edit>Properties or double-clicking it while the Form tool is active. If you choose to edit the properties for multiple fields, only the Appearance tab will appear. To move a field, simply choose the Form tool and then drag the field to a new location, or select the field and use the cursor control keys to move it in increments. To resize a field, drag the field handles to size, or select the field and use the cursor control keys, while the Shift key is pressed, to change the size.

COPYING FIELDS

As you create new fields for a document, you will find that you can't create separate fields with the same name. You can, however, copy and paste to create alternate versions of the same field. Simply select the fields you want to duplicate and then choose Edit>Copy and then Edit>Paste. The new fields will contain the same names as the originals. That is, when the user enters data in one text field, the information is automatically applied to all the fields that share the same name.

You can easily duplicate the fields on a page by holding the Ctrl key (w) or Option key (m) as you drag the field to a new location. The cursor icon indicates that you are copying the selection. A copy of the field appears when you release the mouse.

To duplicate fields onto other pages of the document, choose Tools>Forms>Fields>Duplicate. You can then select the range of pages on which you wish the field to appear. Acrobat duplicates the selected field in the exact location on all or a range of pages in the document.

USING GRIDS/ALIGNMENT

When you create fields, you may want them to be neatly arranged on the page. Unfortunately, Acrobat has no user interface to control the numeric position of the fields. Rather than positioning the fields by eye, you can use the Acrobat grid features or the Alignment commands.

Grid

The grid feature is activated by View>Grid. It displays a series of horizontal and vertical lines in your document. You can have fields automatically line up with the grid lines by choosing View>Snap To Grid. In this way, you can roughly create items and have Acrobat position them along the grid lines.

You can easily customize the grid by choosing Edit>Preferences>General>Layout Grid. The Layout Grid area allows you to specify the distance between the lines, the position of the grid from the left and top edges, the number of subdivision lines in the grid, and the grid color.

Alignment

You can also use alignment commands to align fields along their top, bottom, left, or right edges. Let's say you have a set of ten fields that you want to align along their left edges. Switch to the Form tool and click to select the first field. Then hold the Shift key and select the other fields you want to align. You should notice that the first field is highlighted with a different color than the rest of the fields. This indicates that the rest of the objects will be aligned to that highlighted field. You can highlight a different field by holding the Shift key and clicking the desired field.

Set the alignment by choosing Tools>Forms>Fields>Align. Here, you can choose left, right, top, or bottom edges. You can also align items vertically or horizontally. You can use the Tools>Forms>Fields>Center command to center objects or the Tools>Forms>Fields>Distribute to set the same amount of space between objects. Under Tools>Forms>Fields>Size, you can instruct Acrobat to conform the size of the selected fields to the size of the highlighted field.

KEYBOARD SHORTCUTS FOR FIELDS

There are a few special keyboard shortcuts to keep in mind when working with fields. You can move fields precisely by clicking the Up, Down, Left, or Right arrows on the keyboard. If you hold the Shift key while using the arrow keys, the field resizes incrementally in the direction of the arrow. You can use the F key to select the Form tool.

TABBING ORDER

When you create a document with many fields, you can navigate between the fields by pressing the Tab key. For example, when the user finishes entering her first name, she can tab to enter her last name. The tab order is the order in which the Tab key moves the focus from field to field.

FORMS PREFERENCES

Auto Calculate Field Values When this option is not selected, automatic calculations are suppressed.

Show Focus Rectangle Highlights the currently active form field (the field that has the focus).

Highlight Form Fields This controls whether the selected field is highlighted, and also lets you specify the highlighting color.

Preferences

Forms

- ☑ Auto Calculate Field Values
- ☑ Show Focus Rectangle
- ☐ Highlight Form Fields
  - Highlight Color: ▨

Accessibility
Batch Processing
Color Management
Comments
Digital Signatures
Display
Extract Images
Forms
Full Screen
Identity
JavaScript
Layout Grid
Online Comments
Options
Self-Sign Security
Spelling
TouchUp
Update
Web Buy

Cancel   OK

FIELDS PALETTE

The fields palette is available as a tab in the Navigation Pane and gives you an overview of the fields in the document. The fields are listed in alphanumerical order. You can use the fields palette to navigate, edit, and so forth.

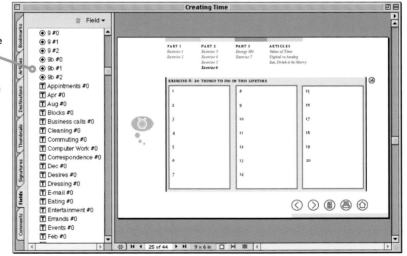

The tab order is automatically created from the order in which you create your fields. The Tab order also determines the layering of the fields. If you have a stack of fields, the field with the highest order number will appear on top.

To rearrange the tab order, choose the Form tool. Then choose Tools>Forms>Fields> Set Tab Order. A number will appear inside each of the fields. These numbers indicate the current tab order. To change the order, click the field that you'd like to be first in the order. Then click the other fields in the desired tab order. When you are finished, simply click on a place outside a field to deactivate the process.

Tabs work on a page-by-page basis. This means that you cannot set the tabbing order across pages, but must start the ordering again when you begin a new page.

SPELL CHECKING FORM FIELDS

Acrobat and Acrobat Approval can spell check the text in Comments as well as the Form fields. (As mentioned earlier, you can choose the option Do Not Spell Check to suppress the spell check from working on the contents of a field.) There are two ways to check the spelling in a document. You can choose Tools>Spelling> Check Form Fields and Comments. This opens a dialog box that lets you move from one word to another.

Alternatively, you can have the spell-check feature automatically underline suspected words as they are typed in a field. Unfortunately, you can't rely on the user to have this option turned on, because it is controlled in the Acrobat Preferences, not in the document. Also note that the automatic spell-checking feature takes quite a lot of resources, and will slow down Acrobat.

EXPORTING FORM DATA

When a user completes a form, the data can be exported in several ways. You can simply create a button that executes the menu command File>Export>Form Data. This creates an FDF file that contains all the information in the document's forms. You can also create a Java-Script command that exports the form data as a FDF file.

THE FIELDS PALETTE

Forms can get quite complicated, with dozens (or even hundreds) of fields. Acrobat 5 has added a Fields palette to allow for the organization of, and quick access to, every field in a document. The new Fields Palette takes form creation, functionality, and work flow to a new level with the ability to quickly access any field from anywhere in a document. This great new feature allows you to sort, delete, rename, lock, and set properties for fields from within a palette.

Select Window>Fields to open the Fields palette from the main menu. This new palette allows you to select and modify fields throughout an entire document, in addition to fields on the page currently in view. The Fields palette can also be docked in the Navigation Pane, where it will appear as a tab along with others, such as Bookmarks. Activate the Forms tool and double-click on a field name or icon in the palette to take you to a field—anywhere in the document. Right-click (w) or Control-click (M) on the field name or icon in the palette to view a context menu. Here, you can choose to jump to the field, rename, delete, lock, or invoke the Field Properties dialog box.

FILLING AND PRINTING FORMS IN ACROBAT READER

Once you have finished and saved your form, it can be distributed electronically to your users on CD-ROM or via website or e-mail. In order to print out the form, users will need the free Acrobat Reader, the inexpensive Acrobat Approval, or the full-version of Acrobat.

Users can view forms in the application window or through the PDF Viewer plug-in in their web browser.

When users open the PDF document, the Hand tool will change when it is placed over or in an active form field. Users can print the completed form, but if they are working with Acrobat Reader, they will not be able to save it (with the filled-in data). If users fill in the form within a web browser, the data can be submitted to a server. To save a form with the filled-in data, the user will need to have the full version of Adobe Acrobat or the inexpensive Acrobat Approval. You may want to explain this to your users in the instructions that come with the document.

FORMS PREFERENCES

Acrobat gives you three preference settings that control how forms are displayed and how they handle calculations. To set the preferences, choose Edit>Preferences and click the Forms category. The setting for Auto Calculate Field Values can be set to automatically calculate the values of set fields. The Show Focus Rectangle shows a fine rectangle in the field that has the focus (is selected). If you choose to set a highlight, you can also set the highlight color. This is the color that is shown when the field is selected or has the focus. Remember, however, that these preferences are set for the application, not the document. This means that your users may not have exactly the same preference settings.

5.2 Creating A Basic Fill-In Form

From the moment you could write your name till your last days on earth, you fill in forms—school forms, baseball sign-up sheets, SAT exams, college applications, product registrations, income tax documents, and health insurance forms. There is an overwhelming need in business, government, and education for billions of different forms. Acrobat's Form tool can help you create a simple form in a matter of minutes. You can use the Form tool to create extremely sophisticated forms as well.

DESIGNING THE FORM

The form shown on the facing page was created by Pattie Belle and Bjørn's design studio, Icehouse Design, for Yale University's Graduate School of Arts and Sciences (YGS). The form was designed to be distributed from the Admissions section of the Yale Graduate School website. At the time of this writing, YGS receives about 6,500 applications a year and about a third of those are printed from Acrobat (Reader).

It was helpful for YGS to have a form that applicants could fill out on screen and print out locally using their own printer. As you might imagine, these forms are designed to hold a large amount of crucial user-defined data. The use of PDF forms helps avoid some of the errors one can expect from forms that are distributed world-wide, such as hard-to-read handwriting and typing errors. PDF forms also allow the user to enter information into the form in a consistent manner. For instance, although the applicant might have entered her date of birth as July 22, 1988, the form field can be set to automatically change the date to 07/22/88. Similarly, a list ensures that the proper two-letter U.S. state abbreviations are entered.

ON THE CD

You will find excerpts from the YGS application forms on the Acrobat 5 Master Class CD. You can also view or download all of the Yale Graduate School PDF documents mentioned in this section at www.yale.edu/graduateschool.

The YGS form was originally designed in QuarkXPress 4.1 to accompany the YGS recruitment catalog (also available by download from the YGS website) and other printed materials produced for the Graduate School.

It was very important that the downloadable PDF version of the form was identical to the print version. Pattie Belle and Bjørn had designed forms that were tailored to the admissions office specific needs, and to the graphic identity of the school. The Icehouse team was concerned with consistency (of design, typography, and color). They also wanted to create easily understandable form fields using feedback that had been collected from previous versions and user testing.

In addition to the print and PDF versions, the same forms are available as an HTML version that is linked to databases. The different formats offer options to students who don't have Internet access or Acrobat Reader.

Interactive Acrobat forms can be created from any page-layout program and converted to PDF. They can also be made by scanning forms that exist only as printed documents. To import scans from the Acrobat menu, go to File>Import>Scan, and convert to PDF. The scanned image then becomes the background artwork on top of which the electronic fields are added. However, note that a scanned

This form for Yale University's Graduate School (as viewed in a web browser) makes use of a variety of form field types, such as check boxes, text fields and combo boxes to enhance the form's appearance and usability. The appearance of simple fill-in text fields can be customized to suit the design of the form by specifying outline and fill colors. Various restrictions, such as the maximum or minimum number of characters allowed in a field, can also be specified in the Field Properties. This is useful for social security numbers and other items, where a missing digit will render the information useless. Drop-down menus called combo boxes help avoid confusion and mistakes by listing all of the codes. This way, users don't have to locate them elsewhere and type them in.

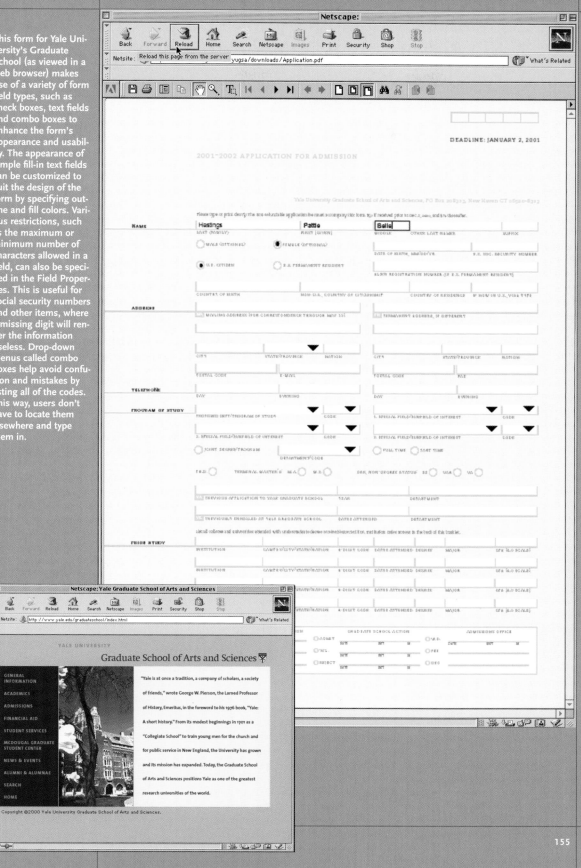

form that prints reasonably well will result in a large file size. If the form is made smaller (by reducing the resolution of the scan), it will be very hard to read—unless it has been processed with an OCR program that converts the scanned text to actual type.

DISTILLING THE FORM

Pattie Belle and Bjørn first created a PostScript file from the Quark document by selecting the Print to File option in the Print dialog box. They then used Distiller 5 to create the PDF. You can also create a PDF document from a Quark file by choosing Utilities>Export PDF from the main Quark menu. This method will locate and use Distiller 5, but also adds the option of automating hyperlinks and Bookmarks in the process. (For more detailed information on Export PDF, Distiller 5, and creating PDFs from other applications, see Chapter 2: Creating PDFs.

Before you make a PDF that will be used as a form, you should know how the form data will be collected. For instance, if the user opens the PDF document in Reader, they can fill out the form fields but they cannot save the new version of the document. This means the form must be printed and requires a higher-quality setting for any graphics than if the form is to be viewed only on screen.

However, if the form is to be electronically submitted, and will not be printed, then it is safe to select the Screen Job Option in Distiller. This lowers the resolution of the graphics and applies more compression to create a smaller final PDF file.

CREATING TEXT FIELDS

Most form documents use text fields for the majority of the form data—name, address, city, and so on. A simple text field holds the text that the user types, while a more advanced text field will also execute actions. Here are the steps to create a basic text field.

Step ① Draw the Text Field

To make a basic text field, select the Form tool and drag it across the area that you want to hold the text information. When you release the mouse button, the Field Properties dialog box automatically opens. Here, you must add a name for the field. Although you can use any type of name, it will help you organize many fields if you use a name that describes the form data, such as "Last Name". (See the next section "Naming Form Fields" for field-naming techniques.)

Use the Type menu to apply the Text category to the field. You'll then see the seven tabs that control text fields. For basic text fields, you only need to set the options in the appearance tab. All the other tab settings retain their neutral default settings.

⚡ CREATING TEXT FIELDS

① Select the Form tool and draw a rectangle. This opens the Field Properties dialog box. For this simple form we left all the settings as default except those found in the Appearance tab. We chose to have no border or background and chose Helvetica as the Font.

Patti Belle and Bjørn wanted to maintain the color and rule lines of the original Quark-XPress document, so they chose the "no border" and "no background" options for their text fields. They also selected Helvetica from the Font list, which sets the type style that will be displayed in the form fields.

CREATING CHECK BOXES
Check boxes and Radio Buttons look almost identical. They have the same Appearance, Options, and Actions tabs. However, there is one crucial difference. You can deselect a check box once it's been selected. You can toggle between choices with Radio Buttons, but they can't be totally deselected once one has been selected. This is the reason Icehouse used check boxes instead of Radio Buttons for the items in the YGS form. Check boxes gave applicants the option of deselecting a choice. Here are the steps to create a check box.

Step ① Draw the Field
Use the Form tool to create a rectangle that will define the check box. The size of the rectangle determines the size of the marker in the check box. The marker will be as large as the width or the height of the rectangle—whichever is the smallest measurement. Next, name the field in the Field Properties dialog and choose Check Box from the Type menu. Set the Appearance options as desired.

Check boxes do not have a text labeling option. Any text description for the box has to come from your layout or an Acrobat text field.

Step ② Define Options
Select the Options tab to choose the style for the type of marker within a check box. The six choices are Check, Circle, Cross, Diamond, Square, and Star. The default Export Value is Yes, but you can change it to any word or numerical value. This is particularly important when creating mutually exclusive Radio Buttons, as you'll see later in this chapter. When using check boxes or Radio Buttons, it is also useful to provide the data in calculation fields, as we'll discuss in the section Enhancing Form Fields. The option Default is Checked means that the marker will automatically appear in the box when the form is reset. When you finish selecting your options, click OK to return to the document.

Repeat the same steps for the other boxes. You can also copy and paste to create a duplicate of a check box. Double-click the duplicate and change the name to create a new field. In this way, all your boxes will be the same size. When you are done, test to make sure your boxes work as desired.

CREATING COMBO OR LIST BOXES
Combo boxes and list boxes are used for items with specific lists to choose from, such as a

---

⚡ CREATING CHECK BOXES

1. Draw a rectangle for the first button. In the Field Properties dialog box, enter the name and choose Check Box.

2. In the Options tab we selected the Circle for the Check Style. Although this looks like a radio button, it is still a check box.

157

country, state, or province. Combo boxes and list boxes provide an advantage over a plain text field in that the user does not have to type in information. As a general rule, you should use list boxes if you want to always show a list, in full or in part, or if multiple selections are possible. List boxes allow the user to select multiple items. Here are the steps to create a combo box or a list box.

Step ① Draw the Box and Define Appearance

Select the Form tool from the menu bar and draw a rectangle to define the area that will contain the box. A combo box field should be deep enough to display one item in the list. The width of the combo box list is determined by the length of the longest item in the list. For a list box, the rectangle should be deep and wide enough to display the scroll bars and several items.

When the Field Properties dialog box opens, name the field. Next, use the Type menu to select combo box or list box. Click the Appearance tab to set the appearance options. The Appearance settings control the look of the field for a combo box or list box. However, the Appearance settings do not control the look of the pop-up menu in a combo box (the look of the pop-up menu is determined by the operating system's standard pop-up menu appearance). If you choose a typeface of 14-point Times, that typeface will be seen only within the field. The typeface settings do not control the look of the items in a list box.

Step ② Setting the Options

You now need to create the list of items that will appear when a user clicks the triangle in the combo box or scrolls through the list box. Click the Options tab. Type the name of the first item in the list into the Item field. It is recommended (though not necessary) to set an Export Value for the item. Click the Add button. The item will appear at the bottom of the dialog box in the scroll field.

Repeat this step for each item in the list. (Sadly, there is no easy way to automate this; automation requires JavaScript or a special FDF document.) Don't worry if an item is out of order. Select the item and then click the Up or Down buttons to move the item until it appears in the correct position.

You may want to sort your items in alphabetical or numerical order. Do this by checking the Sort Items check box. This box automatically rearranges any items already in the list and sorts any new items as they are added to the list. It is extremely helpful for the user when items are sorted alphabetically, especially for long lists. The user can scroll past the early entries to find a listing at the end of the alphabet.

As we prepared the files for this book, we discovered an interesting quirk that might confuse a user. Consider a list of all the two-letter,

---

⚡ CREATING COMBO BOXES

① *We drew a field to create the area for the combo box. We entered a name for the field and chose Combo Box for the type.*

② *In the Options area, we entered each program name, and clicked the Add button. We selected the Sort Items box to alphabetize the list.*

③ *A space at the top of the list created a blank listing as the default item in the list.*

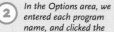

postal abbreviations for each of the fifty states in the USA. Ordinarily Indiana comes before Iowa. However, when you alphabetize postal abbreviations, Iowa (IA) is before for Indiana (IN). This would be confusing for most Iowa citizens who are used to seeing their state name just before Kansas.

Combo Box Options

Normally, you use a combo box to create a uniform list of items. However, you might want to let the user modify the selected items in the list. The Editable option for the combo box allows the users to type their own entry into the combo box field. Additionally, if you set a combo box to be editable, you can choose whether or not you want the form to be part of a spell check.

List Box Options

List boxes do not allow users to enter their own items, so there are no options for editable fields or a spell check. The Options tab for a list box contains the check box for Multiple Selection. Check this option if you want to allow users to select more than one item in the list.

Step ③ Setting the Default Item

When a combo box is displayed, it shows the item that was selected when you finished the list. (This is usually the last item you added to the list.) Occasionally, you may want the field to be blank. If the field is editable, you can simply delete the item in the field and then save your document. If the field is not editable, use the Add button to create an item in the list that consists of a blank space. Then move that item to the top of the list. This creates a blank listing that can be used as the default item in the list.

You can also use spaces or dashes for item names or to create breaks between groups of items in a list. Remember that each item in the list must have a unique name, so if you use spaces you'll have to increase the number of spaces in each listing.

Step ④ Test the field

Before you distribute the form, you should test the combo box or list box in the various Acrobat applications, different operating systems, and on different sized monitors. For instance, if you have a very long list of items, your users may find it difficult to scroll through a long pop-up menu on a very small monitor. In that case, it might be better to use a list box.

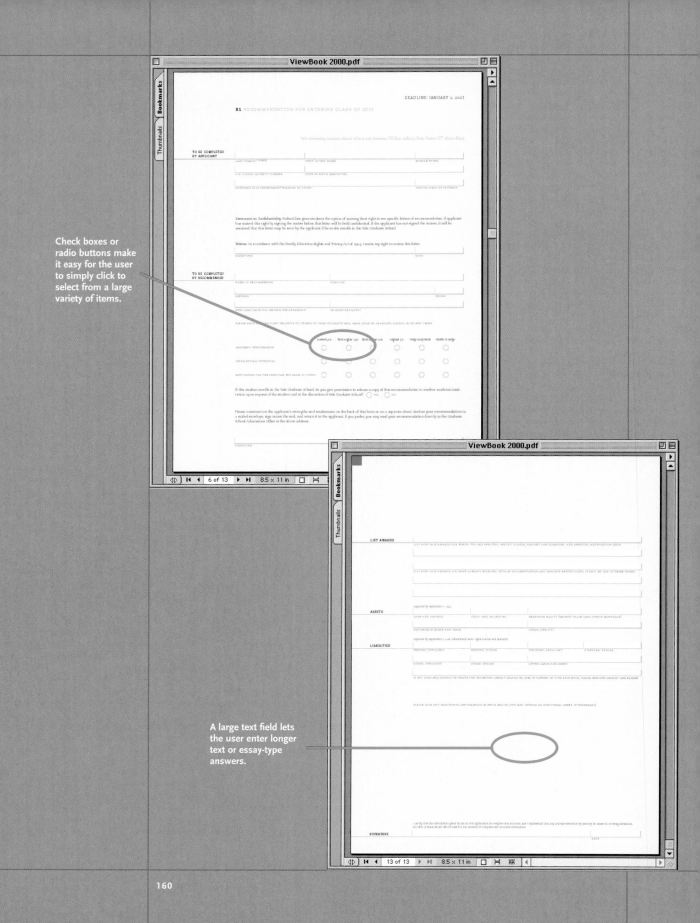

Check boxes or radio buttons make it easy for the user to simply click to select from a large variety of items.

A large text field lets the user enter longer text or essay-type answers.

The most recent version of the YGS application package and forms are available at: www.yale.edu/graduateschool.

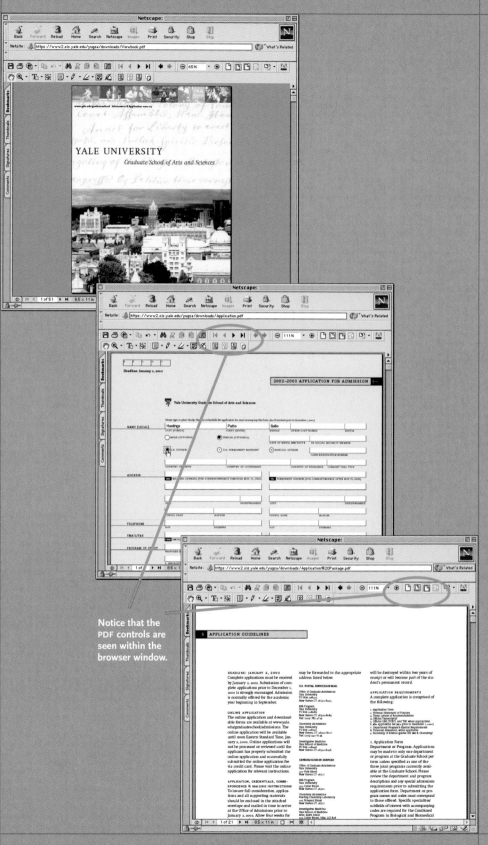

Notice that the PDF controls are seen within the browser window.

5.3 | Naming Form Fields

"What's in a name? That which we call a rose by any other name would smell as sweet." While Shakespeare's Juliet didn't feel that a particular name held any special significance, Acrobat is far less cavalier with how you name fields. Although you may certainly name fields with your own naming conventions, you will find that there are some special advantages to naming fields using Acrobat's special naming conventions.

FLAT OR HIERARCHAL NAMES

Acrobat has two different types of names for fields. The first type is called a flat name. Flat names use ordinary descriptions with no special structure. For instance, Color of Product, Size of Product, and Product Fabric are all flat names. The name describes the various aspects of a product. For most simple forms, it is fine to use flat names.

Acrobat also lets you name fields with a hierarchal structure. (Before you begin naming your forms, check to make sure your organization doesn't have its own forms implementation system and naming strategies already in place.) A hierarchal name creates a structure using a period as a separator for the levels of a name. This type of name would look like Product.Color, Product.Size, Product.Fabric, and so on. This naming convention uses a group name followed by the member name. In this instance, Product is the group and what follows the period is the member. Groups can also have submembers and sub sub-members.

Why would you want to use hierarchal field names? Most older forms systems have been formatted in this way, which means it will be easier to integrate the data submission from the PDF forms, especially when the data transfer format is XML. If you follow naming standards, then authoring and managing forms and fields becomes faster and easier. The hierarchal naming convention also blends well with JavaScript for both field creation and manipulation, and with XML as a data transfer format.

RULES FOR CREATING NAMES

As you create fields, you will notice that you can't close the Field Properties dialog box without entering a name for the field. This is because you must define a name for a field. You may also notice that you cannot define a new field with the same name, but a different field type, as an existing field. Although essentially any character can be used in field names, it is strongly recommended to use only "low-ASCII characters" (numbers, letters, hyphens, and underscores). Avoid diacritical characters, spaces, slash/backslash, quotes of any kind, and double-byte characters.

Name Conflicts

There are some additional rules for working with hierarchal names. Let's say you have one field named Product.Color. If you now try to name a new field Product, you will get a conflict. You can't create a new field that uses the name of a existing hierarchal name. Similarly, if you have a field named Product, you won't

> **NAME THAT FIELD**
>
> PDF *form documents can contain hundreds of individual form fields. Unless you have established a clear naming convention, it can be almost impossible to select certain fields from the long list in dialog boxes.*

These examples by Max Wyss show the hierarchal and numeric naming system applied to a complex interactive form. All actions in this document are executed through JavaScript. There are no other actions assigned to individual fields.

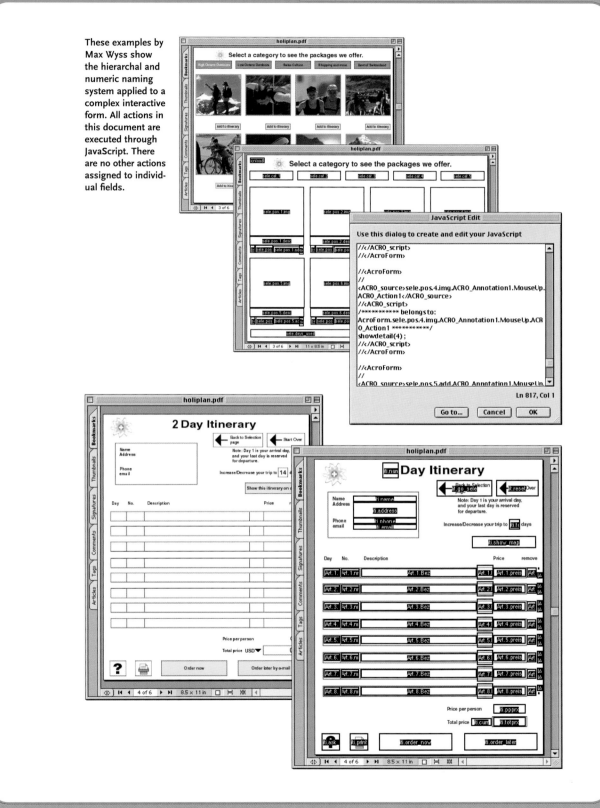

be able to create a hierarchal name Product.Color. Finally, you can create a conflict if you have two fields with the same name and you try to change one of them to a different type of field. Fields that have the same name must also be of the same field type.

Case Conventions

If you use hierarchal or flat names, you need to be aware of inconsistencies concerning upper and lower cases. For instance, the field names "Product.Color" and "product.size" are not part of the same group. The different case structure for the word "product" creates two separate groups. Even if you use simple flat names, you can cause problems by labeling two separate fields "Color" and "color." A form database will recognize the two fields as having the same name. We recommend choosing a strict case convention and sticking to it.

INCREMENTAL NAMES

You may find it helpful to use the incremental naming technique when working with names. This technique allows Acrobat to automatically create new names for existing fields using a numerical suffix. In this way, you can create many fields with different names. The technique also provides you with some special advantages when creating calculations for fields. Sandee has used this technique to quickly make the fields for a student grade sheet.

Step ① Create the First Field

To make the grade sheet, Sandee started with a layout that she created using InDesign. She used InDesign's drop shadows and transparent frames to indicate the areas for the Acrobat form fields. The document was then exported as a PDF file. When she opened the document in Acrobat, all her design elements were in place, except for the fields.

The grade sheet needed two different sets of fields—one for the student names and another for the grades. Sandee drew a field for the first grade and gave it the name grade.1. She then set the field type to Text and set the Format to number, with no decimal places. She also set the Appearance options.

Step ② Create Duplicates of the First Field

Sandee now needed a duplicate of the first grade field. With the Form tool active, she dragged the first field down while holding the Option key on the Macintosh keyboard (Ctrl key in Windows). This created a copy of the grade.1 field. With this duplicate field still selected, she pressed the plus (+) key on the numeric keypad on her keyboard. This automatically changed the name of the field to grade.2. This second field had all the attributes of the first.

Sandee then continued to drag to create copies and renumber them, by pressing the plus key, until she had all seven fields for the grades. This meant that all seven of the grade

 CREATING FORM NAMES

① The layout was created in InDesign and exported as a PDF. In Acrobat the first field was created with the name grade.1.

② A copy was made by holding the Option or Ctrl key as the field was dragged to a new position. After the copy was made, the plus key in the numeric keypad was pressed. This changed the name of the field to grade.2.

fields were sub members of the group field labeled "grade."

She did the same thing with the other set of fields for the students' names. She named the first field student.1, duplicated it, and pressed the plus sign to create student.2, student.3, and so on. (Although Sandee didn't need this feature, she also could have used the minus (-) key to rename the field to a lower suffix.)

Step ③ Create the Calculation Field

Sandee now needed to create a field to display the average of all the data in the seven grade fields. She drew a text field and set its Format to Number. She also set the Common Properties to Read Only so the user wouldn't inadvertently enter a value in that field. She then clicked the Calculate tab and chose to make the Value the Average of the following fields. She clicked the Pick button. This opened the Select a Field dialog box, where Sandee chose which fields she wanted as part of the calculation.

If Sandee hadn't used incremental names, she would have had to choose each of the seven fields for the grades. However, one of the benefits in having created the seven grade fields using the plus key was that another field labeled "grade" was also in the list. This field is the parent of the numbered grade fields. Rather than having to select all seven grade fields to use in the calculation, Sandee only needed to select the group name.

Using numerical suffixes on the field names made it much faster to create multiple fields with the same properties. It also made it easier to use the Calculate tab. If Sandee needed to add more grade fields to a page, she wouldn't have to add them to the calculation list. They would already be included as part of the group field listing.

NAMES IN THE FIELDS PALETTE

Another one of the advantages to using incremental field names is that the fields are automatically grouped by their group names in the Fields palette. The diamond symbol next to the field names "grade" and "student" indicates they are group field names. You can click the plus sign (w) or the triangle (m) to open the group field name listing. This displays the incremental names of the fields in the group.

③ *A new field called Average was set to calculate the value of the average of the grade fields. The parent field name "grade" was chosen from the Select a Field dialog box. The Average function automatically calculates the average of the entries in the grade fields.*

Class Grade Sheet

Student Name	Grade
Daniel	94
Elizabeth	95
August	96
Terry	89
Bonnie	81
Mary	63
Sharon	69
Class Average	84

5.4 Enhancing Forms

There's almost no limit to the actions you can have form fields perform. The built-in capabilities are very flexible and easy to use. You can create forms that crunch numbers, such as mathematical averages based on a range of values entered by the user in some form fields, or the summary of hours in a time sheet. Your form can be made to submit the data as an e-mail, or reset the field values. In addition to the canned functionality, you can integrate virtually any of your own scripts. The form values can be submitted from a web browser to a database for processing. In fact, there's no limit to the complexity of forms you can create. For instance, you can create dynamic forms that change as the user is inputting data.

PROGRAMMING FOR EVERYONE

We have little experience with heavy duty programming. Yet in Acrobat we can add functions to documents that we would previously have had to leave out, or have a techie perform for us. This is an example of technology made available for the masses. While you have almost unlimited configurations available in the properties, there is also the option of adding custom scripts.

Let's take a look at a few of the many things that you can do to forms to make the user experience more interesting and interactive. One easy programmable option is to create fields that automatically calculate values based on information the user enters in various fields.

The calculation function is especially exciting because it contains scripts that make relatively sophisticated features available even to the programming novice. For example, you can create a list of fields that the user fills out with numeric values. The calculation feature adds the numbers up with a total, including tax, as in a web shopping basket. You can cre-

ate fields in which the viewer enters the local temperature for every day of a week, and the average is calculated and displayed. (We showed you an example of creating an average earlier in this chapter in the section on Naming Form Fields.)

CREATING CALCULATING FIELDS

Pattie Belle and Bjørn's *Creating Time* eBook contains some excellent examples of calculating fields. Making a form field is relatively simple, but if this is your first time, the amount of options in the form fields properties dialog box may seem a bit overwhelming. Do not despair. While there are a limitless number of configurations available, there's little you can do to destroy anything, and the programming task is very easy. If you make a mistake, simply select the form field, and edit it or delete it by typing enter on the keyboard.

Step ① Create the Activity Fields

The first step is to use the Form tool to create each of the fields in which the user will enter data. Name the field and choose Text from the Type menu. Use the Appearance tab to set the border and background colors, as well as the appearance of the text.

> **ⓘ FORMS LIBRARY**
>
> *You might want to keep a special document with all your favorite fields and buttons as a forms library. This is especially true for forms that have specialized calculations. You can then copy the form from one document and paste it into another.*

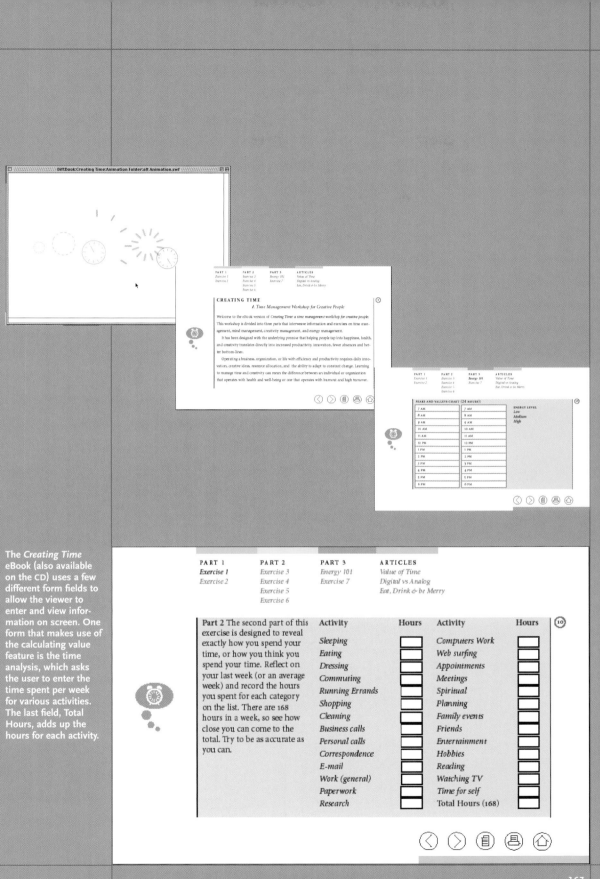

The *Creating Time* eBook (also available on the CD) uses a few different form fields to allow the viewer to enter and view information on screen. One form that makes use of the calculating value feature is the time analysis, which asks the user to enter the time spent per week for various activities. The last field, Total Hours, adds up the hours for each activity.

Step ② Set the Options and Actions

These options control how data is accommo-dated in the fields. Alignment sets the text to the left, right, or center of the field. The Multi-line option creates a form field that can consist of several lines. The Do Not Scroll setting limits the contents of the field to the displayable space. You can also control how many characters a user can enter in the next box. For the example, the *Creating Time* eBook controlled how many characters a user could enter in the activity fields in order to eliminate potential errors. Spell check can be turned on or off according to your need.

For a simple calculating form field, the Action tab has little relevance. For more advanced uses, you might add actions through Mouse events.

Step ③ Set the Format

The next step is to select Number for the Format of the field. The Format tab allows many different styles for form data. Number defines the settings, such as decimal space, currency symbols, negative number style, and decimal style. Percentage controls the display of decimal numbers. Date and Time sets the display of these values with a number of possibilities. Custom allows you to enter your own scripts. Special lets you select displays, such as social security numbers and telephone numbers with preset configurations. Unless you have a cus-tom validation script, leave the Validation tab at the default values. We repeated each of these steps (field creation, options, and format) for all the activity fields.

Step ④ Create the Calculation Field

The Calculation tab sets the calculation instruc-tions. Set this option to "Value is not Calculated" for all the activity fields. Then create another field named Total. This is the field that displays the sum of all the activity fields. Use the same options as you did in the activity fields, but set the Calculation tab for Value Is and choose the sum (+) option. Then click the Pick button and use the Select Field dialog box to select the field values you wish to use in the calculations.

Click done and when you return to the previous box, the form fields you selected will appear in a list. When you've finished, click the OK button.

Picking Fields for Calculations

You might think that only text fields set to the number or percentage format can be chosen as the data for the calculation fields. This is not the case. You can use any type of field to provide the data for a calculation field. For instance, if you sell items in specific quantities, you can use a combo box to have the user choose the specific number of items they want to buy. Simply enter the numbers for each item in the combo box list. When the user chooses that

① We used the Form tool to draw a field for each activity. We then set the Appearance options.

② Under the Options tab, we chose Right alignment and enabled

Do Not Scroll. We also set a Limit of 3 characters.

number, it is added to the calculation.

Calculation fields can even get their data from fields such as check boxes and radio buttons that don't display numbers. For example, you can create a sales sheet that displays various items for sale with the prices listed as non-editable fields. Users simply click a check box next to each item they want to buy. The export value for each check box contains the price of the item. When the user clicks the check box, the export value is automatically added to the calculation field.

MAKING A RESET BUTTON

A reset button returns the values in fields to their default settings. The default setting for a combo box or list box is the top item in the list. The default setting for a text field is a blank field or the entry in the Default field in the Options tab. The default settings for check boxes or radio buttons are either on or off. You may want to create a reset button so that a new user can clear the form before entering data. This is especially useful for kiosk forms. Your users may also need a reset button if they have made errors while filling out the form.

Step 1 Create the Button

Use the Form tool to draw a rectangle that defines the button area. Use any of the techniques described in chapter 4 to set the name, appearance, and options for the button. What makes this a reset button is the action that is assigned to the button.

Step 2 Set the Reset Form Action

Click the Actions tab and select the mouse action that you want to trigger the reset button. The Mouse Up action is the most common choice, as it is prompted when the user releases the mouse button.

Click the Add button. This opens the Add an Action dialog box. Choose Reset Form from the Type menu. Then click the Select Fields button to choose which fields to reset. This will open a Field Selection dialog box that allows you to choose which form data fields you want to reset.

The All Fields option resets all the data, which totally wipes all the fields clean. The "All, Except" option lets you choose the fields that you don't want to reset. This is helpful if you want the button to reset only specific fields such as the person's name and address. The "Only These" option lets you select the specific fields you want to reset. This is useful if there are only a few fields you want to reset.

Step 3 Test the Button

You can test the reset button by switching to the Hand tool. Enter values in various fields and then click the reset button. The forms will reset to their default values.

③ In the Format tab, we chose the Number option. We made sure that we displayed whole hours by setting the decimal places to 0. We kept the rest of the choices at their default options.

④ The Calculate tab is used to set the calculation for the Total field. We set the Value Is the sum (+) and clicked the Pick button. This opened the Select a Field dialog box, where we selected each field for the calculation.

CREATING A SUBMIT BUTTON

As we discussed earlier in this chapter, once the user has entered data in the document's forms, you can have the user submit the data through an Internet connection to your own server. Once the form data has been submitted, server software can store the data, notify others of its availability, or forward the data itself.

There are two parts to submitting data to a server—the easy part and the hard part. The easy part takes place in Acrobat. You create a button that contains an action that submits the form data to the URL of the destination you want the data sent to.

The hard part is configuring the web server to handle the data through a CGI (Common Gateway Interface) application. Designers are not expected to know how to do this! Most likely, you will contact the person in charge of the web server to give you the URL to which the data should be sent. That person will set the server with the necessary software and the proper CGI scripts. There are only a few requirements that the form designer should be aware of. For example, your field names must match the CGI application specifications. Find out from the

web master what those specifications are. Here are the steps, within Acrobat, to create a submit form button.

Step ① Create the Button

Use the Form tool to draw a rectangle that defines the button area. Use any of the techniques described in chapter 4 to set the name, appearance, and options for the button. What makes this a submit button is the action that is assigned to the button.

Step ② Set the Submit Form Action

Click the Actions tab and select the mouse action that you want to trigger the submit button. Click the Add button to open the Add an Action dialog box. This opens a Submit Form Selection dialog box, which is not as complicated as it looks.

First, enter the URL for the web server. Then choose which format the form data should be sent in. Before you get too caught up in these settings, check with the person who is setting up the CGI application and scripts. That person is best qualified to inform you about the proper setup for the exported data.

FDF stands for Form Data Format. This is Acrobat's own format for form data. This format is the most powerful one, and can also be used to import data into a PDF. There is a free toolkit (FDF Toolkit) available to help server scripts parse and generate FDF files. You can

---

SERVER SCRIPTS

If you're ambitious enough to want to program your own server scripts, you might want to start with Perl and CGI for the World Wide Web Visual Quickstart Guide, *by Elizabeth Castro. You can also look at some of the developer tools on planetpdf.com*

⚡ RESET BUTTON

① *Use the Actions tab of the Field Properties dialog box to choose the Mouse Up event that triggers the reset button.*

② *Choose Reset Form from the Type menu in the Add an Action dialog box. Click the Select Fields button. Use the Field Selection dialog box to select which fields should be reset by the button.*

find it at http://partners.adobe.com/asn/developer/acrosdk/forms.html.

HTML stands for the Hypertext Markup Language which is the same format used to transmit forms data from HTML forms to a server, allowing you to use commonly available server scripts.

XML stands for Extensible Markup Language. This is a way to transfer structured information. This information can easily be converted and imported into databases. Transferring data in XML format has become the standard data transfer format in many government to citizen applications.

If you choose PDF as the format for submission, the complete PDF document will be transmitted to the server. Note that this option will not work with the free Reader.

If you choose FDF or XML, you can submit the comments along with the field data. When you choose FDF, you also get the "incremental change" option, which will allow transmission of the information needed to recreate a digitally-signed document on the server.

Use the Field Selection options to control the field data to be exported. This option is similar to the controls in the Reset Form button. You also can choose whether or not empty fields should be included into the data export.

If you have fields that contain dates, you may want to convert the dates to a standard format that can be used in a server application.

Finally, click OK to return to the Add an Action dialog box. Click Set Action. Then click OK in the Field Properties dialog box. The submit form button is completed.

MUTUALLY EXCLUSIVE SELECTIONS

Earlier in this chapter we showed you how to create check boxes and radio buttons. These types of fields reduce the amount of data a user has to enter; a simple click turns a selection on or off. Radio buttons are arranged in groups whose assigned selections are mutually exclusive. For instance, two (radio) buttons with the labels Male or Female are mutually exclusive options. There are cases where no selection should be possible. In these cases, you would want to be able to deselect the selection. This is not possible with radio buttons—as soon as a selection has been made, it is no longer possible to choose "no selection". However, with a set of check boxes set up the same way as radio buttons (same field name, different export value), you can achieve this button behavior.

Pattie Belle and Bjørn created a series of radio buttons as part of their Creative Time document. Each hour has three mutually exclusive selections: L (low), M (medium), and H (high). The assigned buttons represent the reader's energy levels. The reader clicks one of the three choices for each hour of the day. Readers needed to create 24 individual groups

SUBMIT FORM BUTTON

1. Use the Actions tab of the Field Properties dialog box to choose the Mouse Up event that triggers the submission.

2. Choose Submit Form from the Type menu in the Add an Action dialog box. Click the Select Fields button. Use the Submit Form Selections dialog box to choose the URL and the format for the data.

171

of three radio buttons each. Here are the steps to create each group of mutually exclusive selection buttons.

Step ① Creating the Field

Use the Form tool to draw a rectangle to define the first radio button. Name the field with a label that indicates the hour of the day and set the type of field to radio button. Enter Low in the Export Value field.

Step ② Creating the Button Group

You now need to create the two other radio button fields in the group. These buttons need to have the same name as the first field, but different export values. It is easiest to either copy and paste the first field or hold the Alt (w) or Option (m) key as you drag to make each duplicate. Then double-click to open the Field Properties dialog box for the duplicate fields. Change the Export Value to Medium and High. Note: If you wanted this data to be charted in a graph program, you could also set the Export Value to numerical labels, such as 1, 2, or 3.

Step ③ Creating the Other Groups

You'll now need to create the rest of the button groups. Rather than draw a new field, you can simply hold the Ctrl (w) or Opt (m) key as you drag the first group of three fields and then change each field name individually. This

process is somewhat tedious, but you should be able finish the fields for a 24-hour day without too much trouble.

MUTUALLY EXCLUSIVE CHECK BOXES

Almost all Acrobat form designers use radio buttons for mutually exclusive fields. Once the first field is selected, any new clicks can only turn on another field, but cannot deselect them all. However, there may be times when you want to design a form in which the user can deselect all the boxes.

Consider the application for the Yale Graduate School. The fields to select male or female gender are labeled as optional. (This is because United States law forbids discrimination on the basis of gender.) So the gender fields should be optional—if an applicant doesn't want to select the field, he or she doesn't have to. However, what happens if mutually exclusive radio buttons are used for the gender choices? Because they are radio buttons, once the user clicks one of the choices, the button can not be deselected. The user can switch between Male or Female, but she can't deselect both. This is a case in which a mutually exclusive check box can be useful.

Mutually exclusive check boxes are created in the same way as radio buttons; the only difference is that the type of field selected is Check Box. Each group of check boxes gets the same name with different export values assigned to

⚡ EXCLUSIVE BUTTONS

1 Use the Form tool to draw the field for the first l (low) marker. This opens the Field Properties dialog box. Name the field and set the type to radio button. In the Options tab, choose the Square marker style. Set the Export Value to Low.

Field Properties	
Name: 7	Type: Radio Button ▼

Short Description:

Appearance \Options\ Actions

Radio Style: Square ▼
Export Value: Low
☐ Default is Checked

Hint: To create a set of mutually exclusive radio buttons (only one can be on at any time), make sure the fields have the same name but different export values.

[Cancel] [OK]

2 Create two duplicates of the radio button fields and change the Export Values to Medium and High.

Field Pro...
Name: 7
Short Description:
Appearance \Options\ Actions
Radio Style: Square ▼
Export Value: High
...ault is Check

Field Pro...
Name: 7
Short Description:
Appearance \Options\ Actions
Radio Style: Square ▼
Export Value: Medium
☐ Default is Check

3 Each new group of radio button fields uses a different name, but the same three export values. These make the mutually exclusive choices.

10 AM	■	M	H
11 AM	L	■	H
12 PM	L	M	■
1 PM	L	M	■

The *Creating Time* eBook contains a layout with sets of energy labels for each hour of the day. Mutually exclusive radio buttons were added to create the selections.

The labels for each of the groups were added in the QuarkXPress layout.

When the radio buttons are selected, a square marker appears over the selected energy level.

PEAKS AND VALLEYS CHART (24 HOURS):

7 AM	L	M	H		7 PM	L	M	H
8 AM	L	M	H		8 PM	L	M	H
9 AM	L	M	H		9 PM	L	M	H
10 AM	L	M	H		10 PM	L	M	H
11 AM	L	M	H		11 PM	L	M	H
12 PM	L	M	H		12 AM	L	M	H
1 PM	L	M	H		1 AM	L	M	H
2 PM	L	M	H		2 AM	L	M	H
3 PM	L	M	H		3 AM	L	M	H
4 PM	L	M	H		4 AM	L	M	H
5 PM	L	M	H		5 AM	L	M	H
6 PM	L	M	H		6 AM	L	M	H

(28)

PEAKS AND VALLEYS CHART (24 HOURS):

7 AM	L	M	■		7 PM	■	M	H
8 AM	L	■	H		8 PM	■	M	H
9 AM	L	M	■		9 PM	L	■	H
10 AM	L	M	■		10 PM	L	M	■
11 AM	■	M	H		11 PM	L	M	■
12 PM	L	■	H		12 AM	L	■	H
1 PM	L	M	■		1 AM	■	M	H
2 PM	L	■	H		2 AM	L	■	H
3 PM	■	M	H		3 AM	L	■	H
4 PM	■	M	H		4 AM	L	■	H
5 PM	■	M	H		5 AM	L	■	H
6 PM	■	M	H		6 AM	L	M	■

ENERGY LEVEL

Chart your energy over a 24 hour period (based on your average workday) by checking off the corresponding letter.

L – Low
M – Medium
H – High

create each mutually exclusive option. With a group of mutually exclusive check boxes, the user can choose either Male or Female, but not both. However, if a user has already clicked one of the fields and then decides that he or she would rather not submit that information, they can simply click that check box again to deselect it.

USING JAVASCRIPTS IN FORMS

The JavaScript language was developed by Netscape Communications in order to more easily create interactive web pages. Adobe has taken the Core JavaScript language and enhanced it so that JavaScript commands can add interactivity to PDF forms— similar to creating smart forms.

You can use JavaScript in Acrobat forms to format data, calculate data, validate data, and assign actions.

CREATING AN AUTOMATIC DATE FIELD USING JAVASCRIPT

Although teaching JavaScript in Acrobat is beyond the scope of this book, we do want to give you a very simple idea of how to work with a custom JavaScript. We decided to show you how Pattie Belle and Bjørn added an automatic date field to their application form. Since the application form needed a deadline posted at the top, they found it extremely useful to have the fill-in date automatically posted just below the deadline date. Because the date was to be inserted automatically when the document is opened, the JavaScript had to be assigned to the Document level.

Step ① Creating the Field

Use the Form tool to draw a rectangle to define the size of the field. Name the field AutoDate and set the desired options in the Appearance tab. Select the Read Only option in the Common Properties area. This keeps a user from changing the date in the automatic calculation field. (Interestingly, the Read Only option does not protect the field from the Reset Form action. If you create a reset form button as described earlier in this chapter, do not include the Auto-Date field as one of the fields to be reset, or use a second JavaScript action to properly set the field value again.)

Step ② Setting the Date Format

Although the actual date for the field will be automatically inserted in the field, you'll still need to set the format of the date, unless you format it with your script. Click the Format Tab and then choose Date as the category. You can then choose Date Format. In keeping with the look of the existing deadline date, Pattie Belle and Bjørn chose the full month, day, and year format. Once this is done, click OK to close the Field Properties dialog box.

⚡ AUTOMATIC DATE

① The Appearance tab for the "AutoDate" field properties showing the selections for Background, Border, Text, and Read Only.

② The Format tab for the "AutoDate" field properties showing the Date and Format selections.

Step ③ Adding the JavaScript

Finally, insert the appropriate JavaScript at the Document Level. Go to the main menu and select Tools>JavaScript>Document JavaScripts. This opens the JavaScript Functions dialog box. Type the name of the script, AutoDate, in the Script Name field. Click the Add button to open the JavaScript Edit window. This is where you enter the actual JavaScript.

The Edit window opens with default text in place. Delete that text and type the following text exactly as shown below (watch out for extra spaces, missing spaces, and incorrect punctuation. Also, be sure to have correct capitalization of the words).

```
var f = this.getField("AutoDate");
f.value = util.printd("mm/dd/yyyy", new
Date());
```

Understanding the JavaScript code

Once you see the JavaScript, it is not too difficult to figure out what each part of the code does. Let's take it one line at a time.

```
var f = this.getField("AutoDate");
```

This defines the variable f and assigns it a field object connected to the AutoDate field.

```
f.value = util.printd("mm/dd/yyyy",
new Date());
```

This sets the value of our field object to the current date (using the new Date() command), and formats it using the printed method of the Acrobat JavaScript util object, using the pattern "mm/dd/yyyy".

You can also cut and paste the script from the Master Class JavaScript document included on the Master Class CD. However, if you do this, be sure the plain quotes (" ") don't change into smart quotes (" "). Smart quotes create an error report when you close the Edit window. After you type the text, click OK. And then close the Document Level dialog box. The current date will appear in the field that has just been created.

③ Choose Tools>Java-Script>Document JavaScripts. This opens the JavaScript Functions dialog box. Name the script and click the Add button. This opens the Java-Script Editor where you can type the code.

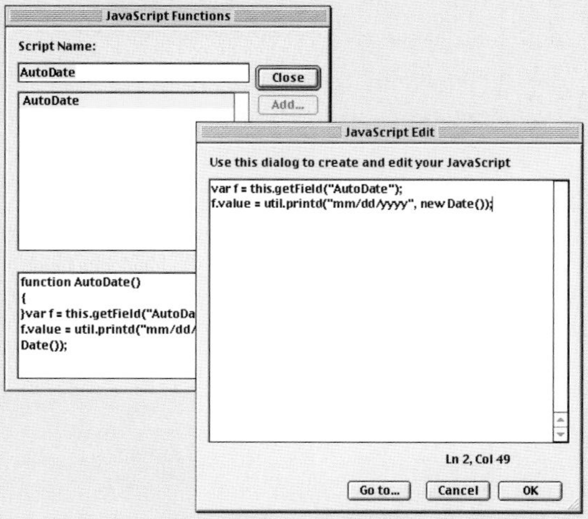

④ The finished Auto-Date field as it appears in the completed form.

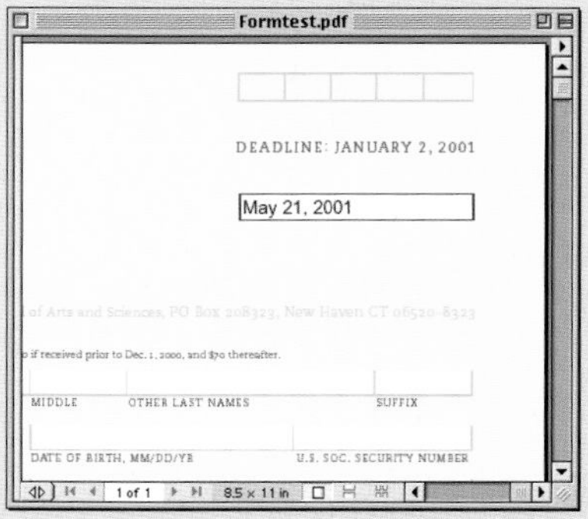

175

5.5 Saving and Signing Forms with Acrobat Approval

Imagine your user has just spent an hour filling out a long form document using Acrobat Reader. Reader has a Print command, but there's no way to save the file or finish it at a later point—if the user closes the file, the data will be lost. Most people will not purchase the full Acrobat product just to fill out a few forms. Acrobat Approval is an inexpensive alternative.

HISTORY LESSON

When Adobe first introduced the PDF technology, there was no free Acrobat Reader. Anyone who needed to view a PDF document was expected to purchase the Reader program. Needless to say, it was only after Adobe began distributing the free Reader software that PDF documents were so widely accepted.

However, Adobe realized that people needed a middle ground between the full-featured Acrobat (selling for around $250) and the free Acrobat Reader. After all, it would not be easy to get people to agree to read and digitally sign documents if they had to spend $250 to do so. That's the reason Adobe created Acrobat Approval (selling for around $40 for a single license at the time of this writing).

COST VS. BENEFIT

Approval is a scaled-down full version of Acrobat. Approval includes the ability to save changes made to documents, export form data, and add digital signatures to files. This makes Approval a great solution for large corporations, in which some users need the full version of Acrobat, while others just need to read and fill out forms. For example, a corporation's employees may need only Approval to fill out and save forms, while the human resource department may need the full version of Acrobat to create the forms.

As an Acrobat form provider, you'll need to consider whether your users will buy Approval when Reader is free. The United States IRS solved this problem by arranging to license Acrobat Approval and distribute it on the CD-ROM that contains PDF versions of IRS tax documents. The version of Approval on the CD is free to the user, but is only licensed for use with the IRS documents.

WHAT'S MISSING?

Because Approval is a downscaled product, it doesn't include Acrobat features such as web capture, Distiller, editing tools, mark-up annotations, or form creation. There are no mark-up comments tools, which makes Approval unsuitable for publishing—where editors and writers need to exchange comments.

USING APPROVAL

Acrobat Approval looks almost identical to Acrobat (or Reader). Forms are filled in the same way as they are in Reader, but Approval lets you save the file or export the form data. Reader only allows you to print the form data. You can also use Approval's Export command to send the form data to another user. Finally, although you can't add a digital signature field to a document, you can use Approval to sign a signature field that has already been inserted in the document.

Acrobat Approval has more features than Acrobat Reader, but fewer features than Adobe Acrobat. Notice that the File menu contains the commands for Save As, Import Form Data, and Export Form Data, which are not found in Reader.

Acrobat Approval contains all the tool bars found in Reader, but does not have the Editing or Annotation tools found in Acrobat.

5.6 | Form Guru

Max Wyss is a consultant and Smart Forms developer who has worked with industrial clients as well as international organizations and various government agencies. He is a well-known member of the PDF community, a frequent presenter at PDF conferences, and is extremely active in the PDF forums. The word "form" doesn't really describe Max's creations, and although the term "smart form" comes a bit closer, it is still inadequate. His documents are actually self-contained PDF applications. We've seen him demonstrate a complex PDF quiz that tests you, grades you, and teaches you all at the same time. In this section, we'll show you an interactive pulley specification application in PDF and a PDF "shopping cart" that Max created. But first we want to pass on some of Max's words of wisdom about smart form design and development.

SMART DOCUMENTS

Max has come up with a simple and useful classification system for electronic forms in general, and PDF forms in particular.

Level 0: Print and Fill out. This is a plain vanilla PDF with no Acrobat form enhancements. A user prints the form and fills it out by hand.

ON THE CD

You'll find both the Pulley Designer and the Swiss Holiday Planner on the Acrobat Master Class CD. Due to the nature of Max's work, both of these documents have been secured to protect his proprietary development work. Nonetheless, we think you'll by amazed by the possibilities that these intelligent documents demonstrate.

Level 1: Fill out and Print. This is a PDF that has had form fields added. In this way, the user can fill out the form on screen and then print the completed form.

Level 2: Smart Form. This is a PDF with fillable form fields, including calculations and scripting that enhance the form's functionality.

Level 3: Attached to Work Flow. These are forms that include the ability to submit and receive data to and from a server environment.

Level 4: Fully Embedded in Electronic Work Flow. This is a PDF form (or forms system) that incorporates the use of digital signatures for securing the workflow.

MAX'S TIPS FOR FORM CREATION

Find out what users know and don't know. Do users know how to fill out the form? Do they know how to handle an electronic form? Do they know how to navigate in a PDF? Are they familiar with the Reader interface? Have they encountered this type of form before?

Figure out your needs. What data do you need to receive and what format do you need it in?

Make forms small but usable. What do you really need to make the form functional and what can you leave out?

Design for readability and usability. The requirements for readability onscreen are different than those for print. A form for use onscreen may appear completely different than its printed counterpart. Balance this tip with the next.

Keep a form recognizable to the printed counterpart for user familiarity. This, of course, may compromise screen usability. In some cases, you must decide between form familiarity versus screen usability. This might be an obvious decision in cases such as the U.S. Government's IRS forms.

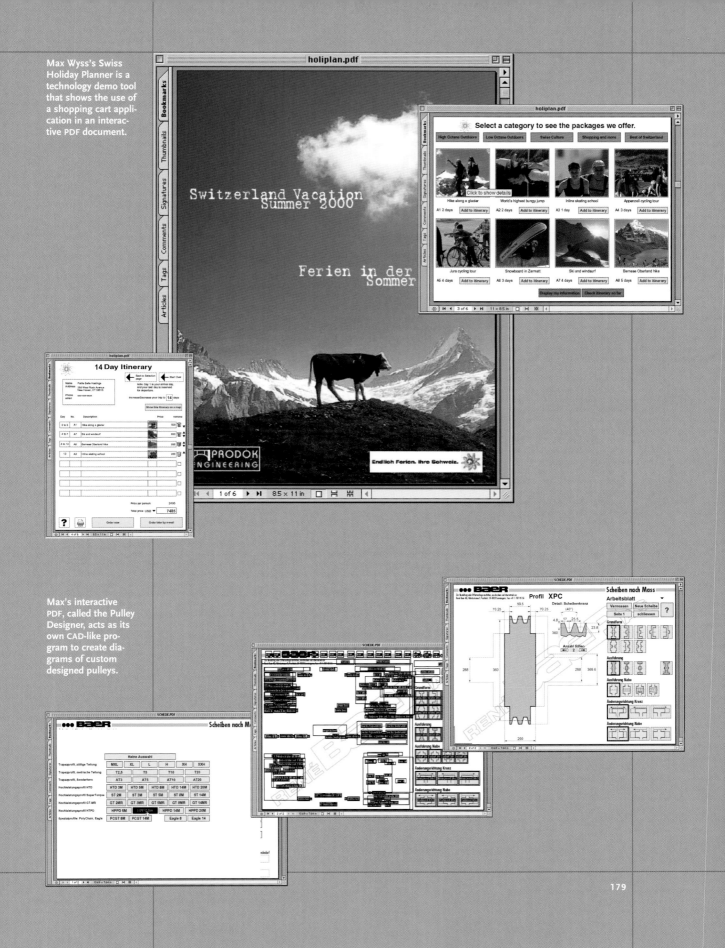

Max Wyss's Swiss Holiday Planner is a technology demo tool that shows the use of a shopping cart application in an interactive PDF document.

Max's interactive PDF, called the Pulley Designer, acts as its own CAD-like program to create diagrams of custom designed pulleys.

Provide help. What questions might your users have while using your document? Find a way to answer these questions within the document.

Whatever you do—don't overdo it! Do we need to explain this? Less is more.

Any form calculation that can be solved mathematically (however complicated) can be executed using JavaScript. The two examples of Max's work pretty much prove this point.

Consolidate scripts. Consolidate scripts by putting the script of a chained calculation into the last element of that calculation. You'll then have full control over that calculation and will not have problems with the calculation order.

Don't optimize smart forms Don't optimize forms of Level 1 and higher for Fast Web View. Byteserving protocol (used to serve Optimized for Fast Web View documents) causes the document to be transferred from the server in individual objects. Because form fields consist internally of several small objects, there will be many objects to be transferred until your form actually is available—each one needing to establish its own connection between server and client. If you don't optimize for fast web view, the form will be transferred in larger chunks of data, speeding the time up considerably (there are known examples where people have gotten a speed up by a factor 20 to 60).

THE PULLEY DESIGNER

Max has a client who produces and trades belt drive components has always relied on a paper catalog to promote the belt drive components he produces and trades. His customers required a high ratio of customization in their orders. Some customers needed to add a notch, others to shorten the hub, and some needed to have additional angles. The client wanted a way to quickly draw these custom pulley designs, so that an exact diagram (including dimensions) could be handed to the sales department for price estimates and then given to the machinists for fabrication. Max began thinking about how this could be done without calling a CAD program to produce the diagrams. His first thought was PDF.

Max wanted to have places to enter data and have this result in a graphic representation of the hub, body, and rim of the pulley. In order to do this in a PDF, he needed to have a controllable number of combinations. First, Max created the diagrams in Illustrator using extreme precision and a registration mark so he could make sure the parts fit together exactly. Then he loaded the diagrams as the icons for Acrobat buttons. (The final PDF document had a stack of approximately 120 fields.)

The next step was to create the logic that would show and hide the appropriate fields. Max developed his JavaScript in BBEdit by BareBones Software, which has a few features

Although the sheer number of fields, buttons, and scripts in Max's documents may seem overwhelming, they are easy to understand when you take them one at a time. Here's the anatomy of one of the fields in the Swiss Holiday Planner.

(1) *As the user adds packages and trips to the itinerary, the number of days for the trip is automatically entered at the top of the itinerary. The number of days of the itinerary appears inside a text field labeled iti.numday.*

(2) *The properties for the iti.numday field are quite simple. The typeface is set in the Text area. The field is set to Read Only so the user does not inadvertently change the amount in the field.*

11 Day Itinerary

Day Itinerary

he finds particularly useful, such as the automatic balancing of parentheses. Max also likes the fact that the program color-codes the text, which helps him avoid about half of the errors that he might make otherwise. BBEdit easily spots typing errors, such as a missing "close quote" or a parenthesis in the wrong place.

Unfortunately, the Macintosh version of Acrobat 5 has no external editor functionality. This means that a Windows user can launch an external text editor from within Acrobat 5, but Mac users cannot. Mac users must launch their script editor and copy/paste the individual scripts between the text editor and Acrobat's JavaScript editor. Even so, the JavaScript improvements between Acrobat 4 and Acrobat 5 can speed up your work significantly.

Once Max has finished the code, he inserts the scripts throughout the document and the result is an incredible cross-platform diagramming tool that can run in Reader and from a CD-ROM.

SWISS HOLIDAY PLANNER

For a while now, Max has been creating PDF client catalogs that function as shopping carts. Because of their proprietary nature, he was barely allowed to present them at conferences and not allowed to distribute them as part of his promotional materials. So he created a fictitious version of a PDF catalog, called the Swiss Holiday Planner, that he could use as a demonstration of PDF technology. In this demo, he uses his shopping cart tool kit.

The document is entirely fabricated. Max used photos (available by permission of the Swiss Tourism Board) to simulate a CD-ROM-based project. After the user specifies the number of people traveling and the number of days for the trip, the document offers a choice of 30 or so activity and destination packages for an imaginary holiday in Switzerland (Max's home). The PDF maintains a table of selected items on the order form page (including a picture icon that acts as a link), calculates the number of available days, calculates the costs, and draws a map of the itinerary. If the sequence of the packages does not make sense on the map, the user can then click the arrow buttons on the form to change the sequence of packages to create a more logical itinerary.

Max says that the most important buttons in this document are the "Add to Itinerary" buttons. All the calculations reside here. The document is also designed to be very flexible and forgiving. The user can delete packages from the order form and try out many different combinations without any limits.

Max and his partner, Makiko Itoh, created the form backgrounds in Illustrator and the photos in Photoshop. Again, Max used BBEdit for the logic—or as Max says, to make the document smart. We think Max is the smart one.

③ *This number for the field is automatically entered as part of a document level Java-Script. Part of 115 lines of code, this simple line sets the value of the iti.num-day field to be the value of the endday field, whose value is the result of calculations of other fields.*

As the user adds packages, the number in the field increases. Notice that the form automatically adds travel days at the front and back of the trip.

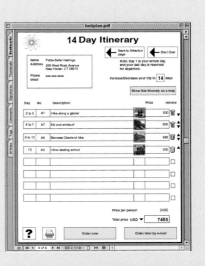

5.7 | PDF Crossword Puzzles

Peter Neese, of Actino Software in Hamburg, Germany, has been fascinated by crossword puzzles since he was a boy. In fact, he started creating his own puzzles when he was young. Over the years, he has created puzzles for various purposes, such as a friend's birthday and his volleyball club. About a year ago, he created his first PDF crossword puzzle for a holiday edition of the Actino newsletter. Peter offered to create a crossword puzzle for us in English (he usually writes in German).

Peter says the real puzzle is writing the puzzle. First, he created the words and configurations, then he came up with the clues. The German puzzles take him about three nights with very little sleep. He says once he starts, it's hard to leave a puzzle unfinished. Why does he do it, you might ask? For the same reason other people solve crossword puzzles—because it's fun.

Once Peter had the puzzle figured out on paper he created a Microsoft Word document for the puzzle itself. Then he created a QuarkXPress document of the clues and left a blank area where the puzzle would go. He made a PDF from the Word document and a PDF from the QuarkXPress document.

He then opened the Quark-XPress PDF in Acrobat and used one of his favorite third-party plug-ins, called Pagelet, by Creo. This plug-in allowed him to place one PDF document as a second layer over another PDF file. He imported the puzzle PDF by going to the Acrobat menu>Pagelet> Import and selected the puzzle PDF and clicked OK. This placed the puzzle on the page. Peter then moved it into place. If he needed to, Peter could also size, crop, rotate, and otherwise transform the placed PDF using Pagelet.

At this point, Peter added his letter fields using the Form tool. He created the first row and then conformed the size of the fields using Control-Click (M) or Right Mouse-Click (W) to invoke the context-sensitive menu. He duplicated the fields down the length of the puzzle. You'll notice the fields that contain the first letter of a word, either down or across, include the clue as a description. Peter specified that the field was limited to one character and he selected centered for the alignment in the Options tab of the Field Properties. In the Format tab, he added a custom Javascript for the fields that changed a character typed in lower case to upper case.

In addition to the fields in his smart puzzle, Peter used links to help the user navigate from the clues to the corresponding portion of the puzzle. He drew a link over the clue number, selected Go to View as the type of link, and then zoomed in on the portion of the puzzle that contained that clue. He selected Fit View for the magnification of the link and clicked Set Link.

ON THE CD

You'll find Peter's puzzle on the Acrobat Master Class CD, as well as a PDF with all the answers. If you want to see his German puzzles, visit www.actino.de and go to the News section>Acrobat PDF World Magazine. You'll find one in the January 2002 issue. His company, Actino Software develops PDF applications and plug-ins. Peter also consults on implementing PDF work-flow solutions. If you want to find out more about Actino Software in English, visit www.actino.com. You can download a fully functioning demo version of Creo's Pagelet at Planet PDF (www.epublishstore.com.)

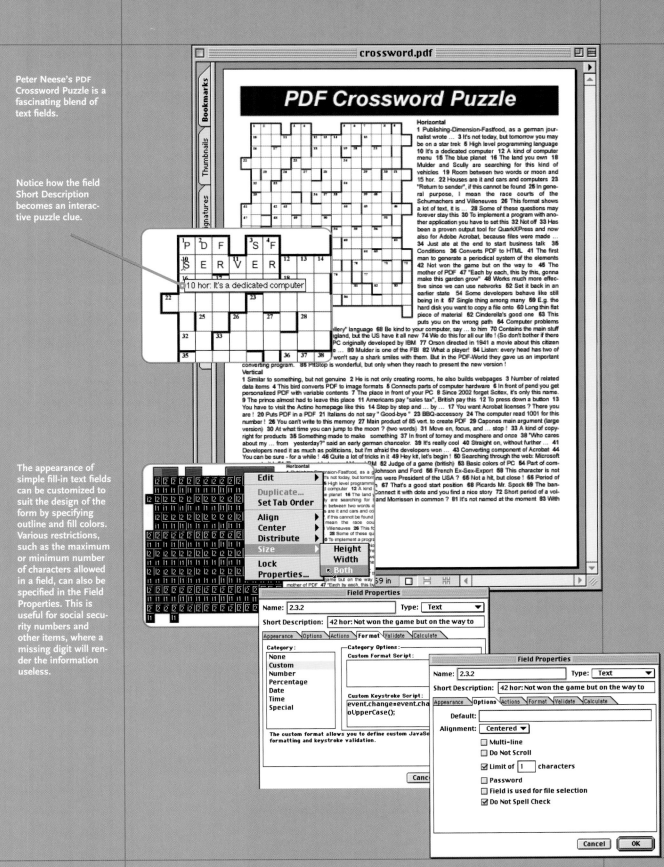

Peter Neese's PDF Crossword Puzzle is a fascinating blend of text fields.

Notice how the field Short Description becomes an interactive puzzle clue.

The appearance of simple fill-in text fields can be customized to suit the design of the form by specifying outline and fill colors. Various restrictions, such as the maximum or minimum number of characters allowed in a field, can also be specified in the Field Properties. This is useful for social security numbers and other items, where a missing digit will render the information useless.

183

6

Comments

Part of what made Acrobat and PDF documents so popular in business and publishing is that they can do so much more than paper documents—especially when it comes to adding interactive links, buttons, bookmarks, and thumbnails. However, there are many people who need Acrobat to work more like old-fashioned paper and pencil. Those who work in publishing, such as writers and editors, need to add editorial and production notes to PDF documents. They need the electronic equivalent of red and blue pencil marks, sticky notes, marker flags, and long comments typed up and pasted on the back of a page. Making PDF documents work like paper is not as simple as it sounds. However, there are advantages to electronic markup. You'll also discover you don't have to be editing documents to make use of Acrobat's comment tools and features.

6.1 Evaluating Acrobat's Comment Tools

We remember the dark ages, when writers, editors, and designers had to learn the cryptic markup symbols for bold, italic, delete text, insert comma, align, move, add space, and so on. We remember dragging out an old copy of Pocket Pal (still published by International Paper) to look up the difference between the symbol for a hyphen and the one for an en dash. These symbols helped each person understand the markup abbreviations used by others. Fortunately, using PDF documents for editorial markup has made it much easier to insert and read the corrections and changes that are added to page layouts.

Once a document has been laid out in a program such as QuarkXPress, it needs to be distributed in a review cycle for corrections and approvals. Before using Acrobat, a designer might have sent a hard copy to each person involved. This could be expensive and time-consuming. Using PDF files allows files to be distributed faster and cheaper—electronically. This method requires that each person has the full version of Acrobat in order to add comments to PDF documents, since neither Reader nor Acrobat Approval allows for this feature.

STRATEGIES FOR USING PDF FILES IN AN EDITORIAL REVIEW CYCLE

Each organization should set up a review cycle work flow in the way that works best. A magazine or book may send a PDF of a document in a linear or sequential order. The designer creates a PDF which is sent to the editor. The editor makes her corrections and then sends the PDF to the author. The author makes his comment on the file, as well as any corrections that the editor requested. The editor reviews the author's comments and then sends the PDF back to the designer who makes the final corrections. Sequential distribution is used when it is necessary for each person to see the comments of others along the line, in a specific sequence.

Another distribution method is radial or simultaneous distribution. Advertising layouts may be distributed in this manner. The designer creates a PDF which is distributed (via e-mail or server) simultaneously to the copywriter, creative director, account executive, and client. Everyone makes their own corrections, unaware of what the others are doing. The comments are sent back to the designer, who combines all the comments into one document. Simultaneous distribution is useful when each person does not need to see what the others say about the file.

Acrobat also allows PDF documents to be commented on through online collaboration. The PDF document is posted on a server and everyone involved can add their comments to the same document through an Internet or Intranet connection. This work flow is a combination of sequential and simultaneous distribution. Those who add their comments immediately after the file is put up on the server may not see what the others say about the document. However, those who comment later can make their own corrections and can discuss the previous comments.

When Sandee wrote the InDesign 2 Visual Quickstart Guide, she e-mailed PDF files of each chapter to her editor, copy editor, and production manager. They used Acrobat's markup tools to make corrections and comments to the files and sent them to Sandee. Before she used PDF files for editorial markups, she spent close to $1,000 in FedEx charges for each book. Using PDF documents has eliminated those shipping charges and saved the time that the packages traveled between New York and California.

The comments can be set to appear as electronic pencil marks, highlights, and small notes. This helps indicate the type of correction or suggestion.

Each person's comments can be set to appear in a distinctive color. In this piece, comments from the production person appear in dark blue, the editor in yellow, and the copy editor in aqua.

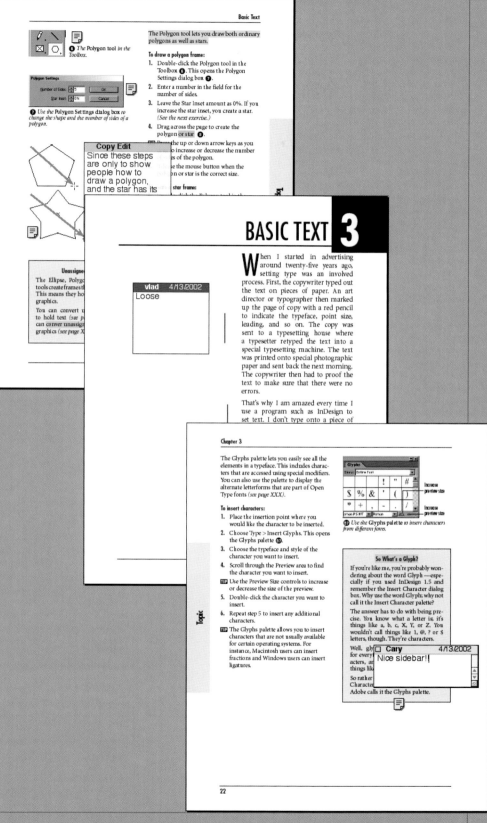

6.2 Adding Comments for Review Cycles

Comments, known in previous versions of Acrobat as Annotations, are an extensive group of features intended for creating, reading, and exchanging notes. Comments are used most often as part of the editorial or document review process. (As you'll see later in Chapter nine, you can also use Comments as part of multimedia presentations.) Acrobat's Comments offer many advantages over their traditional pencil and paper counterparts. For instance, you can distribute copies of the same document for viewing by several different people, and then collate each individual's comments into one single file. Comments allow you to create an editing and approval system where time and distance are of less consequence.

Some of the Comments features have direct equivalents in traditional paper and pencil markup tools. Like the symbols used in traditional markup, you can assign symbols to comments to quickly indicate the type of correction. Like the different colored pencils used by each person proofing a document, each person can have their own color for their Acrobat Comments.

However, Acrobat's Comments offers many features not found in traditional editorial markup. You can easily move or delete markup notes. You can attach your own spoken words to be played back when the comments are reviewed. You can also attach other documents, such as word-processing files, to a document. Comments can be sorted by user, date, or type of comment. Perhaps the greatest benefit is that you don't have to deal with poor handwriting because the notes that accompany comments are typed.

LEARNING TO USE COMMENTS

As the designer of a document, you are not likely to add comments to PDF files you distribute to others. However, you may want to make sure the people who review your document have some general idea of how to set the different Comments features. For instance, it may not be obvious to some users that they can customize the color of their markup notes. Others may not know how to add notes to the markup graphics. You may want to send instructions to educate them about Comments tools.

You may also want to set up certain conventions to help people work with Comments tools. This may mean assigning different colors for each person's comments. You can also choose how the different Comments tools should be used. For instance, background comments about the entire document should be added using the Comment icon of the Note tool. Instructions to insert text should be added using the Insert icon of the Note tool. Conventions make it easier for the person reading comments to decipher a proofreader's intent.

Using the Comments Tools

There are twelve different tools that allow you to add comment objects to the PDF page. While each tool works differently, the general principles are the same. You choose a tool from the tool bar, and then click or drag to create the markup object or symbol on the page. The markup objects can be customized with different colors, icons, or graphics.

SQUARE

This tool lets you draw rectangles or squares (hold the Shift key) around an area on the page. You can set the color of the fill and border, or change the border thickness.

SOUND ATTACHMENT

This tool opens a miniature recorder inside the PDF file that lets you record voice or other sounds. The sound can then be played back later. The color of the speaker symbol can be selected.

STAMP

This tool lets you stamp documents with a number of built-in graphics for different categories. You can also create your own custom graphics to use with the Stamp tool.

LINE

This tool lets you draw callout lines that can be styled with custom colors, thicknesses, and special markers at the start and end points.

NOTES

This tool inserts a symbol onto the document that indicates the type of correction. Notes also open to display small electronic windows where the user can type comments.

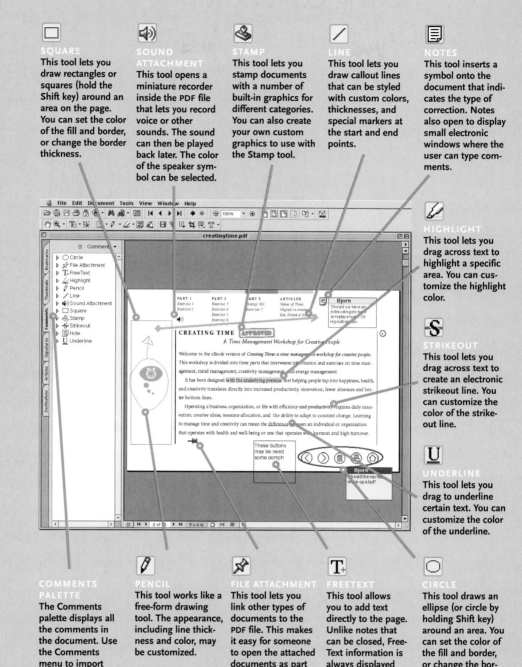

HIGHLIGHT

This tool lets you drag across text to highlight a specific area. You can customize the highlight color.

STRIKEOUT

This tool lets you drag across text to create an electronic strikeout line. You can customize the color of the strikeout line.

UNDERLINE

This tool lets you drag to underline certain text. You can customize the color of the underline.

COMMENTS PALETTE

The Comments palette displays all the comments in the document. Use the Comments menu to import additional comments or sort the comments according to a variety of criteria.

PENCIL

This tool works like a free-form drawing tool. The appearance, including line thickness and color, may be customized.

FILE ATTACHMENT

This tool lets you link other types of documents to the PDF file. This makes it easy for someone to open the attached documents as part of the review process.

FREETEXT

This tool allows you to add text directly to the page. Unlike notes that can be closed, FreeText information is always displayed on the page.

CIRCLE

This tool draws an ellipse (or circle by holding Shift key) around an area. You can set the color of the fill and border, or change the border thickness.

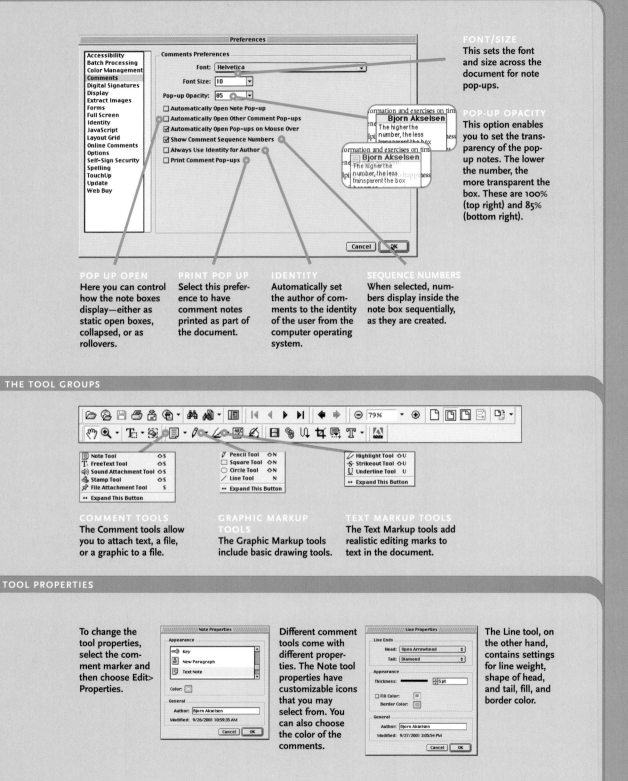

FONT/SIZE
This sets the font and size across the document for note pop-ups.

POP-UP OPACITY
This option enables you to set the transparency of the pop-up notes. The lower the number, the more transparent the box. These are 100% (top right) and 85% (bottom right).

POP UP OPEN
Here you can control how the note boxes display—either as static open boxes, collapsed, or as rollovers.

PRINT POP UP
Select this preference to have comment notes printed as part of the document.

IDENTITY
Automatically set the author of comments to the identity of the user from the computer operating system.

SEQUENCE NUMBERS
When selected, numbers display inside the note box sequentially, as they are created.

THE TOOL GROUPS

COMMENT TOOLS
The Comment tools allow you to attach text, a file, or a graphic to a file.

GRAPHIC MARKUP TOOLS
The Graphic Markup tools include basic drawing tools.

TEXT MARKUP TOOLS
The Text Markup tools add realistic editing marks to text in the document.

TOOL PROPERTIES

To change the tool properties, select the comment marker and then choose Edit> Properties.

Different comment tools come with different properties. The Note tool properties have customizable icons that you may select from. You can also choose the color of the comments.

The Line tool, on the other hand, contains settings for line weight, shape of head, and tail, fill, and border color.

Using the Note Pop-up Windows

Nine of the Comments tools also provide a note pop-up window where you can type your own notes about the comment. (The three tools that don't contain a note pop-up are the Sound Attachment tool, the File Attachment tool, and the FreeText tool.) You don't have to worry about running out of space, as the pop-up windows can contain up to 5,000 characters. Pop-up windows also show the name of the person who created the comment and the date the comment was created.

When you first click with the Note tool selected (depending on your preferences), the pop-up window opens automatically. To open the pop-up window for the other types of Comments tools, select the Hand tool or the tool that created the comment and double-click the comment graphic or symbol. In the Comments properties dialog box, you can choose whether or not notes will pop up automatically.

After you finish writing the text in a pop-up window, you can close the window by clicking the icon on the left side of the title bar. If you close the window, make sure the person who will be reading the comments knows that there is a pop-up window associated with that comment. Otherwise, they will see an icon on the page, but may not know what you want them to do.

You can also reposition the pop-up window away from the comment icon. For instance, you might want to move a pop-up window over to the margin of the page to make the document or the notes easier to read. There is nothing wrong with this method, as long as you make it clear which pop-up window goes with which comment.

Pop-up windows are removed by deleting the comment they are associated with. Select the comment with the Hand tool, or the tool that created the comment, and then press the Delete key on the keyboard. If you want to delete many comments, use the Shift key to select multiple comments in the Comments palette. Hold the Ctrl (w) or Cmd (m) key to select non-contiguous comments. Once you have made your selections, press the delete key or click the the trash icon in the Comments palette.

Setting the Comments Properties

Each of the comments has a Properties dialog box. Because the Comments tools are very different in nature, their properties vary greatly. Almost all types of comments let you change the color of the object and the note pop-up. Many Comment tools let you choose new graphics for the comment object. Others contain specific properties, such as the thickness of the Line tool.

All types of comments have a field that contains the name of the author of the comment. By default, this is the name of the user of the computer. If you are a guest on someone else's computer, you can enter your own name as author by opening the Properties dialog box.

Open the Properties dialog box by selecting the comment in the Comments panel or the comment object with the Hand tool, or the tool that created the comment. Then choose Edit> Properties. Make any changes you want to the author, color, or other comment properties.

If you are using someone else's computer, you may not want to constantly open the Properties dialog box to change the author for each comment. Open the Comments Preferences (covered immediately below) and deselect the preference for Always Use Identity for Author. This changes Acrobat's settings so the last name entered as an author becomes the default author for all future comments.

Setting the Comments Preferences

The Comments Preferences affect the way comments are displayed on each individual computer. To change preferences, choose Edit> Preferences>General and click the Comments category. The first options control the typeface, point size, and opacity of all the note pop-ups in the document. (Since other users may have other preference settings, there is no way to control how pop-ups are displayed on other computers.) Set the opacity for any value between 0-100%. Watch out, though—if your note pop-ups are over other text and graphics, values under 75 are often impossible to read.

The first three preference check boxes control how note pop-ups are opened. Automatically Open Note Pop-up means that each time the user clicks with the Note tool, the pop-up window opens. The default for this option is turned on, which helps you recognize that comments created with the Note tool have pop-ups.

Automatically Open Other Comment Pop-ups means that each time the user creates any comment that has a note pop-up, the note pop-up immediately opens. The default for this option is turned off, which is unfortunate because many people don't recognize that there are pop-ups associated with all the text markup and graphic markup tools. We've seen users highlight text and then add a note comment next to it because they they did not know there was a pop-up window associated with the Highlight tool. You may want to instruct others in your review cycle to change this preference, especially if they want to use the text markup and graphic markup tools.

Automatically Open Pop-ups on Mouse Over turns the comment icons into rollover buttons that automatically open the pop-up window when the user pauses over the icon. This option is very helpful if you need to read many comments very quickly. Mouse Over also lets you use comments as primitive buttons that show and hide information in their pop-up windows.

Show Comment Sequence Numbers adds a small number next to each comment on the page. These numbers are added according to the sequence in which the comments were created. These numbers do not change if you modify any of the comments.

Always Use Identity for Author instructs Acrobat to insert the name of the user of the computer as set in the operating system as the author for each comment. This option is turned on by default. (If you have not set a user name for your computer, the author name will be set as Default.) We recommend that you deselect this option if you'll have many people adding comments on a single computer.

Print Comment Pop-ups options refers to printing the contents of the note pop-ups. To print the note pop-ups, you also need to choose to print comments in the print dialog box. If you choose Comments without this preference, you'll print only the symbols, not the pop-up windows. You can't print the pop-up windows without the checking the corresponding preference setting.

WORKING WITH THE TOOL GROUPS

Adobe has divided the Comments tools into three categories: Comment, Graphic Markup, and Text Markup. When you first open Acrobat, there are three Comments tools shown in the tool bar: Note tool, Pencil tool, and Highlight tool. Behind the Note tool are the rest of the Comment tools. Behind the Pencil tool are the rest of the the Graphic Markup tools. Behind the Highlight tool are the rest of the Text Markup tools. You can choose other tools in the group by clicking the small triangle next to the tool icon. This opens the menu that contains all the tools in that group. You can display all the tools in a particular group by choosing Expand This Button from the menu.

THE COMMENT TOOL GROUP

The Comment tool group includes the Note tool, the FreeText tool, the Sound Attachment tool, the Stamp tool, and the File Attachment tool. They all allow you to attach an item (text, graphic, sound, or external graphic) to a comment.

Note Tool

Click or drag with the Note tool to place a note comment on the page. Depending on the preference settings, the note pop-up window appears, which allows you to enter text in the comment. If you drag with the Note tool, you set the size for the note pop-up. When you release the mouse, the cursor changes to an I-beam. This indicates that you can type text in the pop-up window.

Open the Note Properties dialog box to choose one of the seven note icons. These icons are representations of various markup commands, such as insert text, break a paragraph, add a new paragraph, and so on. The Properties dialog box also lets you change the color of the note icon and the pop-up window. Once you change the icon for a note, it becomes the icon for all new notes.

The FreeText Tool

Click or drag with the FreeText tool to create a rectangle. Here, you can type text for a note that is displayed on the document page. You can resize the text area by using the Hand tool to drag the corners of the rectangle. Use the Hand tool to reposition the rectangle anywhere on the page. Use the Properties dialog box to set the fonts, point size, and alignment of the text inside the rectangle. You can also set the border color, the thickness of the border, and the fill color.

Sound Attachment Tool

This tool lets you record spoken comments directly into the file. It also lets you attach sound files saved in the AIFF (.aiff) and WAV (.wav) sound file formats. Click with the Sound Attachment tool and the Record Sound dialog box appears.

If you want to attach a spoken message, click the Record button. (You need to have a microphone hooked up to your computer or an internal microphone to record sounds.) Speak and then click the Stop button. You can preview your message by clicking the Play button. If you don't like the recording, click the Record button to change the message. When you are satisfied with the sound, click the OK button. The sound file will be embedded into the PDF file.

To attach a prerecorded sound, click the Choose button and navigate to find the sound you wish to attach. Preview the sound you have chosen by clicking the Play button. Once you have the sound you like, click the OK button. This embeds the sound file into the Acrobat document.

The Sound Properties dialog box allows you to control the color of the sound icon. You can also write a description for the comment. This description appears as a tool tip when the user pauses over the sound comment. Add a description to the sound comment to help people understand what they are listening to when playing sounds.

It is very easy to play sound comments. Just double-click the sound icon. However, once you have started listening to a sound there is no simple way to stop it except to close the file. (You can even open another PDF file and the sound will continue to play!) It's also important to remember that each sound file adds to the final size of the PDF document. If you're planning on using long audio clips, you'll need to first experiment with the file size it yields to make sure that it doesn't make the file size prohibitive for the user.

File Attachment Tool

The File Attachment tool lets you embed any file on your computer into a PDF document. This allows you to send one PDF document instead of lots of individual files. Of course, the user must have the corresponding application to view the file.

ATTACHING FILES

The custom icons for the File Attachment tool. The icons indicate, but don't control, the content of the attached file.

Graph

Paperclip

Attachment

Tag

To create a file attachment, select the File Attachment tool and click the place in the document where you want the icon to appear. When the Open dialog box appears, you can navigate to find the file you wish to attach. If you want to attach a file other than a PDF, you'll have to change the setting of the Show list to All Files. Click the Select button to choose the file. This opens the File Attachment Properties dialog box. Here, you can select between four different icons to represent the content of the file you are attaching. The choices are Graph, Paper Clip, Attachment, and Tag. (The content of the File Attachment is not sensitive to the icons so don't feel constrained about which icon you choose.)

Once you have placed a file attachment, the viewer must double-click the icon to access the content. Ever-cautious Acrobat displays a dialog box that warns you that the attachment may contain macros or viruses that "can potentially harm your computer." Unless you have a reason to suspect the files, click OK to open the file in the application that created the attachment. File attachments cannot be opened in Reader or Approval.

The Stamp Tool

The Stamp tool is the electronic equivalent of a traditional rubber stamp (remember those?). Click or drag to create the area that contains the stamp graphic. Acrobat displays the last stamp graphic that was applied. You can use the Stamp Properties dialog box to change the stamp graphic. Acrobat 5 comes with stamp graphics in four categories: Standard, Faces, Pointers, and Words. Although Sandee likes the Happy faces, Pattie Belle and Bjørn wouldn't be caught dead using any of them. They all like the idea that they can use their own artwork as a stamp graphic. Any image that can be turned into a PDF can be used as a stamp graphic. You can use any graphic application to create a stamp graphic. Pattie Belle and Bjørn use Adobe Photoshop or Adobe Illustrator. Sandee uses Adobe InDesign.

As with the other tools, the Stamp Properties dialog box allows for color specification and naming of author.

CREATING CUSTOM STAMPS

1 *We used Adobe Photoshop to rasterize an Illustrator file of our company logo. We then used it as a stamp element in our Acrobat/PDF files. Remember to save your stamp graphics file as PDF files.*

2 *Type a suitable title for the stamp. This title will be the one used when the stamp is accessed from the stamp library. Leave the other options untouched.*

CREATING A STAMP GRAPHIC

Creating custom stamp graphics makes it easy to insert your own graphics in PDF documents.

Step ① Create the Graphic in a PDF

Use any illustration or photo-manipulation program to create the graphic you want to use as a stamp. Use the Save or Export commands within the program or Acrobat Distiller to create a PDF document that contains the graphic. Note: If you use a multi-page program such as InDesign or Macromedia FreeHand, you can put different stamp graphics on each page. Each graphic becomes a separate graphic within the stamp category.

Step ② Add a Title to the Stamp PDF File

You'll need to create a title for the PDF document. This is not the same as the document's file name; it is part of the Document Summary. Open the PDF document in Acrobat and go to File>Document Properties>Summary. Type the title (without extensions) of the file. This is the category that will appear in the Stamp Properties dialog box. Other information, such as Subject, Author, and so on is not absolutely necessary for the custom stamp option.

Step ③ Create a Page Template

You'll now need to make each page in the PDF document a Page Template. (This has nothing to do with layout templates; it is the convention that Acrobat uses to add pages from a PDF document as stamp graphics.) Choose Tools> Forms>Page Templates. The Page Templates dialog box appears. Name the page template as follows: <Title><PageName>=<PageLabel>. For instance, in a document with the title "IcehouseLogo", you might want the name Library to appear as the name for the stamp graphic. The Page Template would be named exactly as seen below: IcehouseLogoLibrary=Library. Do not put any spaces between the items in the name. Click the Add button. Click Yes when the dialog box asks if you want to create a new Page Template. Then click the Done button.

If your PDF document only has one page, you can move to step 4. If you have a multi-page document, move to the next page in your PDF and repeat step 3. Do this for each page of the PDF. When Sandee created a six-page PDF with a series of fingers pointing in different directions, the PDF title was Fingers. She named her page templates FingersRight=Right, FingersLeft=Left, FingersUp=Up, and so on until she had all six pages labeled.

Step ④ Add the PDF to the Stamp Library

Once you've set the title and page templates, save your PDF document in the proper location. In order for Acrobat to see the custom stamp file, it needs to be saved under the following path: Adobe Acrobat: Plug-ins: Annotations. When the PDF file is saved in the

③ *We created a Page Template by going to Tools>Forms>Page Template. Here, we entered the file title that we defined, IcehouseLogo, followed by Library=Library. All new stamps must follow this naming convention to work. The resulting file name is IcehouseLogoLibrary =Library. When done, we entered Add and clicked Done.*

④ *To be of use in Acrobat, the stamp must be placed in the Stamps folder. We used the Save As option to navigate the following path: Adobe Acrobat>PlugIns>Ann otations>Stamps.*

proper location, it becomes available for use as a custom stamp.

Step ⑤ Using the Custom Stamp

Select the Stamp Attachment tool, and click or drag to create a new stamp comment. The last stamp comment used will be the default graphic. Open the Stamp Properties dialog box and choose the category for the PDF you created. Choose Custom Stamp from the page template list. Your custom stamp can be used like any other graphic.

GRAPHIC MARKUP TOOLS

The graphic markup tools are the Pencil tool, the Square tool, the Circle tool, and Line tool. They work a lot like the drawing tools in programs such as Illustrator or CorelDraw. Each tool has a pop-up window that can be opened after you have created the markup object. We recommend using these markup tools to indicate broad areas of the page that need attention. Then you can type your corrections in the pop-up window for each comment.

✏ The Pencil Tool

This tool lets you create any mark on the page, much like a real pencil. If you draw very quickly, multiple pencil marks produce only one com-

> **ⓘ PENCIL POINTS**
>
> *Acrobat's Pencil tool is too clunky to create the fine lines needed for traditional editorial markup symbols. Unless you draw very quickly, each Pencil mark on the page is listed as its own comment. This causes chaos for anyone trying to summarize comments. We recommend that you use the Pencil to outline irregular areas and then type in a comment to specify what needs to be done.*

ment. Reshape or resize pencil marks by selecting the mark and dragging the handles. Move pencil marks by holding the mouse button down and dragging the cursor to a new position. Use the Pencil Properties dialog box to change the thickness and color of the mark.

▢ The Square Tool

The Square tool creates an object that can be used to outline a large area. Drag to create a rectangle or hold the Shift key as you drag to create a square. Resize and reshape the resulting object by dragging the corner handles on the box selection. Move the object by holding the mouse button down inside the rectangle and dragging the cursor to a new position. In addition to setting the border color and thickness, you can add a fill color to the object.

If you use the Square tool to outline an area of text, the pop-up window will automatically contain the text within the outlined area. This makes the Square tool ideal for selecting large blocks of text and then making corrections in that area. The Pencil and Line tools do not automatically copy outlined text.

◯ The Circle Tool

The Circle tool creates an elliptical object that can be used to outline a large area. Drag to create an ellipse or hold the Shift key as you drag to create a circle. Use the same techniques as described for the Square tool to resize and

---

⚡ CREATING CUSTOM STAMPS

⑤ When we clicked the stamp tool in our PDF document, it invoked the last stamp used. We selected the current stamp and went to Stamp Properties (Edit>Properties) to retrieve the custom stamp from the previous steps. From the resulting dialog box, we opened the category to find our new stamp, and selected OK.

The new stamp appears in the place of the older version, as a selection (see the black outline with corner handles) to be resized and repositioned. The stamp is now fully functional and may be used in any PDF document.

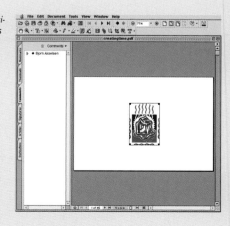

customize an object. Like the Square tool, the Circle tool automatically copies the text within the outlined area into the pop-up window.

✏ The Line Tool

This tool creates straight lines that can be used to point to specific objects or areas. Hold the Shift key to constrain the line to 45-degree angles. The Line Properties are rather extensive. You can add shapes, such as a circle or square, to the head and tail of a line. You can add a fill color inside those shapes. You can also set the thickness of a line and its color.

TEXT MARKUP TOOLS

The text markup tools consist of the Highlight tool, the Strikeout tool, and the UnderLine tool. Each tool allows you to draw objects on a page to indicate markups and corrections. To use the text markup tools, select the desired tool, move the I-beam cursor over text, and drag to create the mark along the text. The smallest selection the tools recognize is a single word and they always mark entire words, not letters. You can drag down to mark multiple lines.

> **ⓘ LINE MARKERS**
>
> *The five markers for the Line tool are the open arrowhead, closed arrowhead, square, circle, and diamond.*

However, if the text is in columns, this action will highlight both text columns as you drag. To select just a specific area of text as you drag, hold the Alt key (w) or Option key (м). This creates a rectangle that defines the text to be marked.

All three Text Markup tools automatically place the marked text into the pop-up window for a comment. Sandee instructs people who mark up her documents to use the tools in the following way. The editor uses the Highlight tool to select the text that needs corrections. In the pop-up window, she makes any changes to the text. The editor doesn't add any other comments in the pop-up window. When Sandee reviews the marked up PDF file, she opens the pop-up window for each highlighted comment and copies the text from the window. She then switches over to her page layout file and replaces the incorrect text with the contents of the pop-up window. This technique is useful for text corrections that don't need explanations or comments.

The only customization element of the text markup tools is the ability to change the color of a mark.

✏ The Highlight Tool

The Highlight tool creates a mark similar to a highlighter pen. When you print the document, the mark is converted from a solid color to an outline. This makes it easy to read highlighted text. Try to avoid very dark highlight colors. They are difficult to read and people are most comfortable with highlighter colors that are electric pink, yellow, or green.

S The Strikeout Tool

This tool works like the highlight tool, except that instead of a highlight, it draws a line through the text. The position or thickness of the strikeout mark cannot be altered.

U The Underline Tool

This tool works like the Highlight tool, except that instead of a highlight, it draws a line under the text. The position or thickness of the underline cannot be altered.

EXPORTING/IMPORTING COMMENTS

During a review process, it's common to have several copies of a document being reviewed by different people at the same time. What do you do with the comments added to different files? The answer is simple; you can export the comments from one PDF file and then import them into another. To export comments, open the PDF document that contains the comments and choose File>Export>Comments. Name the file and add the .fdf (Forms Data Format) extension. Now open a second PDF document, and choose File>Import>Comments. (You can also choose Import from the Comments palette menu.) Navigate and choose the FDF file. All the comments are imported into the second file (in the same position as in the first file) with the same author identity and identification color.

While this technique is useful for merging comments from two or more PDF files, Sandee uses this feature even though she receives comments from just one source. In New York, she creates a PDF for a chapter and sends it to her editor in California. The editor adds the comments to the PDF file. Instead of sending back the entire PDF file, the editor e-mails the FDF file. Since the FDF file is much smaller than the PDF, it can be sent quickly for anyone who does not have a high-speed Internet connection. When Sandee gets the FDF file, she imports it into her original PDF document. (In case you were wondering, the FDF file doesn't have to be imported back into the original PDF. It can be imported into any PDF file—even one with blank pages.)

MANAGING COMMENTS

It is possible for a single document to have hundreds of comments from many different reviewers. Rather than scroll around from page to page, trying to find comments from specific authors, you can use the Comments palette to look at the comments in a document. To access the Comments palette, open the Navigation Pane and then click the Comments tab.

Navigation with Comments

You can use the comments in the Comments palette to move through a document. Click the name of the comment in the palette to jump to a particular comment. If you double-click the name of the comment, the comment will open its pop-up window.

Sorting Comments

Comments in the palette can be displayed according to their type, page, author, or date. Open the Comments palette menu to change how comments are displayed.

Searching Through Comments

Use the Find command in the Comments palette or choose Tools>Comments>Find to search for a specific word or phrase in the Comments pop-up windows. This makes it easy to find a specific correction or those corrections that deal with a certain topic.

Exporting Selected Comments

Unlike the Export command in the File menu, the Comments palette offers a special command that lets you export just the selected comments in the Comments palette. This is very helpful if you want to export all the comments from a specific author, or those made after a certain date. Use the Shift key to select a range of comments, or hold the Ctrl key (w) or Cmd key (m) to select non-contiguous comments. Then choose Export Selected from the Comments palette menu. This creates an FDF file that contains only the comments you selected.

Filtering Comments

If a document has numerous comments, you may find it difficult to review the comments if they all appear on the page at the same time. The Filter options let you display only certain sets of comments at one time. Choose Tools>Comments>Filter. The Filter Comments dialog box will open. Use the Modified list to choose the time frame of the comments you wish to view. The options are Anytime, Within the last 24 hours, Within the last 6 hours, Within the last hour, or Within the last 30 minutes. Then select or deselect author's comments that you want to see. Finally, select or deselect which types of comments you want to see. You can

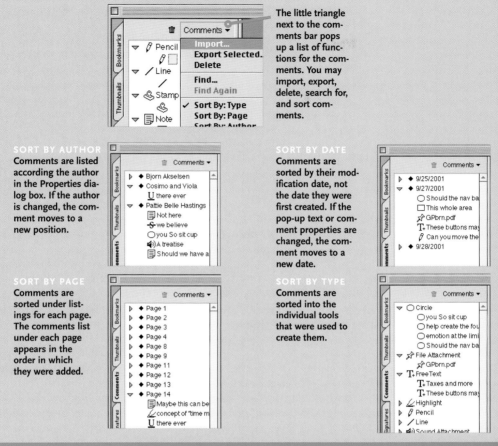

The little triangle next to the comments bar pops up a list of functions for the comments. You may import, export, delete, search for, and sort comments.

SORT BY AUTHOR
Comments are listed according the author in the Properties dialog box. If the author is changed, the comment moves to a new position.

SORT BY DATE
Comments are sorted by their modification date, not the date they were first created. If the pop-up text or comment properties are changed, the comment moves to a new date.

SORT BY PAGE
Comments are sorted under listings for each page. The comments list under each page appears in the order in which they were added.

SORT BY TYPE
Comments are sorted into the individual tools that were used to create them.

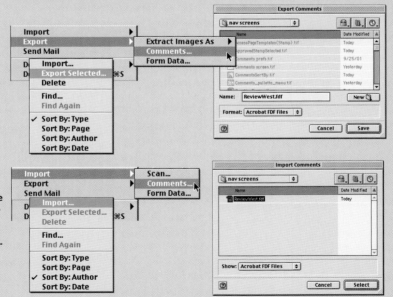

EXPORTING
Choose File>Export> Comments. Or use the Comments Palette menu to export just selected comments. Comments are saved as an FDF (Forms Data Format) file.

IMPORTING
Choose File>Import> Comments. Or choose Import from the Comments Palette menu. Choose the FDF file that contains the comments you want to import.

also use the Select All or Deselect All buttons to quickly make these selections.

Once you have filtered the comments, the excluded comments remain hidden until you choose the Filter option again, or until you close and reopen the document. If you use the Export command, only the visible comments will be exported.

Summarizing Comments

You can also summarize the comments in a document in a separate PDF file. This creates a file with all the comments listed. This list includes the author, date, time, and text from the pop-up window. Reading through these printed PDF pages of comments can be easier than navigating through the Comments palette or the document pages. You can also export the text from the summary PDF document as a RTF (rich text format) text file. This makes it easy to import the summary text into another application.

CREATING A COMMENT SUMMARY

You can use the features for exporting, filtering, summarizing, and inserting pages to add PDF pages of comments to the original PDF document. This allows you to create an introductory page of comments that serves as a table of contents for the comments on the pages that follow.

Step ① Summarize The Comments

Choose Tools>Comments>Summarize. The Summarize Comments dialog box lets you choose how the summary document will be sorted: by author, page, date, or type.

Step ② Filter The Comments

If you want, you can summarize only certain comments. Click the Filter button in the Summarize Comments dialog box. In the Filter Comments dialog box, choose which comments you want as part of your summary. Use the Modification list to include only those comments that were modified within the last 24 hours, 6 hours, hour, or 30 minutes. (Acrobat designers must work on a very intense timetable!) You can also choose to include only the comments from specific authors or you can choose to summarize only certain types of comments. For instance, it may not be meaningful to summarize pencil marks that have no pop-up text associated with them.

Step ③ Create the Summary Document

When you have set all the filter and sort options, click OK in the dialog boxes. A new PDF file is created with the temporary name "Summary of Comments on <Name of Document>." This file contains a print out of all the comments you summarized. If you want to keep this document, it must be saved. You can also choose to rename the file.

⚡ SUMMARIZING COMMENTS

① Choose Tools>Comments>Summarize. The Summarize Comments dialog box lets you choose how the summary will be sorted. Click the Filter button to control which comments should be summarized.

② Use the Filter Comments dialog box to choose which comments will be summarized. The choices are by modification time frame, author, and type.

Step ④ Insert Summary into Original

The summary PDF is a separate file from the original document, but you can easily add it to the source file. Switch back to the original PDF document and choose Document>Insert Pages. Select the summary file and add it to the front or back of the original PDF.

📝 SPELL CHECKING COMMENTS

If your comments will be used as the corrected text in the original page layout, you may want to check the spelling of the text. Choose Tools>Spelling>Check Form Fields and Comments.

The Check Spelling dialog box works like the spell check feature found in other programs. The Start button begins the check. The check stops when it finds a suspect word. You can ignore suspect words or choose from the entries in the Suggested Corrections list. If you don't see the correct suggestion, you can edit the text directly in the Not in Dictionary field. Click the Change button to make the change or Ignore to continue. The Add button allows you to add suspect words to the Spell Check dictionary.

③ *Once you click OK in the various dialog boxes, a new PDF document appears. This document contains a neatly printed list of all the comments you have summarized.*

④ *Open the original document and choose Document>Insert Pages to add the summary pages. Use the Insert Pages dialog box to place the pages in the correct position.*

6.3 Setting Up an Online Collaboration

As mentioned in the previous chapter, it is possible to collate PDF comments from various sources into one document. But what do you do if you want everyone to see each other's comments? That was the challenge faced by the three authors, two technical editors, and project editor of this book. Fortunately, we were able to use the most current technology available: the online collaboration features in Acrobat 5.

When we first starting working on this book, Pattie Belle was put in touch with Adam Z. Lein. She had been told that he was an excellent book tester, but soon found out he had even more valuable skills.

Adam wears a lot of hats at Roher Sprague Partners, a comprehensive design firm located just north of New York City. His responsibilities include new technology management, network administration, and graphic artwork creation. Adam also has experience with 3D animation, photography, photo retouching, vector illustrations, web design, database maintenance, and active server page programming. Why are we telling you all of this? Well, if it weren't for Adam, we'd never have gotten our Acrobat WebDAV online collaboration to work. (In case you were wondering, WebDAV stands for Web-based Distributed Authoring and Versioning. It is a set of extensions to the HTTP that allow users to edit and manage files on remote web servers.)

When Pattie Belle first contacted Adam, he said that the new collaborative ability in Acrobat 5 was the most interesting aspect of the

application. He suggested we set up a test site for the book. Pattie Belle said "Go for it!" Not only would we be able to edit the book using online collaboration, but we'd then be able to write about it.

For those of you who aren't familiar with this feature, Adobe Acrobat's Online Comments allows multiple users to add comments to a document—while online within a web browser. It is even possible for this to take place simultaneously in real time. This meant that their tech editor in Switzerland could comment at the same time a co-author in Connecticut responded, and the managing editor in California proofread.

To use Online Comments, the PDF document is posted on a server without any special treatment. The comments exist as FDF files, which are saved into what Adobe calls a repository, outside of the PDF document. The repository can be a database, network folder, or a folder on the web. The collaboration can be set up to operate on the Internet or on an Intranet.

Adam put on his IT hat and began setting up a test site. Although Acrobat's Online Comments can be configured in a number of ways, WebDAV allows for Windows users and Macintosh users to collaborate, without having to be connected to the same internal network. This was an important consideration for us. This solution works cross-platform and stores

> **ⓘ REQUIREMENTS**
>
> *Before you go rushing out to create an online Acrobat collaboration, make sure you can fulfill these WebDAV Requirements: The server must be Microsoft IIS 5.0 or Apache 1.3.14 with mod_dav 1.0 or newer. You must set up a site to store the comments and make it accessible to the collaborators via HTTP. You must get your IT department to set this up correctly—that is, unless you are the IT department. Collaborators need to use Mac OS 9.x or Windows 98, Windows NT 4.0, Windows Millennium Edition, Windows 2000, or Windows NT. And, of course, everyone involved needs to have the full version of Acrobat 5 and a PDFViewer compatible browser.*

The Acrobat Master Class Collaboration site was created using Webdav IIs5 (Microsoft Internet Information Server 5) running on Windows 2000 with Share Point Team Services 2002 installed. The Internet Information Services MMC (Microsoft Management Console) is used to create a sub web for use as the FDF repository. Create a sub web by right-clicking on a current web and choosing New>Server Extensions 2002 Web.

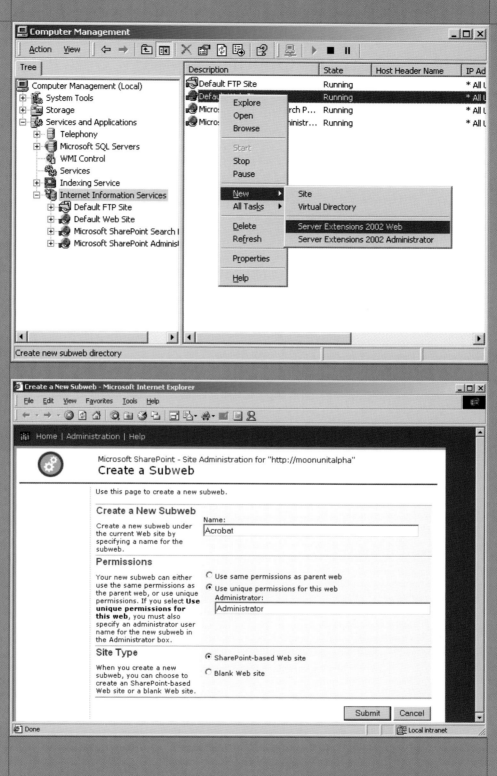

each collaborator's comments as an individual FDF file in a repository on the WebDAV server. This method also allows collaborators outside of a firewall to participate in the review process. Adam used Windows-based systems, software, and servers to set-up the collaboration and all of the editors and authors of Acrobat 5 Master Class were on Macs.

IF AT FIRST YOU DON'T SUCCEED

The Acrobat Master Class Collaboration site was created using WebDAV IIS5 (Microsoft Internet Information Server 5) running on Windows 2000 with Share Point Team Services 2002 installed.

When we began this experiment, Adam created a folder on the web server to store our Acrobat PDF chapters and our FDF repository (in the same sub web). In order to keep the PDF files secure, Adam added user names and permissions that allowed users to access the PDF files.

The WebDAV server (IIS5) was set in the Acrobat 5 preferences, and a PDF was made available in the Acrobat folder on IIS. We then tried our first test. When we opened the PDF through a web browser, the Acrobat client made a subfolder in the FDF repository. The name of this subfolder was associated with the particular location of the PDF file that was opened. Things looked good at first. Our Mac users could prepare comments. When they pressed upload, the server asked for the user name and password. However, no comments appeared to upload or download in the browser. The IIS5 server log showed that a username FDF file had been created on the server, but when we tried to

> **MORE HELP**
>
> In addition to these instructions, you can find a well-written PDF document on setting up online collaboration on the Acrobat 5 application CD. It's called Online Comments and it is located in the Collaboration folder. This file provides various scenarios for setting up a collaboration site.

> **CAUTION!**
>
> An unsecured sub web with author permissions, such as those needed for cross platform FDF sharing, can be a potential security problem. Make sure that all executables and directory browsing are disabled and that only authorized personnel are aware of the FDF repository location. Another way to increase the security of the FDF repository is to give the location a long, difficult-to-guess name.

locate the file, it was nowhere to be found. It showed an attempt to create an FDF file from the Mac client, but returned a 401 (unauthorized) error. The process did work with Windows-based clients; it just wasn't working for the Mac users.

Adam put on his detective hat and set out to solving the crime. To make a long story short, we discovered a glitch in how Acrobat 5 for the Macintosh works. We found that Acrobat 5 for the Macintosh is not able to authenticate itself (apply an ID and password) properly against IIS5, so the comments were not being accepted on the server. (Remember, all our online collaborators use Macs.)

So Adam created a second folder for the FDF repository. This folder was created with anonymous authoring permissions, so that any user could post and view the comments in the FDF repository. (If your users are on Windows only, you can also apply permissions to the FDF repository, or use the same sub web as the location in which your PDFs are stored.) We had to create a separate FDF repository that all our users could access. This should not be a problem if you use an Apache WebDAV server.

Try Try Again

After Adam found out the source of the problem and had it confirmed by Adobe, he set out to work around this limitation (bug). Here are the steps he took to create our site.

Step ① Create the Repository

First, use the Internet Information Services MMC (Microsoft Management Console) to create a sub web to use as the Acrobat comments sharing (FDF) repository. Create a sub web by right-clicking on a current web and choosing New>Server Extensions 2002 Web. You can also use an entirely new web site as a WebDAV Acrobat comments repository. By creating a sub web, we were able to change the

Create user names and permissions for people to access the PDF files on your server. This step is unnecessary if you are not worried about unauthorized access to the PDFs.

In order to bypass the need to enter a password every time you synchronize comments to the WebDAV server, turn on Anonymous access permissions and allow anonymous users Author permissions so they can post comments to the WebDAV FDF repository. This also allows Macintosh clients to collaborate with online comments sharing.

Folders created in the FDF repository are named with a hash encoding scheme that associates that folder with the specific location of the PDF the comments apply to. If you move a PDF with Online comments to a different server location, the comments will no longer be associated with the PDF. If you add comments to a relocated PDF, a new folder will be created in the FDF repository. You can move the FDFs associated with the PDFs previous location into the FDF repository for the new location and the old comments will be restored.

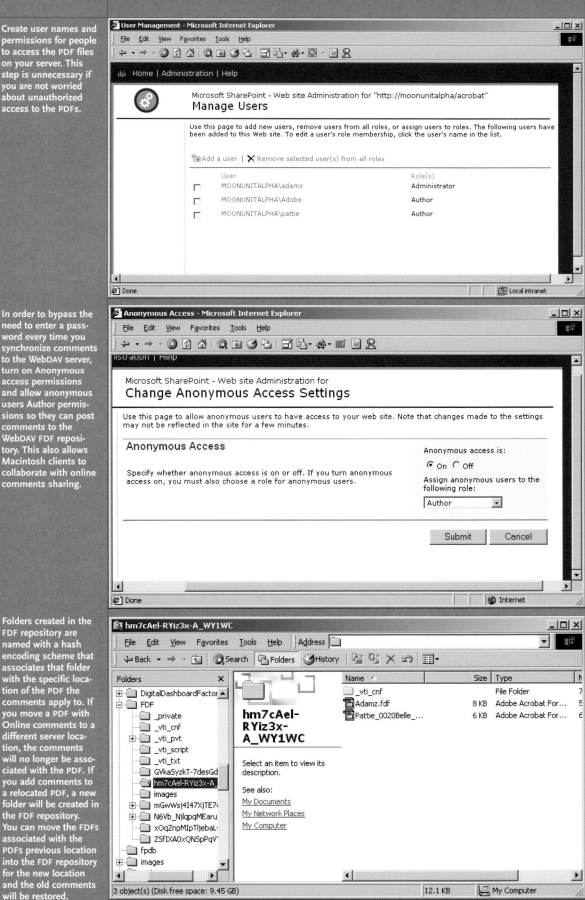

access permissions of the repository without having to create a new site.

Step ② Create the Sub Web

When you choose to create a new Server Extensions 2002 sub web from the IIS management console, Internet Explorer opens and launches the web-based Create Sub Web application. This is a part of the SharePoint Team Services Administration application. Type a name for the new sub web. If you choose to create unique permissions for this sub web, you'll be able to control who has what access, independently of the root web. If you create a Sharepoint-based sub web, a collaboration site will be generated within the new sub web, but this is not necessary for the Acrobat repository (PDF or FDF). Adam doesn't recommend creating a Sharepoint-based sub web for the FDF repository, but it's nice to have for sharing the PDF documents.

Step ③ Create the Summary Document

After you've created a sub web for the repository, you can create users and assign them author permissions so they can add and view Acrobat shared comments. Do this through the Web Site Administration pages that were created for your new sub web.

Alternatively, you can create a sub web that gives authoring permissions to all users by default. This way, people won't have to enter a password when opening a PDF through the web browser (and Mac users will be able to use comments sharing). You can do this in the Web site Administration's "Change Anonymous Access Settings" page in your FDF sub web.

Step ④ Set Acrobat WebDAV Preferences

After you've created a WebDAV comments repository sub web for Acrobat 5 clients, you'll have to distribute the address of the repository's location to the collaborators so the URL can be entered into the Acrobat Online Comments Preferences. Adam sent e-mails with the instructions to the small group of collaborators on this Master Class book. Each person then set the Online Comments Preferences in Acrobat (this can't be done in the browser). You can also embed JavaScript code into the PDF files to automatically reconfigure the Acrobat client. You can also create an FDF file that users can open, which will auto-configure their Acrobat to use the server as the WebDAV comments repository.

When an Acrobat 5 user opens a PDF in her browser, the PDF client goes to the comments-sharing WebDAV file store specified in the Acrobat 5 preferences. It then looks for a folder name referencing the opened PDF. If there is no folder for this PDF, it will create one. If there is a folder, it will download and display the comments found in that folder. A separate FDF file is saved for each user who contributes comments to each PDF document.

UP AND RUNNING

Finally, after a bit of trial and error, we got our WebDAV server working. Although there are other ways to set up the servers, we think this is the easiest method currently available for cross-platform remote collaboration. After our initial struggles, it really was quite a simple solution. We then developed our online collaborative work flow, which we'll describe in the following section.

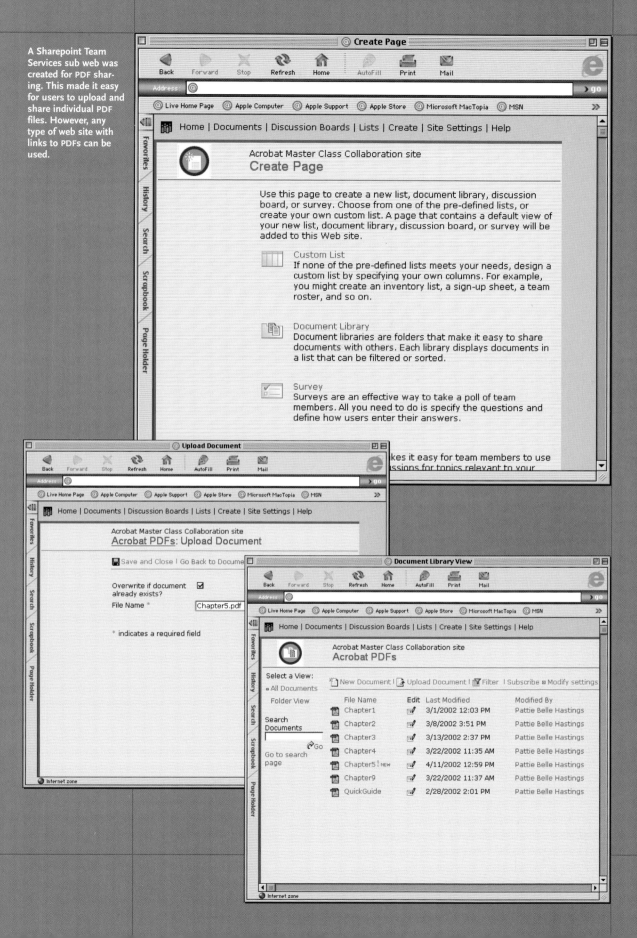

A Sharepoint Team Services sub web was created for PDF sharing. This made it easy for users to upload and share individual PDF files. However, any type of web site with links to PDFs can be used.

6.4 | Collaborating Online

Once your IT department has ironed out the wrinkles, it's time to step into the virtual world of online collaboration. Using a WebDAV server, multiple users can add comments to PDF files, all at the same time, from many different locations. This technology allows users to make comments and respond to the comments of others. However, just like any group collaboration, you will need to set up some ground rules to coordinate how everyone will work together.

SETTING THE ONLINE PREFERENCES

Before beginning their online collaboration, users need to set Acrobat's Online Comments preferences. Fortunately, this is not a complex process. In the case of the online collaboration for this book, our IT person, Adam Z. Lein, sent each of the collaborators an e-mail that contained the instructions to manually set the preferences. We each chose Edit>Preferences and then clicked the Online Comments category. We used the Server Type menu to choose WebDAV. This indicated that the online collaboration would occur through the Internet. Select the Network Folder option if the comments sharing requires access to a hard disk on a network through a file-sharing network protocol. The setting for None turns off online collaboration.

Adam also sent each user the web address to enter for the Server Settings. This is the address for the FDF repository. The server settings remain in effect until changed, which means that if you only work on a single site you may never have to touch these again. This is fine for those who work at a single company where all the online collaboration takes place from a single server.

This setup may not be appropriate for all collaborations. Consider an author or technical editor who collaborates on several projects at the same time—all with different publishing houses. This person may have to change her server settings every time she switches from one project to another. Using a single server setting, she would need to write down the previous server settings, and then enter new ones. It is possible to create scripts that automatically set the correct preferences when a user logs into a collaboration site or opens an FDF file. However, it is the rare IT manager who will create special scripts just for one or two freelancers. We expect that as online collaboration becomes more popular, Adobe will make it easier for one person to log onto many different collaboration sites.

ACROBAT ONLINE TOOLS

When you view Acrobat pages through a web browser as part of an online collaboration, the Acrobat tools appear just underneath the browser tool bars. Because you don't have access to the Acrobat menus, you must use the icon buttons for commands such as Save, Print, Next page, and so on. You will also notice three new online tools in the tool bar. These are the icon buttons for the Download Comments, Upload Comments, and Upload and Download Comments commands.

Each user logs onto the Home Page of the collaboration pages for the Adobe Acrobat Master Class book. The Announcements section provides an area where users can post messages to the other collaborators. The Quick Launch section provides links to the other collaboration pages.

The Acrobat PDFs page contains the links to each of the PDF documents for the book.

The PDF documents open within the browser window. Comments appear with a unique color and name for each collaborator.

The additional online collaboration tools appear in the browser version of the Acrobat tool bar.

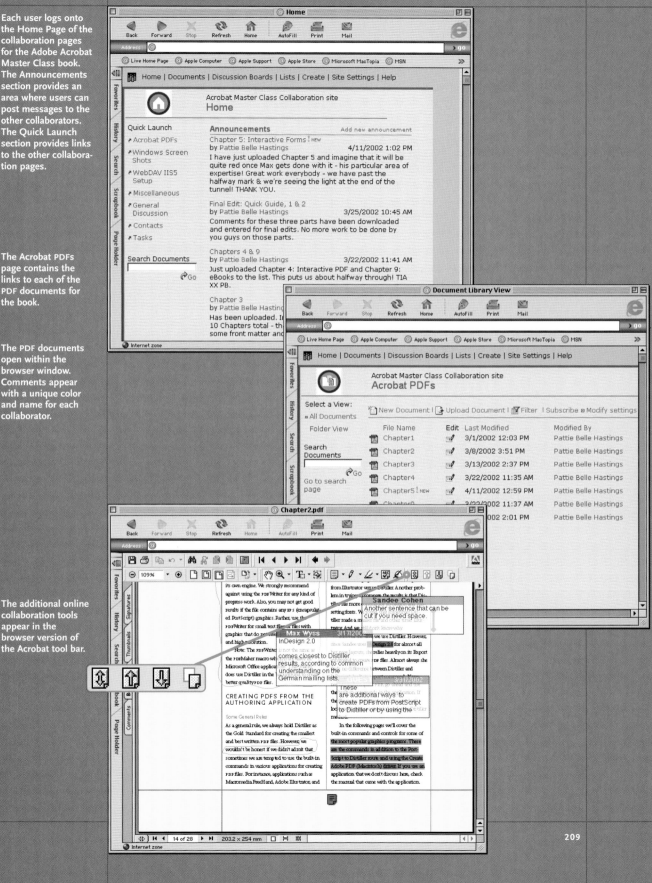

⬆ Upload Comments

The comments that each user adds to the PDF in the browser window need to be uploaded to the server FDF repository so the other collaborators can see them. Once a user creates a comment, the Upload Comments button becomes active. Comments are automatically uploaded if you close the browser window or navigate to another web page.

⬇ Download Comments

Since multiple users may be adding comments at the same, the Download Comments button receives additional comments that may have been uploaded after the page was initially opened.

⬍ Upload and Download Comments

This button makes it easy to synchronize the comments you need to upload, and at the same time download any additional comments that may have been posted.

Show/Hide Comments

This button temporarily hides all the comments displayed online. This makes it easier to read the online PDF—especially if you have a technical editor like ours, Max Wyss, who adds many comments to files. You can download and view any additional comments that may have been posted since beginning the editing session.

WORKING ONLINE

Working online is similar to working with comments on your own computer, with a few exceptions. It's similar in that you can use any of the comment tools to markup the document. In Acrobat 5, you can set the tool properties, such as the color, icon, thickness, and so on for any of the comment objects with one exception. You can't change the comment author. This is set as part of your log-in information. You can open or close any of the other user's comments, but you can't move them to other positions, nor can you change what the other person has written. (This keeps people from changing each other's comments.)

The steps for collaborating online are very simple. First log onto the website and open the PDF document. Next, use any Comments tool to add your own comments to the document. You can also select and delete any comments you've previously created. Use any navigation buttons or tools to move from one page to another. Remember, just because you see the comments up on the page doesn't mean that the rest of the team can see what you've done. You must click the Upload Comments or the Upload and Download Comments buttons to actually send your comments, or changes to comments, to the FDF repository.

You may want to set up some ground rules for the collaborators. For instance, we wanted a way to easily identify each person's comments

---

⚡ WORKING ON & OFF LINE

1 *If you can't collaborate completely online, you can download the files to work offline. Log onto the WebDAV server and click the Save button on the tool bar. Save the file onto your hard disk.*

2 *Use Acrobat to add any comments you wish to the file saved on your hard disk. Save your work. If you must transfer the file to another computer, you must eventually reload the file back onto the computer that originally saved the file.*

by color. Since Max Wyss had already written his comments with red highlights, he retained that color. Sandee chose aqua. Pattie Belle chose purple and Adam chose yellow.

You may also want to instruct people as to which Comment tools should be used for what purpose. Sandee believes that highlight comments should only be used to set new text. She would rather see notes used for general comments. However, these are just suggestions for working with online collaborators, not requirements.

Finally, we discovered, to our surprise, that you can create sound comments online—just as you would with an off-line PDF file. We also discovered that even a very short sound file added a lot to the file size. For this reason, we don't recommend using sound files with online collaboration.

COLLABORATING ON AND OFFLINE

There are times when it may not be feasible for a user to work totally online. For instance, although Sandee has a cable-modem connection in her home/office, she often travels and works out of hotel rooms that have expensive charges for modem phone calls. Sandee needs a way to download the files at home, add her own comments on the road, and then upload those comments to the server when she gets back to New York. These are the steps she takes to work on- and offline.

Step ① Log on and Save the File

Start by logging onto the WebDAV server and opening the PDF file you want to download. Because there are no Acrobat menus when working in the browser, clicks the Save button on the Acrobat tool bar. This opens a normal Save As dialog box which you can use to save the file to your hard disk.

Step ② Add Comments Off-line

Use Acrobat to open the saved file and add any comments. Save the work to the hard disk. If you need to, you can move the file to another computer, but you must transfer the file back to the computer that originally downloaded the file in order to upload the comments back to the WebDAV server.

Step ③ Upload the Saved Comments

When you are able to connect to the WebDAV server, choose File>Upload Comments from the Acrobat menu. Acrobat launches the web browser and logs onto the WebDAV server. The upload seems to happen automatically and a congratulatory message appears.

When you choose the Upload Comments command, Acrobat sends your comments to the browser window. It does not change any of the comments created by others.

You can use this feature for your own benefit. When you download the PDF file, you may find it difficult to read the document due to all

③ *When you go back online, choose File> Upload Comment. You must do this from the same computer that downloaded the file. Also, you'll need the PDF that you were commenting on to be opened in the full version of Acrobat.*

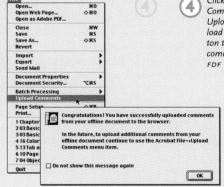

④ *Click the Upload Comments or the Upload and Download Comments button to send your comments to the FDF Repository.*

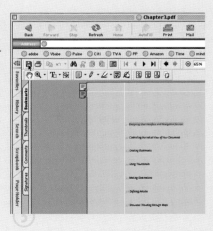

211

the other users' comments. If you don't care to see the other comments, you can delete all the other comments by choosing Tools>Comments>Delete All. This should make the document easier to read. (You can also choose Tools>Comments>Filter to hide the other user's comments.) You can now add your own comments to the file. When you choose File> Upload Comments, you'll notice that your own comments have been added, but the other users' comments have not been deleted.

EXTRACTING ONLINE COMMENTS

There are some people who can't work with online collaborations. For example, Cary, our editor at Peachpit Press, wasn't able to work online. It was no problem to send Cary her own PDF document, but we also wanted her to see Max Wyss's online technical comments. So Pattie Belle created a specialized work flow to extract Max's FDF comments from the online collaboration chapters.

Step 1 Export the Online Comments

Pattie Belle logs onto the WebDAV site and opens the Comments palette. Sorting the comments by author, she selects Max Wyss's comments. Since she doesn't have access to the File menu, she uses the Comments palette menu to choose Export Selected. She saves the comments as an FDF file.

Step 2 Import the Comments

Pattie Belle then opens a clean version of the PDF chapter and choose File>Import>Comments. She selects the FDF file that contains Max's comments and imports it into the PDF document. She then sends the file to Cary.

⚡ EXTRACT FDF COMMENTS

1 *In order to send a PDF with just one person's online comments, select that person's comments and choose Export Selected from the Comments palette menu. Save the file as an FDF.*

2 *Open a clean version of the PDF document and choose File>Import>Comments. Select the FDF file. The comments appear in the PDF document.*

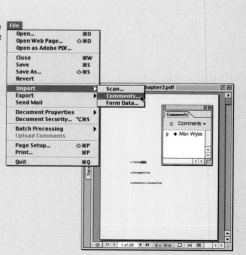

Those fun folks at planetpdf.com have created a demo page with no passwords so that anyone can see what it is like to participate in an online collaboration. To log on, set your Online Comments preferences as shown here. Then move to the web address shown in the Address bar.

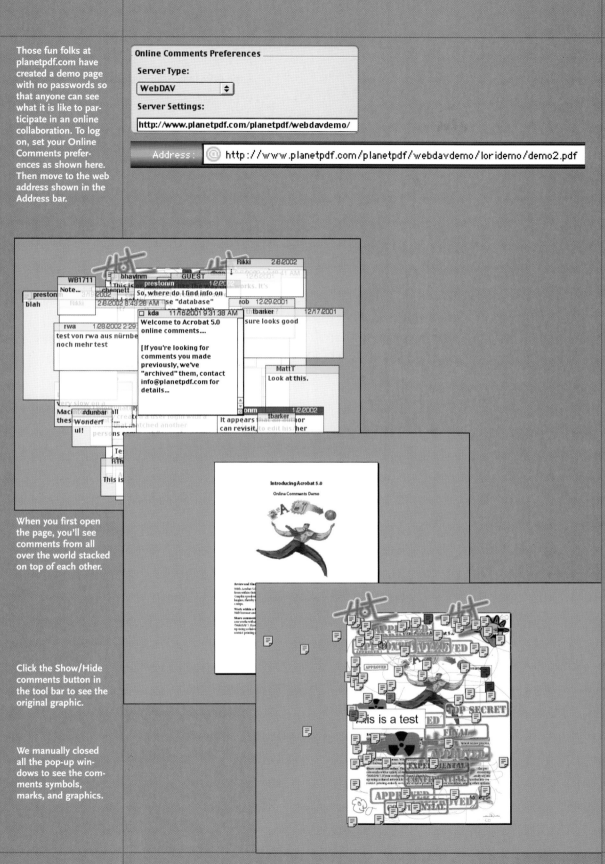

When you first open the page, you'll see comments from all over the world stacked on top of each other.

Click the Show/Hide comments button in the tool bar to see the original graphic.

We manually closed all the pop-up windows to see the comments symbols, marks, and graphics.

7

Editing PDF

As you work with PDF, you may need to apply commands and make changes to many documents at the same time. This is when batch processing options come in handy. Also, even though a PDF file is meant to "freeze" the text and layout from the original file, you may need to edit the text and graphics in a PDF document. You may also want to prepare your documents so they can be viewed on portable devices or meet accessibility requirements.

7.1 Batch Processing

Most applications take a similar approach to batch processing. You choose one or more commands (a command string) that you wish to apply as a single instruction. These are usually commands from the menus and dialog boxes. You then select the files that you want to alter. The command string is automatically applied to each of the selected files, allowing you to take a break or talk to your co-workers. Acrobat 5's batch processing feature is now highly evolved. It gives you a host of preset functions, as well as unlimited customization possibilities.

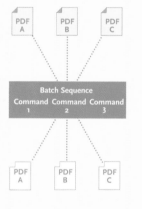

WHEN TO USE BATCH PROCESSING

There are two benefits to using batch processing. The first benefit is the ability to record a series of steps into a single command (or a batch of commands). This is very helpful if you frequently find yourself repeating the same commands over and over. Instead of choosing separate commands from different menus, you can string all the commands together into a single batch sequence which can be easily applied with a single command.

The second benefit is the ability to apply a batch sequence to many files. You don't need to manually apply the command; Acrobat does it all automatically.

For example, let's assume that every month you create a set of PDF manuals in different languages. These manuals need to include an updated language reference at the end of the document. Rather than opening each individual file, inserting the new and updated page at the end of the document, and then saving the file, the batch processing feature lets you record these steps into one simple instruction, which you can then apply to all the files in a directory that you choose.

> **ⓘ BACKUP FILES**
>
> *If you aren't comfortable using the Batch Processing commands, copy all your source files (the files that you want to batch process) into one folder. This makes it easier to process multiple files and reduces the chance of overwriting files that you want to keep unchanged.*

If you are involved with repetitive/reoccurring PDF creation, a little planning now can save you enormous amounts of time in the future. If you repeat certain tasks over time, think about how certain tasks can be automated and consolidated. Although the process may seem tedious at first, the potential time saved can be staggering.

DEFINING A BATCH SEQUENCE

Part 1: Setting the Commands

You may feel overwhelmed by all the steps necessary to batch process files. Instead of looking at all the steps at once, divide them into smaller tasks. The first task is to define the batch sequence or the command string. In the following example, we would like to create a batch sequence that will apply our favorite Open Options to many files at the same time.

Step ① Create a New Batch Sequence
Choose File>Batch Processing>Edit Batch Sequences. The Batch Sequence dialog box appears. The existing batch sequences (such as the ones that ship with Acrobat) appear in a list on the right.

To add a new sequence to the list, click the New Sequence button. This opens the Name Sequence dialog box where you can enter a

The Batch Process-ing submenu con-tains the existing batch sequences, as well as the Edit Batch Sequences command.

The existing batch sequences are dis-played in the Batch Sequences dialog box. You may edit, rename, or delete a sequence. You can also create a new sequence or run an existing sequence.

The Batch Edit Sequence dialog box contains three areas from which you can select com-mands, choose the to run commands on, and select out-put location and options.

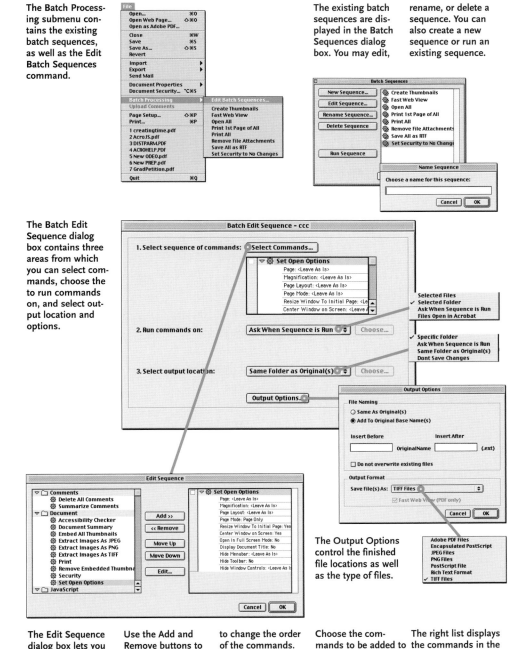

The Output Options control the finished file locations as well as the type of files.

The Edit Sequence dialog box lets you choose and edit the commands to be combined.

Use the Add and Remove buttons to control the com-mands in the string. Use the Move Up or Move Down buttons

to change the order of the commands. Use the Edit button to control the spe-cific settings of the command.

Choose the com-mands to be added to the sequence from the list on the left.

The right list displays the commands in the sequence. To see the details of the com-mand, click on the tri-angle to expose the settings.

name for the sequence. Click the OK button. This automatically opens the Batch Edit Sequence dialog box.

Step ② Choose the Sequence Commands

Choose the command that you want to make part of the sequence from the list on the left side of the Batch Edit Sequence dialog box. For instance, to change the Open Options, select the Set Open Options command and then click the Add button, which adds the command to the list on the right side. Do this for as many commands as you want to string together. Use the Move Up or Move Down buttons to change the order of the commands in the sequence. Use the Remove button to remove commands from the sequence.

Step ③ Choose the Sequence Commands

If a command has editable options, you can set those options by selecting the command in the right-hand list, then clicking the Edit button. This opens the dialog box for the command. For instance, you can edit the Set Open Options command to choose all the controls for opening files. Commands with no further settings, such as Remove All Comments and Remove Embedded Thumbnails, can't be edited.

When you have set the options for the command, click OK to close the dialog box. This returns you back to the Edit Sequence dialog box. If a command has editable options, you can click the arrow to the left of the name to display the settings for the command. When you have entered all the commands and the custom settings that you would like to be included in the Batch Sequence, click OK. This returns you to the Batch Edit Sequence dialog box, which displays the command string under the Select Commands button. Don't close this dialog box yet, as you'll need to set the options for Parts 2 and 3.

Part 2: Choosing the Files to Batch

If you have just finished the previous steps, you should be in the Batch Edit Sequence dialog box. (If you're not, click OK to close any dialog boxes on top of the Batch Edit Sequence dialog box.) Your next task is to select the files to which you want to apply the batch sequence.

Step ① Selecting the Files to Batch Process

Use the Run Commands On menu to choose which files should be batch processed. Choose Selected Files or Selected Folder and click on the Choose button to choose the files or folder that you want to process. Note: If you choose these options, the batch process command will always be tied to those files or folders. This means you have to edit the batch sequence in order to choose other files. We recommend that you choose Ask When Sequence is Run. This allows you to choose the files you want to process at the time you run the command. If you choose Files Open in Acrobat, you will have to open the files before you can batch process them.

Step ② Setting the Source File Options

If you choose Selected Folder, the Source File Options button appears. Use it to select which types of files (in addition to PDF files) should be used as part of the batch sequence. These file types are the same as the files that are available in the Open as Adobe PDF command. There are several ways to use these non-PDF files. For instance, you can use the Insert Pages command to select a folder full of images and add them to a PDF document. When you have set the Run Commands On options, return to the Batch Edit Sequence dialog box.

Part 3: Setting Destination controls

Once again, if you have just finished the previous steps, you should be working in the Batch

Edit Sequence dialog box. Your final task is to select a destination and the output options for your files.

Step ① Select the Output Location

Back in the Batch Edit Sequence dialog box, you can choose the location for the files created during the batch processing. Use the Select Output Location menu to choose the destination for the processed files. If you select the Specific Folder setting, click the Choose button to select a destination folder.

The option Ask When the Sequence is Run lets you to choose a specific folder. This may be better than choosing a specific folder in advance as you may not want the same folder used for all batch processing.

If you use the option for Same Folder as Originals, you'll need to understand that this may replace the original file with the batch-processed version. This could cause a problem if you find the batch sequence has changed the original in a way you did not anticipate.

The final option, Don't Save Changes, may seem baffling—after all, why would you apply a batch sequence if you're not going to save the changes? However, this option is useful for those files that have been processed using Java-Scripts or have had their form data exported. In these cases, the exported data is saved, but no changes are applied to the original files. Unless you understand how to use this option, it is doubtful you will find much use for the Don't Save Changes command.

Step ② Select the Output Options

If you choose to save the processed files in the same folder as the original version, you may have difficulty distinguishing the new and the old files from each other. Click the Output Options button in the Batch Edit Sequence

ⓘ DESTINATION

Unless you are very experienced, we strongly recommend creating a separate folder to hold the processed files. It is much easier to tell the original from the new files if they are in separate directories.

dialog box to open the Output Options.

The File Naming options let you choose to name the processed file with the same name as the original. If you have chosen to save the processed files in the same folder as the original, this option will replace the original files with the processed ones.

Rather than give the processed files the same names as the original ones, you can choose the option to Add To Original Base Name(s). When this radio button is chosen, the fields for Insert Before or Insert After become available. If you choose Insert Before, you can add a prefix such as New- in front of the file name. So the file names One.pdf, Two.pdf, and Three.pdf are processed and saved as New-One.pdf, New-Two.pdf, New-Three.pdf. If you choose Insert After, you can add a suffix such as -New after the base name, but before the file extension. So the file names One.pdf, Two.pdf, and Three.pdf are processed and saved as One-New.pdf, Two-New.pdf, and Three-New.pdf.

The option Do Not Overwrite Existing Files is a protection to make sure that you don't inadvertently replace an existing file in the same folder. With this option turned on, Acrobat will return an error message and refuse to run the batch sequence if it will cause a file to be replaced by the results of the batch processing.

The Output Format allows you to choose any of the Export or Save file formats. Under most circumstances, you would leave this as Adobe PDF files. However, you can use the alternate options for batch extracting of text and images from files. For instance, if you set the format to RTF, and then run a batch sequence with no command on a folder of files, you extract all the text from those files.

Once you have set all the output options, click the OK button to close the Edit Batch Sequence dialog box. This returns you to the Batch Sequences dialog box. The new sequence appears with the list of existing batch sequences.

① Choose File>Batch Processing>Edit Batch Sequence. Click the New Sequence button in the Batch Sequences dialog box. This opens the Name Sequence dialog box. Name the sequence and click OK.

② Click the Select Commands button in the Batch Edit Sequence dialog box. This opens the Edit Sequence dialog box. Choose the command from the left side and click the Add button. With the command selected on the right, click the Edit button. This opens the dialog box that controls that command and lets you specify options for the sequence.

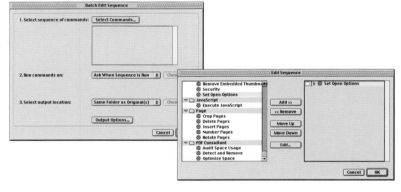

③ This step changes depending on which command was selected in the second step. Here, the Set Open Options dialog box appears. Choose the options you want to apply during the batch sequence. Then click OK. Those changes are reflected on the right side of the Edit Sequence dialog box.

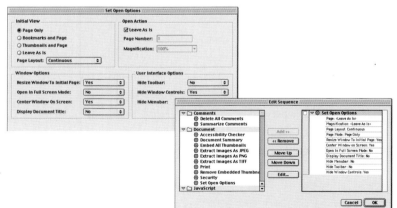

① In the Batch Sequences dialog box, choose one of the settings in the Run Commands On list. If you choose Selected Files or Selected Folder, a dialog box opens from which you can select the files or folder to process.

② If you choose Selected Folder, the Source File Options button appears. Click it to set which types of files (other than PDF) should be processed.

① In the Batch Sequences dialog box, choose one of the settings in the Select output location list. If you choose Specific Folder, a dialog box opens where you can select the destination folder.

② You can select the naming conventions and file format for the processed documents in the Output Options dialog box.

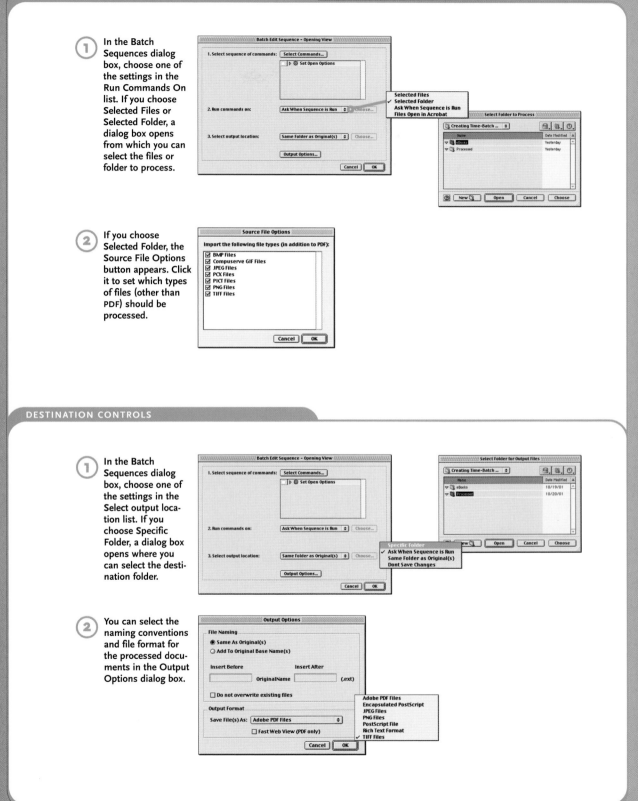

It also appears in the Batch Processing sub-menu. Click the Close button to close the box, or keep it open to run the batch sequence.

Creating an Interactive Batch Sequence

Ordinarily, we enjoy creating batch sequences that are totally automatic. We start the sequence, point to a folder of files, and go make a cup of coffee while Acrobat does all the work. However, you may want to have a little more control over the batch sequences. For instance, if you add the Document Summary to the batch sequence, you might want to open that dialog box to enter your own title or keywords.

To create an interactive sequence, open the Edit Sequence dialog box and select the command for the batch. Click the Toggle Interactive Mode rectangle 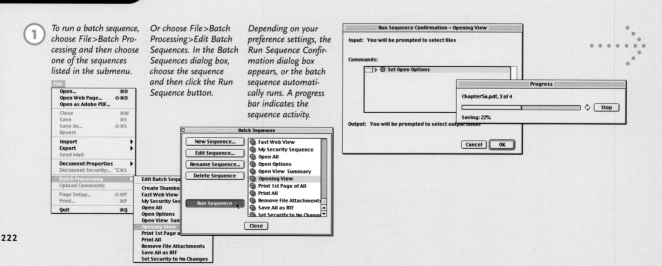 to the left of the name of the command. A filled rectangle indicates that the command will stop and open the dialog box for that command.

Editing Batch Sequences

Once you have created a batch sequence, you may want to make changes—either to the commands, the source files, or the final output options. Simply choose File>Batch Processing>Edit Batch Sequence. In the Batch Sequences dialog box, choose the batch sequence and then click the Edit Sequence button. This opens the Batch Edit Sequence dialog box where you can make changes.

RUNNING A BATCH SEQUENCE

This can be extremely simple—you choose the batch sequence and let Acrobat go to work. Or, you may have a few controls that you'd like to set during the batch sequence.

Step ① Choose the Batch Sequence

There are two ways to start the batch processing. You can choose File>Batch Processing and then choose one of the batch sequences listed in the submenu. Alternatively, you can choose File> Edit Batch Sequence. This opens the Batch Sequence dialog box. Select one of sequences listed and click the Run Sequence button.

Depending on your preferences (covered below) the Run Sequence Confirmation dialog box may appear. This dialog box gives you a final check to review the options that have been set for the sequence. If you are satisfied with the sequence settings, click OK to start the batch processing. A progress bar will appear as the files are processed. The following steps may or may not be required, depending on the settings for the batch sequence.

Step ② Choose the Source Files (Optional)

If you have selected the option to Run Commands On Ask When Sequence is Run, a dialog box now appears in which you can select the source files for batch processing. Use the navigational tools to find the files you want to process. Click to select the first file. If you want

⚡ RUNNING A BATCH

① To run a batch sequence, choose File>Batch Processing and then choose one of the sequences listed in the submenu.

Or choose File>Batch Processing>Edit Batch Sequences. In the Batch Sequences dialog box, choose the sequence and then click the Run Sequence button.

Depending on your preference settings, the Run Sequence Confirmation dialog box appears, or the batch sequence automatically runs. A progress bar indicates the sequence activity.

to process multiple files, hold the Shift key and click to select the desired files.

Step ③ Choose the Destination (Optional)

If you have selected the option for Select Output Location for Ask When Sequence is Run, a dialog box will appear. Select the folder in which you'd like to store the finished files.

Step ④ Set Interactive Dialogs (Optional)

If you have set any dialog boxes to be interactive, those dialog boxes will appear for each file that is processed. Set these dialog boxes and apply the settings by clicking the OK button.

Step ⑤ Read Warning and Errors (Optional)

When the batch sequence finishes, Acrobat may display a dialog box that shows warnings or errors that occurred during the processing. These messages provide information that can help you edit the sequence so it runs correctly.

Examining the Processed Files

We make it a habit to always inspect a few randomly selected files to make sure that the procedure was successful. If you're not satisfied with the results, you can go back and modify the various input and/or steps in the process to get it right. Go back to the Batch Sequences dialog box and click Edit Sequence. Since your commands are saved, you can easily experiment with and tweak the settings without having to go through all the steps you took to set up the sequence in the first place.

OPTIMIZING WORK FLOW

We have tried to illustrate a very simple work flow in the QuickSteps. However, you may create more complex sets of instructions to fit a unique process. One of the best things about the flexibility of Acrobat is that it lets you go back and edit your commands, or the batch sequence, as many times as you like.

BATCH PROCESSING PREFERENCES

You can also control how batch sequences run by setting the batch processing preferences. Choose Edit>Preferences>General and click the Batch Processing category. Deselect the option for Show Run confirmation dialog to omit that step as you run the batch sequence. Use Save Warnings and Errors in Log File to create a record of all messages generated during batch processing. Choose the location in which the log should be stored.

Finally, you can use the Security Handler list to choose how Acrobat should handle batch processing that requires security settings. Choose Do Not Ask for Password to apply security without stopping for a password. Or you can choose to apply Acrobat Standard Security or Acrobat Self-Sign Security.

---

② If the Run Commands On option has been set for Ask When Sequence is Run, a dialog box appears. Here, you can select the files for processing.

③ If the Selected Output Location option has been set for Ask When Sequence is Run, a dialog box opens. Here, you can set the destination folder.

④ If you have set a command for the interactive mode, you will see the dialog box for that command. Enter the settings and then click OK to continue the sequence.

⑤ If there have been problems executing the sequence, read the messages in the Warnings and Errors dialog box.

7.2 Editing Text

We're old enough to remember how print houses corrected errors on film separations by scratching out a misplaced comma or stripping in the correct price. This method wasn't easy, but it was sure faster than setting new type and creating new separations. Of course if we had to rewrite an entire paragraph, we would have to reset the text. The same principle applies to editing text in Acrobat. It's possible to make some changes to text, but after a certain point you may need to go back to the original page layout application.

Although there are quite a few ways to edit text in Acrobat, there is one important caveat to the process—you can only edit text one line at a time. If you add or delete long amounts of text, the text does not reflow to accommodate the changes. So extensive text edits should be viewed as a last resort. You should also make the same corrections to the authoring application document.

If you do change the document in the authoring application, you'll need to create a new PDF file. If your changes are only on one or two pages, you can make PDF files of these pages and then insert them into the main PDF document, or replace the appropriate pages.

A WORD ABOUT FONTS

Before you edit text, remember that font status affects how you can edit the text. If you try to edit text in a font that is embedded or subset, a dialog box appears that asks you to unembed the font. Once you unembed the font, you still need to have the font installed on your computer in order to add or change text characters. You can always delete characters, but if you want to edit the text by adding characters, you have to install the font on your system. Otherwise you can only make changes to attributes such as color, tracking word spacing, baseline, margins, and justification.

If you try to add characters to an embedded font that is not installed on your computer, you'll receive a message that asks if you want to remove the embedding—the only way to add characters is by removing the embedding. If the embedded font is not on your system, you'll get a message that says "You cannot edit this text font."

You can embed or unembed fonts using the Text Attributes palette, but you can only embed additional characters if the font is installed. Single-byte (Roman) fonts are fully embedded when you choose Embed from the Text Attributes palette. Multibyte fonts (Asian) are always subset embedded. This also happens when you choose Embed on the Text Attributes palette.

USING THE TOUCHUP TEXT TOOL

T Click with the Touch-up Text tool to insert a cursor inside a line of text. Drag to select the text. Double-click to select the entire line. You can cut, copy, and paste text with the TouchUp Text tool. (Note: The TouchUp Text tool is the only tool that lets you modify text. The Text Select and Column Select tools are used to copy large areas of text to be pasted into other applications—not to modify text. If you need to extract all the text in a document, use the Save As command and then choose the Rich Text Format.

The TouchUp Text tool and the Text Attributes palette allow you to edit text in PDF files. This before and after set of pictures shows some of the text changes that are possible within Acrobat. While these changes were not too extensive, there still were some limitations as to what could be changed.

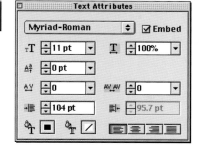

BEFORE
The extra period before the ellipsis needs to be deleted.

Wrong text color.

Price needs to be set differently.

Needs to be italic.

Needs to be larger point size.

At the Old Ball Game....

There's a Dad explaining to his kid the strategies of throwing to a left handed batter with a man on third.
There's a young man on a first date buying a $5.00 hot dog for a girl who can't tell a strike from a bunt.
And an old man who watches as if he was still a kid.
It's all at the old ball game.

AFTER
Using the text editing tools, the document is changed. However, notice that the text does not rewrap where the price was changed. This is one of the limitations of editing text in Acrobat.

At the Old Ball Game...

There's a Dad explaining to his kid the strategies of throwing to a left handed batter with a man on third.
There's a young man on a first date buying a $5 hot dog for a girl who can't tell a strike from a bunt.
And an old man who watches as if he was *still* a kid.
It's all at the old ball game.

You can also insert a new line of text—just a line—using the TouchUp Text tool. Hold the Ctrl key (w) or Option key (м) and click with the TouchUp Text tool where you want the text to begin, and then type the text.

When you select a line of text, you'll notice two "handles" on the left end of the line. These are called the Line Markers. Grabbing the selected line by these handles allows you to move the line horizontally by dragging to the left or right. If you want to move text up or down, you need to use the TouchUp Object tool described in the next section.

USING THE TEXT ATTRIBUTES PALETTE

Open the Text Attribute palette by choosing Tools>TouchUp Text>Text Attribute. Select the text and then use the Text Attributes controls to change the font, point size, baseline shift, tracking, word spacing, horizontal scale, alignment, indents, color, and alignment. These are similar to the controls found in graphics programs.

FIT TEXT TO SELECTION

If you select and then retype text, you will discover that the new text doesn't always fill the previous width. This can be a problem when trying to substitute text within a justified text format—text that fills the entire column width. Fortunately, Acrobat has a command that helps avoid problems when retyping text so that it fits the original column width.

Step 1 Select the Text to be Changed
Click inside the line of text with the TouchUp Text tool and then double-click to select the text you want to change. This is usually the entire line, but can be a portion of the text within the line.

Step 2 Choose Fit Text To Selection
Choose Tools>Touchup>Fit Text to Selection. The Line Markers disappear, indicating that the command has been applied.

Step 3 Insert the New Text
Type the replacement text. As you type, the text automatically fills the selected area. If there is only a single word, Acrobat adds or deletes the space between the letters to fill the selected area. If there is more than one word, Acrobat adds or deletes the space between the words to fill the selected area. Note: If you try to insert too much text in the selected area, the characters will be stacked together into one unreadable mess.

⚡ FIT TEXT TO SELECTION

1 To change text to fit within the original column width, click with the TouchUp Text tool inside the line. Double-click to select all the text in the line.

> I don't change InDesign's keyboard shortcuts to follow all those other programs. I find it easier to concentrate on learning InDesign's shortcuts. It's the

> I don't change InDesign's keyboard shortcuts to follow all those other programs. I find it easier to concentrate on learning InDesign's shortcuts. It's the

2 Choose Tools> TouchUp Text>Fit Text to Selection. The Line Markers disappear from the selected text.

Tools
Comments
Compare
Digital Signatures
Self-Sign Security
Spelling
Web Capture
Accessibility Checker...
Catalog...
Distiller
Forms
JavaScript
Locate Web Addresses
PDF Consultant
TouchUp Text
Ari's Ruler
Stratify PDF
Formatix Paginierung
Create Adobe PDF Online
Paper Capture Online
Search Adobe PDF Online

Text Attributes
Text Breaks
Fit Text to Selection
Insert
✓ Show Line Markers

> I don't change InDesign's keyboard shortcuts to follow all those other programs. I find it easier to concentrate on learning InDesign's shortcuts. It's the

3 Type the replacement text. The word spacing automatically adjusts to fit the original selection.

> I don't change InDesign's keyboard shortcuts to follow those other programs. I find it easier to concentrate on learning InDesign's shortcuts. It's the

Choose Tools> TouchUp Text>Text Attributes to open the Text Attributes palette. Select the desired line of text with the TouchUp Text tool and apply one of the text attributes to change the text.

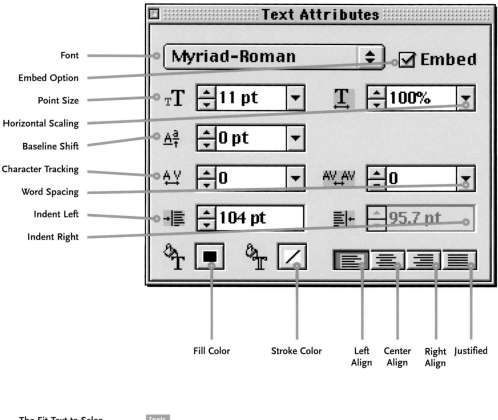

Font
Embed Option
Point Size
Horizontal Scaling
Baseline Shift
Character Tracking
Word Spacing
Indent Left
Indent Right

Fill Color — Stroke Color — Left Align — Center Align — Right Align — Justified

The Fit Text to Selection command helps avoid unequal lines of text.

Instead of a short column of text, the Fit Text to Selection command expands the space between words to fit the justified column.

I don't change InDesign's keyboard shortcuts to follow those other programs. I find it easier to concentrate on learning InDesign's shortcuts. It's the

I don't change InDesign's keyboard shortcuts to follow those other programs. I find it easier to concentrate on learning InDesign's shortcuts. It's the

7.3 Editing Graphics

As you may have noticed, there are no drawing or painting tools in Acrobat. The program was never meant to be an illustration or retouching application. Yet there are many times you may need to change the graphics in Acrobat documents. Rather than make the changes in the original author-ing application and then recreate the PDF document, there are several techniques you can use to edit graphics and graphic objects in PDF files.

THE TOUCHUP OBJECT TOOL

The TouchUp Object tool allows you to select and manipulate objects on a page. Acro-bat objects can be placed images, rectangles, lines, curves, text paragraphs, or clipping paths (masks) around graphics. Working with the TouchUp Object tool is quite simple. Click to select an object; drag to move it.

OBJECT COMMANDS

You can also use any of the editing commands to work with objects selected with the TouchUp Object tool. These commands are available in the Edit menu or in the contextual menus. Right-mouse (w) or Ctrl-click (m) to access the contextual menu.

Cut: removes the object from the document and places it on the clipboard.

Copy: places a copy of the object on the clipboard.

Paste: places the contents of the clipboard into a selected object or onto the page.

Select All: selects all the objects on the page.

The next set of commands are available only through contextual menus.

Paste in Front: places the contents of the clip-board in front of the topmost selected object, or on top of everything on the page if nothing is selected.

Paste in Back: places the contents of the clip-board behind the bottommost selected object, or behind everything on the document page if nothing is selected.

Delete: removes the selected objects.

Select None: deselects any selected objects.

Delete Clip: deletes the objects that mask the selected objects. For example, shapes, such as circles, are usually used to clip or mask images or text into non-rectangular shapes.

TOUCHUP EDITORS

Acrobat has no retouching or drawing tools of its own. (The Comments tools may look like drawing tools, but they are used only to create comments.) You can link Acrobat to an image or graphic editor, such as Adobe Photoshop or Adobe Illustrator to edit selected images and objects. Choose Edit>Preferences>General. Then select the TouchUp category from the list. Click the Choose Image Editor button and navigate to choose an image editor, such as Adobe Photoshop. Click the Choose Page/ Object Editor button and navigate to choose an object editor, such as Adobe Illustrator. Click OK to set the editors.

If you want to select non-Adobe applica-tions as the external editors, choose All Appli-cations from the Show List.

USING PHOTOSHOP

In the TouchUp preferences, click the Choose Image Editor to select an application, such as Adobe Photoshop, to edit pixel-based images.

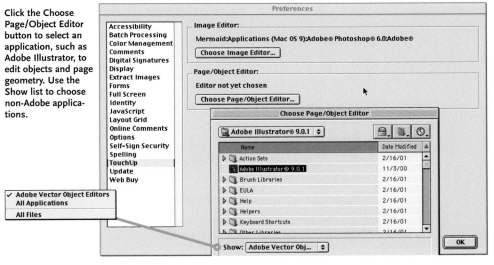

To edit and save images back into the Acrobat file, you must have Adobe Photoshop (5.0 or later). With Photoshop 5.0/5.5, you need the PDF Format Photoshop plug-in installed in the Photoshop plug-ins folder. If the graphic image is in a format supported by Photoshop 6.0, the edited image will be saved back into the PDF. If the graphic image is in an unsupported format, Photoshop 6.0 handles the image as a generic PDF and saves it as a file instead of into the PDF document.

MACINTOSH EDITORS

Click the Choose Page/Object Editor button to select an application, such as Adobe Illustrator, to edit objects and page geometry. Use the Show list to choose non-Adobe applications.

You must have Adobe Illustrator (7.0 or later) to act as the Acrobat page/object editor. If you use Illustrator 10 or Photoshop 7 for the Macintosh as a page/object or image editor, you must do the following before you select the page/object editor. Control-click the Illustrator or Photoshop package in the application folder to reveal the contextual menu. Choose Show Package Contents. Open the folder Contents and then MacOS Classic. Create an alias of the application icon and move the alias to the desktop. Use the All Files setting to select this alias as the editor.

USING EXTERNAL EDITORS

Once you have set the external editors for images or page/objects, you can use the TouchUp Object tool to edit images and objects in the document.

Step (1) Select the Image or Object and Edit

Use the TouchUp Object tool to select the image, object, or page, as follows. Position the cursor over an image to select and edit it. Position the cursor over an object to select and edit it. (Each individual path in a vector shape is considered a separate object.) Drag to select and edit multiple images or objects. (If you select a mixture of both objects and images, they will be edited using the page/object editor.) Position the cursor over an empty area of the page or outside the page to edit the page as a whole.

Right-mouse-click (w) or Ctrl-click (m) to open the contextual menu. Depending on the selection, choose Edit Image(s), Edit Object(s), or Edit Page. This launches the external editing application. The image or objects appear in a new document window. (Notice that the title bar displays a temporary file name and PDF as the file format.)

Step (2) Make Changes in the Editor

Use any of the editing tools or commands to make changes to the image or objects. If you change the size of the image or objects, they may not have the same position when brought back into the PDF file.

If you edit a native Photoshop file with a transparency mask—created by placing a transparent file into InDesign 2—you can make any changes you like to the original layer, but you can't add any new layers to the image.

For all other file formats, you must flatten the image in order to bring it back into the PDF document.

Step (3) Save the Changes

In the external editor, choose File>Save and close the file. Instead of saving the file to disk, the edited image or objects are applied to the PDF document.

EXTRACTING IMAGES AND OBJECTS

You can save the pages of a PDF as individual images by going to Save As and selecting JPEG, EPS, PNG, or TIFF. Each page in the PDF file is saved as a separate image file. You can extract all the images in a PDF file to an image format by going to File>Export>Extract Images As> JPEG files, TIFF files, or PNG files.

You can use the same steps with the TouchUp Object tool and external editors to select objects and images and then save them as their own separate documents. For instance, if you have a logo that only exists in a PDF document, select and use the Edit Object command to open it in Adobe Illustrator. There, you can save the object as a native Illustrator file or any other format. You can also save the extracted object as a PDF document. This makes it possible to save portions of a page as separate PDF files.

COPYING INDIVIDUAL GRAPHICS

To copy graphics to the clipboard, select the Graphics Select tool, drag a rectangle around the graphic you want to copy, and choose Edit> Copy. To paste the graphic in Acrobat choose Edit>Paste.

1 Position the TouchUp Object tool over an image or graphic. Or position the TouchUp Object tool over the page. Use the contextual menu to choose the Edit command.

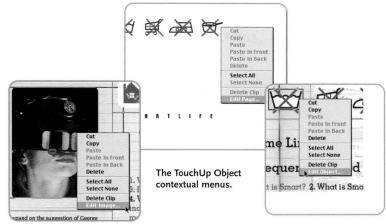

The TouchUp Object contextual menus.

2 Use the external editor to make any changes to the image or objects.

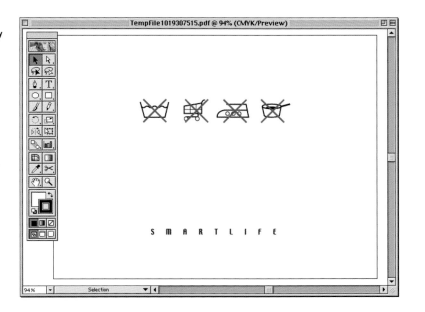

3 Choose File>Save and then close the temporary file. Or just close the file and click the Save button. The changes are automatically applied to the PDF.

Stratify PDF

What is the one feature that would make Acrobat more like it's sibling Adobe products Photoshop, Illustrator, and InDesign? Without hesitation, our answer is layers!

Since the Acrobat team hasn't given us layers, Lantana Software has created a plug-in for Acrobat 4 and 5, called Stratify PDF, that adds layers to PDF documents. With Stratify PDF, you'll be able to show and hide layers, add objects to layers, and merge and delete layers. You can also set individual layers to be password protected. Stratify PDF also makes it easy to create alternate content PDFs. This means that with one layered PDF, you can produce multilingual versions and variations on products or information.

You can also use Stratify PDF's Convert Pages to Layers command on a multi-page document. This automatically combines all the pages into a single multi-layered page. You can use the Add Page as Layer command to convert a single page in the document into a layer.

Unlike ordinary programs that put each object on its own layer, Stratify PDF lets you assign one object to be on several different layers. This makes it possible to have one image that appears on the layers for several different languages.

The layer functionality also includes the ability to move objects and layers forward and backward. You can lock layers or print only the exposed layers.

Stratify PDF also makes it easy to select all the objects on a layer. This is especially helpful if you need to select an object that is behind several others.

Stratify PDF is currently available for U.S. $249. You can download a demo version of Stratify PDF from the Lantana Web site: www.lantanarips.com. The demo version allows you to create layers, but does not allow you to save changes to documents.

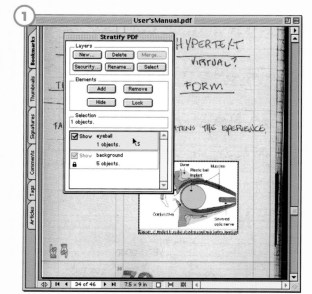

1 Use the Stratify PDF palette to create layers for a document and add objects to those layers. Once a layer has been created, click the Show option to see the objects on the layer.

2 Select a layer and then click the Security button to add a password to protect a layer.

3 Select a layer and then click the Select button to select all the objects on that layer. This makes it easy to select complex text and graphics.

PDF Imageworks

As you've seen, you can modify placed images using an external editor, such as Adobe Photoshop. But what if you would like an internal editor within Acrobat? Lantana Software has created an Acrobat-native, image editing plug-in called PDF ImageWorks.

Instead of editing images outside of Acrobat, you can do so without ever leaving the PDF document.

PDF ImageWorks allows you to resize, rotate, and crop images within a PDF. But that's just the beginning. It also lets you adjust the hue, saturation, brightness, and contrast of a single image or all of the images in a document.

The Edit Image window contains painting tools that allow you to cut, copy, paste, erase, crop, and retouch images directly in Acrobat.

PDF ImageWorks also allows you to create/repair OPI links, and control both the image in the PDF or on the OPI server, providing you flexibility in OPI, web and print document implementation.

PDF Imageworks is currently available for U.S. $249. You can download a demo version from the Lantana site: www.lantanarips.com.

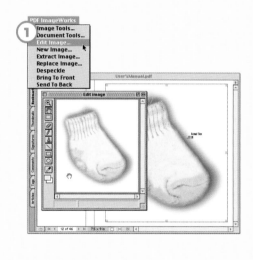

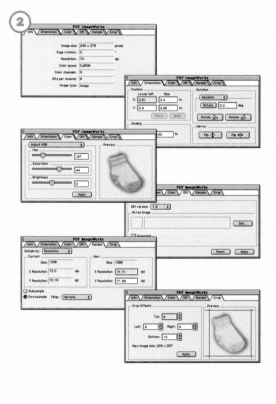

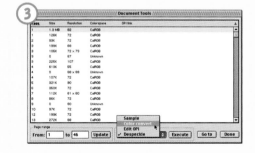

① Once you have selected an image, you can choose Edit Image from the PDF Imageworks menu. This opens the PDF Image-works image editing tools. These tools allow you to paint, retouch, erase, and draw directly on an image.

② The seven Image Tools tabs control the specific characteristics of a selected image.

③ The Document Tools let you manage and control all the images in a document. This is especially helpful for converting color spaces and working with OPI images.

7.4 Moving and Copying Pages

Although it's not a page layout program, Acrobat offers quite a few options for working with pages. Pages can be easily moved from one place to another, copied from one document to another, rotated, or deleted. This is very helpful if you suddenly realize you would like to expand a certain section in a project, or if you'd like to add pages from another document and they need to be rotated into position. It can also be helpful if you would like to post sample pages on the Web to entice readers to read an entire book.

We admit there are some limitations to text editing. Surprisingly, there are very few limitations to page editing. Perhaps this is because PDF files are used as part of prepress operations, where printers have to move and rotate pages into position for printing. Whatever the reason, you'll be pleased to see that Acrobat's page arrangements are quite flexible.

CREATING A BLANK FILE

One of the commands we miss the most in Acrobat is File>New. There is no built-in way to create an empty PDF file into which you can combine pages from other documents. One way to work around this is to create your own reusable blank PDF file. Simply go to whatever authoring application you usually use to create PDF files, and create a single, blank page PDF file. When you would like to combine pages from other PDF documents, you can open your blank document, and add as many pages as you want. Then delete the blank page and save the file under a new name. Your blank document serves the same function as choosing File>New.

COMBINING PDF FILES

The simplest way to combine PDF files is to choose Document>Insert Pages. This opens the operating system dialog box where you can choose the files you want to insert.

(Although the feature is labeled Insert Pages, you actually insert the entire file into the current PDF document.) You can use the Shift key to select multiple documents at the same time. When you have chosen the files to insert, the Insert Pages dialog box appears. Here you can choose where to insert the new pages.

DRAGGING AND DROPPING (W ONLY)

Windows users have an extra technique for inserting a file into their PDF documents. Arrange your monitor so you can see both the Acrobat window and the Windows Explorer window. Select the icons for the PDF files you want to insert, and drag and drop them from the Explorer window into the document area of the PDF. If you have selected multiple files, hold the Ctrl key to insert all the files.

MOVING/COPYING WITH THUMBNAILS

Once you have your pages in a document, you can easily move them around using the Thumbnails palette. Press and drag the page icon from one position to another. (Use the Shift key to select a range of pages; use the Ctrl key (w) or Cmd key (m) to select non-contiguous pages. To copy the page to a new position, hold the Ctrl key (w) or Opt key (m) as you drag. You can also drag the thumbnails from one document into the Thumbnails palette in another.

EXTRACTING PAGES

Choose Document>Extract Pages to extract pages from a PDF document and save them as a separate file. A new document opens with the name Pages from <name.pdf>. This document must be saved.

Extracted pages will contain all comments, form fields, and links—but bookmarks and articles are not extracted. To delete the pages from the document during the extraction process, select the option Delete Pages After Extracting.

DELETING PAGES

You can delete pages by choosing Document> Delete Pages or the Delete Page command in the Thumbnails palette. The Delete Pages dialog box will appear. Choose the pages to be deleted. (You can also select the pages ahead of time in the Thumbnails palette.) Use the Save As command to reduce the file size after deleting pages. You can't delete all the pages; one page has to remain.

REPLACING PAGES

You may need to replace one PDF page with another. For instance, you may need to make extensive changes to a page in the original authoring document. You can then export that page as its own PDF file. Only the text and graphics on the original page will be replaced. Interactive elements on the original page are not affected, which means that you will not have to redo all the linking or adding interactive elements; you only have to relocate them if needed.

Open the file that contains pages to be replaced. Choose Document>Replace Pages or Replace Pages in the Thumbnails palette. Navigate and select the document that contains the replacement pages. The Replace Pages dialog box will appear. Under the Original section, enter the page numbers to be replaced in the original document. Under the Replacement

section, enter the first page of the replacement page range. Acrobat automatically calculates the last page based on the number of pages selected in the Original section. You can only replace equal numbers of pages. Click the OK button to replace the pages.

You can also replace pages using the Thumbnails palette for click-and-drag flexibility. Open two documents so you can see the Thumbnails in both. Move to the Thumbnails palette of the document that contains the replacement pages. Select as many pages as you want using the Shift key for a range or Ctrl key (w) or Cmd key (m) to select non-contiguous pages. Drag the selected thumbnails into the Thumbnails palette of the target document. Position the cursor over the page number box of the first page you want to replace. Release the mouse button. The pages from the first file will replace the same number of pages in the target document.

ROTATING PAGES

You can also rotate pages to a different orientation. Choose Document>Rotate Pages or choose Rotate Pages from the Thumbnails palette. The Rotate Pages dialog box appears. Choose the Direction from the pop-up list. In the Page Range controls, choose the pages you want to rotate. You can rotate all of the pages selected in the Thumbnails palettes, or a page range. You can limit your pages to odd or even pages. You can also rotate all landscape pages (wider than tall) or portrait pages (taller than wide).

7.5 | Creating Tagged PDF

If your only idea of tagging is "Tag—You're it!," don't worry. You're not alone. There are very few designers who are familiar with the concept of tagging, what it does, and how to add tags to their documents. Tagging is a way to add special codes to the various items in a document. This is called a logical structure. What is a logical structure? Imagine you are moving from one home to another, but you don't know the layout of the new house. One way to tell the moving men where something belongs would be to describe its function. Instead of saying that the stove belongs in the kitchen, you would apply a tag to describe its function—in this case, "Cooks food." The moving men would then decide the appropriate room for the object. Tagging allows you to create documents that are more flexible and can be used in a variety of situations.

Tagging is a form of coding similar to HTML (hypertext markup language) or XML (extensible markup language) that tags the organization of a document's content, such as headings, captions, paragraphs, and images.

Tagging allows documents to reflow text for use on mobile devices such as Palm and Pocket PC. Reflow means that when the page is viewed on different-sized devices, the text changes to fit the allotted space. This is extremely important for documents viewed on the Palm OS and Pocket PC.

Another reason to tag a PDF is to make the document accessible to users with disabilities, such as blindness or impaired vision. This is important to companies and U.S. government agencies that need to make their information and websites accessible to all viewers. (The U.S. Government's Section 508 mandates accessibility of all government information, including its websites.) Unlike HTML web pages, which can be translated into spoken language using screen readers, ordinary PDF documents appear to screen readers as blank pages. (Screen readers are a type of software that converts text to

speech.) Adding accessibility to a PDF allows people with impaired vision to listen to the document. Adding a tag structure to a PDF document gives the screen reader software the reading order of the content and alternate text for graphics and images.

Tagged PDF documents work better for text export, saving as RTF, and exporting to the clipboard. It's also easier to repurpose Tagged PDF content to HTML, XML, and other formats using Adobe's Save as XML plug-in (available from the Adobe website). Tagged PDF documents do have larger file sizes because they contain more information than the untagged version of a document.

TAGGING OPTIONS

Although we are still at the dawn of tagging, there are many options for creating Tagged PDF documents, and we expect more to come as tagged documents become more ubiquitous. Here are some of the ways to create Tagged PDF documents: Acrobat 5 Open Web Page command automatically tags the elements converted from HTML; create Adobe PDF Online

Here's the route that a tagged document created in InDesign took to be read in Acrobat and on a Palm IIIc.

(1) A document laid out in InDesign. Although not necessary, XML tags were applied to each of the elements as seen in the Structure panel.

(2) After it was exported from InDesign as a PDF with eBook Tags, the document is opened in Acrobat. The tags are visible in the Tags palette.

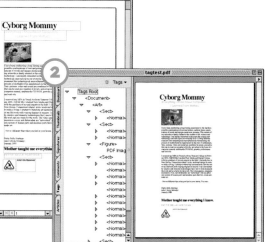

(3) You can also see the tagged objects by choosing the Object TouchUp tool (not available except for tagged documents).

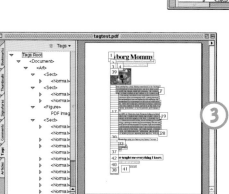

(4) Tagged documents reflow to the shape of the document window.

(5) A Tagged PDF document can also be displayed on portable devices such as a Pocket PC (left) or a Palm OS device (right).

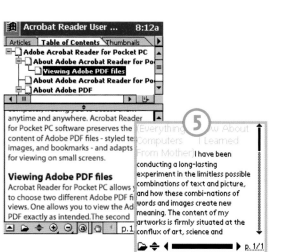

for paid subscribers (North America only), Microsoft Office 2000+ (w); the Make Accessible Plug-in for Acrobat 5 (w); Acrobat Capture with the Tagged PDF Agent add on; PageMaker 7; InDesign 2; FrameMaker 7; manually applying tags in Acrobat 5.

These tools for tagging are in their first incarnation—their infancy. This is why we have found so little information on the subject. The number of people putting tagging tools to the test are few and far between. XML and content repurposing are not yet the hot topics among graphic design professionals. However, we expect that to change as time goes by.

DESIGNING FOR TAGGED PDF

Perhaps we should say "undesigning" for Tagged PDF, because this is basically the approach you'll need to take. All the cool design techniques we don't think twice about for print and web, such as special fonts, rule lines, bullets, graphics, and images, make it more difficult to successfully tag PDFs for repurposing and accessibility. Complex elements such as columns and tables also make it more difficult to tag the document.

If you are creating a Tagged PDF for accessibility purposes, this should be taken into account before the design process begins. Every document design decision should be made with consideration for accessibility to screen readers—no small feat. The simpler the layout, the better chances it has of being an accessible document.

The main thing to remember when it comes to designing a tagged document is to keep it as simple as possible. The next important lesson is to test, test, test with screen reader software and mobile devices. Then go back and redesign the document as necessary.

Pattie Belle, our tagging expert, has been working in this area for a while. Here are a few of her recommendations.

Stay with the Base-14 fonts and leave out graphic embellishments.

Watch for characters that a screen reader won't recognize. These are usually the Alt + number characters (w) or Option characters (m) such as bullets, dingbats, hyphens, em dashes, accents, and ligatures.

Match your images to your end device, such as a grayscale or 256-color Palm. Consider whether graphics or images are truly necessary and consider the screen size of the final device.

Collect alternate text for images, graphics, and charts during the creation process and not after the fact.

Screen readers balk at table data. If you have to incorporate tables into your document, use rules to clearly delineate the table's columns, rows, and cells.

Logos, charts, and other vector graphics may be recognized in the tagging process as multiple parts. Your company logo could have a dozen tags instead of one. One possible (but not guaranteed) method to prevent this is to place all vector graphics inside a ruled border box within the authoring application. This can help Acrobat recognize that the vector graphic is a single element.

Any design embellishment can negatively affect the success of a screen reader. Pull quotes, side bars, captions, and multi-column text confuse the logical reading order. If your document has to have these things, you will more than likely have to use Acrobat's Touch Up Order tool to make sense of the reading.

If you use charts, graphics, or images, you'll need to provide an alternate text description of those graphics that can be translated by screen readers. (This is similar to the alt tag text in web pages.) We'll cover how to add alternate text to graphics later.

SCREEN READERS

If your main reason for tagging PDFs is accessibility, then you must test your efforts on the common screen readers. Alva Access Group has a screen reader called outSPOKEN, which is available for Windows and Macintosh. There are also some other popular products for the Windows platform, including Freedom Scientific's Jaws and GW Micro's Window-Eyes.

EXAMINING THE TAGS

You can see the tags in a PDF document by opening the Tags palette. Choose Window> Tags or click the Tags palette tab in the Navigation Pane. The main level of the tags is the Tags Root. This is the topmost level in the logical structure tree. Click the plus sign (w) or triangle (M) to open the interior levels of tags. The tags are labeled with the type of objects, paragraphs, figures, and so on.

You can also see the individual tagged elements by choosing the TouchUp Order tool in the tool bar. This tool is only available if the document is a Tagged PDF. Each object appears inside a numbered rectangle. The numbers refer to the reflow order of the objects. For instance, the object labeled number 1 will appear before number 2, which in turn appears before number 3, and so on.

ON THE CD

If you'd like to quickly get your hands on some Tagged PDF documents, look on the CD-rom in the Tagging folder. We've created some Tagged PDF files for you to open and explore.

REFLOWING A TAGGED PDF

When Adobe first introduced PDF documents, one of the important benefits was that PDF files would not reflow text like native files. A designer could send out a PDF document and know that the text and images would appear exactly where they were created in the original authoring application. This is not the case with Tagged PDF documents.

Unlike ordinary PDF documents, Tagged PDF files can reflow to accommodate the size of the viewing screen. This makes Tagged PDF documents ideal for viewing on different devices. These includes electronic book readers and hand-held personal digital assistants, such as Palm and Pocket PC devices.

To see an example of reflow, open any Tagged PDF document and choose View> Reflow. Then change the size of the document window and watch how the text reflows to fit the width of the page. This illustrates how Tagged PDF documents can accommodate various viewing devices.

CREATING A TAGGED PDF

Enough of the background stuff—by this time you'd probably like to get your hands on a Tagged PDF document to see what all the fuss is about. Here are a few of the ways you can create your own Tagged PDF files. You'll also have an opportunity to see how various layouts are translated for reflow.

Open Web Page

The quickest way we know to see what a tagged document looks like is to choose File>Open Web Page. Web pages converted into PDF documents can create Tagged PDF files if the Add PDF Tags option is checked in the Conversion settings. Select Open Web Page from the File Menu. Click Conversion Settings in the Open Web Page dialog box. Click the General tab and make sure that the Add PDF Tags option is selected. This will produce a Tagged PDF from the captured web pages.

CREATING A TAGGED PDF FROM INDESIGN 2

Of course, in most cases, you would like to create your own document and then convert it into a Tagged PDF. The simplest way we know that is available for both Windows and Macintosh users is to create a document using InDesign 2 or PageMaker 7. Both of those programs add tags to the PDF files they create. Here's how Pattie Belle created a Tagged PDF document in InDesign 2.

Step ① Create the document in InDesign

Create the InDesign document. Keep the elements simple and avoid stacking text over graphics. Don't use images as background elements. They will disappear during any reflow.

The stacking order—from back to front—of the items in the InDesign file determines the initial reflow order of the tagged elements in Acrobat. For instance, in our first attempt to create a Tagged PDF, we had an image positioned near the top of the page, but at the very front of the stacking order. When the file was converted to a Tagged PDF, the image was positioned at the very bottom of the layout. When we changed the InDesign layout so that the image was stacked just in front of the headlines, the reflow order kept it next to the headlines.

Step 2 Export as a PDF document

Choose File>Export and then choose Adobe PDF as the file format. Name the file and click the Save button. This opens the Export PDF dialog box.

In the General category, check the eBook Tags, in addition to the other settings you want.

Step 3 Verify the tagging in Acrobat

Open the document in Acrobat. The Tags palette shows the main level Tags Root. You can open that tag to see the other tags in the document. That's it! The export feature from InDesign has automatically created a Tagged PDF.

Step 4 Tag Within InDesign 2 (Optional)

InDesign 2 also comes with a plug-in called XmediaUI (cross-media), that extends InDe-sign's tagging capabilities with a built-in Tags palette. This allows you to use PDF structure commands, as well as define custom tags to extend the control over the resulting Tagged PDF. This plug-in allows you to map InDesign paragraph style names to Acrobat 5.0 tagged Adobe PDF paragraph styles; change the reading order of document content; and mark or hide artifacts (rules, bullets, etc.), text, or images so that they won't appear when reflowed in Acrobat 5.0.

PageMaker 7

The steps for using PageMaker are very similar to the ones for InDesign. You can create a Tagged PDF file by exporting the PageMaker document as a PDF file. Then make sure to check the Embed Tags option in the General tab of the PDF Options dialog box.

Microsoft Office 2000+ (W)

When you create a Microsoft Word document for the purpose of converting it to a Tagged PDF, you must format the text using styles such as titles, headings, and paragraphs. Styles provide the structure information for the conversion to a Tagged PDF document.

To create a Tagged PDF from a Microsoft Office application choose Acrobat>Change Conversion Settings, and select the Office tab. Make sure Embed Tags in PDF is turned on and Page Labels is turned off. Select the styles

---

⚡ CREATING A TAGGED PDF

1 Create the document in InDesign 2. Keep the layout simple and avoid stacking images and text.

2 Choose File>Export and choose the Adobe PDF format. Click Save. Make sure the Include eBook Tags is turned on in the Export options.

you want for the Adobe PDF bookmarks. Then choose Acrobat>Convert to Adobe PDF or click the Convert to Adobe PDF button on the tool bar.

Make Accessible Plug-in (W)

The Make Accessible plug-in allows you to convert existing untagged PDF files to Tagged PDF documents. It is available as a free download at the Adobe web site, but is only available for the Windows platform at this time. Once you have installed the plug-in, a Make Accessible command will appear in the Acrobat menu. To convert an untagged PDF, choose Document>Make Accessible. This plug-in is known to have quite a few limitations, including the inability to deal with font encodings, tables, complex layouts, and layer order.

TAGGING INFO

For more information on Tagged PDF documents, see http://access.adobe.com.

Create PDF Online

Subscribers to create Adobe PDF Online have the option of converting files to Tagged PDF files. The accepted file formats include Microsoft Office files, HTML files, and web pages. Hyperlinks in Microsoft Word and Microsoft Excel files will be also retained in the converted PDF. Note that this service is available only for users in North America.

MANUALLY TAGGING IN ACROBAT 5

What if you want to add tags to a PDF file that was not created with a tagging application? Can you add the tags yourself in Acrobat? In spite of what you may have read elsewhere, you can create a Tagged PDF manually. (This method is best used for very simple documents.) We'll go through a step-by-step exercise to manually tag a document; but before we do, here are some of the things that you should know in order to create a Tagged PDF from scratch or to modify the structure tree of an existing Tagged PDF.

Element Tags

When you open the Tags palette, you will most likely need to click the nesting icons to see past the initial Tags Root level. As you go down the list, you will see a sort of outline listing all the elements in the file. This is the logical structure tree. Each line in the structure tree represents an item on the page—a section, an article, a block of text, or an image. The tags next to the elements tell what type of item it is. If the element is text content, then part of the text will be shown to help you identify that element.

Element Hierarchy

The logical structure tree also arranges the file as to how it should be read and reflowed. For instance, look at the columns of text on this

(3) Open the document in Acrobat and inspect the logical structure tree in the Tags pane.

(4) As an option, you can also apply tags within the InDesign document using its Tags palette and Structure panel.

page. You know how to read them because you've been taught that columns have a specific order. But screen readers don't know that—so the logical structure tree arranges the elements as to how they should be read. The order that the elements are read is controlled by the logical structure tree in the Tags palette.

The tree begins with a level called the Tags Root. Inside the Tags Root is a container element that represents the document <Document>, or a section <Sect> of the document. The next element may be for an article <Art> or a section. Any element that contains other elements is called a parent. The elements within a parent are called children. Two children at the same level under a parent element are called siblings. Parents give their children some attributes. For instance, if you specify a language to the parent elements, that language is inherited by the child elements. Also, if you move or delete a parent, all the children go along for the ride.

Another type of element is an artifact. Artifacts are extraneous elements that are not considered important to repurposing the document. The colored line between the columns on these pages is considered an artifact. Other artifacts include comments, page numbers, running heads, decorative ornaments, and crop marks.

Element Properties

Each element in the logical structure tree has its own properties. The properties of all elements are set using the Element Properties dialog box. These properties include element name, tag type, actual text, alternate text, and language.

The following is a very simple exercise that lets you manually tag a PDF file. This may help you understand the logical structure tree of Tagged PDF documents. Note: This exercise is for demonstration purposes only to help you understand the logical structure tree. It is not a recommendation for real document production; it's just our way of helping you understand Tagged PDF files.

Step ① Create the PDF document
Create a simple text-only PDF document with no tags. (We created a text-only file in InDesign and exported it with no eBook Tags.) Open the untagged PDF document. Open the Tags palette in the Navigation Pane or chooseWindow> Tags. The only comment in the Tags palette should be No Tags Available.

Step ② Create the Tags Root
Choose Create Tags Root (the only command) from the Tags palette menu. The Tags Root element appears in the Tags palette.

⚡ MANUALLY TAGGING

① Open an untagged document in Acrobat. The Tags palette shows the label No Tags available.

② Choose Tags>Create Tags Root.

③ Choose Tags>New Child Element>Document Element. This adds a <Document> tag under the Tags Root. With the Document tag selected, choose Tags> New Child Element>Article Element. This adds an <Article> tag under the Document tag.

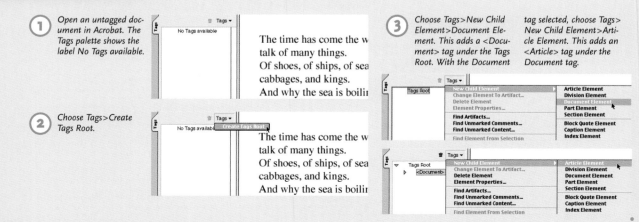

Step ③ Create the Child Elements

You now need to create a child element for the Tags Root. Choose Document, which is one of the high-level elements. Select the Tags Root in the Tags palette and then use the Tags palette menu to choose Tags>New Child Element> Document Element. With the Document tag selected, choose Tags>New Child Element> Article Element. This shows the basics of the logical structure tree: one type of element is contained within another.

Step ④ Convert Text to Child Element

At this point, all we've done is set up the logical structure, but there is no object inside the structure. This is like buying a house without ever moving into it. The logical structure tree (house) needs content (family). Right now, the only content in the document is unmarked—that is, it is not a tagged element inside the logical structure.

Use the TouchUp Object tool to select the text object. The object will be highlighted. Then choose Tags>Create Child Element from Selection. This adds the text content under the Article tag. Our logical structure tree now has content.

Step ⑤ Set the Document To Tagged

Finally, you'll need to tell Acrobat to look at the tags in the document. Choose Tags>Document is Tagged Adobe PDF.

Step ⑥ Add Line Breaks (Optional)

One thing this method doesn't do is break the text into individual objects. This means that when the document reflows, the text from one paragraph flows back into the previous one. Fortunately Adobe has added the ability to add line breaks to the ends of paragraphs. We used these line breaks to help the document reflow correctly.

Use the TouchUp Text tool to place an insertion point at the end of a line that needs to stay separated from the next line. Choose Tools>Touchup Text>Insert>Line Break. This keeps the next line from flowing into the previous line when the text reflows.

HIGHLIGHTING ELEMENTS

To view the association between elements displayed in the Tags panel and the actual page content, select Turn On Associated Content Highlighting in the Tags palette menu. Then select an element in the Tags palette and the content associated with the selected tag will be highlighted in the document.

If you want to do the reverse, find the element tag from the content and use the Text Selection tool or Graphic Selection tool to select the content in the document. Choose Find Element From Selection in the Tags palette menu and the logical structure tree will highlight the element tag of the selection.

④ Select the text object on the page and choose Tags>Create Child Element from Selection. This adds the text as an element contained inside the Article tag.

Tags ▾
New Child Element ▸
Change Element To Artifact...
Delete Element
Element Properties...
Find Artifacts...
Find Unmarked Comments...
Find Unmarked Content...
Find Element From Selection
Create Child Element From Selection
Set Span Expansion Text...
Set Span Language...
Edit Class Map...
Edit Role Map...
Document is Tagged PDF
Turn On Associated Content Highlighting

me the walrus said, to
ngs.
ps, of sealing wax, of
ings.
a is boiling hot.
gs have wings.

Tags ▾

Tags Root
  ▽ <Document> Docum
    ▽ <Art> Article
        The time has

The time has come the wal
talk of many things.
Of shoes, of ships, of sealin

You can rearrange elements in the structure tree by clicking and dragging the element to the desired position. You can also delete elements by selecting them and choosing Delete Element from the Tags palette menu, or by using the context menu. This does not delete the content from the document; it only deletes the associated structural element.

REFLOW TESTING AND EDITING

You can easily test to see if a document will reflow. Click the Reflow icon 🖹 on the tool bar, or choose View>Reflow. Change the size of the document window or the zoom factor. The text will reflow to fit the size of the document area. You must exit the Reflow mode to do any work on the document. Choose Actual Size, Fit in Window, or Fit Width on the tool bar or in the View menu to return to the Tagged PDF document in an unreflowed state.

You can also change the order that elements appear in the document with the TouchUp Order tool 🔳. (The TouchUp Order tool is not available for non-tagged documents.) Choose the TouchUp Order tool in the tool bar. Click the object you wish to be first. The number 1 appears in the rectangle for the object. Do the same for the rest of the objects. If you need to start over, choose any other tool in the tool bar and then go back to the TouchUp Order tool.

You can also change the order of just one or two objects in the middle of a sequence. Right-mouse click (w) or Control-click (m) with the TouchUp Order tool on the object that you want to move to a new reflow position. Choose one of the following commands: Make First, Make Last, Swap with Previous, Swap with Next, Bring to Front, Bring to Back, Bring Forward, or Send Backward. This will change the order of the selected object.

ACCESSIBILITY CHECKER

Once you've created a Tagged PDF, you can use the Accessibility Checker to see if the document meets accessibility standards. Choose Tools> Accessibility Checker. The Accessibility Checker Options dialog box opens. Under Options, you can choose to create a logfile that will list all the problems found in the document. If you choose this option, you can also choose where the logfile should be created. You can choose to create Comments around the areas that have problems, with notes explaining the problems. Use the Pages area to choose which pages should be checked. In the Check For area, select the items you wish to check. If you want your document to be totally compliant with current accessibility standards, leave all these options checked.

⚡ MANUALLY TAGGING

⑤ *Choose Tags>Document Is Tagged PDF. This sets the document as a Tagged PDF.*

⑥ *You can add line breaks where needed by using the TouchUp Text tool to place an insertion point at the end of the line. Then choose Tools>Touchup Text>Insert>Line Break. This keeps the next line from reflowing into the previous line when the text reflows.*

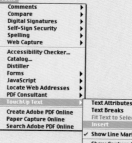

Setting the Alternate Tags

One of the most common problems the Accessibility Checker finds is the lack of Alternate Tags for graphics. (We found a missing alternate tag in the PDF file we exported from InDesign 2.) The alternate tag gives the screen reader the text that describes the information inside a graphic. Here's how you can set the alternate tags for objects.

Step ① Run the Accessibility Checker

You can find objects that are missing their alternate tags by running the Accessibility Checker. Choose Tools>Accessibility Checker and set the options to include the accessibility features you want to be in compliance with. Click OK to run the check. A dialog box will return the results. If you have chosen the Comments option, you'll also get comments around each of the problem objects.

Step ② Review the findings

Read the notes and delete the comments. If you have a figure that contains individual vector paths, you will have many comments in one position. Choose the Hand tool. Select and delete the comments.

Step ③ Open Element Properties

Use the TouchUp Object tool to select any object that has recorded an accessibility problem. If it is a series of vector paths, drag a rectangle around all the objects to select them as one object.

Choose Tags>Element Properties. Type the image description in the Alternate Text field. Click OK. Repeat for each additional element in the document. If you are having a hard time finding the element in the Tags palette, select Turn On Associated Content Highlighting from the Tags palette menu. Each item you select in the Tags palette will be highlighted in the document.

Document Language

If you are striving for Section 508 compliance, you'll need to specify the language of the document. The Accessibility Checker shows an error if the document language has not been specified. To specify an element's text language, find and select the element in the Tags palette (as high in the document structure tree as possible) that does not have a text language specified. Choose Tags>Element Properties from the context menu. Choose a language from menu in the dialog box and click OK.

Tables

If your authoring application has a built-in table function, use it. Professional application tables can be tagged more easily when the document is converted using a software application that supports Tagged PDF, or by using the Make Accessible plug-in.

Vector Graphics

Each line of a vector graphic can be interpreted as an individual object. This can cause tagging and accessibility problems for logos. If this happens, you have to delete the entire structure associated with the logo in the logical structure tree and create a new structure element manually. This is not fun.

READER FOR MOBILE DEVICES

In addition to accessibility standards, there is an even more important reason for creating Tagged PDF files: the ability to read PDF documents on portable digital assistants (PDA), such as Palm OS and Pocket PC devices. Tagged PDF documents can be transfered to your PDA and read at your convenience.

> **i** LANGUAGE
>
> *The language encodings for Tagged PDF are based on the International Organization for Standardization (ISO) standards.*
> *Brazilian Portuguese: PT-BR*
> *Chinese: ZH*
> *Danish: DA*
> *Dutch: NL*
> *English: EN*
> *UK English: EN-GB*
> *US English: EN-US*
> *Finnish: FI*
> *French: FR*
> *German: DE*
> *Italian: IT*
> *Japanese: JA*
> *Korean: KO*
> *Norwegian: NO*
> *Spanish: ES*
> *Swedish: SV*
>
> | |
> |---|
> | PT-BR |
> | ZH |
> | DA |
> | NL |
> | EN |
> | EN-GB |
> | EN-US |
> | FI |
> | FR |
> | DE |
> | IT |
> | JA |
> | KO |
> | NO |
> | ES |
> | SV |

We've done it—at least Sandee did. (Pattie Belle couldn't get the Acrobat for Palm software to work with her older Handspring device.) Sandee was not very impressed. Graphics were scaled down so much that reading the numbers on a chart was nearly impossible. In addition, the document has to rearrange text and shrink graphics. Normally, a PDF is meant to maintain the layout and visual integrity of a document. Because there is a great deal of undesign necessary to get a PDF file to work on a PDA device, Sandee wonders if it's worth it. Why not use another format to get the text and graphics onto a PDA?

Pattie Belle (who is much more of a pioneer than Sandee) counters that this is just the infancy of PDF on PDA. She says, "Give it time!" Imagine what the future of PDF on PDA could be—interactive demonstrations with forms, comments, buttons, movies, even sound!

Adobe Acrobat Reader for Palm OS

The Acrobat Reader for Palm OS is, as of this writing, in a beta test of version 2. The software is available for some, but not all, Palm and Handspring devices, depending on the software installed on the PDA itself and the Palm desktop software. There are two components of the software: The Acrobat Desktop software translates PDF documents into a format that is compatible with the PDA and then works with the Palm Desktop to transfer the files to the PDA during a Palm HotSync. The second component is the Reader software that resides on the PDA.

Adobe Acrobat Reader for Pocket PC

The Acrobat Reader for Pocket PC also has two components. The ActiveSync filter (available for Windows only) prepares untagged Adobe PDF files into a suitable format for the Pocket PC and transports the files into the user's device. The Acrobat Reader is a Pocket PC application that provides two ways to view any PDF document. The first way lets you view the document exactly as intended. This may require scrolling around if the document is not a Tagged PDF. The second way reflows Tagged PDF documents to fit the screen.

(1) Choose Tools> Accessibility Checker and set the options to specify types of problems to check for. Run the check. The dialog box tells you what types of problems were found.

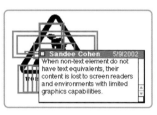

Accessibility Checker Options

Options
☑ Create Logfile   [Choose...]
☑ Create Comments in Document

Pages
● All Pages
○ Selected Pages
○ Pages from [1]   to [1]

Check for
☑ Alternate descriptions provided
☑ Text language specified
☑ Reliable character encodings
☑ All content contained in the document structure
☑ Form fields have descriptions

[Cancel] [OK]

> The checker found problems which may prevent the document from being fully accessible.
> 21 element(s) with no alternate text.
>
> [OK]

(2) If you have chosen to Create Comments in Document, you will see comments around the problems in the document. You can use the Hand tool to select and delete the comments. Vector objects may be interpreted as multiple objects.

Sandee Cohen 5/9/2002
When non-text element do not have text equivalents, their content is lost to screen readers and environments with limited graphics capabilities.

(3) Use the TouchUp Object Tool to select the problem object. Then choose Tags> Element Properties. Add the Alternate Text in the field. Run the Accessibility Checker again to make sure you have fixed all the problems.

Element Properties

Main Properties:

Title: [Logo]
Type: [Figure]
Actual Text: [ ]
Alternate Text: [Work in Process logo]
Language: [▼]
ID:
Revision Number: 0
Number Of Children: 1

Classes and Attributes:

▷ Classes:
▷ Attributes:

Classes:
[Add Class]
[Delete Class]

Attributes:
[Add Key]
[Change Key]
[Delete Key]

> The checker found no problems in this document.
>
> [OK]

[OK]

Security & Search Enhancements

This is where you get to step back and look the features that work with the

document as a whole. For instance, once you have enhanced your fabulous

PDF document and you're ready to distribute it, you should consider whether

you need to protect the file from unauthorized changes, using the security

options. You can also look at the Find and Index features, which let you

search through documents for specific information.

8.1 Restricting Viewing and Editing with Security

Distributing your finished PDF document to others may feel like sending your 5-year old daughter off to kindergarten for the first time. You want your child to meet other children, but you also need to protect her from talking to strangers, going to the wrong school, losing her lunch money to bullies, or even from telling other children your personal family secrets. Fortunately, there are several different ways you can protect PDF documents by setting the built-in security options.

Document security is an increasingly important factor in PDF work flow, particularly for documents that will be shared through e-mail, CD-ROMs, intranets, or the Internet. There are many different levels of security needed for PDF documents. For example, companies may send advance notice of new documents to their retail sales partners. The company doesn't want others to be able to open these documents. Another company may send a price sheet that they want to protect from someone altering the prices. An author may want to post a chapter from her book, but doesn't want anyone to be able to extract the text or graphics to use in their own documents. A publishing house may distribute books as PDF files, but not allow the books to be printed.

Acrobat lets you set a password at two different levels. The User password is required to allow people to open the document. Once the document is open, a Master password is required to change the security settings. In Acrobat version 5, the type of security encryption has been increased. This makes it harder for someone to break into a document. It also allows users to share documents between peo-

> **i MORE SECURITY**
>
> *There are lots of security add-on options for Acrobat PDF files. As of this writing, we know of at least 11 companies that provide security features that can be integrated into PDF documents. These companies include Entrust Technologies, FileOpen Systems, and Appligent.*

ple or locations with less fear of unauthorized viewing, printing, or editing. (Remember, no security solution is foolproof, but we'll cover that later.) Acrobat security settings can be specified when you first create a PDF file or at any time after the file has been created. Once you set the security restrictions, the tools and menu items related to the restricted features are dimmed in the tool bar and the main menu. This means that these tools are no longer accessible in the document.

PROTECTING WITH PASSWORDS

A PDF file can be protected with two passwords. A lower-level User password is set as the password required to open the document. A higher-level Master password is set as the password required to change any of the security options. You cannot choose the same password as both the User and the Master passwords. If a file has been protected with both a User and a Master password, you can use either one to open the file. If you open a file with a User password, you'll still need to enter the Master password in order to change the security options. Any restrictions on modifying and printing the document remain in effect. If you open a file with the Master password, you can also change the security options and all modifying and

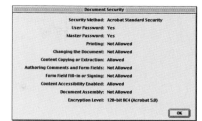

Document Security options control which features are active for a particular document, in either Acrobat or Acrobat Reader.

Don't think you can get around the security options by saving a copy of the file. The security options stay in place for the new file.

When a user password had been set, the password dialog box appears as the file is opened. The user must enter the correct password to open the file.

The Document Security dialog box shows which options in the document are allowed or not allowed.

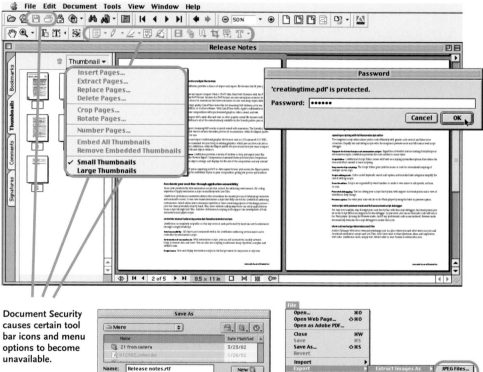

Document Security causes certain tool bar icons and menu options to become unavailable.

Even commands that appear to be allowed, such as saving text, will be denied.

printing restrictions can be turned off. (That's why we call the Master password the high-level security option.)

The most common method of securing a document is to set only the Master password. This lets anyone open the document without any restrictions, but only the master can change the security settings. If a User password has been set, but there is no Master password, then anybody who opens the document can change the security settings. Obviously, this type of security would be pointless. Yet we receive many PDF documents that have precisely this sort of brain-dead security setting. We also get a lot of documents that have very specific security settings, but no Master password at all. In these cases, anyone can march right in and change the security options.

Please be cautious and fastidious about documenting, tracking, and storing the passwords to your documents. If a password is lost or forgotten, there is no easy way to recover it. There are third-party solutions out there that will attempt to recover a password from a document, but this could take days or weeks, if recovery is successful at all. Legitimate password-recovery companies also require verification that you or your organization are the legal owners of the secured files and that the password recovery solutions will not be used for illegal activity. In general, the longer the password—the more difficult and longer the recovery.

At the basic software level, Acrobat does provide a measure of built-in protection. If you need added security, there are companies such as FileOpen and Appligent that offer plug-ins, add-ons, and server-based solutions that increase PDF security. Just as in real life, tighter PDF security comes with a price tag that might include usability issues. Digital rights management solutions for eBooks are an example of security measures that often result in an unusable document. Many eBook users complain that that when they upgrade system software, the eBook file is no longer recognized or that they can't transfer it to a new computer or PDA. We're all for protecting intellectual property, but the cost in time and frustration may simply not worth the added security.

With that said, let's get on with the basics. Acrobat has two basic built-in security options; Standard Security and Self-Sign Security. Both are accessed from File>Document Security, and both choices contain numerous options for restrictions and levels of document encryption.

ⓘ PASSWORD CHOICES

The longer a password, the harder it is to break into a document. Nonsense combinations of letters such as "zxcv" are harder to decipher than real words. Also, mixing cases, numbers, and symbols such as "Zx$2" is even more secure. Whatever password you choose, don't pick one like the password we found in a PDF file from a company we'll call "Acme Software." Someone set the Master password for a document we got from them as "Acme."

⚡ STANDARD SECURITY

① Add security to a document using the Document Security options. Choose File>Document Security to open the dialog box. Choose Acrobat Standard Security from the Security Options list. The Standard Security dialog box opens.

② Set the user password to enable the basic password security feature. All users must enter a given password to access the file. Passwords are case sensitive.

③ The 40-bit encryption offers backwards compatibility with Acrobat 3.x and 4.x. It provides four options for document permissions.

SETTING STANDARD SECURITY

The Standard Security option is the most common and easiest type of security to apply. It is used with documents that will be distributed to people you do not know.

Step (1)   Open the Security Options

Open a PDF in Acrobat 5 and choose File>Document Security. Choose Acrobat Standard Security from the Security Options list. This will automatically open the Standard Security dialog box.

Step (2)   Enter the Passwords

If you want to restrict certain Acrobat features, such as editing and printing, select Master Password and then type that password into the Master Password field. To restrict opening of the document to only those who have a password, select User password and then type that password in the User Password field. Passwords are case sensitive.

Step (3)   Set the Encryption Level

Use the Encryption Level list to set the complexity of the encryption of the document. The 40-bit encryption is a weaker level of encryption that is also used with Acrobat 3 and 4 documents. This setting should be used if you anticipate that the document will be opened by Acrobat 4 or Acrobat Reader 4. The 128-bit encryption is stronger, and works only with Acrobat 5 or Acrobat Reader 5. A document with 128-bit encryption settings cannot be opened by Acrobat version 4 or 3.

Step (4)   Control the Permissions

Although the two encryption levels are worded differently, the results are similar. However, the 128-bit encryption does provide a finer control over the options.

Enable Content Access for the Visually Impaired allows the document to be read by screen readers or other such devices. When this option is turned on, the security of the document is lowered.

Allow Content Copying and Extraction lets the user select and copy text and graphics. It also lets them extract images or save the document in a text format. Turn this off if you don't want others using your text or images in their own work.

The Changes Allowed list lets you choose what type of changes can be made. The options go from bottom to top in order of increasing level of restriction.

The Printing list lets you choose three options for printing. Fully allowed lets the user print with complete fidelity to the original images. Low Resolution limits the printing to the screen resolution of images and fonts.

> **ⓘ TOTAL SECURITY**
>
> *In case your mother never warned you, there are nasty, evil people out there. Just because you add security to a document doesn't mean that someone (like a 12-year old kid) won't try to hack into your document. There are constant reports of security flaws discovered in Acrobat and other electronic media. If your life's work would be lost if someone breached your document's security, then don't distribute it as a PDF file.*

(4) *Once you have chosen the encryption level and whether you need compatibility with Acrobat 4, you can select from a variety of permissions for the document.*

These are the options for setting 128-bit permissions. The permissions for both encryption levels are similar; but worded differently. 128-bit encryption is slightly more flexible.

Standard Security

Specify Password
- ☐ Password Required to Open Document
  - User Password: _____
- ☐ Password Required to Change Permissions and Passwords
  - Master Password: _____

Permissions
- Encryption Level: 128-bit RC4 (Acrobat 5.0) ⬥
- ☑ Enable Content Access for the Visually Impaired
- ☑ Allow Content Copying and Extraction
- Changes Allowed: General Editing, Comment and Form Field Authoring ⬥
- Printing: Fully Allowed ⬥

Cancel   OK

None
Only Document Assembly
Only Form Field Fill-in or Signing
Comment Authoring, Form Field Fill-in or Signing
General Editing, Comment and Form Field Authoring

Not Allowed
Low Resolution
Fully Allowed

RESTRICTING ACCESS WITH DISTILLER

You can also secure documents at the same time they are created. Start Distiller, and choose Settings>Security. You will be given the same 40-bit encryption dialog box that you see when setting document security in Acrobat. If you want to apply 128-bit security to your documents, you must first create a custom Job Options set. Start by choosing which set of Job Options you want to base your custom settings on (eBook, Print, Screen, etc.) and then select Settings>Job Options>Compatibility Acrobat 5. If you have based this new set on one of the "canned" Acrobat job options, then it will ask you to name and save this new set in the Job Options folder. Now, when you select Settings>Security, you'll see the dialog box for 128-bit encryption. You can also apply these security settings to the job options assigned to Watched Folders.

REMOVING SECURITY

There are times when you need to remove the security from a document. We remove security settings (especially the User password) when we're opening, closing, and making changes to a document. As long as you know the Master Password, removing security is easy. Go to File>Document Security. When the initial dialog box appears, select No Security from the Document Security pull-down menu. If you did not use the Master Password to open the document, a dialog box appears that asks for the Master Password. Acrobat will also ask if you are sure that you want to remove the security. Choose Yes, and the security is lifted.

SETTING SECURITY FOR BATCH PROCESSING

If you'd like to apply the same security settings to a group of PDF files, you can use Acrobat's built-in batch processing capabilities. Whatever you do, don't run the pre-made sequence that ships with Acrobat 5 labeled "Set Security to No Changes." While it will indeed set the security on all the chosen documents to No Changes, it does not add a Master password to keep someone from changing the Security Options (brain-dead security).

Fortunately, it's not too hard to create your own batch processing security setting.

Step 1   Create a New Batch Sequence
Choose File>Batch Processing>Edit Batch Sequences. In the Batch Sequence dialog box, click the New Sequence button. Enter a name for the sequence and click OK.

Step 2   Add Security to the Sequence
In the Batch Edit Sequence dialog box that

---

i   SEARCH & SECURITY

If you want users to be able to use the Catalog and Search functions on documents that don't allow content extraction, they must be sure to select the Certified Plug-ins Only option in their Options preferences. You may need to include instructions on how to change the preferences. Choose Edit>Preferences>General>Options. Check the box by Start Up>Certified Plug-ins only and restart Acrobat.

⚡ ADDING BATCH SECURITY

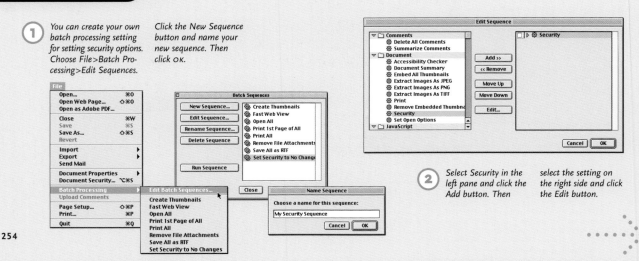

1. You can create your own batch processing setting for setting security options. Choose File>Batch Processing>Edit Sequences.

Click the New Sequence button and name your new sequence. Then click OK.

2. Select Security in the left pane and click the Add button. Then select the setting on the right side and click the Edit button.

opens, click the Select Commands button and then choose Security in the Document group in the left pane. Then click the Add button. This adds the Security listing to the right side of the dialog box. You now need to define the security options.

Step ③ Define the Security Options

Select the Security listing and click the Edit button. This opens the Document Security dialog box. Choose Acrobat Standard Security and click the Change Settings button. This opens the Standard Security dialog box. Define the security options you want for your batch sequence—make sure you enter a Master password. Click OK as many times as necessary to close the dialog boxes. The new sequence appears in the Batch Processing submenu. See the Batch Processing section in the previous chapter for more on running batch sequences.

CREATING SELF-SIGN SECURITY

Acrobat 5 provides additional security with the Self-sign Security option, which is essentially part of the digital signature system. Here, the documents are not secured with passwords, but with public keys that come from certificates provided by the intended recipients of the document. This means that you secure the document for one specific person. And it is only that person who can open the document (by using his own private key and password). This also means that you can customize the set of permissions for that individual. For instance, an editor may be allowed the ability to copy text and print the document, while the client can only read and approve the document.

Note that documents secured with Self-Sign security are harder to crack than "normal" password-secured documents. Acrobat also supports third-party signature tools and verification, such as the ones from Entrust and Appligent.

Setting up an Acrobat Self-Sign security system/work flow takes a bit of advance planning and preparation, as does any digital signature system. All participants in this chain must have the full version of Acrobat 5 or Acrobat Approval 5 in order to provide and approve User Certificates. Each participant must create a User Certificate and send it to you. On the other hand, the procedure is pretty simple, and your request for a certificate e-mail can be created automatically by Acrobat. You must then import these certificates into Acrobat. Here are the steps we took so that Bjørn could send Sandee and Pattie Belle PDF files encrypted with Self-Sign security. (This is just an example—we're not really that rigid about sending each other PDF files.)

③ *Choose Acrobat Standard Security from the Security Options, and then click the Change Settings button.*

Set the Standard Security options for the batch sequence.

Document Security

Security Options: [Acrobat Standard Security ⇕]

[Change Settings...]

[Close]

Standard Security

Specify Password
☐ Password Required to Open Document
User Password: [   ]
☑ Password Required to Change Permissions and Passwords
Master Password: [●●●●●●]

Permissions
Encryption Level: [128-bit RC4 (Acrobat 5.0) ⇕]

☑ Enable Content Access for the Visually Impaired
☑ Allow Content Copying and Extraction

Changes Allowed: [Only Document Assembly ⇕]
Printing: [Fully Allowed ⇕]

[Cancel] [OK]

Step ① Set the Self-Sign Preferences

Adobe recommends that you use the standard PKCS#7 format for the Self-Sign signature. This makes the signature compatible with other signature handlers, such as those from third-party vendors. To do this, all three of us set the Acrobat Self-Sign Security preferences by choosing Edit>Preferences>General. Select Self-Sign Security in the left pane of the Preferences dialog box, choose Use Certificate Message Syntax (PKCS#7 format) Signature, and click OK.

> **ⓘ PKCS#7 FORMAT**
>
> *The standard pkcs#7 format is specific to Self-Sign Security. You can't import certificates created by other applications, such as Microsoft Office.*

Step ② Create User Profiles

Each member of the team needs to create his or her own user profile. We chose Tools>Self-Sign Security>Log In, and then clicked New User Profile. In the Create New User dialog box, each person entered a name for their profile, created a password containing at least six characters, and confirmed the password. It was as simple as that. This created a password-protected file containing each person's name, password, and some other basic information. It also stored important information used for security purposes.

Step ③ Export/Collect User Certificates

As the content creator, Bjørn didn't have to do this step, but the other members of the group needed to export and send him their user certificates. These are FDF files that contain a unique set of serial numbers to make sure only the right person opens the PDF document. To export her user certificate, Sandee chose Tools>Self-Sign Security>User Settings. She chose User Information from the list on the left, and then clicked Export to File. She used the the Export Certificate As dialog box to name and select a location for the file. A dialog box explained that the file had been successfully exported. She wrote down the Fingerprint number strings that were displayed. Sandee then e-mailed the FDF file to Bjørn. When Bjørn got the file, he saved it on his hard drive.

Step ④ Create the Trusted Certificates

Once Bjørn collected the user certificates from Sandee and Pattie Belle, he used them to create a list of trusted certificates. He chose Tools>Self-Sign Security>User Settings. He then selected Trusted Certificates, clicked Import from File, and selected the FDF files from Sandee And Pattie Belle. The Verify Identity dialog box displayed descriptive information about the certificate. Although not necessary for our work flow, Bjørn could verify each user's certificate by having Pattie Belle and Sandee e-mail or phone him with the numerical fingerprint of their certificates.

Step ⑤ Assigning Recipients and Security

As the final step, Bjørn assigned each user her

⚡ SELF SIGN SECURITY

① *To make your certificates more compatible with other signature handlers, choose Edit>Preferences>General. Then select the User Certificate Message Syntax in the Self-Sign Security preferences.*

② *To create your own user profile, choose Tools>Self-Sign Security>Log In. Then click the New User Profile button. Enter your user attributes and password.*

own security settings. He opened the PDF and chose File>Document Security, then Acrobat Self-Sign Security. In the Self-Sign Security-Encryption Settings dialog box, he selected a name from the Trusted Certificates list, and then clicked Add to add it to the Recipients list. (The content creator's name is included in the Recipients list because that person is always viewed by Acrobat as a recipient of their own documents.)

Bjørn selected each recipient and specified the security options by clicking User Access, and then clicked User Permissions. In the User Permissions dialog box, he selected the access options. These are the same options you would set in Standard Security.

DIGITAL SIGNATURES

The Acrobat Digital Signature feature takes the security process even further by adding signature authorization and verification for approval of documents and legal transactions. Digital signatures allow you to electronically sign a document using a password-protected, encrypted electronic "certificate," and to e-mail your certificate to others to verify your signature.

Digital signatures can be used to authenticate all sorts of transactions, from tax forms to applications to contracts.

In the summer of 2000, a bill was signed into law that gives digital signatures the same legal status as a handwritten signature. This law applies to various legal documents (specific ones vary on a state-by-state basis). Not long after the U.S. law was passed, the European Union also approved legislation to recognize digital signatures as the legal equivalent to a handwritten signature.

The same User Certificates we discussed in the previous section can also be used as authentication for signatures in an approval process or document signing procedure, such as legal papers of various kinds. Like a conventional signature, a digital signature uniquely identifies the person signing a document. This means that people can sign your electronic document, instead of a printed one.

The application of a digital signature also applies a time stamp to the document, and associates the signature with the state of the document. This means that the viewer of a document can tell if there have been any changes made after a document has been signed.

The Signatures Palette

If you have digital signatures in a document, you can see a list of those signatures in the Signatures palette which is available in Acrobat 5 and Acrobat Approval 5. Choose Window>Signatures or select the Signature tab in

③ *Each user needs to export their own security certificate. Choose Tools>Self-Sign Security>User Settings. Then click the Export* *to File button. Name and save the file. The confirmation message lets you know the file has been successfully exported.*

These fingerprints can be used to verify the authenticity of the certificate with the owner.

the document window. The palette lists all the signatures in the document, and includes the name of the person who created the signature, the date, and the verification status. A question mark means the signature is unverified and a checkmark means it is verified. You can use the Verify All Signatures command in the Signatures palette menu to verify all the signatures in a document at once. The Signatures palette also displays a red alert icon that lets you know if a document has been modified since the signatures were applied.

DIGITALLY SIGNING A DOCUMENT

If you want to sign a PDF digitally, you first have to create a user profile in the same way you create a certificate for Self-Sign Security. The digital signature can be displayed with text information or custom graphics, such as your scanned handwritten signature or company logo. Document recipients can verify your signature's authenticity when you e-mail them your certificate. This feature is as secure as any password-protected document. Just as with the Self-Sign security work flow, you'll need some advance planning. In addition, everyone in the digital signature work flow needs the full version of Acrobat 5 or Acrobat Approval 5 in order to participate. Let's say Pattie Belle wants Sandee to digitally sign an agreement to work on their next project. Here are the steps they would take.

Step 1 Set Preferences and User Profile

Both Sandee and Pattie Belle need to set the application that will handle the certification of their digital signatures. They choose Edit> Preferences>General and then select Digital Signatures. They then choose Acrobat Self-Sign Security from the Default signature handler list. (If you have installed third-party security plug-ins, they'll appear in the Default signature handler list.) Both of them also need to create their own user profile. This is the same method as for Self-Sign security, so if you have done this for Self-Sign security, you don't need to do it again. Choose Tools>Self-Sign Security> Log In, and click New User Profile. Enter a name and password and save the profile.

Step 2 Signing Documents

Pattie Belle then sends Sandee the PDF agreement. After Sandee reads the document, she chooses the Digital Signature tool to create a signature field. After she releases the mouse button, the Sign Document dialog box appears. Sandee enters her password, as well as any other information she wants included in the signature field. This can be a message in the Reason For Signing field, her location, or contact information, such as a phone number. Sandee clicks the Save button which creates the digital signature and saves the file. Sandee then sends the signed PDF document back to Pattie Belle.

⚡ SELF SIGN SECURITY

④ *The user certificates are added as Trusted Certificates by choosing Tools>Self-Sign Security>User Settings and* *then choosing Trusted Certificates. Click Import from File to import the certificates. The certificates can be* *verified by having the user send separate confirmation of the numerical fingerprints.*

⑤ *Trusted certificate users can be added to the Recipients list. Then the User Access for* *that recipient can be set for specific access.*

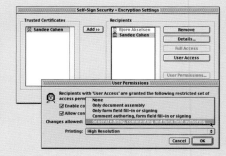

1 Each user starts by setting the Default signature handler in the Digital Signatures preferences. The user also needs to create a user profile. Choose Tools>Log In, then click the New User Profile button. Enter the name, other information, and password.

2 Use the Digital Signature tool to drag a rectangle for the digital signature field. This opens the Sign Document dialog box. Enter the password and other information and click the Save button. The signature appears in the document.

3 If a digital signature's validation is unknown, double-click the field to open the Validation Status. This opens the Verify Identity dialog box, which displays the numerical fingerprints for the signature. These numbers can be checked with the person who signed the document.

Step ③ Verifying the Signature

Pattie Belle has never received a user certificate from Sandee; so when Pattie Belle opens the document, Sandee's signature is displayed as not verified. Pattie Belle needs to add Sandee's name as a trusted certificate. In addition to getting the certificate from an FDF file (as described earlier), Pattie Belle can create a trusted certificate directly from the digital signature in the PDF file. Pattie Belle double-clicks the digital signature field, which opens the Validation Status dialog box. This opens the Verify Identity dialog box that displays the numerical fingerprints for Sandee's signature.

Pattie Belle calls Sandee (using the phone number given in the contact information) and asks for her fingerprint numbers. If Sandee never wrote these numbers down, she chooses Tools>Log In, enters her password, and clicks the User Settings button. She then clicks the Details button. This opens the Certificate Attributes dialog box, which displays the numbers. She reads the numbers to Pattie Belle. Since they match, Pattie Belle clicks the Add to List button, which validates the signature.

Invisible Signatures

You don't have to create a visible signature to sign a document. Using Acrobat, you can choose Tools>Digital Signatures>Invisibly Sign Document. This launches the same dialog boxes as if you had used the Digital Signature tool.

The only difference is that after you finish signing the document, the only display of the signature is within the Signatures palette.

Signing in Acrobat Approval

If you have the full version of Acrobat, you can add a digital signature using the Digital Signature tool (this tool does not exist in Acrobat Approval). What happens if you send a document to someone with Acrobat Approval? Can they sign the document? Absolutely; you just need to prepare the document ahead of time. First, using the full version of Acrobat, choose the Form tool and draw a field on the page. In the Field Properties dialog box, set the type of field to Signature. Enter text for the Short Description that indicates that this is the field to be signed. You may want to add a background or border appearance so the user can identify the field.

The user also needs to create a user profile in Acrobat Approval. The steps are the same as in the full version of Acrobat. When the user opens the document, they can click inside the field to sign the document.

CREATING GRAPHIC AND CUSTOM SIGNATURES

You can customize your signature by using a picture or a combination of graphics and words. You might want to use your company logo or a scan of your handwritten signature.

⚡ GRAPHIC SIGNATURES

① Create the graphic or scan an image. Use whatever application you want to save the image as a PDF document.

② Choose Tools>Self-Sign Security>Log In. Then choose Signature Appearance. Click the New button to create a new signature appearance. Click the PDF File button and then the Browse button to select the PDF file that contains the signature graphic.

Step ① Create the Graphic

Start by creating a graphic in any authoring application. Then convert the graphic into a PDF document—it has to be a PDF. Pattie Belle opened the IceHouse Studio logo in Adobe Illustrator. Sandee used Illustrator's Brush tool to scribble her own name in vector art. If your artwork is on a transparent background, it remains transparent when converted to the signature graphic. Scanned images, such as handwritten signatures, will have a white background behind the image. You don't have to worry about the size of the signature because Acrobat also automatically scales the graphic to fit in the signature field.

Step ② Add the Graphic to the User Profile

You must be logged into Acrobat using your User Profile. (Choose Tools>Self-Sign Security> Log In. Then click User Settings in the Alert message or choose Tools>Self-Sign Security> User Settings.) Select Signature Appearance in the left pane of the User Settings dialog box, and click New to create a new signature appearance. You can create several different appearances, depending on the type of document you are signing, or on your mood. In the Configure Signature Appearance dialog box, enter a name for the signature that will help you identify it later. Your current signature appears in the preview box.

To add the graphic to the signature, choose the Imported Graphic option and click the PDF File button. This will open the Select Picture dialog box. Here, you can browse to select the PDF document containing the signature graphic.

Step ③ Configure the Signature Text

Digital signatures may contain text along with the image. Choose each of the options in the Configure Text area as follows. Name shows the ordinary name of the user. Location shows the information in the Location field of the Sign Document dialog box. Distinguished Name shows the user attributes defined in the profile, like name, organization, and country. Date adds the date the signature was applied. Logo adds a pink Acrobat logo behind the signature. Reason displays the information entered in the Reason field of the Sign Document dialog box. Validity text adds text to the validation checkmark or question mark. Finally, the Labels option adds explanation labels to all the text elements in the signature. When you are done, click OK in Configure Signature Appearance, and close the User Settings dialog box. Drag with the Digital Signature tool to see your graphic signature.

If you want to edit your signature, log in to Acrobat Self-Sign Security and choose Tools> Self-Sign Security>User Settings. Select the Signature Appearance in the left pane of the User Settings dialog box.

③ *The final appearance of the signature is a combination of the options selected in the Configure Appearance dialog box and the information entered in the Sign Document dialog box.*

DOCUMENT COMPARE

You can also use Digital Signatures to track changes to a document between signings, or to track differences between two versions of a document. Acrobat highlights the changes made between signatures and summarizes them. The summary shows what changes were made when, and by whom. The versions can be viewed side-by-side in a tiled window.

Step ① Create the Signed Documents

Start with two signed versions of a document, or a single document that was signed on two separate occasions. Then choose Tools>Compare>Two Documents or Tools>Compare> Two Versions Within a Signed Document.

Step ② Set the Comparison Options

The Compare Document or Compare Document Revisions dialog boxes appear. In the Compare Document dialog box, use the Choose buttons to select the two different documents. In the Compare Document Revisions dialog box, use the Compare and To lists to choose which versions of the document to evaluate.

In the Type of Comparison area, choose how you'd like to view the differences. The option Page by Page With Visual Differences looks for any type of differences between the documents. This may include adding comments or fields, moving items, changing text or graphics, modifying colors, or changing pages. The comparison shows the pages with differences outlined. You can also set how sensitive Acrobat should be to differences between the pages. High sensitivity looks for changes as small as a pixel. The option for Text Only outlines the changes to text. The options for Text Including Font Information outlines text changes that also include changing font size, typeface, etc. Click the OK button to make the comparison.

Step ③ Set the Comparison Options

When you compare documents, Acrobat creates a new PDF file. This new document contains opening pages that summarize the differences between the documents. The new PDF also contains side-by-side pages from the two documents with the differences outlined using Acrobat's Pencil tool.

Acrobat does not actually list the changes that have been made. It only outlines the differences between the documents. In order to know what changes were made, you'll need to look for what is different within the outlined areas.

1. Choose one of the two commands in the Compare submenu to compare two separate signed documents or two versions of the same signed document.

2. Use the Compare: and To: menus to choose which two documents to compare or which two versions of the document to compare. Set the Type Of Comparison for visual differences, differences in text, or text including font changes. If you choose visual differences, set how sensitive Acrobat should be to differences.

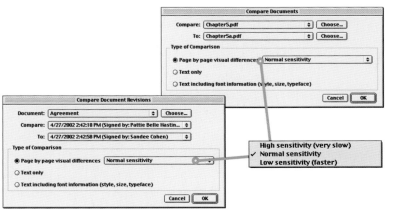

3. Scroll through the side-by-side documents to see where the changes have been made. Some changes may be too small to be recognized by ordinary examination.

8.2 Using Find and Search Commands

We can barely remember where we left the house keys, so the idea of remembering which page of a PDF file contains a specific word or phrase is out of the question. Fortunately Acrobat contains two separate features that let you quickly look through PDF files for specific text phrases. We only wish we had such features for the other parts of our lives.

Although Find and Search may seem like synonyms for the same feature, they are two separate commands that differ in both range and complexity. The Find command is limited to looking for text within a single PDF document —for instance, a single chapter in a book. The Search command is more powerful and can look through multiple documents—for instance, all the chapters in a book.

Think of a company that sends out newsletters as PDF documents every month. When a recipient receives a copy, she can use the Find command to look through the open file for specific topics. She then carefully files each month's newsletter with dozens of others in a single directory. She uses the Search command to look through all the the newsletters for a specific topic. The command returns a list of all the newsletters that contain the topic. She doesn't even have to have those documents open.

Which should you use? The Find command is available at any time—without any extra work on your part. The Search command requires you to plan ahead and create an index of all the files to be scanned.

For a single, short document, the Find command is all you need. It may even be useful for quickly scanning two or three short files. However, if you work with text-heavy, complex documents it may be worth the extra effort to create a Search index.

ACROBAT READER FIND AND SEARCH

The basic Acrobat Reader download contains the Find command. However, you'll need to download Acrobat Reader with Search and Accessibility for Windows, or Acrobat Reader with Search for Macintosh, in order to get the Search command. These are separate and distinctly different versions of Acrobat Reader, both of which are available from the Adobe website. However, only the full-version of Acrobat can create the indexes that are necessary for the Search command to work.

THE FIND COMMAND

The strength of the Find command is in its simplicity—it can be applied to any PDF document at any time with no advance preparation. Open the Find dialog box by clicking the Find icon in the tool bar or by choosing Edit> Find. Type the text string you want to look for in the Find What field.

Text String Strategies

Carefully consider the text string you enter in the Find What field. You don't want to enter too generic a term or Acrobat will stop too often. For instance, in a geography book, it is much faster to look for "Mississippi River" than just "river". Watch out, though—you don't want to get too specific. If you enter the term "Pres. of the United States," the Find command does not stop at "President of the United States."

You can open the Find dialog box by clicking the Find icon in the tool bar or by choosing Edit>Find.

The Find command returns the results as highlighted words in the document window. To move to the next result—on a page-by-page basis—click Find Again in the Find dialog box.

The Find dialog box allow you to refine the Find criteria by selecting Match Whole word only (excludes words that contain your find word as part of it), Match Case

(case sensitive), Find Backwards (search back all the way from the current page) and Ignore Asian Character Width (leave this unchecked).

The Find button changes to Find Again after the first initial search. Keep clicking Find Again to move through all the results successively.

File   Edit   Document   Tools   View   Window   Help

100%

Creating Time

PART 1   PART 2   PART 3   ARTICLES
Exercise 1   Exercise 3   Energy 101   Value of Time
Exercise 2   Exercise 4   Exercise 7   Digital vs Analog
               Exercise 5   Eat, Drink & be Merry
               Exercise 6

HAVING A LIFE WHILE MAKING A LIVING—PART 1

Almost forty years of time management books, theories, techniques, workshops, and planning systems... and where has it gotten us? Do we have more time? Are we less stressed? Are our lives more fulfilled? The answer for most of us is, resoundingly, No.

We don't have the forum here to give you a sweeping overview of why this may be the case, though consider this:

The term "time management" is somewhat of an oxymoron. Einstein demonstrated that time does not exist on its own. You can't manage time.

You can only manage your passage through it. (But you

have also radically transformed the way we work. In virtually every area, companies accomplish more with fewer workers, millions of people find them-

selves in "one-person" companies or as busy freelancers, and

efficiency. Great if you're making widgets in a world that never changes.

Find

Find What: [time   ]   [**Find Again**]

☐ Match Whole Word Only   [Cancel]
☐ Match Case
☐ Find Backwards
☐ Ignore Asian Character Width

5 of 45   9 × 6 in

You can also choose any of the following options to narrow the results when you use the Find command.

Match Whole Word Only

This option limits the search highlight to only whole words based on the text string you enter. For instance, searching for the word "record" will not highlight a portion of the word "recording." This option affects both single and multiple word searches. For example, if you check this option, a search for the text string "news report" does not return the phrase "news reporter".

Match Case

Check this feature to make your search case sensitive. So a search for the word "Earth" (as in planet) does not return the word "earth" (as in ground). Similarly, a search for the word "buffalo" (as in the animal) doesn't return "Buffalo" (the city).

Find Backwards

The Find command usually searches forward from the current position to the end of the document. If you select this option, the Find works backwards from the current position to the beginning of the document.

Ignore Asian Characters

Leave this box unchecked unless you are working with the Asian version of Acrobat and need to search for Asian characters. When the Find command finds a match, it stops and highlights the term. You can stop, or click the Find Again button to look for more instances of the text string. Repeat this process until you reach the end of the document.

THE SEARCH COMMAND

At first glance it may seem that the Search command is simply a multi-document Find command. Far from it—the Search command offers an incredible set of sophisticated search options. The Search command lists all the matches instead of moving through the highlights one by one. The command is not limited to finding just the exact text string; it can find derivatives of a search word. It can search for two or more words that are in close proximity to each other. The Search command can also search for other information about the document. The Search command does require some advanced preparation.

CREATING A SEARCHABLE INDEX

There are two parts to using the Search command. First, the creator of the PDF must create a searchable index (for the end-user of the PDF to perform searches). This is a set of documents that contain references to the PDF documents. Instead of plowing through the original PDF files, the Search command looks through the index documents; then it displays the PDF files

⚡ CREATING AN INDEX

1 Choose Tools > Catalog to open the Adobe Catalog dialog box. Then click the New Index button.

2 Enter an Index Title and Index Description. Click the Options button to open the Options dialog box. Type the words to exclude from the index. Also, set the other controls to exclude numbers, optimize for CD-ROM, add IDs for Acrobat 1 files, and add the Word options. Click OK when done.

that contain the search criteria. This makes the Search command much faster and more powerful than the Find.

Before you create the index for a group of files, it is a good idea to make sure the documents are proofed and checked. You may also want to gather the files into a single directory. This is important since the index and the PDF documents it references need to be in the same relative positions on the hard drive in order to work with each other. Keeping all the files in a single directory makes it easy to move them to other drives or burn to a CD.

Step ① Define and Name the New Index
Choose Tools>Catalog. This opens the Adobe Catalog dialog box. Click the New Index button to open the New Index Definitions dialog box.

Step ② Set Title, Description and Options
In the New Index Definition dialog box, enter a descriptive name for the index in the Index Title field. This is not the name of the index file, but a descriptive name that lets the user know which files the index is referenced to. You can also enter additional information in the Index description.

Click the Options button. If you want, you can add words that you don't want indexed such as but, not, and the. This helps reduce the size of the index and makes the searches faster. However, excluded words can't be used

as part of a search. So you may need to instruct other users that they have been excluded from the index. You can also choose to omit numbers from the index.

Check which Word options you want to be able to search for. Case sensitive recognizes the difference between upper and lower case words. Sounds Like finds words that are spelled differently, but sound alike. This lets you find differences in spelling of proper names, such as Pattie Belle and Patty Bell. Word Stemming looks at the root of a word and then finds derivatives of the words. This means a search for the word "create" will also find "creative".

The Optimize for CD-ROM organizes the index files in a way that makes it easy for them to be copied onto a CD-ROM. It also turns off the alerts that appear if the original files are modified after the index has been created.

Step ③ Save the Index and Choose Files
Click the Save As button to create and name the index file. Mac users should add the extension .pdx so that the index can be used in a cross-platform environment. We save the index in the directory that contains the PDF files. This makes it easier to move the PDF documents and index to other volumes or to burn them onto a CD-ROM. Click the Add button in the Include These Directories area to choose the actual PDF files from which the index will be built. When making the index, make sure that

③ Click the Save As button to name and save the file. Use the Add button in the Include These Directories to select the files you want to index. Use the Add button in the Exclude These Subdirectories to skip other files.

④ Click the Build button in the New Index Definitions dialog box to create the index. This returns you to the Adobe Catalog dialog box. A progress bar shows the status of the index.

you choose all directories you want to include. You can select more than one. Use the Add button in the Exclude These Subdirectories area to exclude certain sub-folders.

Step ④ Build the Index

Click the Build button. This closes the New Index Definitions and builds the index. If you didn't save the index in the previous step, a dialog box opens, giving you an opportunity to can save the index.

When you create an index, the Catalog command creates the following items: the index.pdx file, a folder that includes nine sub-folders, and a file called index.log. Keep these files with the original PDF documents. If you need to move the files to a new volume, keep them in the same relative path positions on the new disk.

USING THE SEARCH COMMAND

If the Search command were only a way to scan multiple documents at once, it might not be worth all the advance preparation. But the Search command offers a variety of features that make it much more intelligent than the Find command. Some of these features, such as the Case sensitive, Sounds Like, and Word Stemming are available only if you have set those options when you built the index.

> **ⓘ SEARCH OPTIONS**
>
> If you are interested in using operator characters, Boolean operators (AND, OR, and NOT), and other advanced search techniques, you can find more information in the Acrobat Support Knowledge-base on the Adobe website.

Other features are available regardless of how the index was built. These include using the Boolean operators: AND, OR, and NOT. This allows you to search for documents that contain both House and Senate. You can also use wild-card characters such as * which lets you match none, one, or more characters. For instance, a search for "U*S*" returns a match for "U.S.," as well as "United States."

PERFORMING A SEARCH

Once you have created the index, you can set the variables for the Search command.

Step ① Opening the Search Dialog Box

Choose Edit>Search>Query or click the Search icon 🔍 in the tool bar. This opens the Adobe Acrobat Search dialog box. (You can customize the look of this dialog box as explained later in this section.)

Step ② Set the Search Term and Options

Type the text you want to search for in the Find Results Containing Text field. Check the Options to control the text matches. (Some options are not available depending on how the index was created.) Word Stemming finds derivatives of the search term. Sounds Like finds alternate spellings of proper names. Thesaurus finds synonyms of the search term. The Proximity option limits searches so that the words are within three pages of each

⚡ PERFORMING A SEARCH

① Click the Search icon or choose Edit>Search> Query. This opens the Adobe Acrobat Search dialog box.

② Type the text string in the Find Results Containing Text field.

③ Click the Indexes button in the Adobe Acrobat Search dialog box to open the Index Selection dialog box. Click the Add or

Remove buttons to change the list of available indexes. Click the check box to select the indexes to be used in the search.

other. (Thesaurus is not available if Proximity is turned on.) Match case limits the search to the same upper or lower case words. (Match case turns off Word Stemming, Sounds Like, and Thesaurus.)

Step ③ Choose the Index

Your final option (before the search) should be to select the indexes to be used during the search. Click the Indexes button in the Adobe Acrobat Search dialog box. This opens the Index Selection dialog box, which displays a list of all indexes that have been defined and added to the list. Click the Add button and navigate to the folder/directory where the new index.pdx is located. Use the Remove button to remove an index. You're not limited to searching through just a single index. Use the check boxes to choose as many indexes as you want. When you have chosen the indexes, click the OK button.

You can also choose File>Document Properties>Associated Index to automatically apply an index to a file. However, note that you can attach only one index to a given file.

Step ④ Run the Search

Click the Search button in the Adobe Acrobat Search dialog box to start the scan. The Search Results dialog box displays a list of all the documents that contain the search term.

Step ⑤ Display the Match Highlights

Choose one of the selected documents and then click the View button. The results are displayed as highlighted selections in the document window. If there are multiple pages in the document with the search term, click the Next Highlight button ▶ to view the search results on the next page, or the Previous Highlight button ◀ to view the previous highlights. You can also use the commands in the Edit> Search submenu to move through the document.

If you have too many results from the search, you can use Boolean terms to refine the results. For instance, if the original search was for the text "New York City" you can add AND "downtown" to narrow the search. Hold the Alt key (w) or Option key (m). The Search button changes to Refine. Click the Refine button to see the shorter list of search results.

WORD ASSISTANT

When you add the options for Thesaurus, Word Stemming, and Sounds Like as part of a search, the results will include words other than the text typed in the search dialog box. You may want to know what words these options will add. Use the Word Assistant to see which words will be added.

Choose Edit>Search>Word Assistant. This opens the Word Assistant dialog box. Enter the search word in the Word field. Choose one of the options from the Assist menu. The three settings, Word Stemming, Sounds Like, and

④ *The Search Results dialog box displays the documents that contain the search terms. The pie chart graphs show the amount of relevance each document has to the original term.*

⑤ *Choose a document and then click the View button in the Search Results. The document opens with the words highlighted.*

Use the Next Highlight or Previous Highlight icons on the tool bar, or the commands in the Edit>Search menu, to move to each match.

269

The Search command is accessed by clicking in the tool bar or by choosing Edit>Search>Query. The tools available in the Search category include:

Search Query

Search Results

Next Highlight

Previous Highlight

The Search command must be enabled through the Catalog tool by creating indexes. You can index many PDF files simultaneously.

The Search command returns the results as highlighted words in the document window. Search displays all occurrences on the same page simultaneously. To move to the results on the next page, click Next highlight or Previous highlight to go back a page at the time.

HEADLINES

Set the Search to Thesaurus to find synonyms for the search term. Here, a search for images with

Thesaurus turned on returned the words "pictures" and "shows".

Set the Search to Proximity to find two separate terms on the same page.

The pie-chart symbols next to each result shows how close the result matches the original search term.

Select each result and click View to go to the match. Click Info to find Info about the document that contains the match.

Thesaurus correspond to the options in the Search dialog box. Click the Indexes button to choose the indexes that will be used for the search. You can then click the Look Up button. This provides you with a list of the words that will be found as part of the search.

SEARCH PREFERENCES

Choose Edit>Preferences> Search to open the Acrobat Search Preferences dialog box. These preferences let you control how the Search command performs.

Document Options: Check this option if you want to search for the information in the Document Properties>Summary dialog box. This includes document title, keywords, author, and so on. Of course, it does no good to choose this option if you have not set any of the document properties.

Word Options: This is the default option that lets you search using text strings.

Date Filtering: This lets you search by the document's creation or modification dates. This is especially helpful in searching through the indexes for newsletters and other periodicals.

Sort By List: Use this to control the order in which the search results are displayed.

Show First: Set this to the number of searches you want to have displayed.

Next Highlight List: Choose how highlights are displayed: by page, by word, or not at all.

Hide Query Dialog on Search: Check this option to close the Adobe Acrobat Search dialog box after you press the Search button.

Hide Results Dialog on Search: Check this option to close the Search Results dialog box after you press the View button.

Automount Servers: This controls the indexes on servers.

CATALOG PREFERENCES

The Catalog preferences control how the index is built and how the Catalog features perform. You can open the Catalog preferences by using Tool>Catalog and then clicking the Preferences button. There are five preference categories. In most cases, you can leave the settings at their defaults.

General

Delay Before Purge (seconds): This setting lets you set an amount of time that the Purge command waits before discarding inactive links in an index. The default setting delays the command by 15 minutes. This gives others who may be using the index on a network time to stop using it. If you are the only one using the index, you can choose a shorter time.

Document Section Size (words): This refers to the amount of memory allocated to process the document. The more memory you allocate, the faster the search is processed. A small amount is considered 200,000 words; medium is 400,000 words; and large is 800,000 words. If the document exceeds this setting, Acrobat creates additional indexes for the document.

Group Size for CD-ROM: This controls the number of documents indexed. Do not exceed the maximum number of documents, which is 4,000.

Index Available After x Documents: This controls how fast a (partial) index is available after revisions. You can use a range from 16 to 4,000.

Minimum Range for Building Indexes (KB): The higher you set the value, the less likely that indexing will be aborted as a result of the disk cache falling below the set value. The larger the setting, the faster the result. If you experience memory issues while working with the Search command, increase this amount.

Allow Indexing on Separate Drive: This lets you create indexes on separate drives.

Make Include/Exclude Folders DOS Compatible: This is used for cross-platform indexing. Mac users must use the DOS compatible naming conventions.

Index Defaults

These are default settings that can also be changed in the Options dialog box when creating an index.

Do Not Include Numbers: When you exclude numbers from the index, the search and updating will be faster.

Optimize For CD-ROM: We always enable this option, as it speeds up searches on CD-ROMS.

Add IDs to Acrobat 1.0 PDF Files: This is important for files created with Distiller 1.0.

Word Options: Case Sensitive, Sounds Like, Words Stemming: If these are not checked, you won't have the options available when searching the index.

Logging

Whenever you create an index with the Catalog function, a log file is created that contains specifics about the index. The Logging preferences determine how you want the log file to appear. You can leave these settings at default unless you are familiar with logging.

Enable Logging: This must be checked for the logging function to work.

Log Search Engine Messages: Leave checked if you want the log to function.

Log Compatibility Warnings: Check this option if you want compatibility warnings to be part of the log file.

Maximum Log File Size: Use the default size of 1 mb unless you have reason to suspect that the file will need to be larger.

Log File Name: Use the default Catalog name that appears unless you have reason to use another name.

Save Log File In: Unless you specify another location, the log file will be saved inside the Acrobat application folder by default.

Index File Location: This option gives you control over the index.pdx file.

Default Index Name: This lets you choose the name that first appears when you save the index.pdx file.

Save Index: This lets you choose a custom location for the file. We leave this as the default location so we can maintain the relative path locations.

Custom Fields

You can create your own custom fields in the PDF document. You can then add the definitions for these fields in the Catalog preferences. For more information, see the Acrobat Java-Script Object Specification and the documentation for the Acrobat Software Development Kit (SDK).

Should you accidentally make changes and forget the defaults, you can restore the original default settings by clicking in the Restore All Defaults button in the lower-left corner of the Catalog Preferences dialog box.

Choose Tools>Catalog and then click the Preferences button to open the Catalog Preferences. Click each of the five categories on the left of the dialog box.

These preferences control how the Catalog command builds new indexes and works with existing indexes.

Catalog Preferences

General
Index Defaults
Logging
Index File Location
Custom Fields

Index
Delay before purge (seconds): 905
Document section size (words): 250000
Group size for CD-ROM: 4000
Index available after: 1024 documents
Minimum memory for building indices (KB): 128
☑ Allow indexing on separate drive
☐ Make include/exclude folders DOS compatible

Restore All Defaults   Cancel   OK

Catalog Preferences

Index Defaults
☐ Do not include numbers
☐ Optimize for CD-ROM
☐ Add IDs to Acrobat 1.0 PDF files

Word Options:
☑ Case sensitive ☑ Sounds like ☑ Word stemming

Catalog Preferences

Logging
☑ Enable logging
☑ Log search engine messages
☐ Log compatibility warnings
Maximum log file size: 1024 Kilobytes
Log file name: Catalog
Save log file in: Application Folder
Custom Folder...

Catalog Preferences

Custom Fields

Field Name:

Field Type:
✓ Integer
Date
String

Remove

Custom field changes in an existing index will occur, the
purge and re-build the index.

Catalog Preferences

Index File Location
Default index name: index.pdx
Save Index: Inside First Include Folder

Cancel   OK

Choose Edit>Preferences>Search to open the Acrobat Search Preferences dialog box. Choose the options in Results to control

how the documents are displayed. Set the Display list to control the highlights for matches. Set the View Dialog Options to show or

hide the Query and Results during the search. Set Indexes to Automount Servers.

Select the options for Document Information or Date Filtering to add to the default setup of the Adobe Acrobat Search dialog box.

Include in Query
☐ Document Information
☑ Word Options
☐ Date Filtering

Acrobat Search Preferences

Include in Query
☐ Document Information
☑ Word Options
☐ Date Filtering

OK
Cancel

Results
Sort By: Title
Show First: 100 documents

Display
Next Highlight: Show By Page

View Dialog Options
☑ Hide Query Dialog on Search
☐ Hide Results Dialog on Search

Indexes
☑ Automount servers

Score
✓ Title
Subject
Author
Keywords
Created
Modified
Creator
Producer

✓ Show By Page
Show By Word
No Highlighting

Adobe Acrobat Search

Find Results Containing Text

Search
Clear
Indexes...

Options
☐ Word Stemming   ☐ Thesaurus   ☐ Match Case
☐ Sounds Like   ☐ Proximity

Searching in the Chapters to CaryID 2 YQS index.

☑ Document Information
☑ Word Options
☑ Date Filtering

Find Results Containing

Search
Clear
Indexes...

With Document Info
Title
Subject
Author
Keywords

With Date Info
Creation after   /   /   before   /   /
Modification after /   /   before   /   /

Options
☐ Word Stemming   ☐ Thesaurus   ☐ Match Case
☐ Sounds Like   ☐ Proximity

Searching in the Chapters to CaryID 2 YQS index.

Multimedia

Nothing has the potential to capture your attention like multimedia and inter-

activity. However, the cost to deliver multimedia content—in time, as well as

money—has been prohibitive for most people. With software such as Acrobat,

sound and movies can be integrated and delivered with relative ease. Though

Acrobat 5 does not come with as many powerful features as some of the stand-

alone multimedia and interactive software, it removes the steep learning curves

often associated with multimedia applications. It may be may be helpful to

think of Acrobat as a stage on which all sorts of tricks can be performed. Acrobat

enables all these multimedia components not only to coexist with other power-

ful interactive features, it has the flexibility to integrate multimedia content you

would never believe was carried by a PDF.

9.1 | About Multimedia Capabilities

Hooray for Hollywood! Ever since Edison played back his own voice reciting Mary Had a Little Lamb, the world knew the power of recorded sounds. Ever since the first Nickelodeon movie theater in downtown Pittsburgh, people have recognized the thrill of moving pictures. However, it took computer-graphics engineers to create the new experience of interactive multimedia. At first, interactive multimedia could only be created using very complex programs. Today, it is very easy to create and display interactive multimedia documents using Adobe Acrobat and Acrobat Reader.

The ease with which you can add media clips and interactivity to a PDF document is changing the nature of business and educational presentations. Instead of slide shows with simple words and limited graphics, Acrobat allows you to add an exciting array of movies, sounds, and animation effects. However, as exciting as this technology is, it does come with special considerations.

COMPATIBILITY ISSUES

Adding sounds and movies to PDF documents is not as simple as you might hope. As soon as you add a movie to a document, you open a whole host of compatibility issues.

Playing Movies

Before your viewers can play the movies or sounds in your PDF documents, they must have the appropriate software installed. Windows users will need Apple QuickTime version 2.5 or later or Microsoft Video. Macintosh OS 9 or Classic users will need Apple QuickTime version 2.5 or later. This is only the absolute minimum requirement—Adobe recommends installing Apple QuickTime 4 or later. If you want to use MPEG files, the minimum requirement is Apple QuickTime 5 or later.

Testing

If you use multimedia content, you must also make arrangements to test the documents on a wide range of equipment and operating systems. For Windows users this means running Windows 95, 98, 2000, and NT at the very least. Macintosh users need to run Macintosh OS 9, OS X, and OS X running in the Classic mode, at the very least. If you expect your PDF files to be read through web browsers, you should test back to at least Internet Explorer 5 and Netscape 4.7.

ANTICIPATE PROBLEMS

You'll need to think of every possible thing that could go wrong when you distribute your document. For instance, when you add movies to a PDF document, those files do not become part of the file, but are linked to the document. If the PDF file is moved from a CD-ROM to the user's hard disk, the user may not also transfer the movie file. (This also affects sound files that are not embedded, but are placed as movies into documents.) You need to create Read Me files that tell your users how make sure their multimedia content plays correctly. To find the type of problems that can happen, send your files to some non-expert friends and see what they do with them.

Pattie Belle's Cyborg Mommy presentation consists of a series of frames that each display multimedia content in a fresh way. The presentation is non-traditional for PDF formats, and relies on linear, as well as non-linear, navigational devices. Most of the 9 rectangles in the grid contain some sort of multimedia content: a button or link to websites; other PDF documents; or other pages in the presentation. Rollover sounds, animations, text links, and page actions enhance the content and utilize a series of built-in tools and custom features.

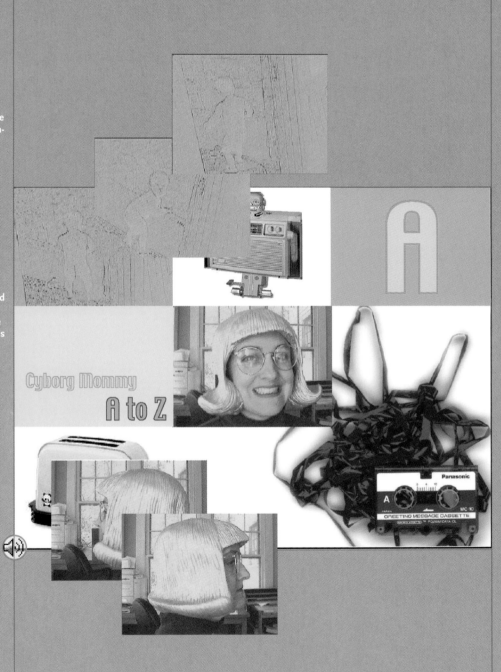

Since the printed page can't do justice to a multimedia experience, we have included an excerpt of Cyborg Mommy on the CD-rom for you to enjoy.

9.2 Integrating Movies

Movies can be added in a variety of ways: as buttons, links, bookmarks, and page actions. Though the Movie Properties dialog box seems to give you limited control of playback, the tools are actually quite customizable. There are essentially two main ways to deliver media clips. You may use a movie as an integrated, invisible layer in the document, activated by certain actions such as a rollover, page action, etc. Alternatively, the movie can be clearly delineated. You can give the viewer control over playing a movie by posting a frame of the movie with the movie controller bars. Regardless of what your goals are, Acrobat gives you a variety of simple, yet effective, controls.

Before you add moving images, we must warn you that, unlike sounds that are actually embedded in PDF files, movie clips are not embedded. A movie does not become a part of the PDF; it is only referenced. All movie files are linked to a source file, which means that whatever file you insert in the document, it must be distributed along with the PDF. As for the path, the movie source file should be in the same location, relative to your PDF document. This means that if the movie is moved to a different disk, the relative path may be broken. This is the primary reason why users get an error box asking for the location of a placed movie.

MOVIE FILE TYPES

There are only two types of video files that can be used for Acrobat: Apple QuickTime which works on Macintosh and Windows, and AVI, (Audio Video Interleave) format which works on Windows only.

If you want your presentation to be played on both Macintosh and Windows, you must choose the QuickTime format. For cross platform publishing, it's important to consider that most Macintosh users have QuickTime installed as it comes packaged with the operating system. Windows users must install it

separately, whether it's from the Acrobat installer disk, or from another source.

ADDING MOVIES

In order to play a movie, you must add the movie to the document in the location that you want it to play. Use the Movie tool 🎞 to create a movie object that links to the external movie file. You can start the movie in several ways. The movie object contains its own trigger area that you can click in to start the movie. You can also click a button on the page, or a bookmark in the Navigator Pane, to trigger the movie. Finally, you can set a page action to automatically play the movie as the page opens or closes.

The way in which you trigger the movie is important. A button with a label that says Play Movie tells the user that what they are seeing is a movie—something that is separate from the rest of the document. However, a page action that automatically starts the movie as soon as the page opens integrates the movie with the document. The movie isn't separate from the document, but is a natural part of the presentation.

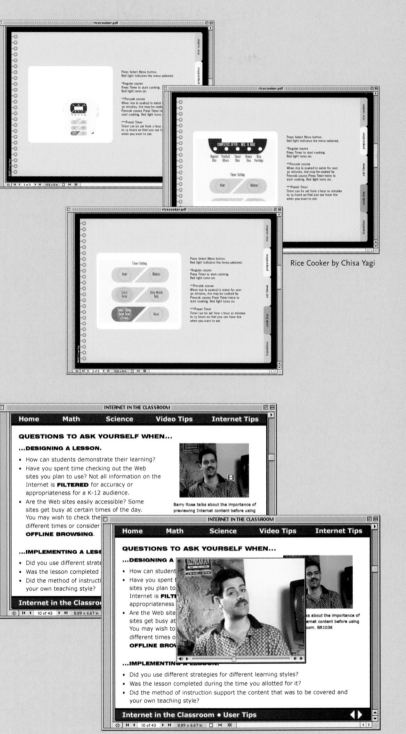

INTEGRATED MOVIES

In an integrated movie, the movie or animation appears as part of the page design and does not require any actions on the part of the viewer. In this presentation, the rice cooker animations are coordinated with the rest of the page elements. There are no user controls for the movie, which starts automatically when the page is first opened.

Rice Cooker by Chisa Yagi

FLOATING WINDOW MOVIE

In this example, the user makes the deliberate decision to play the movie by clicking the area inside the image that describes the featured video. The movie then plays in its own window, which gives the user controls to start, rewind, change the sound, and stop the movie.

The Connected Classroom by J. Kaye Baucom

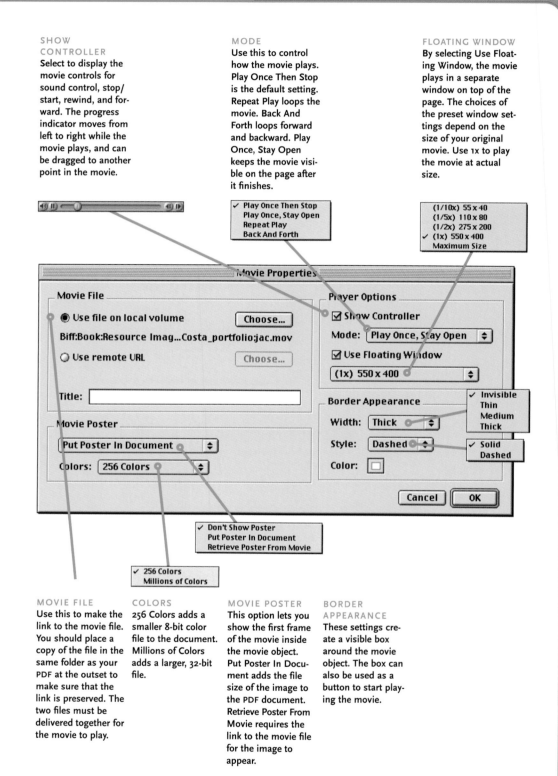

SHOW CONTROLLER
Select to display the movie controls for sound control, stop/start, rewind, and forward. The progress indicator moves from left to right while the movie plays, and can be dragged to another point in the movie.

MODE
Use this to control how the movie plays. Play Once Then Stop is the default setting. Repeat Play loops the movie. Back And Forth loops forward and backward. Play Once, Stay Open keeps the movie visible on the page after it finishes.

FLOATING WINDOW
By selecting Use Floating Window, the movie plays in a separate window on top of the page. The choices of the preset window settings depend on the size of your original movie. Use 1x to play the movie at actual size.

✓ Play Once Then Stop
Play Once, Stay Open
Repeat Play
Back And Forth

(1/10x) 55 x 40
(1/5x) 110 x 80
(1/2x) 275 x 200
✓ (1x) 550 x 400
Maximum Size

Movie Properties

Movie File
◉ Use file on local volume   Choose...
Biff:Book:Resource Imag...Costa_portfolio:jac.mov
○ Use remote URL   Choose...

Title:

Movie Poster
Put Poster In Document
Colors: 256 Colors

Player Options
☑ Show Controller
Mode: Play Once, Stay Open
☑ Use Floating Window
(1x) 550 x 400

Border Appearance
Width: Thick
Style: Dashed
Color:

✓ Invisible
Thin
Medium
Thick

✓ Solid
Dashed

Cancel   OK

✓ Don't Show Poster
Put Poster In Document
Retrieve Poster From Movie

✓ 256 Colors
Millions of Colors

MOVIE FILE
Use this to make the link to the movie file. You should place a copy of the file in the same folder as your PDF at the outset to make sure that the link is preserved. The two files must be delivered together for the movie to play.

COLORS
256 Colors adds a smaller 8-bit color file to the document. Millions of Colors adds a larger, 32-bit file.

MOVIE POSTER
This option lets you show the first frame of the movie inside the movie object. Put Poster In Document adds the file size of the image to the PDF document. Retrieve Poster From Movie requires the link to the movie file for the image to appear.

BORDER APPEARANCE
These settings create a visible box around the movie object. The box can also be used as a button to start playing the movie.

Creating a Movie Object

There are two different ways to create a movie object with the Movie tool. You can click to create the movie object, or you can drag the movie tool to define the movie's size. If you click for a floating movie, the size is set by the floating window menu controls. If you click for an integrated movie, the size is automatically set to the actual size of the movie.

Be aware that if you click to create a movie and then set it to be displayed as a floating movie, the size of the movie object becomes microscopic. That is, the movie object is only 1 pixel wide and 1 pixel tall. There is nothing wrong with having a movie object this size, though it makes it very difficult to select the movie object in order to make changes later. The only way we know to find such microscopic movie objects is to give them thick, colored frames when they are created.

SETTING MOVIE PROPERTIES

Each movie object has its own Movie Properties dialog box that controls how the movie appears in the document. These settings control how the movie is viewed with the PDF file. For example, the movie object can be an invisible element on the page, that is automatically activated when the page first opens. This gives the viewer the feeling that the animation is an integral part of the design of the page. The movie object can also be a framed object: When the user moves the cursor inside the movie object, a movie symbol ▣ appears. The viewer can click inside the movie object to start the movie. The movie can be played as an element separated from the rest of the document, with a control bar that let the user play and stop the movie. Thus, the settings you choose determine how the movie is perceived within the document.

Movie File

The movie object does not contain the movie itself, rather the movie object serves as a link to an external movie file. The Movie File settings let you choose that external movie file on either a local disk or a remote server.

The option Use File on Local Volume lets you select a file that is contained on the same volume as the PDF document. This option sets the movie to play at the best quality, since there is no need to retrieve the file from remote servers or over a web connection. If you set your file up in this way, you must remember to ship the movie file along with the PDF document. The best choice is to place the movie file in the same folder or directory as the PDF file. This means that if the documents are moved from one disk to another, the movie keeps its relative path to the original PDF document.

The option to Use Remote URL lets you store the movie file on a remote server. This option lets you ship the PDF document without the movie file. However, it should be used only for situations where you can be assured there is a high-speed or Intranet connection to the movie file.

Player Options

Show Controller This option adds the Quick-Time movie controller to the bottom of the movie area. The movie controller contains the play/pause button, sound volume slider, start and end buttons, and a progress bar. For short movies that add just a slight bit of animation to a page, the controller is not necessary. However, for movies that provide educational information, you may want to give the viewer the controls to start, stop, and replay parts of the movie.

Use Floating Window Ordinarily, a movie is seen inside the movie object. The Use Floating Window option plays the movie in its own separate window above the rest of the page. The floating window is centered on the monitor screen, even if the movie object is positioned in another area. The size of a floating

MOVIE IN DOCUMENT

For the opening animation for the Creating Time workshop, the Show Controller and Use Floating Window options are not chosen. The movie plays as an element within the page. This keeps the user within the PDF presentation.

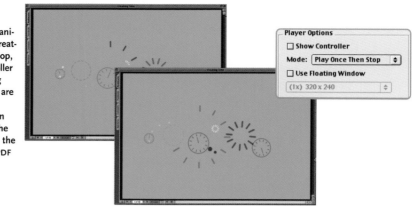

CONTROLLED MOVIES

In this movie showing a road map, the controller is turned on to let the viewer start, stop, and rewind the movie. With the floating window, the movie appears as a separate element from the page.

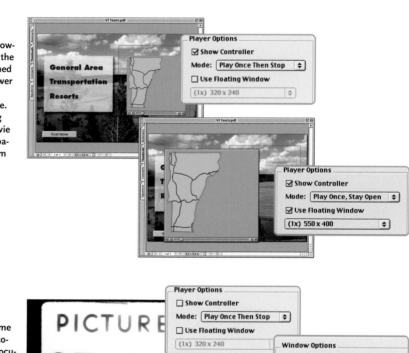

FULL SCREEN MODE

Using a QuickTime movie from Photo-Spin.com, this document opens with the look of an old 16-millimeter movie. With no controller and a full screen mode, there are no clues that this is a PDF document.

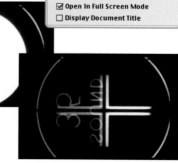

movie is determined by the choice you make in the Movie Properties. The sizes in the list are determined by the size of the original movie file. Small-sized movies offer more choices than larger ones. If your movie comes from a video source, you should not use the enlargement (2x) setting, because it will pixelate the images in the movie. However, if your movie was created using a vector program, such as Macromedia Flash, you can enlarge the movie to any size without a loss of resolution.

Mode This pull down menu controls how the movie plays. The first option, Play Once then Stop, plays the movie; stops after the last frame; and discards the controller if it was visible. It also closes the floating window if it was chosen. This is the best option for most movies.

The second option, Play Once, Stay Open, plays the movie; stops after the last frame; and leaves the controller in place if it was visible. It also leaves the floating window open if Floating Movie was chosen. This option can cause serious problems for your viewers. It leaves a floating window open over the document page. Unless the viewer knows she needs to press the Escape key on the keyboard, there is no way to close the window. If you want to use the Play Once, Stay Open option, we strongly urge you not to make it a floating movie.

The third option, Repeat Play, plays the movie over and over after it reaches its last frame, like a loop. This option is even more dangerous than the previous one when applied to a floating movie. Not only is there no way to close the window, but without a controller, the movie plays endlessly. Even if the viewer moves from one page to another, the floating window will continue its endless loop. We strongly urge you not to set floating movies with this option.

People often wonder how to set a movie to loop a certain number of times and then stop. The answer is, you can't—not in Acrobat; however, there is a trick you can use to create the same effect. In the application that creates the movie, repeat all the frames for the movie as many times as you want the movie to run. For instance, if you want the movie to play three times and then stop, you would have three sets of the same frames. Then set the movie mode to Play Once Then Stop. The movie appears to play three times and then stops.

The final option, Back and Forth, plays the movie to the final frame and then plays it backwards to the first frame. This is repeated endlessly, so you should not use this option with the floating window setting.

If you set an integrated movie for Repeat Play or Back and Forth, you can still access the controller, even if you have not set it to be displayed. As the movie plays, click inside the movie area. A movie symbol appears in the lower-left corner. Click the symbol. The controller appears below the movie.

Border Appearance

The movie object can be set to have a visible border. The Width options are Invisible (no border), Thin, Medium, and Thick. You can also set the Style to Solid or Dashed. Finally, you can choose a color for the border.

Movie Poster

In addition to setting a border, you can also choose to place a graphic from the first frame of the movie within the movie object. This is called the movie poster. There are three choices on the menu. Don't Show Poster leaves the area inside the movie object empty. Put Poster in Document and Retrieve Poster From Movie both add the image from the movie inside the movie object. Put Poster In Document adds the graphic to the PDF file and will increase the size of the document a bit. Retrieve Poster From Movie uses the link between the PDF file and the movie to retrieve the image, but does not store the image in the document. This keeps the size of the PDF file smaller.

If you add a poster, you can set the colors to 256 colors or millions of colors. The 256 colors creates a smaller file, but does not look good with photographs. If you choose Retrieve Poster from Movie, it automatically retrieves the best quality image.

ⓘ MOVIE ESCAPE

If you are going to add movies (especially long movies) to a document, it is vital that you include an instruction to tell the viewer that she can stop and close a movie by pressing the Escape key on the keyboard.

MOVIE SIZES AND ASPECT RATIO

As you work with movies, the size of your document page becomes important. If you want a movie to fill the entire page, you can drag with the Movie tool to create the movie object. However, as soon as you choose the movie file, the size of the movie object changes to the proportions of the movie file. Therefore, a movie you thought would fill the page may not. In addition, if you expect to project your presentations in full screen mode from a computer onto a screen, you may want to make sure that your PDF pages are sized to neatly fill the projected image.

One way to ensure the above is to size your documents according to the video aspect ratio. The aspect ratio is the height of a computer screen compared to its width. Most computer monitors have a 4x3 aspect radio. This means that if you divide the width of a document by 4 and the height by 3, the results will be the same number.

An 8x6 inch document has the right aspect ratio, but it's not the right format if you want to play movies at their actual size. Most movies are created with the same 4x3 aspect ratio, but their actual size, in pixels, is 640x480. So, if you want to play a movie at its actual size, the 8x6 inch page is a little too small. Instead, you should use a document that is 9 x 6¾ inches. This maintains the aspect ratio and is the same size as a 640x480 pixel movie.

ADDING A MOVIE OBJECT TO A PAGE

In order to play a movie on a page, you must add a movie object to the page. Use the following steps to add a movie object linked to an external movie file.

Step ① Create the Movie Object

Select the Movie tool in the tool bar. Click or drag to create the movie object. This opens the Movie Properties dialog box.

Step ② Set the Movie Properties

In the Movie Properties dialog box, set the options, as described in the Setting Movie Properties section earlier in this chapter.

USING THE MOVIE OBJECT TRIGGER

The simplest way to trigger a movie is to instruct the viewer to move their cursor inside the movie object. This changes the cursor into the movie symbol. A single click plays the movie. The drawback to this technique is that you have to educate the viewer about how to use the movie object. Even a movie poster may not clearly show that the movie object can trigger the movie. This may mean adding text inside or below the movie object with instructions about how to start the movie.

One way to ensure that the viewer sees the movie symbol cursor is to draw the movie object so that it totally covers the page. No matter where your viewer moves the cursor, they will still see the movie symbol. However,

⚡ CREATE MOVIE OBJECT

① To add a movie object to a page, click or drag with the Movie tool. Drag to set the movie object to a specific size. This can scale the movie larger than the original. Click to create a movie object the actual size of the original file. If you click and then choose Floating Window, you'll create a microscopic movie object.

② Set the options in the Movie Properties dialog box. The option for Use Floating Window is not available until you have chosen the actual movie file.

ACTUAL-SIZE OBJECT: INTE-GRATED MOVIE

Click with the Movie tool and then deselect the Floating Movie option in the Movie Properties dialog box. This automatically sets the size of the movie object to the actual size of the movie.

OFF-SIZE OBJECT: FLOATING MOVIE

Drag with the Movie tool to create a movie object at any size, then deselect the Floating Movie option in the Movie Properties. The movie object stays the size that you defined while dragging. The size of the movie is controlled by the Floating Movie menu.

OFF-SIZE OBJECT: INTEGRATED MOVIE

Drag with the Movie tool to create a movie object at any size. Set the Movie Properties to something other than Floating Window. The movie object changes shape to maintain the proportions of the movie.

FLOATING MOVIE: OFF-PAGE OBJECT

Drag with the Movie tool to create a movie object at any size. Set the Movie Properties to Floating Window. The off-page movie object plays the movie, but is not an interactive element on the page.

you may want a more automatic way to play a movie.

MOVIE PLAYED BY PAGE ACTION

You can also play a movie by setting it as part of a page action. This means that when the page opens or closes, the movie automatically begins to play. In order to set the movie to play as a page action, there must be a movie object on the page. (Use the previous exercise to create a movie object.)

Step ① Choose the Page Action Command

Choose Document>Set Page Action. In the Page Actions dialog box, choose either Page Open or Page Close. An action set to Page Open plays the movie when the page opens. An action set to Page Close plays the movie when the viewer moves to another page in the document. Click the Add button to open the Add an Action dialog box.

Step ② Define the Page Action

In the Add an Action dialog box, select Movie from the Type menu and click the Select Movie button. This opens the Movie Action dialog box. Use the Select Movie list to choose the movie you want to control with the page action. Use the Select Operation list to choose whether to Play, Stop, Pause, or Resume the movie.

A Word About Page Actions

At first glance, we had little idea why we would want to use Page Close as a movie action. With a little brainstorming, we came up with a few ideas. Remember our admonition earlier not to use a floating movie that repeats endlessly? There's no way to stop the movie as it repeats. Well, what if you set the Page Close action for the movie to stop? That would solve the problem of the floating movie that repeats endlessly.

You may also want to test your page actions to make sure they work correctly. With the Acrobat navigation tools, go back and forth between pages to see that the movie file opens and plays whenever you return to the movie page.

MOVIE PLAYED BY BUTTON OR LINK

You can also set a button or link to trigger a movie. This gives you great flexibility in controlling a movie. For instance, you can position the movie object off the page and use the button or link to trigger the movie in a floating window. Before you can trigger the movie with a button or link, you must add the movie object to the page.

Step ① Draw a Link or Button Area

Use either the Link tool or the Form tool to create a link or a button on the page. If you have drawn a link, the Link Properties dialog box appears. Set the Action Type to Movie and

⚡ MOVIE PAGE ACTION

① Open the page from which you want the movie to play. (A movie object must be defined on the page.) Choose Document>Set Page Action. In the Page Actions dialog box, choose either Page Open or Page Close. Then click the Add button. This opens the Add an Action dialog box.

② Use the Type menu to choose Movie as the type of action. Click the Select Movie button. This opens the Movie Action dialog box. Use the Select

Movie list to choose the movie on the page. Use the Select Operation list to choose the type of action for the movie.

then choose the movie. If you have drawn a button, the Field Properties dialog box appears. Enter a name for the button and set the Type list to button. Set the button appearance and click the Actions tab.

Step ② Set the Movie Actions

If you have drawn a button, choose one of the events in the Actions tab in the Field Properties dialog box and then click the Add button. The Add an Action dialog box appears. Set the movie action.

MOVIE PLAYED BY BOOKMARK

One of the limitations to using page actions, links, or buttons to play movies is that the movie can only be played when the viewer is on a specific page. There is no such limitation when you add the movie action to a bookmark. Although this technique is not very common (we've actually never seen it used in a presentation), we think it holds promise for new and creative ways of playing movies and sounds.

First, add the movie files to the document. We suggest drawing a small movie object on the pasteboard area of any page. Then set the movie to play as a floating window. This means that even though the movie object is positioned off the page, it will still play in the center of the computer screen. (You can set the movie object to play as an integrated movie, but that requires the movie object to be positioned on

an actual page, not the gray pasteboard area.)

Create the bookmarks and set their properties to play the movie file. Unlike the movie played by a page action, movies played using bookmarks can be set to play any movie that has been linked to the document. In addition, the bookmark does not go to the page that contains the movie. The movie appears as a floating window over the current page.

Step ① Create the Movie Objects

Zoom out so you can see the pasteboard of the page that will contain your movie object. Use the Movie tool to create a small movie object and set the movie to play as a floating window. Repeat this series of actions to create as many movie objects as you wish. Stay on the page that contains the movie objects for the next two steps. You may want to add a visible border to the movie object so you can find it later.

Step ② Make New Bookmark

Open the Bookmarks palette in the Navigation Pane. Choose New Bookmark from the Bookmarks palette menu. Give the bookmark a descriptive name that helps the viewer understand that it's a movie.

Step ③ Set Bookmark Properties

Click the bookmark icon to select the bookmark. Then choose Bookmark Properties from the Bookmark palette menu. This opens the

MOVIE LINK OR BUTTON

① Use the Form tool to create the hotspot area that controls how the movie plays. This opens the Field Properties dialog box.

Or use the Link tool to draw a link object. This opens the Link Properties dialog box. Use the Action area to choose the Movie action. Use the Select Movie button to select the movie object on the page.

② Using the Form tool, set the Field Properties to button, then choose the event you want to trigger the movie. Then click the Add button. This opens the Add an Action dialog box. Use the Select Movie button to choose the movie object on the page.

Bookmark Properties dialog box. The settings here are similar to the ones for a page action. Use the Type menu to choose Movie. Then click the Select Movie button to open the Movie Action dialog box. Choose the movie object from the Select Movie list. Use Select Operation to choose whether the bookmark will start, stop, pause, or resume playing a movie. You can also choose a unique color and type style for the appearance of the movie bookmarks (available only in Acrobat 5). Click the OK and Set Action buttons to finish setting the bookmark. Repeat this for as many other bookmarks as you want. You can also move the movie bookmarks to one location under their own bookmark in the Bookmarks palette. This makes it easy to explain to your viewers how to play the movies.

Test the bookmark by moving to any other page in the document and clicking the bookmark. The floating movie opens in the center of the screen with the current page in the background. Move to another page and the bookmark will still work.

MOVIES AND FULL SCREEN

When playing presentations that use movies, be sure to set the Document Properties Open Options to play the document in the full screen mode. The full screen mode hides all Acrobat or Acrobat Reader tool bars, menus, document window, and other interface elements. It is an excellent way to engage the viewer completely in the presentation without any onscreen distractions. The full screen mode is an excellent choice for self-running kiosk-style presentations or those that are always run by an expert presenter. For instance, Sandee uses full-screen presentations for her speaking engagements. Since she is the only one who uses it, she doesn't need to educate any users about how to move through the show.

If you want other people, such as members of a sales force, to run your presentation in the full-screen mode, make sure you give them instructions about how to use it. Make sure you have added custom navigation controls that allow users to move from one page to another, as well as to start and stop movies. The presenter should know to press the escape key to stop a movie that was inadvertently started.

If you send a presentation to the general public, you may not want to use the full screen mode at all. Inexperienced computer users may become concerned when the menus and tool bars on their computer screen disappear. If you provide a button to close the presentation, make sure you return the viewer's screen to its regular mode.

MOVIES AND FILE SIZE

Here's where we come back down to earth and look at practical matters associated with adding movies. Photographic (pixel-based) movies,

⚡ BOOKMARK AS MOVIE

① Use the Movie tool to create a movie object in the pasteboard area of a page. Choose the movie and set the movie to play in a floating window.

② Open the Bookmark palette and create a new bookmark. Select and name the new bookmark.

such as video clips, can make for large file sizes. Even a small 320 x 240, 10-second, silent video clip can be 200K in size. Make the movie longer; the screen size larger; and add sound, and the file becomes a megabyte or more. As a producer, you must consider how your presentation will be distributed. If you publish on a CD, through Intranets, via looping kiosk displays, or if you present from your hard drive, you will not have the same file size concerns or delivery issues that you will if you distribute through e-mail or the web.

Any presentation that uses the web for delivery still has limitations in terms of bandwidth. Even if you expect that most of your audience will have high-speed Internet connections, you can't rely on it. Fortunately, vector-based (SWF) animations created in Flash and exported as QuickTime movies are small in size—even in long segments.

Even if there are no file size or delivery issues, consider whether the movie is worth the time it takes to watch. Too often, we have been forced to watch movies that are nothing more than a presenter talking. Just as they make for bad television, these "talking heads" are a waste of the time it takes to sit through them. This sort of content can just as easily be written out as text. If you want to use video in a presentation, make sure it has a purpose.

③ *Choose Bookmark Properties from the Bookmark palette menu. Then choose Movie as the Action Type and use the Select Movie button to select the movie.*

You can give the movie bookmarks their own distinctive typeface. You can also color and nest them in their own bookmark group.

289

9.3 | Making Movies

We hope that you're now excited about the possibility of creating your own movies to add to PDF presentations. Before you run out to buy video-editing software, look at what's already on your computer. You may already possess an application that allows you to create QuickTime movies. The choices for video-editing software range from professional software to inexpensive alternatives. You also need to figure out how to get video into your computer. This short section describes some of the choices you have for creating movies, as well as the benefits and drawbacks of each.

FROM CAMERA TO COMPUTER

We're assuming you want to shoot your own video clips and transfer them into the computer. If you have an analog camera, you may need a device that converts the video and audio from the camera into the computer's USB port. You may also need a video capture device to convert an analog signal into a digital signal.

If you have a digital camera, it has an IEEE 1394 output (also called Firewire). If your computer has a Firewire input port, then all you need is a Firewire cable between the camera and the computer. Newer Macintosh computers starting with the blue-and-white G3 models and the Pismo Powerbooks have at least one Firewire built-in port. Windows users may need to install a Firewire card. Check with the camera manufacturer to make sure the camera is compatible with the computer.

PROFESSIONAL APPLICATIONS

As tempting as it is to work with the same applications used for network television, carefully consider how much you're going to use the software. If you're going to add just a few short movie clips straight from the camera, you may not need these expensive products, which have a steep learning curve.

Adobe Premiere

This is a professional product that is available for both the Windows and Macintosh platforms. Adobe Premiere automatically imports video from digital cameras. It also imports graphics from Adobe Photoshop and Illustrator. You can use Premiere to edit audio components. Premiere export formats include QuickTime, as well as MP3 audio, RealVideo, and videotape.

Adobe After Effects

Although After Effects doesn't import video, it provides you with a full arsenal of video effects, such as motion blur, layering, feathered images, and masking, as well as 2-dimensional and 3-dimensional compositing. If you've ever wanted your movies to swoop into position, this is the program that makes it happen. After Effects is fully compatible with Premiere and is available for both Macintosh and Windows.

Apple Final Cut Pro

Macintosh users can also choose Final Cut Pro from Apple Computer. Final Cut Pro fully supports digital video import through a Firewire connection. Final Cut Pro offers complete editing tools, including color correction. Effects include cross-dissolves, fades, and several types of screen wipes. At almost $1,000, Final Cut

Pro is definitely not for the occasional video editor.

HOME/SMALL BUSINESS APPLICATIONS

If the price tag of the professional products has you in sticker shock, consider these affordable applications.

Apple Quicktime Pro

QuickTime is not just a free player or a movie format. If you upgrade to QuickTime Pro, it can be used to import video and audio from a wide variety of formats. You can edit and combine movie clips. You can also select the frame that will appear as the movie poster in Acrobat. At $30, and available for both Macintosh and Windows, it is a worthwhile choice.

Apple iMovie

Free with Macintosh computers, iMovie also imports video and lets you edit clips and apply transitions and special effects, such as adjusting colors, or adding ripples, and blurs.

INTERACTIVE ANIMATION

When most people hear the word movie, they think photo images. However, some of the best animations come from graphic programs that work with vector or line art.

Macromedia Flash

Flash is the basis for an entire world of websites that use SWF (ShockWave Flash) technology. One reason is that SWF files are incredibly small. In Acrobat 4, you could import SWF files directly into a PDF presentation. This is no longer true with Acrobat 5. However, it's simple to export SWF animations as QuickTime movies. Given their vector source, these movies can be scaled without any pixelation.

WHAT'VE YOU ALREADY GOT?

You may not need to go out and get any new software. We've discovered two products you may already have that can edit video.

Adobe ImageReady

Adobe ImageReady can import QuickTime movies into ImageReady frames. Once the frames are in ImageReady, you can move them around, delete them, or duplicate them. You can export those frames as QuickTime movies. The compression is nothing like a video editor and there is no support for soundtracks, but if you want to create a rough sample for a client, this could be all you need.

Adobe GoLive

We're quite impressed with the movie-editing features in GoLive. Although the program was originally intended for posting movies as part of a website, there is no reason Acrobat users can't also use GoLive's features. When you open a movie in GoLive, the Layout tab lets you position, resize, manipulate and combine tracks in a movie. You can also add soundtracks to movie tracks and skew or rotate tracks. As you are working, you can use the Preview tab to play the movie and set its properties. Finally, when you are done, you can save the movie or export it. We don't recommend editing long movies using GoLive; but it can help you out in a pinch.

ROYALTY-FREE STOCK MOVIES

You don't need to shoot video to use video. Many online services will sell you the rights to use stock video clips. Photospin.com, for instance, has a excellent collection of stock footage that you can purchase and download instantly. Read the license agreement carefully. You may have the right to present the video yourself, but since movies are not embedded in the PDF document, you may not have the right to distribute the movie to others.

The QuickTime movies in Acrobat don't have to start as photographic videos. Macromedia Flash also exports in the QuickTime format, so you can use Flash to create PDF movies.

One of Pattie Belle's students, Chris von Achen, created this PDF document using a movie originally created in Flash. The still images were combined to give the impression of the hands turning the pages. Flash buttons were added to create the back and next hotspot areas. These Flash buttons maintain their interactivity, even when exported into the QuickTime format.

The opening animation for the Creating Time eBook starts with a Flash movie. Even though the movie fills the entire screen, it is not a large file. This is because Bjørn used only vector objects, which maintain their small file size even when transferred to QuickTime.

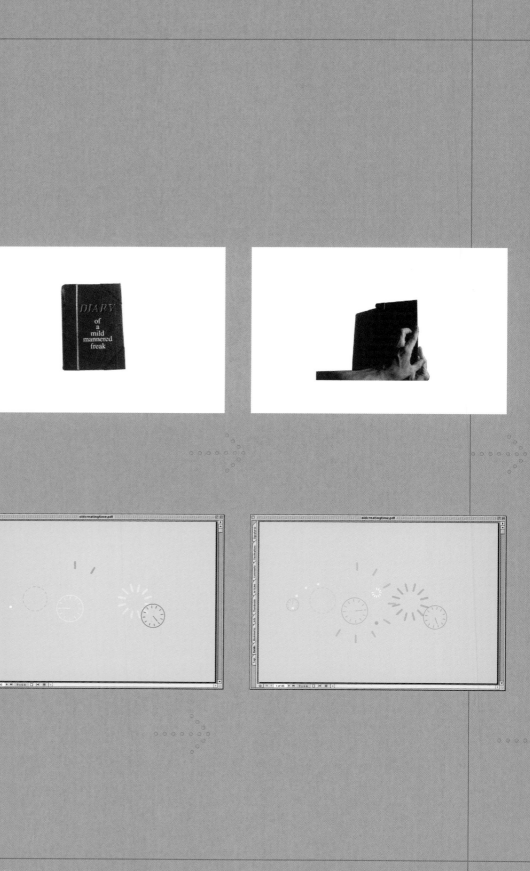

this morning I opened
the newspaper to the
obituaries, only to
discover that chivalry
was indeed dead.

.........I then ate 6
bowls of Cap'n
crunch and jogged
naked for 5 miles

next

CREATING TIME

CYBORG MOMMY

Cyborg Mommy is electronic art that uses PDF as its performance platform. The next two spreads examines some of the interactive elements in the piece.

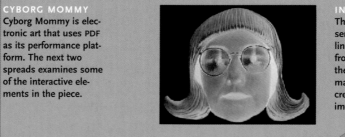

INTERACTIVE LINK

The top middle frame serves as an interactive link. By selecting Inverse from the links properties, the image reverses. This makes it unnecessary to create a mouse down image.

ROLLOVER/BUTTON

This button uses two distinct mouse events to both play a sound and trigger a movie. Moving the cursor inside the button area (Mouse Enter event) activates a sound. A mouse click inside the frame (Mouse Down event) starts a movie in the center of the bottom frame, which replaces the original image with the animation of a beehive.

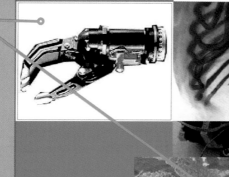

EXTERNAL LINK

Some buttons are linked to external websites, such as the one for bust.com.

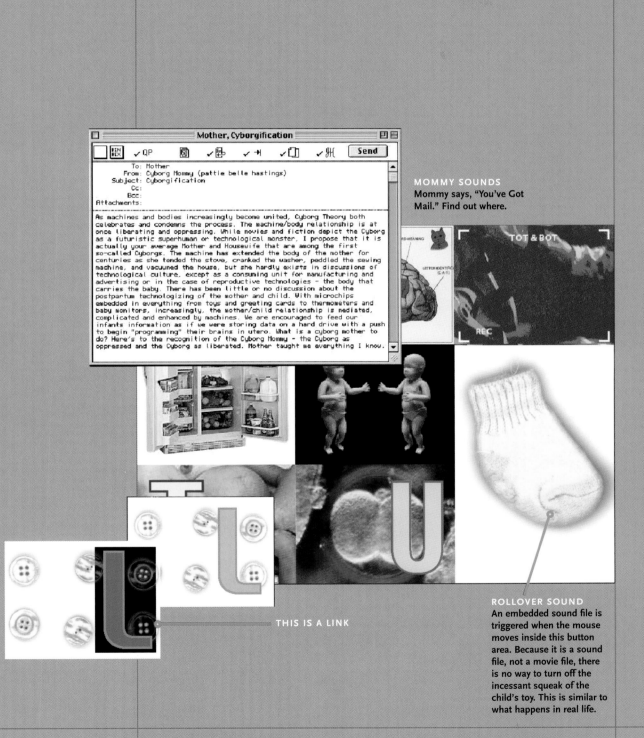

Mother, Cyborgification

To: Mother
From: Cyborg Mommy (pattie belle hastings)
Subject: Cyborgification
Cc:
Bcc:
Attachments:

As machines and bodies increasingly become united, Cyborg Theory both celebrates and condemns the process. The machine/body relationship is at once liberating and oppressing. While movies and fiction depict the Cyborg as a futuristic superhuman or technological monster, I propose that it is actually your average Mother and Housewife that are among the first so-called Cyborgs. The machine has extended the body of the mother for centuries as she tended the stove, cranked the washer, peddled the sewing machine, and vacuumed the house, but she hardly exists in discussions of technological culture, except as a consuming unit for manufacturing and advertising or in the case of reproductive technologies – the body that carries the baby. There has been little or no discussion about the postpartum technologizing of the mother and child. With microchips embedded in everything from toys and greeting cards to thermometers and baby monitors, increasingly, the mother/child relationship is mediated, complicated and enhanced by machines. We are encouraged to feed our infants information as if we were storing data on a hard drive with a push to begin "programming" their brains in utero. What is a cyborg mother to do? Here's to the recognition of the Cyborg Mommy – the Cyborg as oppressed and the Cyborg as liberated. Mother taught me everything I know.

MOMMY SOUNDS
Mommy says, "You've Got Mail." Find out where.

THIS IS A LINK

ROLLOVER SOUND
An embedded sound file is triggered when the mouse moves inside this button area. Because it is a sound file, not a movie file, there is no way to turn off the incessant squeak of the child's toy. This is similar to what happens in real life.

9.4 | Adding Audio

Like movies, sounds can enhance a PDF tremendously. Audio files can be added to, or recorded inside, a document. They can also be embedded in a file. Sounds can be activated in numerous ways: as a sound comment (described in Chapter 6), in a link or a button, or as a page action. The versatility of Acrobat makes audio very easy to integrate.

AUDIO FORMATS

Acrobat combined with QuickTime can give you a wide range of sound files that can be played inside PDF documents. If you want to use sounds within Acrobat, you can choose either AIF or WAV files. These sound formats can be embedded as part of the PDF document. If you want to play external sounds through the PDF document, you can use AIF, WAV, or any format that QuickTime supports. These are AIFF/AIFC, Audio CD, MP3, Sound Designer II, System 7 sound, uLaw (AU), and WAV files.

CAN YOU HEAR ME?

This may seem obvious, but unless the viewer of your file has sound capabilities on their computer, or more importantly, the sound turned on, they will not hear your message. Imagine a button that says "Click for Important Message." If the sound is not turned up, someone could click endlessly expecting some sort of text page. If you're wondering how many people don't have the sound turned up, it's actually quite a few—especially those in noisy offices, those working in libraries and student labs where sounds are unwelcome, and Sandee, who can't hear anything on her powerbook unless she plugs in the external speakers.

THE SOUNDS OF PDF

There are three primary types of sound experiences in a PDF document. The type of sound experience you choose depends on how you want to use a sound.

Sounds as Comments

As we discussed in Chapter 6, you can add sounds using the Sound Attachment tool. These sound comments are recorded using a microphone attached to the computer. You can also import native sound files, not QuickTime sounds, into a sound comment. Sound comments cannot be extracted from the document. Because you can grab a microphone and record a sound quickly, sound comments are very good for creating soundtracks for presentations. However, the sounds recorded as comments using a microphone can't be combined with page actions, buttons, links, or bookmarks as other types of sounds can.

Sounds as Sounds

If you choose Sound from the Type menu in the Add an Action dialog box, you can import any AIF or WAV sound files into a PDF document. This can be part of a page action, bookmark, button, or link. The steps are similar to the steps outlined earlier for movie actions.

The sounds that are imported when you choose a sound are embedded into the PDF document. Unlike movies, which are only

Lonn Lorenz created this PDF-controlled version of Crafts-men's Jeopardy even before he worked for Adobe. The game uses a combination of buttons, sounds, and JavaScript commands.

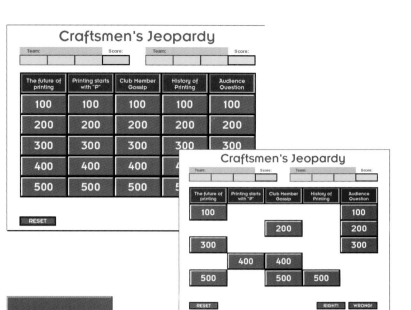

Each button on the game board jumps to a new page in the document. Click any-where on the page that contains the question to move to the page that con-tains the answer. Click the page that contains the answer to move back to the game board.

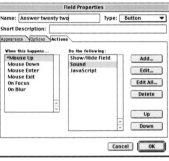

The real brains of the game are in the doc-ument's JavaScripts.

linked to the file, the sound file becomes part of the PDF file. You don't have to send the separate sound file along with the PDF document and it doesn't have to maintain its path. However, each sound that you embed in the PDF document does adds to the size of the PDF file. Also, embedded sounds continue to play even if the user pounds madly on the Escape key. The only escape from embedded sounds is to close the document.

Sounds as Movies

Sounds can also be added as movie objects. Use the Movie tool to draw the movie object. In the Movie Properties dialog box, instead of linking to a QuickTime movie, use the Choose button to select a sound file or QuickTime sound. Movie sounds can be made part of a page action, bookmark, button, or link.

The advantages of creating a sound as movie is that the sound file does not add to the size of the document. You can also use the QuickTime controller to stop, play, rewind, or fast forward the sound. You can even use the controller to lower the sound volume. Also, movie sounds can be stopped by pressing the Escape key.

The disadvantage is that you must remember to send the sound along with the PDF document. Also, because it is a separate file, you may not be able to distribute clip art sounds as part of a license agreement.

LAYERING SOUNDS WITH MOVIES

One of the rules of Acrobat multimedia is that you can't play two sounds at the same time. The second sound stops the first. You also can't play two movies at the same time. As soon as you launch the second movie, the first one stops playing. You can, however, play a movie and a sound at the same time. Sandee has used this trick to add a long background soundtrack that starts as a page action. She also adds clicking sounds that play when a button is selected. These sounds are imported using the Movie tool and played using button actions. The clicks are heard over the soundtrack.

You can also use embedded sound files to add a soundtrack to a silent movie. Although the sound may not be in perfect sync, this feature does provide an easy way to add commentary or background music to a movie.

Step ① Create the Movie Objects

Use the Movie tool to create the movie object. Use the Movie Properties dialog box to choose the movie and set the controls. We suggest setting the movie to play as a floating movie without a controller. This will prevent the viewer from starting and stopping the movie while the soundtrack continues to play in the background. If you create a floating movie, you may also want to position it on the pasteboard so that it is not inadvertently triggered.

⚡ SOUNDS AND MOVIES

① Use the Movie tool to draw a movie object positioned off the page. In the Movie Properties dialog box, choose the movie and set it to play in a floating window. Click OK.

② Use the Form tool to draw a field object. Set the Type as Button. Set the Appearance and Options. Click the Actions tab.

Step ② Create the Movie Trigger

Although there are four different ways to trigger movies and sounds, only page actions and buttons let you combine two or more actions together. As an example, let's create a button that plays the movie. Start by using the Form tool to draw the field object. In the Field Properties dialog box, name the field and set the type to Button.

You may want to give the button a special appearance. If you have access to an image-editing program such as ImageReady, you can open the movie and extract a single frame. You can then save the frame as a TIFF or PDF graphic. Use the Appearance tab of the Field properties to apply that graphic as the icon for the button. If you can't apply the custom icon, you can use text to indicate that the button is the movie trigger.

Step ③ Set the Action to Play the Movie

Click the Actions tab in the Field Properties dialog box. Choose the mouse event that will trigger the action. (We chose Mouse Up which triggers the action when the mouse button is released on a click.) Then click the Add button. This opens the Add an Action dialog box. Use the Type menu to choose Movie and then click the Select Movie button. This opens the Movie Action dialog box. Use the Select Movie list to choose the movie that was added to the movie object created in step one. Click OK and then Set Action. The word Movie appears as the action for Mouse Up. Keep the Field Properties dialog box open for the next step.

Step ④ Set the Action to Play the Sound

With the Mouse Up event still chosen under the Actions tab, click the Add button again. This time, use the Type menu to choose Sound. Then click the Select Sound button. The Open dialog box will appear. Navigate and choose either AIF or WAV sounds. The sound is then added to the file. Click Set Action. The word Sound will appear under the Movie. The order in which the sound and movie are listed is not important. They both play as soon as the mouse button is clicked.

Click OK to close the Field Properties dialog box. Use the Hand tool to test the button. The movie and sound play together when you click the mouse.

③ *Choose a mouse event, such as Mouse Up, and then click the Add button. Set Movie as the Action Type and use the Select Movie button to choose the movie object in the Movie Action dialog box. Click OK and Set Action, but leave the Field Properties dialog box open.*

④ *Click the Add button again and choose Sound as the Action Type. Then click the Select Sound button to choose the sound. Click Set Action and then OK to close the Field Properties dialog box.*

SOUND COMMENTS

Click with the Sound Attachment tool to create a sound comment. Use the Record Sound dialog box to record, stop, and play the sound. You can also choose a sound file to import into the comment. Choose Edit>Properties to set the Appearance and Author of the sound comment.

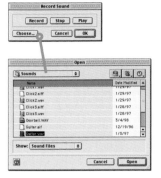

SOUNDS IN BOOKMARKS

Create a new bookmark and then choose the Bookmark Properties. Use the Type menu and Select sound button to add a sound to the bookmark. You can also use bookmarks to play sounds added as movies.

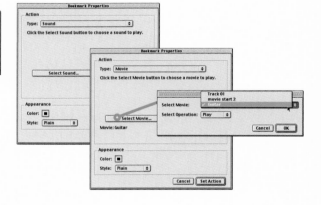

SOUNDS IN LINKS

Use the Link tool to draw a link object. In the Link Properties dialog box, set the Type of Action to Sound. Then select the sound. You can also use links to play sounds added as movies.

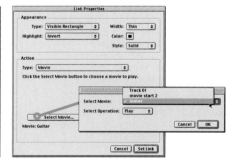

IMPORT SOUNDS AS MOVIES

Use the Movie tool to draw a movie object. In the Movie Properties dialog box, click the Choose button to select a sound file or a QuickTime compatible sound file. The movie object can then be played like any other movie.

SOUNDS IN PAGE ACTION

Choose Document> Set Page Action. Choose the page event and then click the Add button. In the Add an Action dialog box, use the Type menu and Select sound button to add a sound to the bookmark. You can also use page actions to play sounds added as movies.

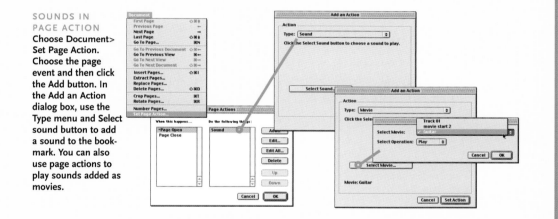

SOUNDS IN BUTTONS

Use the Form tool to draw a field object. In the Field Properties dialog box, set the object to Button. In the Actions area, choose the mouse event. Click the Add button. In the Add an Action dialog box, use the Type menu and Select Sound button to add a sound to the button. You can also use buttons to play sounds added as movies.

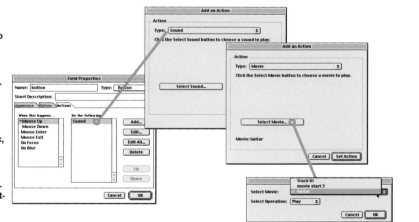

9.5 | Making Sounds

Don't underestimate the power of sound. Even a half-second click added to a button can provide important feedback for interactive buttons. Long, self-running presentations may feel very empty without some sort of background music or transitional sounds. If you want to experience the power of sound, try the following experiment. Close your eyes and listen to the evening news for a few minutes. Then turn off the volume and watch the program without any sound. In which mode did you understand more information? Finding a good sound source is one of the most important steps in the process of adding audio to your document. How you create and edit sounds depends on your needs. You can make the sound yourself, hire someone to create the sounds for you, purchase a sound CD, or download sounds from a website.

When it comes to creating and delivering audio, there are a few things to keep in mind. Hardware configurations for sound are much less standardized than those for graphics. While almost all Macintosh computers have good sound cards and output, some older Windows computers in offices have no sound at all. Most Macintoshes can mix and play several channels of sound without much difficulty, but some Windows configurations have problems playing more than one sound channel. These issues will directly effect how difficult it may be for you to work with audio files and how difficult it might be for your end user to experience them. Check the hardware requirements before you invest in any sound-editing software.

VOICE-OVER NARRATIONS

We assume that you do not have a professional sound studio. (If you do, you don't need to read this section.) However, you may want to use your computer's built-in microphone to record voice-over narrations for PDF presentations.

If your computer shipped with a microphone and audio input, or a built-in microphone, you may be tempted to use it to record sound. Those choices are fine for in-house presentations or quick sound comments added with the Sound Attachment tool. However, they are not at all suitable for professional presentations. You'll need a good-quality microphone if you want to provide extensive voice-over narration for a professional presentation.

You'll also need a quiet room in which to record your sound. Find a room—if possible without windows—away from the noise of your office. You'd be surprised to notice how much noise you may have become accustomed to: phone rings, elevators, doors, computer beeps, sirens, and so on. If you record your sound directly into your computer, position the microphone far enough away so that it doesn't pick up the noise from the hard drive, fan, and external devices.

> **COPYRIGHTS**
>
> *You may be tempted to grab your favorite artist's latest CD and use it as the background music for your presentation. Don't do it! You need permission to use other people's music in presentations—even if it's only going to be played in your own office. You are much better off using royalty-free music that is specifically made for presentations.*

RECORDING SOFTWARE

Sound applications do more than simply record the sound that comes into your computer. Some features you may want in a sound editor include output in various formats, including aif, wav, RealAudio, and MP3; mixing multiple tracks; cross-fades and effects such as echo and reverbs; and looping. Professional programs should be able to compress sound files so they are at their smallest without sacrificing quality. These programs should be able to clean up clicks, pops, and hisses in the audio track.

You can use the sound editing features of a high-end video editing program, such as Premiere or Final Cut Pro. You can also use professional audio applications, such as Bias Peak and Bias Deck (M), or Sound Forge and WaveLab (W).

There are also low-cost shareware and freeware applications you can use. Some of the most popular are CoolEdit (W) and Sound Studio (M). For a complete list of available applications, visit Version Tracker at http://www.version-tracker.com or ZDNet Downloads at http://downloads-zdnet.com.com/. (That's not a typo, the end of the URL is ".com.com".)

HIRE A PROFESSIONAL

Sound experts know what sounds to use, how to use them, and have the equipment to create clean sound. They know how to avoid distortion and background noises. They have the same years of experience working with sound files that you have with your area of expertise. If your PDF project requires professional audio, you may want to hire a musician, sound editor, or professional voice-over actor.

BUYING ROYALTY-FREE SOUND

Another excellent source for sound and music are audio CDs. This is similar to purchasing stock photos or clip art, but instead of graphics, you get royalty-free sound files. This does not mean there will be no restrictions on use, so you need to familiarize yourself with the license of any sound files you purchase to be sure to avoid copyright issues. For instance, if you use a sound file embedded in the PDF document, the sound file cannot be extracted and used for other purposes. If you use a sound file as a movie object, the sound file is not embedded in the document. You may have the right to distribute sound files that are embedded in the document, but not sound files that are distributed separately from the PDF document. Some license agreements allow you to use sounds in PDF presentations, but not in documents that will be sold commercially.

Many companies create license-free CDs with music or sound effects. These come in various formats and sometimes have a choice of sample rates and resolutions.

DOWNLOADING SOUNDS

You can download or buy audio files from many sites on the web. Beware—some sites offer illegal sound clips of copyrighted material, such as movie themes and famous dialog. Just because you got it "off the web" doesn't mean you have the right to use it yourself.

There are several reputable sites for purchasing music and sound effects, such as www.sounddogs.com and www.sfxsearch.com. We particularly like these sites because they let you preview the sounds using QuickTime web streaming. Both of these sites also offer complete sound collections for sale on CD.

9.6 How to Read a Film

We have seen the future of interactive multimedia. It is a DVD *disc called* How to Read a Film: Multimedia Edition *by James Monaco. James is a film expert, author, former university professor, and president of* UNET, *a multimedia software firm. The* How to Read a Film DVD *contains the* PDF *version of four of James's books on film theory—but that's just the start. Using Acrobat as the platform, James has created hundreds of additional* PDF *documents that are all linked to the* PDF *books. These* PDF *files contain film clips illustrating the various lessons in the book, audio interviews with the author and noted members of the film industry, and interactive diagrams.* How to Read a Film *is not just an exceptional way to learn about film theory, it is a great lesson for anyone interested in using* PDF *for delivering multimedia content.*

The following is adapted from the hilarious 12-page account (featured on the disc) describing how James Monaco created *How to Read a Film: Multimedia Edition*. The story is an excellent lesson in how a project can be stymied by problems with new technology and legal issues. Yet, the irony is that without all the delays, James would never have used Acrobat as the platform for *How to Read a Film*.

The story tells how, back in 1991, James Monaco has lunch with a friend who runs a multimedia publishing company. The friend suggests that the book, *How to Read a Film*, that James had written in the 1970s would make a good multimedia project. James immediately agrees!

James goes to the the publisher of the printed book, who rejects the idea. The publisher says the CD-ROM rights belong to them (despite the fact that electronic media, such as CD-ROM, didn't exist in 1975 when the original book contract was signed). Despite the dispute with the publisher, James decides to go ahead with the project.

In 1993, the multimedia company starts work on the disc. By 1994, James has hired a production crew. They plan to produce multimedia enhancements, such as a short film that will provide the footage for the various editing labs on the disc. James records audio notes for the chapter introductions.

By June of 1995, the production team has finished editing the film for the labs and has assembled the rest of the film clips. All the source material is delivered to the multimedia company. A few sample elements are sent to James. He is not pleased. There is too much text and the graphics make it hard to read. He doesn't feel the animation is right. He knows that as little as eight seconds of animation can make a reader impatient. A few months later, Apple introduces QuickTime Virtual Reality. James's team is one of the first to buy the equipment to shoot panoramic images of Hollywood studios.

In December of 1995, the team decides they need a new platform for the presentation. They choose Oracle Media Objects over HTML.

These shots show some of the PDF documents in *How to Read a Film*. Each area of the splash screen has a link object that takes you to a different part of the book.

The small icons in the margins of the text pages link to diagrams, movies, and interviews that illustrate the main text. Here, the author offers introductory comments on the chapter.

All pages that contain a movie open with a short click sound effect. This sound cues the viewer to place the cursor over the image to trigger the movie.

Movies, such as this one of the sky-cam in action and the zoetrope, help illustrate parts of the text in ways that no print text and still photos ever could.

In June of 1996, the team feels the disc is sluggish and buggy. Fortunately, just a few months later, Oracle kills the Oracle Media Object software. By December, the disc is on its third producer. James sends an ultimatum to the multimedia company. They must finish the disc or step aside.

In 1997, the multimedia company bows out of the project and James and his team reformat the disc in HTML. They believe that HTML has become the standard for multimedia content. The problem is that they have little control over how a reader views the product. Nevertheless, by June they have a working version of the disc in HTML. James is pleased and feels they should have gone with HTML the year before. (Why didn't the team use Macromedia Director like most most multimedia producers did at that time? The answer is that they had large amount of text in the four books on the disc. Director doesn't handle text very well.)

By July, the DVD format has been introduced. This proves to be a fortuitous development. Rather than produce the book on CD-ROM, they decide to switch to DVD-ROM. DVD has a greater capacity than CD, which means they should be able to fit more than three hours of video on the disc. DVD also has a faster speed, which makes it able to handle the movie content better. The added space means the artwork can be resaved at "millions of colors" instead of 256. The question still remains, will anyone have DVD-ROM drives to play the disc? The industry promotion is that by early 1998, most PCs will ship with DVD-ROM drives.

By June of 1998, computers are not shipping with DVD-ROM drives the way everybody said they would. The team takes the opportunity to redo all the film clips, since the newer compression codecs are superior to the ones they'd used four years ago. There are still some browser issues—especially the lack of control —which makes it difficult to choose either Netscape or Internet Explorer. For the rest of the year, the project is put on hold.

By the middle of 1999, James has solved the legal issues with his book publisher. They will publish the book version; James can publish the multimedia edition. In the fall, James makes an important decision. He decides to eliminate the browser issues entirely and shift the delivery platform to Acrobat. James had been thinking of this choice for several years. Acrobat gives a publisher control over layout and fonts that is missing with HTML. Acrobat 4, released in the spring of 1999, appears to have solved all the production problems. Since the team has used Framemaker to format the four books on the disc, they can easily be exported as PDF files. Although all the parts of the disc are in place, it is going to take several months to reshape the disc. There are four huge books, thousands of illustrations, over a hundred movie clips, and assorted notes and pop-up elements to arrange and format.

Six months into 2000, the team is still working out the kinks in the disc. Although Acrobat is cross-platform, there are issues with how the software works on Macintosh and PC. In the fall of 2000, the disc is finished and sent out for replication.

Since its publication, the disc has received high praise from critics who have called it "The best visually rich, interactive and stimulating eBook available. Highly recommended!"— Shlomo Perets, MicroType. "…the closest thing to a film school in a box that you're likely to find for $39.97."—Orlando Sentinel. The disc also received the DVD Excellence Award for 2001 from the DVD Association. For information on *How to Read a Film*, visit www.readfilm.com.

One of the most extensive uses of movies in *How to Read a Film* is the Cutting Room section. This contains the unedited footage for the various types of shots used in the short film produced for the disc. These shots let the viewer see the differences between camera angles, two-shot, and pan. The disc also shows the difference between a director's cut and the editor's cut. The raw footage is also included on the disc so students can create their own edit of the movie.

The disc also takes advantage of the interactive features of QuickTime movies. For instance, the diagrams are movies that consist of several static graphics. The viewer moves over the QuickTime triggers to see the difference between the illustrations.

Not all interactive elements are movies or sounds. Footnotes are displayed as links that open small separate PDF files.

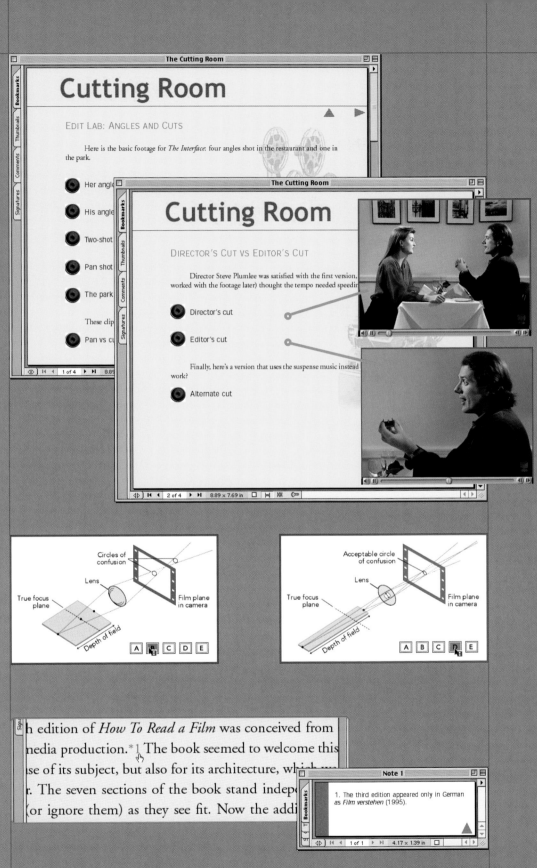

Presentations

We can hear some of you asking, "Hey, with all those interactive buttons, can I use Acrobat to make my presentations instead of Microsoft PowerPoint?" It's never occurred to us to use PowerPoint for presentations—most likely, due to our graphic design background. We have, however, noticed countless questions and threads in PDF discussions about how to convert PowerPoint presentations into PDF documents. We also see a trend—graphic designers who want to use their professional layout tools as the basis for creating dynamic presentations. This is all possible using Acrobat and PDF.

10.1 | Creating Dynamic Presentations with Adobe Acrobat

With Acrobat's full screen feature, any PDF can instantly become a presentation. Think about it. You don't have to do anything to the document other than go into full screen mode or specify that the document opens in full screen mode. Presto—instant presentation. If the presenter knows the keyboard commands for the hand, zoom, scroll, page forward, and page backward tools, this instant presentation can appear seamless and very professional.

Before we go any further, let us state unequivocally that we have nothing against Microsoft PowerPoint. PowerPoint is a terrific program for salesmen and other non-designers to use to organize their thoughts and create internal slide presentations. Unfortunately, many people feel that the same slides they present to their colleagues are suitable to present to potential clients and the general public. Would you use Microsoft Word to create an important annual report or brochure? Of course not. Yet that's exactly what you do when you use PowerPoint for a public presentation.

There are many reasons to use Acrobat instead of PowerPoint. For example, you can't rely on someone having the same version of PowerPoint. So your presentation may not play on other people's machines with the same effects that you created. (Although there is a free PowerPoint player, it is much less widely distributed than the Acrobat Reader.)

You don't have to worry about the viewer having the same fonts as you. Although PowerPoint 2002 has the ability to embed the fonts used in the document, we've seen presentations in the past ruined by missing or substituted fonts. PDF documents are inherently cross-platform and can easily be posted on websites and viewed through web browsers. PowerPoint

documents need to be converted to HTML files before they can be viewed on the web, whereas PDF files do not.

Acrobat is the perfect convergence of content and media created from other applications, such as Illustrator, Photoshop, Premiere, Final Cut Pro, Flash, QuarkXPress, PageMaker, InDesign, Microsoft Word, Excel, and even PowerPoint. In other words, Acrobat plays well with others.

It's easy to re-purpose existing print content into a quality presentation without limitations on typography, layout, and color. For example, if you use the high-quality typography in Adobe InDesign, you get the same quality typography in a PDF document. The transparency features in Photoshop, Illustrator, or InDesign also translate into PDF documents.

Acrobat's value-added interactive features, such as rollover buttons, links, movies, and sound, are easy to learn and implement. If created with the proper settings, PDF file sizes are usually much smaller than PowerPoint files. Of course, this doesn't mean that any PDF document automatically makes a good presentation—but more on that later.

Let's say you've traveled across the country and the laptop you were going to use for a

Glenn Page is the principle director of GPMC, a marketing and sales consulting firm. GPMC creates interactive marketing presentations for its clients that can be sent by e-mail or downloaded from a website. Using PDF as the platform, these iBrochures are excellent presentations that go far beyond the typical slide show. These are just a few frames from the opening of the company's own interactive sales piece.

Although simulated here in print, the transitions from one page to another create a dramatic opening for the presentation.

The combination of vector graphics and sound effects make the presentation look like a Flash movie.

Notice the effective use of contrasting color.

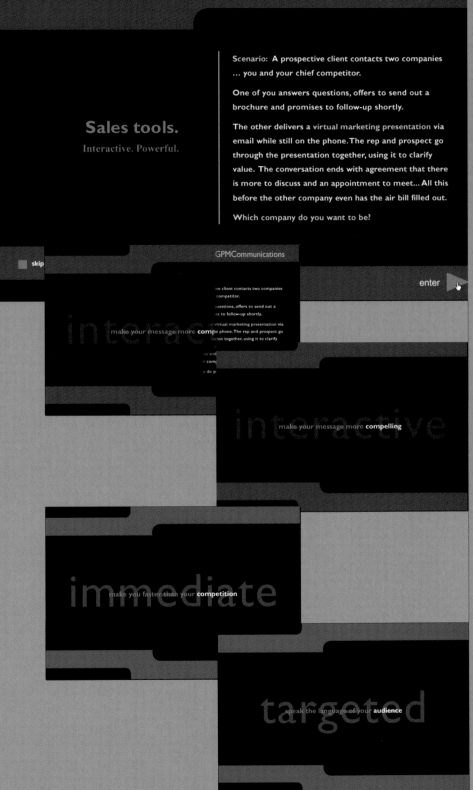

presentation has a problem. (This actually happened to Pattie Belle and Bjørn in Bergen, Norway.) If you have posted your PDF presentation on the web, you can use anyone else's machine (Windows or Mac) to present the document. You can even download the Reader software to the backup computer. (Pattie Belle and Bjørn recommend e-mailing the presentations to yourself before leaving the office, so you have the option to download your PDF file from anywhere in the world.) As frequent speakers around the country and around the world, we've experienced and seen quite a few problems while on the road. See the Planning for the Worst-Case Scenario section, later in this chapter.

Though we do promote PDF for presentations, there are some disadvantages. PDF is a final format. Even with the Touchup tools, you will want to edit a presentation back in the original authoring application. Acrobat is not template-driven like PowerPoint. You can't just grab style #42 and throw in the text. (Fortunately, this also means that your presentation is less likely to look the same as the fellow who just preceded you onstage.)

Acrobat doesn't have the single focus on presentation that PowerPoint does. Acrobat doesn't have as many slide show effects as PowerPoint. (But then again, we think people have a tendency to over-use and misuse the transitions and special effects in PowerPoint.)

PRESENTATION DESIGN

Design your presentation with the authoring application of your choice. Pattie Belle and Bjørn mainly use QuarkXpress and Illustrator, although they agree with Sandee that the future will include InDesign. Here are a few presentation design fundamentals to keep in mind during the pre-PDF process.

Layout Grid

Just as any print document is designed on a grid of some sort, your slide designs should incorporate a basic underlying grid for the placement of text, images, media, logos, etc. The goal is to present a clear, easy-to-read, and memorable message. The layout should direct the audience to the key points, while at the same time present information in a visually interesting format.

Define the overall visual theme and style for the presentation. Create master slides (master pages if you use QuarkXpress or InDesign) for the presentation using the same grid, fonts, colors, graphics, and object placement. To create continuity, rhythm, and flow, use different layout variations (but the same underlying grid) for slide variety.

Design a system of page layouts based on the use of your grid and the repeating elements of the presentation. The unexpected changes in layout will help to keep audience attention during the presentation. Don't get too elaborate. You may end up destroying the reception of your information with too much visual competition. Don't be afraid of white space. This is the term for the amount of slide (or page) that is not covered by image and text. White space provides a visual pause, or rest, for the viewer's eyes.

The size of your slides should be in close ratio with your screen for best results. Power-Point creates slides that are 10 x 8 inches, but we usually base our slide size on a standard video size of 640 x 480 pixels. We round this figure off to 9 x 6 inches if we're working in an application that does not support pixel measurement. Create a bank of your own "slide templates" for future use. We keep blank documents of these sizes with basic grid formatting in all our favorite application formats. If we have to throw together a quick presentation, we open one of these templates and bring in the content.

Color

Just as you start with an underlying grid for structure, you should also create a simple color palette before you begin creating your slides. Contrast and legibility are the key concerns when it comes to using color in presentations. All projectors are not created equal and color variation from your monitor to the actual projection scenario can be quite dramatic. In some instances, color variation can even destroy the legibility of the presentation. The only way to have absolute control over this is to provide the projector yourself—not always feasible. Play it safe and stick to a simple, high contrast color palette. This should improve as the baseline for projector technology improves.

Copy

Keep the number of words per slide and per sentence to a minimum to get the message across. Slides are meant to be visual aids for the audience, not a script for the presenter. Use short sentences. Use numbered lists or bulleted lists. Use charts, graphs, and illustrations.

On the other hand, it is possible to have too little copy in the slide. A slide with just three bullet points that is projected for more than ten minutes of discussion is great way to put your audience to sleep.

Presentation Typography

When it comes to slide typography, the number one concern is readability. Let's start with point size. If your presentation is going to be projected in front of an audience, you want to err on the larger size. How can you tell what will be legible to an audience from looking at your monitor? Well, you can't. In an ideal scenario, you would be able to test your presentation using the actual projector setup in the

presentation room. However, that is rarely possible. Allow us to offer some gross generalizations that should keep the back of the room from getting out their binoculars.

Our fail-safe recommendations are 36-point or larger type for headings and titles, and 24-point type for body text. Pattie Belle often uses 14- to 18-point type for body text. She's lucky—she speaks in front of various audiences several times a week, week in and week out. This allows her to test her documents on a variety of projectors, and in a wide range of spaces.

Don't get crazy with your font selection. Create a style sheet for your font choices, sizes, and colors. Pick two families that complement each other, such as a serif and san-serif, and use one for the headings and titles and one for the body text and captions. Italics and all-caps may be harder to read than plain text, so use them sparingly. If you are using bullet points, try to tighten the language to simple phrases rather than long sentences. This helps the audience focus on the key concepts of the presentation.

Visuals

Visuals can enhance slides and increase audience retention of key points. Use photographs, illustrations, charts, graphs, symbols, and icons to illustrate your content. Media elements, such as movies, sound, and animation can also act as information enhancements. Rollover text buttons and show/hide fields can be used to enhance the visual aspects of the presentation. For example, if your slide has a question that you are discussing, the answer can be revealed with rollover text.

HYPERLINKS AND CROSS-DOCUMENT REFERENCES

A presentation can also be greatly enhanced by hyperlinks, cross-document references, and web links. The success of these techniques depends upon the presentation scenario, web access, document library, dependent applications, etc. This method is probably the easiest way to customize a presentation on the fly.

Perhaps you realize that your audience expects more details on a key subject. A few hyperlinks to the appropriate website can instantly provide the added material. Instead of creating a one-size-fits-all presentation, build a library of interconnected PDF files that can be customized on the fly to fit the audience. Remember, in most presentation settings, your audience does not know what you plan to present. They never need to know you changed the content at the last moment.

PREFLIGHTING PRESENTATIONS

"The best-laid schemes o' mice an' men Gang aft agley" (Robert Burns). "Be prepared!" (Boy Scout motto). "Anything that can go wrong, will go wrong." (Murphy's Law).

Obviously, things went wrong long before computers and electronic presentations. That's why you need to consider every possible scenario for what might go wrong and how you can fix it. You wouldn't believe the number of backup operating system and application disks we take on the road for our speaking and training assignments. Here are the preflight checklists we use as we create PDF presentations.

Author Application Checklist

Make sure you do the following while in your authoring application. Spell-check and proofread the document. Remember, Acrobat's Spelling command only works on comments and forms, not the text from the authoring application. But don't rely on spell check for everything. It can't find errors if they are "reel" words. Check the spelling of proper nouns, names, and terms not included in the application's dictionary. Check the links for placed images, charts, graphs, and illustrations. Check colors, typefaces, capitalization, punctuation,

and layout for consistency. Electronic style sheets can help avoid errors. Also, use the book feature to coordinate styles and colors across multiple documents. Proof for bad line breaks and stray single words.

During PDF Creation

Do the following during the process of distilling the document, or saving as a PDF file. Double check the page-size specifications in the Document Setup dialog boxes. Even if you are going to present the document on your own machine, make sure all the fonts are embedded. You never know when you'll have to work on someone else's computer.

After PDF Creation

Set the following options in Acrobat. Specify appropriate open and full screen options (covered in the next section). Test your page transitions and timing. Test all sounds, movies, and links. This is especially important if you have moved the files from one computer to another. Memorize the keyboard commands for all navigation tools.

Worst-Case Scenario Back-up Plan

Your file gets corrupted. Your hard disk fails. Your computer is stolen. Take the following steps and you'll be able to work on anyone else's computer. Burn a cross-platform CD and pack it separately from your laptop. Upload your presentation to a website or e-mail the PDF to yourself at an address you can access from any computer.

A new approach to creating charts came from this study of the coffee-making experience by student designer Melissa Olsen. Instead of a series of links leading from one page to another, this document is one very long chart. The viewer uses the Hand tool to scroll along the document. As the cursor moves over the different elements, new images appears and sounds are triggered.

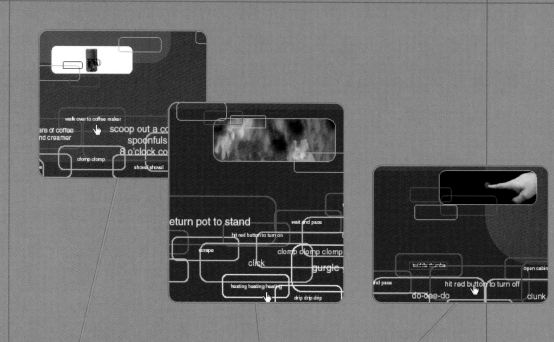

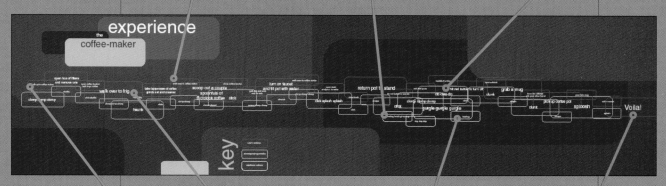

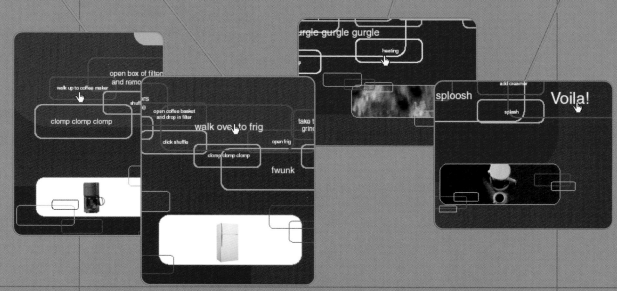

When Sandee was asked to teach an Illustrator session for Russell Brown's ADIM (Art Director's Invitational Master) class, she used the special relationship between Illustrator 10 and Acrobat to create these interactive training materials.

The document was created in Illustrator and then saved as a PDF file.

Sandee added comments and sounds to include instructions on how to create the art.

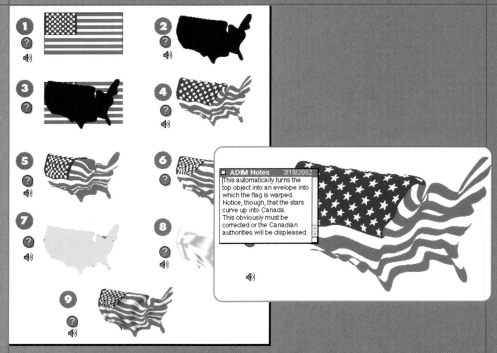

You'll find a copy of this document included on the CD.

Sandee also extracted the comments as their own PDF files and added those pages to the first page. This lets her students read all the steps necessary to create the art-work.

When the document is opened in Illustrator, the comments and sounds are not visible. When the file is reopened in Acrobat, the comments and sounds are visible.

Pattie Belle teamed up with Sharon Steuer to create Zen of the Pen, a workshop on how to use the Pen tool in Illustrator, FreeHand, and several other applications. It can be purchased online at www.zenofthepen.org. The materials are divided up into small packages so students can download just the files they need to use.

The PDF document consists of exercises that contain Quick-Time movies which explain the various steps.

The course also contains templates that can be used to understand the principles of working with the Pen tool. These templates are available in the five applications covered by the course. You'll find a Zen of the Pen Demo on the Master Class CD.

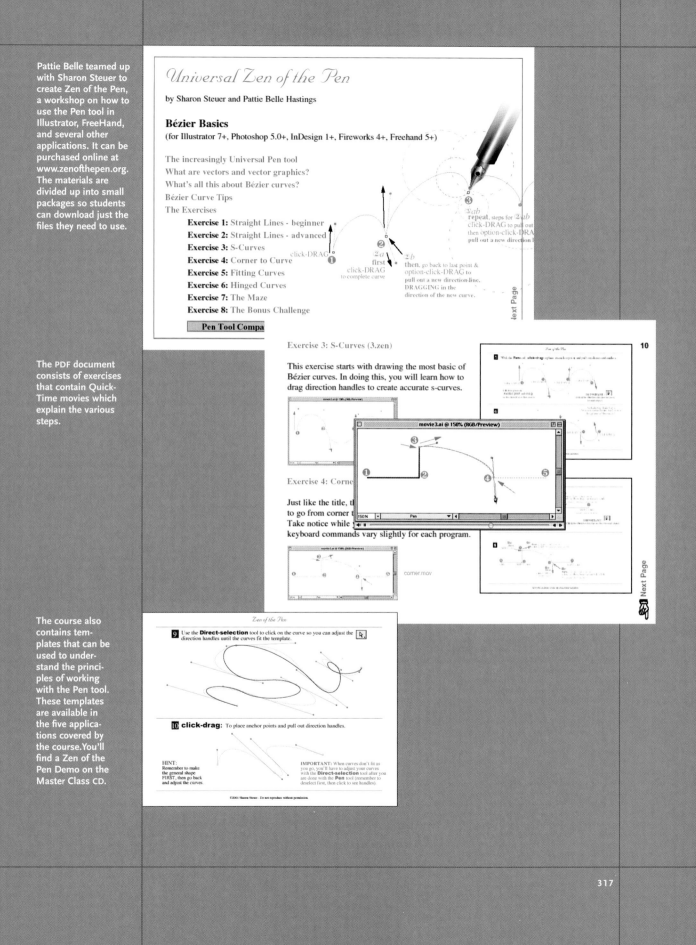

10.2 | Full Screen Mode

What's the most important part of an Acrobat presentation? The opening. You don't want the first thing that your audience sees to be you resizing a document window; moving the title bar up to the top of the screen; madly clicking to close palettes and tool bars; and then zooming in and out to the correct magnification. This is the electronic equivalent of watching the Three Stooges trying to get their act together.

OPEN IN FULL SCREEN MODE

Back in Chapter 3, we looked at the Document Open Options. These options control how the document appears when it is first opened. The Open in Full Screen Mode in the Document Open dialog box is an important setting for presentations.

The Full Screen mode hides everything that isn't part of the presentation. The document opens with none of the following elements visible: menus, tool bars, palettes, document window, computer desktop, icons, other applications, operating system controls. Furthermore, if the document window does not fit exactly inside the computer screen, a background color will appear around the document. In the Full Screen mode, no one ever needs to know you are working in Acrobat. After you choose Open in Full Screen Mode, the document doesn't automatically change into the Full Screen mode. You have to close the document and then open it to see the Full Screen setting, or you can choose View>Full Screen.

You can't count on the fact that someone will stay in the Full Screen mode. Anyone who knows the keyboard command for View>Full Screen (Ctrl-L for Windows or Command-L for Macintosh) can switch to the normal view.

SETTING FULL SCREEN PREFERENCES

Once you have set a document to open in the Full Screen mode, you'll still need to set the full screen behavior. Choose Edit>Preferences> General and then click the Full Screen category. The Full Screen Preferences will appear.

FULL SCREEN NAVIGATION

The full screen navigation options are very helpful if you want to create a self-running kiosk-style presentation. These options control how you can move from one page to another. If you have memorized the shortcuts for the navigation commands under the Document menu, or you use navigational elements contained within the document, you probably won't need to set these options.

Advance every [number] seconds sets the presentation to run automatically with a specific time interval between each page. Even if this setting is turned on, you can still use manual clicks and keyboard shortcuts to override it and move through the document.

Advance On Any Click allows you to move through the presentation by pressing the mouse button. This is very useful for kiosk displays in which you don't want the user to use the keyboard to close the document or quit the program.

Loop After Last Page turns the presentation into a never-ending document. Unless you want to mesmerize a seated audience, this option is better left for kiosk displays.

Choose File>Document Properties>Open Options to set the Window Options to Open In Full Screen Mode. Use the Full Screen Preferences to set the behavior for the full screen mode.

Document Open Options

Initial View

- ● Page Only
- ○ Bookmarks and Page
- ○ Thumbnails and Page

Page Number: 1 of 2
Magnification: Default
Page Layout: Default

Window Options

- ☐ Resize Window To Initial Page
- ☐ Center Window
- ☑ Open In Full Scr
- ☐ Display Docum

User Interface Options

- ☐ Hide Menubar

Preferences

Accessibility
Batch Processing
Color Management
Comments
Digital Signatures
Display
Extract Images
Forms
Full Screen
Identity
JavaScript
Layout Grid
Online Comments
Options
Self-Sign Security
Spelling
TouchUp
Update
Web Buy

Full Screen Navigation

- ☑ Advance Every 5 Seconds
- ☑ Advance On Any Click
- ☑ Loop After Last Page
- ☑ Escape Key Exits

Full Screen Appearance

Default Transition: Random Transition
Mouse Cursor: Always Visible
Background Color: ■

Blinds Horizontal
Blinds Vertical
Box In
Box Out
Dissolve
Glitter Down
Glitter Right
Glitter Right-Down
No Transition
✓ Random Transition
Replace
Split Horizontal In
Split Horizontal Out
Split Vertical In
Split Vertical Out
Wipe Down
Wipe Left
Wipe Right
Wipe Up

✓ Always Visible
Always Hidden
Hidden After Delay

Cancel | OK

The five basic transition appearances (from left to right): Blinds, Box, Dissolve, Split, and Wipe.

Escape Key Exits designates the Escape key to exit from the Full Screen mode to the normal view. The Escape key function used to stop a movie supercedes this command, so if a movie is running you'll have to hit the Escape key twice to exit Full Screen.

When you set a document to run in the full screen mode, you may frighten inexperienced users who may think your presentation has taken over their computer. They may not know that they can press the Escape key; close the file; or quit Acrobat to get back to their computer. For those users, you might consider creating a button that executes the menu item View>Full Screen. Give the button a name such as "Back to the Computer Screen" to let users know that they can escape from the full screen.

FULL SCREEN APPEARANCE

These options offer refinements relating to how the Full Screen mode should be displayed. It is important to remember that all of these options are not contained within your document. This means that you cannot rely on the same settings when your presentation is shown on another computer.

Transitions are the graphic devices that replace one page with another. Acrobat offers 19 transition choices in the Default Transition menu. These choices can be grouped into five categories: Blinds, Box, Dissolve/Glitter, Split, and Wipe. The option for Random Transition

```
Blinds Horizontal
Blinds Vertical
Box In
Box Out
Dissolve
Glitter Down
Glitter Right
Glitter Right-Down
No Transition
✓ Random Transition
Replace
Split Horizontal In
Split Horizontal Out
Split Vertical In
Split Vertical Out
Wipe Down
Wipe Left
Wipe Right
Wipe Up
```

uses an assortment of the listed transitions. The setting for No Transition and Replace may appear identical, but there is a difference. No Transition lets one page replace another without any control over the visual display. This may cause some page elements to flicker or redraw poorly. If that happens, choose the Replace transition, which forces a better page replacement.

The options in the Mouse Cursor menu let you set what should happen to the mouse cursor. Always Visible keeps the mouse cursor visible throughout the presentation. Use this setting especially if you want your user to click buttons or other onscreen elements. Hidden After Delay hides the mouse cursor a few seconds after the Full Screen mode begins. However, if the user clicks or moves the mouse, the cursor reappears. This is an excellent choice to keep the screen uncluttered without immobilizing the user from using the mouse. Always Hidden hides the mouse cursor immediately after moving into the Full Screen mode. It does not reappear even if the mouse is clicked or moved.

If the PDF document does not completely fill the screen, you'll need some sort of fill around the document. The Background Color option lets you choose the color for that fill. The default setting is black which means that most people will have a black color surrounding their document. Sandee routinely changes

① Choose File>Document Options>Open Options. Set the Window Options to Open in Full Screen. Save the changes.

Document Open Options

Initial View
● Page Only
○ Bookmarks and Page
○ Thumbnails and Page

Page Number: 1 of 2
Magnification: Default
Page Layout: Default

Window Options
☐ Resize Window To Initial Page
☐ Center Window On Screen
☑ Open In Full Screen Mode
☐ Display Document Title

User Interface Options
☐ Hide Menubar
☐ Hide Toolbar
☐ Hide Window Controls

[Cancel] [OK]

her background color to match one of the highlight colors in her presentations such as the red in the text.

CREATING A SELF-RUNNING PDF
The following steps can be used to set a document to automatically advance from one page to another with a transition.

Step ① Set the Open Options
Choose File>Document Properties>Open Options. Choose Open in Full Screen from the Window Options. Set the Magnification to Fit in Window to see the entire presentation. Set the Page Layout to Single Page to see one page at a time. Click OK and then save the changes to the file.

Step ② Set the Document to Repeat
Choose Edit>Preferences>General. Then click the Full Screen category. The Full Screen Preferences appear. To create a self-running document, choose Advance Every [number] seconds. Set the time to reflect the length of time you feel it would take a moderate reader to read the page. To create a document that runs continuously, choose Loop After Last Page.

Step ③ Set the Transition
In the Full Screen Preferences, choose one of the transitions in the Default Transition menu. Close the preferences.

To test the settings, close the document and then reopen it. Watch the document run at least twice to make sure the advance, loop, and full screen settings work correctly.

OPENING MULTIPLE DOCUMENTS IN FULL SCREEN
Sandee discovered this technique recently when she had to quickly present 30 different PDF documents as a single presentation. The Full Screen mode can also be used to string separate single-page documents into what looks like one presentation. Open all the documents in Acrobat. Set the the Full Screen Appearance as desired. Switch to the Full Screen mode. The first document appears. Use the keyboard shortcut to close the document. The next document appears in the Full Screen mode with the transition you selected. Close each document to continue through the presentation.

Transitions set in the Preferences are different on each machine. You also can't set different transitions for each page in the Preferences. The next section shows how to create transitions that can play anywhere.

---

② *Set the Advance Every [number] settings for the amount of time you'd like between the pages.*

Preferences

Accessibility
Batch Processing
Color Management
Comments
Digital Signatures
Display
Extract Images
Forms
Full Screen
Identity
JavaScript
Layout Grid
Online Comments
Options
Self-Sign Security
Spelling
TouchUp
Update
Web Buy

Full Screen Navigation
☑ Advance Every [5] Seconds
☑ Advance On Any Click
☑ Loop After Last Page
☑ Escape Key Exits

Full Screen Appearance
Default Transition: Random Transition
Mouse Cursor: Always Visible
Background Color: ■

Cancel   OK

③ *Set the Default Transition for the document. Close the document and then reopen it to test the settings.*

Blinds Horizontal
Blinds Vertical
Box In
Box Out
Dissolve
Glitter Down
Glitter Right
Glitter Right-Down
No Transition
✓ Random Transition
Replace
Split Horizontal In
Split Horizontal Out
Split Vertical In
Split Vertical Out
Wipe Down
Wipe Left
Wipe Right
Wipe Up

10.3 | Embedding Page Transitions

The major limitation associated with using page transitions is that they are controlled by the preferences on each user's machine. Fortunately, there are several ways to embed the instructions for page transitions within the document. This makes it possible to create sophisticated page transitions that play anywhere, without relying on the user's preference settings.

ACROBAT PDFMARKS

Back in the days of Acrobat 3, the Acrobat CD contained a folder of transition EPS files. You imported an EPS into the page layout. When the document was distilled, the transition was embedded as part of the page. These transitions overruled the preference settings and allowed different transitions for each page. If you have access to an Acrobat 3 CD, you can still use those files.

EMBEDDING PAGE TRANSITIONS FROM THE JAVASCRIPT CONSOLE

These days there are easier ways to embed page transitions. The JavaScript Console lets you type in commands (calls) that control page transitions. Using the JavaScript console, you can set different transitions for the various pages. You can also set the length of time each transition runs. More importantly, these transitions work in the normal and full screen modes. This method of embedding transitions also works when the document is viewed in Reader 4.

Is this easy? We asked the most code-phobic member of our team (Sandee) to try it. Here are the steps she took to add the Box In transition for the first two pages of a document. Don't try to understand the code, right now;

> **ON THE CD**
>
> *The JavaScript from this section is included on the Acrobat Master Class CD. You can copy and paste it from our text file into the JavaScript Console.*

we'll explain it all after you've followed the steps and seen it work.

Step (1) Open the JavaScript Console

Choose Tools>JavaScript>Console. The JavaScript Console dialog box appears. Don't worry about any text that may be in the console area. The main concern should be the new text you enter.

Step (2) Type the JavaScript

Click inside the white area of the console, and make sure you're on a new line. Enter the following code as one line, exactly as written. (Watch for the spaces after the colons and commas.)

```
this.setPageTransitions({nStart: 0,
aTrans: [-1, "BoxIn", 1], nEnd: 1});
```

Press the enter key on the numeric key pad to send the code from the console into the document. If you've entered the text correctly, you will see the word "undefined" appear in the console text area. If you're on a keyboard that doesn't have a numeric keypad, hold the Alt key (w) or Control key (m) when you press Enter (Return) to execute the script.

Step (3) Save and Test

Save the file, close the document, and then reopen it. Use any of the navigation controls to move between pages. The first two pages

PDFMARK

If you still have your CD from Acrobat 3, look for the Trans (W) or Transitions (M) folder in the Utility folder. Place the EPS files onto the page in the authoring application. Then distill the file. The transitions are embedded in the file. This is how the code looks in a text editor, such as BBEdit.

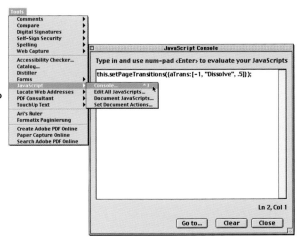

JAVASCRIPT CONSOLE

This is quite an easy method, even if you are not familiar with JavaScript. Go to Tools>JavaScript> Console and type the script into the console. Hit Enter on your numeric keypad and the word "undefined" will appear. You can test your results by moving from page to page. You must save the document for the transitions to be permanent.

THIRD PARTY PLUG-INS

These products provide an interface for setting page transitions. They can all be purchased from the Planet PDF ePublish store at www.epublishstore.com.

Actino Software's Presentation Tool (W), $75, lets you set the duration and page advance, in addition to the transition.

Kas Thomas' TransitionAny (W) $50, does page transitions only.

ARTS PDF Tools (W/M) $149, does page transitions and a whole lot more.

will appear with the Box In transition. The other pages will appear with whatever transition has been set in the Full Screen Preferences. If you want to modify your embedded page transition, you must enter the new call in the console and then press the Enter key to send it to the document.

UNDERSTANDING THE JAVASCRIPT PAGE TRANSITIONS CODE

Here's a breakdown of the JavaScript code in the previous exercise.

```
this.setPageTransitions({nStart: 0,
aTrans: [-1, "BoxIn", 1], nEnd: 1});
```

This phrase says the script is to set the page transitions.

```
this.setPageTransitions({nStart: 0,
aTrans: [-1, "BoxIn", 1], nEnd: 1});
```

nStart specifies the page of the document for the transition. Acrobat starts numbering pages with 0.

```
this.setPageTransitions({nStart: 0,
aTrans: [-1, "BoxIn", 1], nEnd: 1});
```

aTrans sets the definition array for the transition.

```
this.setPageTransitions({nStart: 0,
aTrans: [-1, "BoxIn", 1], nEnd: 1});
```

The information in the square brackets is an array, and sets the definition of the transition. The first number controls how long (in seconds) the page is displayed. The value of -1 turns off automatic page advancing.

```
this.setPageTransitions({nStart: 0,
aTrans: [-1, "BoxIn", 1], nEnd: 1});
```

This is the name of the transition as it appears in the preferences. Type the name of all transitions without any spaces.

```
this.setPageTransitions({nStart: 0,
aTrans: [-1, "BoxIn", 1], nEnd: 1});
```

This number sets the duration of the transition. The 1 here stands for one second.

```
this.setPageTransitions({nStart: 0,
aTrans: [-1, "BoxIn", 1], nEnd: 1});
```

The nEnd number stands for the last page you want the transition applied to. If you want only one page to have the transition, you can delete this part of the code.

Applying a Transition to All the Pages

If you want to apply a transition to all the pages in a document, use this code. (Here, we changed the transition to Dissolve.)

```
this.setPageTransitions({aTrans:
[-1, "Dissolve", 1]});
```

Deleting the Embedded Code

What if you want to get back to a normal document without embedded transitions? You'll have to send a command to delete the embedded transitions. (Clearing the JavaScript Console won't work.) Here's the code to delete the transitions from the first two pages.

```
this.setPageTransitions({nStart: 0,
nEnd: 1});
```

⚡ EMBEDDING TRANSITIONS

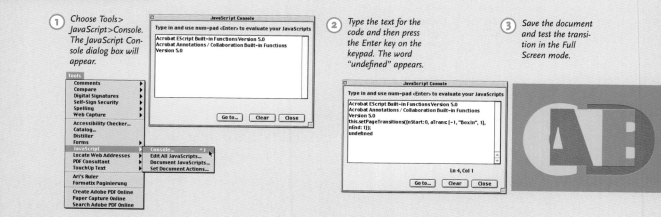

1. Choose Tools> JavaScript>Console. The JavaScript Console dialog box will appear.

2. Type the text for the code and then press the Enter key on the keypad. The word "undefined" appears.

3. Save the document and test the transition in the Full Screen mode.

ARTS PDF Tools

Pattie Belle calls ARTS PDF Tools her Acrobat time management system. It's actually a customizable tool bar that comes with more than 70 pre-defined tools and advanced Acrobat commands. You can also make and edit your own tools.

Imagine, if you will, having a button on your tool bar that instantly applies all your favorite Open Document options! The Set Open Options button allows you to define any or all of your favorite Docu-ment Open Options: Open with the page only, with bookmarks or thumbnails; page number, magnification and layout; open in normal or full screen mode; and hide or display the menu, tool bar or window controls.

You can add any of the pre-defined tools by selecting them and importing them onto the tool bar. You can also make new tools by selecting your own commands and menu items, and then assigning a tool bar button to them. You can copy and share your custom tools with other users by using the Import/Export feature. You can even create a new blank PDF from within Acrobat.

Although ARTS PDF Tools is available for both Mac and Windows, it is the first product that provides a user inteface to customize and embed page transitions on the Macintosh. It comes with three tools for page transitions: Apply Transition to Current Page, Apply Transition to All Pages, and Display Current Page Transition.

ARTS PDF Tools also gives you access to advanced tool creation with JavaScript. Many of the plug-in's built-in tools contain JavaScript that is completely open to modification. This means it can be used in the creation of other custom tools.

The demo version allows you to use five tools before you have to restart Acrobat. ARTS PDF Tools is available for $149 at www.epub-lishstore.com.

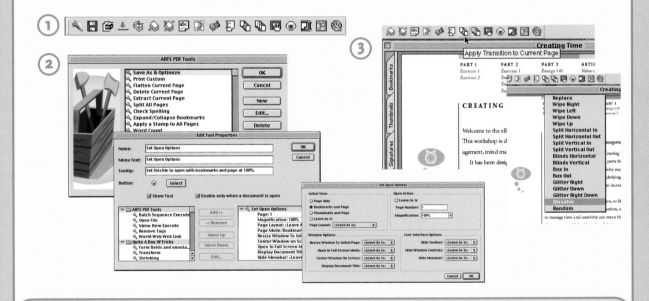

1 Some of the ARTS PDF Tools as they appear on the Acrobat tool bar.

2 Want those instant Document Open Options? Click on the Wrench to open the tool box, select the Open Options tool from the list and click Edit. The dialog box lets you select all your favorite settings. From that point on, all you have to do is click the Open Options button on the tool bar and the options will be instantly set.

3 Click the Apply Transition To Current Page button to pick from the list of Acrobat's built-in page transitions. These can be applied to individual pages, as well as the entire document.

10.4 Transition Magic

When we first saw Glenn Page's PDF presentations we were blown away! They were unique—they looked more like Flash movies than Acrobat files. When we found out how he created them, we were even more amazed. The first thing you'll notice when you view his documents is that they seem to be self-running presentations. Then, they stop and let the user interact with the elements. Certainly, that can't be possible—but there it is. Here's a little background on Maestro Page, and some of the secrets behind the curtain.

Glenn Page calls himself a corporate consultant, but that hardly does justice to his talents as a designer, copywriter, salesman, voice-over announcer, and PDF-magician.

FROM PRINT TO INTERACTIVE MARKETING

Glenn is the principle director of GPMCommunications, a corporate sales and marketing firm. Several years back, Glenn felt he had reached a creative dead-end with print documents and decided to make the move to digital marketing. He had been working in QuarkXPress and InDesign and was looking at the possibilities of multimedia and interactive presentations using Macromedia Director. Then one of his client requested a PDF proof of a project.

While researching the features of Acrobat, Glenn came across information on interactive PDF files in Ted Padova's PDF Bible. His interest was piqued. Unlike Director, Acrobat and PDF allowed him to use his familiar print software and still create animated, interactive projects. He also had much better control of text. Acrobat was the multimedia application he had been looking for.

Glenn's first project was an interactive portfolio for himself. He was immediately impressed with Acrobat's ability to transform print-based documents into multimedia experiences. He also realized that interactive, PDF brochures (Glenn calls them iBrochures) are much more than ordinary slide presentations. They give the viewer a range of options for navigating through the document. The more time a viewer spends playing with one of Glenn's iBrochures, the more likely they are to call or e-mail for more information.

BEHIND THE SCENES AT GPMC

Glenn uses his own small studio with professional audio equipment and software. This is very important, as he makes ample use of sounds and voice-over narration.

His Acrobat files start in InDesign with a page size of approximately 9 x 6 inches. This allows them to fit neatly into most computer screens, with just a little background color.

The iBrochure presentations are designed to be downloaded from a company's website or sent as an e-mail attachment. The animation for the iBrochures comes not from movie objects, but through the clever use of page transitions. This helps keep the size of the iBrochure to a minimum.

For the page transitions, Glenn used BBEdit to open the EPS files from the Acrobat 3 CD. He then changed the timing of the transi-

ON THE CD

Samples of Glenn Page's PDF presentations can be found on the Acrobat Master Class CD. You can find more information about Glenn's work at www.gpmconnect.com.

GPMC iBrochures are designed with all the care of print documents. This type of control is not possible with other presentation applications.

tions—faster or slower—to suit his needs. The timing of these transitions is actually the most critical aspect. The transitions can't be too long or too short. Glenn spends a lot of time testing the transitions.

He then imports these EPS files onto their own layer on the appropriate pages in InDesign. He can also put one transition on a master page to apply it to all the pages in the document. He then converted the InDesign documents to a PDF document using Distiller. Although InDesign has an Export as PDF feature, that feature does not recognize the EPS transition files.

CREATING A CUSTOM AUTO-RUN PRESENTATION

Glenn uses the EPS page transition files from the Acrobat 3 CD. However, you can achieve the same effect by embedding page transitions using the JavaScript Console. The following steps show how to use page transitions and page actions to create a custom self-running presentation. The benefit of using the embedded transitions is that they override any transitions set on the user's machine.

The presentation opens in the Full Screen mode. When the document opens, the first five pages are automatically displayed with custom transitions that wipe from left to right. The

> **FOLLOW ALONG**
>
> *Look on the CD for before and after versions of the Autorun document featured in these steps. You can open the after version to see the finished effect. Then open the before version to follow along with the steps.*

visuals create a countdown effect: 05 04 03 02 01. On the fifth page, the presentation stops. A button lets the viewer move to the next page. On the last page, the viewer clicks a button which exits the full screen mode.

Step (1) Set the Page Transitions

Our first step adds the code to the JavaScript Console. Choose Tools>JavaScript>Console. Click in the Console field and enter the following code.

```
this.setPageTransitions({aTrans:
[-1, "WipeRight", 1]});
```

This code set applies the Wipe Right transition to all the pages with a one-second transition time. We set the timing for all the pages so we could control the appearance for the entire document.

Don't set the timing too fast. At first we tried a tenth of a second and found that Acrobat couldn't combine the page transition with the page actions at that speed. The presentation just jumped to page five without any transitions at all.

Don't forget to save your work. The code isn't embedded in the document until it is saved.

Step (2) Set the Page Actions

Now you'll need to set the page actions for the first four pages. This moves the presentation automatically through the numbers 05, 04, 03,

⊘ AUTO-RUN PRESENTATION

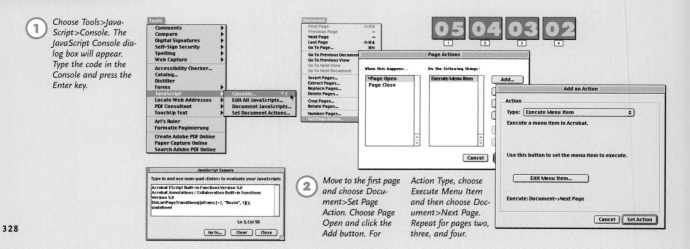

(1) *Choose Tools>JavaScript>Console. The JavaScript Console dialog box will appear. Type the code in the Console and press the Enter key.*

(2) *Move to the first page and choose Document>Set Page Action. Choose Page Open and click the Add button. For*

Action Type, choose Execute Menu Item and then choose Document>Next Page. Repeat for pages two, three, and four.

and 02. It then stops on the page that contains the number 01.

Move to the first page (numbered 05) and choose Document>Set Page Action. Click the Page Open event and click the Add button. In the Add an Action dialog box, set the Action Type to Execute Menu Item. Then click the Edit Menu Item button. Choose the Document> Next Page menu command. Click OK and Set Action to close the Add an Action dialog box.

Move to the next page (numbered 04) and repeat this step. Then move to the next page and repeat the step. Continue until you get to the fifth page, (numbered 01). Then stop. Don't apply a page action to that page. That's where we want the presentation to pause for the viewer's input.

When you set Page Actions to advance from one page to another, you may find it difficult to go back and edit the pages. As soon as you go to the page, the Page Action takes you to the next page. Set the View to Continuous-Facing. This stops the Page Actions, so you can edit pages. You may have to increase the magnification so the odd-numbered pages touch the left-side of the document window. That's how Acrobat recognizes that you're working on a specific page.

Step ③ Create the Buttons

At this point, we want the presentation to stop moving from page to page, in order to allow the viewer to control page navigation. To do this, you'll need to add a custom navigation button. (Glenn Page's presentations are much more complex than this simplistic example, but the principle is the same.)

On page five, (numbered 01), use the Form tool to draw a button. Name the button, and set the action to Execute the menu item to go to Document>Next Page.

On the last page, (labeled AB), use the Form tool to draw a button. Name the button and set the action to execute the menu item View>Full Screen. If the document is in Full Screen, the command exits the mode.

Step ④ Set the Open Options

As a last step, choose File>Document Properties>Open Options. Set the Window Options to Open in Full Screen. Set the Magnification to the size that is appropriate for your document. We chose Fit in Window. We also chose the Page Layout as Single Page. This forces us to remember to reset the document from Continuous-Facing to Single Page.

Save your work and close the document. Reopen the file and test all the transitions and buttons.

③ On page five, use the Form tool to create a button with the Document>Next Page command.

On the last page, use the Form tool to create a button with the View>Full Screen command.

④ Choose File>Document Properties>Open Options. Set the Window Options to Open in Full Screen. Set the Magnification as desired. Set the Page Layout to Single Page.

eBooks

The world of publishing is in the midst of a Gutenberg-sized revolution—the birth of the eBook. Like most birthing processes, it has not been painless. The publishing industry is not new to change—in the 20th century alone there have been countless dramatic technological changes in print production (from movable type to linotype to desktop publishing) that have completely transformed the industry. While some people were quick to adopt the new technology, others have protested—just as when the paperback or "pocket book" was introduced. Similarly, in the infancy of the eBook, history repeats itself as formats change and companies struggle, compete, merge, or buy each other out. While this goes on, there is an enormous amount of debate about the merits and drawbacks of digital publications. These discussions range from in-depth analysis of reading on screen to securing content via digital rights management.

11.1 Creating eBooks for the Acrobat eBook Reader

One seismic shift in the publishing landscape is evident in financial allocation. With eBook publishing, the costs of printing, shipping, and warehousing are eliminated, which should greatly reduce expenses. However, while the financial investment can now be focused on the author, design, content and promotion, the true costs of developing, designing and building websites, servers, tech support, and digital rights management systems are enormous—eating up any potential savings from the elimination of traditional expenses. It's hard for us to imagine that there will be a significant reduction in the costs of e-publishing in the near future. While it seems to make sense that an eBook should cost less than its printed counterpart, that is not always the case. In fact, many eBooks cost as much as bound books.

In spite of industry and standards chaos, and despite the resistance of some readers, we believe the eBook is here to stay.

For the narrow scope of this book, we will discuss Acrobat PDF eBooks, and for the even narrower scope of this chapter we will discuss PDF eBooks created specifically for viewing in the Acrobat eBook Reader. We won't argue the merits or defects of eBooks and eBook technology—we'll leave that to the various Internet forums and pundits. In this section, we'll present the basic information necessary for the design and creation of eBooks for Acrobat eBook Reader. Watch carefully for the differences in our discussions about the Acrobat Reader vs. the Acrobat eBook Reader.

> **ⓘ EBOOK GLOSSARY**
>
> **Encryption** *translates digital content into code that can't be accessed without a "key" or password.*
>
> **Digital Rights Management** DRM *systems are used to control viewing access to digital content, such as Adobe's Content Server.*

WHAT IS AN EBOOK?

One of the challenges in working with eBooks is defining exactly what an eBook is. We take a fairly broad definition. An eBook is an electronic document that contains any of the following elements: text, graphics, video, sounds, or animations. These elements are linked together into a single electronic unit. What this means is that a folder on your hard drive full of text files and graphics is not an eBook. But if you use a program to link all the text and graphics together into a purposefully designed document, then it is an eBook.

The term eBook does not define the type of software or hardware device that displays information. There are several competing formats for displaying eBooks. A PDF eBook is an eBook created using the Portable Document Format created by Adobe Systems Inc. A PDF eBook may be able to be read by Acrobat Reader or may require the special Acrobat eBook Reader.

ADVANTAGES OF THE PDF EBOOK

There are a few distinct advantages of eBooks over bound books. These include speed of delivery; no warehousing needed; non-predetermined number of copies; the ability to contain and transport a large numbers of books in a single device; an instantaneous dictionary; advanced hyper-linking, cross-referencing, and search capabilities; and the ability to contain media-rich content, such as sound and movies. eBooks allow for a new kind of reading experience, not unlike the introduction of other historical content delivery systems, such as radio, film, television, and the World Wide Web. And like the eBook's technological predecessors, its existence does not mean the extinction of the previous form (i.e., the printed-page book), especially since it does not easily fulfill the 4B-criterium: to be read on the Bus, in the Bed, in the Bath, and at the Beach.

There are a variety of formats for eBooks—some that are tied to a device, and some that are tied to a specific software or programming language. Currently, the advantages weigh heavily on the side of the PDF eBook. A few of these advantages include visual fidelity, the familiarity of pages, compact file size, the ability to annotate readings, cross-platform viewing and distribution, re-purposing of existing content, and the fact that there are millions of Acrobat Reader users. There are also software, systems, and servers in place for the encryption, digital rights management, and distribution of PDF content.

DESIGNING EBOOKS

The first rule of eBook design is that it should not be a direct digital translation of the printed work, but a completely separate version designed specifically for the screen. In the same way that the design for printed matter does not translate well to broadcast television, the design for a printed page does not always translate well to viewing on a computer screen. An eBook should also be approachable, easy to use, and easy to navigate. Many people widely recommend testing design for the web, and we suggest the same for ebook design—test, test, and test again. This means looking at your eBook design on as many different computers, monitors, and platforms as you can find. How does the typography perform? How does the color appear? Test for usability by actually observing how people read the eBook, or solicit user observations from friends and colleagues. Most important of all, don't throw out a successful model entirely; learn what you can from 500 years of book design.

Page Format

If you are designing for the Acrobat eBook Reader, we recommend that you use a format of 6 inches wide by 9 inches tall. If you are designing your book to be read in Acrobat Reader, then you have a choice of whether to go portrait or landscape (tall or wide). Some early eBook designers advocated for a wide format that is more in ratio with the computer screen. Others advocated for standard book and page ratios, based on their printed counterparts. It's too early in the lifespan of the eBook to rule out any particular format. You must make a decision about size based on

Here are a few sample grids for placing the main body of a text on the 6x9 inch page format.

The top and bottom page margins can be different from each other, but in order to have a smooth transition while turning the pages, the left and right margins must be the same width. Be sure to look at your design in single page view and as two page spreads. Books that rely less on text and more on images have more flexibility in terms of grid and margins.

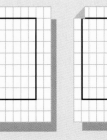

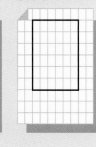

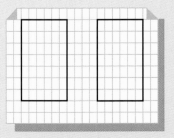

the content of the book, how it will be used, and the technology used for viewing and distribution.

Keep in mind that, unlike website design, books need a lot more white space for the eye to rest. In other words, don't cram the page with text, images, or other elements. White space is the term used to describe an area not containing images, text, or graphics. That doesn't mean it is literally a white space, but rather an area that is open. (Much of the white space in this book is actually a light yellow.) You can use margins to help create some of this white space, but keep them consistent and equal on the left and right sides. The gutter margin of a bound book is traditionally wider than the outer margins, but often your reader will be viewing an eBook as single pages and not spreads. You don't want the margin to jump back and forth from page to page.

Commit the same attention to detail and careful formatting as you would to a high quality printed book. If you are designing for the Acrobat eBook Reader, be sure to use its Open Document feature to test your designs in the actual software.

Typography

You'll need about 10 to 12 pixels in height for a text line to display properly onscreen. You'll want to keep this measurement in mind when testing type sizes. The general consensus on type size for eBooks falls between 12–14 points depending on the font family, x-height, and weight. Compare that to the standard 10 pts for body copy in printed books. We also recommend that you use generous leading (space between the lines of text). These two factors (larger type size and over-leading) contribute

> **ⓔ ADOBE CONTENT SERVER**
>
> *This is Adobe's software for packaging, encrypting, and distributing eBooks for the Acrobat eBook Reader. It works between the database and the web server by applying security and rights, or permissions, to individual books. These permissions include the ability to print, copy, give or loan a book, and whether the text to speech function is enabled. For more information on Adobe Content Server, visit the Adobe website.*

the most to legibility and comprehension of screen reading. Looser tracking (the space between letters) is also recommended. Some designers debate whether serif or sans-serif type is more readable on screen. We are not going to take a side on this one. We like to use both and make our decision based on the content, design, and testing of the document. If you wish to use a serif font, it needs to be a little chunkier—not too fine as the serifs might be too delicate to display. Line length should be kept short for readability—about 70 characters per line, maximum.

The more complex the content, the more important it is to design for a hierarchy of information. This means using headings, sub headings, captions, and call-outs to differentiate and lead the reader through the content. Remember, most of all, design your typography for readability.

Interactivity

You wouldn't be taking advantage of the special qualities inherent in an eBook if you didn't build in some interactivity. Usually, one of the first levels of interactivity to address is navigation, but the eBook Reader has the basic navigation built into the software. If you are designing a book that is not meant to be viewed in eBook Reader, then you'll want to design a navigation system that is consistent throughout the book. (For more on this subject, refer to "Navigation for PDFs" in the Interactive PDF Chapter.) The most minimal navigation system would be Next Page and Previous Page.

Your book should, at the very least, contain a hyper-linked Table of Contents (TOC). If it is a work of nonfiction or a reference book, then we also recommend that you include a link back to the table of contents from every page. If your readers haven't yet placed a bookmark on the TOC page, it can be annoying and cumbersome to grope around using the eBook

Reader's navigation. The same can be done for an index, if one exists for the book. You can also create hyperlinks to additional source materials and references on related websites.

Dynamic elements, such as rollovers and buttons, add movement and provide access to additional text, images, captions, figures, diagrams, or illustrations. eBooks viewed in the Acrobat Reader can contain sound and movies. But for the time being, the Acrobat eBook Reader cannot display movies or play sounds. So books viewed using the eBook Reader can only link to media-rich websites to deliver audio and video content.

Keep It Simple, Keep It Small, and Other Miscellaneous Advice

Don't bother with Acrobat Bookmarks and Thumbnails when designing for the eBook Reader. They add file size with no real benefit to the user.

When creating your original files in Quark-XPress, PageMaker, or InDesign, place as many of your repeating visual and interactive elements (destinations, links, and navigational buttons) on the Master Page as possible. This will greatly reduce the final file size when you distill the PostScript file.

If you want your document page numbers to match the Reader interface page numbers, you must go through the process of renumbering pages in Acrobat 5.

Use thin rules (.5) with caution or not at all. Acrobat 5, Acrobat Reader 5, and Acrobat eBook Reader do not display them consistently, even with anti-aliasing turned on. Some lines appear thick and some appear thin, even though they were created with the same specifications. There are workarounds for this, but they are a bit complex and involve adding special Post-script code in the Distiller stream.

This point size and font comparison chart was captured from the screen in Acrobat 5 and is shown at 100%. Notice the wide variety of sizes and widths among the different fonts within the same point specification. Also notice that the .5 line rules are not displayed consistently.

12pt.	13pt.	14pt.	
Aa	Aa	Aa	Helvetica
Aa	Aa	Aa	Adobe Garamond
Aa	Aa	Aa	Verdana
Aa	Aa	Aa	Minion
Aa	Aa	Aa	Arial
Aa	Aa	Aa	Time New Roman

The screen shots on these two pages were taken in Acrobat 5 and are shown at actual size. This is a size and leading comparison between two popular typefaces, using a 65 character line length based on 12 point Minion Regular. Notice the difference in legibility, especially the difference between the samples with standard two point leading and the samples with over-leading.

Helvetica 12/14
The general consensus on type size for eBooks falls between 12–14 points depending on the font family, x-height, and weight. It is also recommended that you use generous leading between the lines. These two factors (larger type size and "over-leading") contribute the most to legibility and comprehension of screen reading.

Helvetica 12/18
The general consensus on type size for eBooks falls between 12–14 points depending on the font family, x-height, and weight. It is also recommended that you use generous leading between the lines. These two factors (larger type size and "over-leading") contribute the most to legibility and comprehension of screen reading.

Helvetica 14/16
The general consensus on type size for eBooks falls between 12–14 points depending on the font family, x-height, and weight. It is also recommended that you use generous leading between the lines. These two factors (larger type size and "over-leading") contribute the most to legibility and comprehension of screen reading.

Helvetica 14/22
The general consensus on type size for eBooks falls between 12–14 points depending on the font family, x-height, and weight. It is also recommended that you use generous leading between the lines. These two factors (larger type size and "over-leading") contribute the most to legibility and comprehension of screen reading.

Minion 12/14
The general consensus on type size for eBooks falls between 12–14 points depending on the font family, x-height, and weight. It is also recommended that you use generous leading between the lines. These two factors (larger type size and "over-leading") contribute the most to legibility and comprehension of screen reading.

Minion 12/18
The general consensus on type size for eBooks falls between 12–14 points depending on the font family, x-height, and weight. It is also recommended that you use generous leading between the lines. These two factors (larger type size and "over-leading") contribute the most to legibility and comprehension of screen reading.

Minion 14/16
The general consensus on type size for eBooks falls between 12–14 points depending on the font family, x-height, and weight. It is also recommended that you use generous leading between the lines. These two factors (larger type size and "over-leading") contribute the most to legibility and comprehension of screen reading.

Minion 14/22
The general consensus on type size for eBooks falls between 12–14 points depending on the font family, x-height, and weight. It is also recommended that you use generous leading between the lines. These two factors (larger type size and "over-leading") contribute the most to legibility and comprehension of screen reading.

11.2 | Using Acrobat eBook Reader

Acrobat eBook Reader is Adobe's free software for viewing and organizing electronic books. It's main similarity to Acrobat Reader is that it allows you to view PDFs—other than that, it has been designed for books, book type content, and screen reading. For those familiar with Acrobat Reader, certain tools and functions of eBook Reader follow the same logic. In addition to being a vehicle for the display of books, the software adds the ability to combine reading with online communications. Think of the eBook as a portal to online bookstores, subject-related content, and media-rich resources (such as movies and sound). Even with the eBook in its infancy, a future is visible where reading books will become a truly interactive experience.

The single main purpose of Acrobat eBook Reader is the ability to control digital rights through distribution. This is something that can't yet be done with Acrobat Reader.

eBook Reader offers a number of options that can be customized, such as page view, library settings, text annotations, bookmarks, and connections with bookstores. It is also quick, intuitive, and easy to set up.

SETTING THE PREFERENCES

In the menu, you may set viewing preferences, such as fine tuning CoolType settings, text to speech (Read Aloud function) and rotation of the pages. As with any document, the preferences you specify will dictate how the eBook Reader displays the rest of the pages in the book.

NAVIGATING

Like Acrobat Reader, or a hard copy book, Acrobat eBook Reader allows you to view books as single pages or in spreads. This feature lets users customize their reading according to their needs. Though this may seem like a mundane function, the fact is that eBooks are designed differently, which can affect the way in which a book is best viewed.

Most of the titles available for the Acrobat eBook Reader have been designed for its format (6 x 9 inches). The display can be rotated so viewers can read the eBook on a laptop computer as if it were an open book. (The computer itself is rotated so that the screen is taller than it is wide.) Though this may seem cumbersome to some users with larger displays, it works well on some of the smaller and lighter notebook computers.

There are two main ways you can navigate through an eBook. The first is to use the forward and backward buttons. You can also use the page number bar at the bottom of the window.

Page view can be enlarged and reduced by clicking on the Zoom tool.

LIBRARY OF BOOKS

You can add any PDF or HTML document to the library by clicking Open File on the menu, or by dragging and dropping files onto the eBook Reader window.

> ### ⓘ COOLTYPE
>
> *CoolType is a cross-platform screen rendering technology designed to improve the legibility of text on flat screen displays, laptops, LCD, and hand held devices. It is currently available in Acrobat 5, Acrobat Reader 5, and Acrobat eBook Reader. CoolType is cross-font compatible, and works with Type 1, True Type, and Open Type fonts. The technique is called color anti-aliasing and uses sub-pixel font rendering. This means that the individual sub-pixels of red, blue, or green are controlled to give more definition to individual characters. This creates the appearance of smoother edges on the characters by increasing the horizontal resolution. CoolType can be fine tuned and can be turned on or off in Acrobat 5 and Acrobat 5 Reader.*

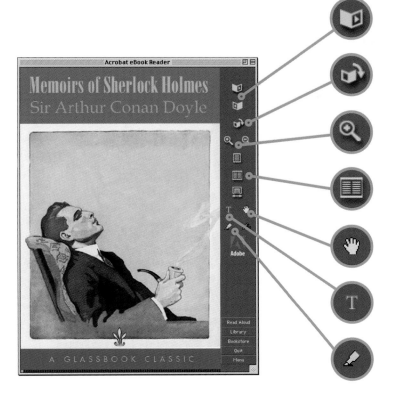

Next Page and Previous Page navigation buttons.

The Rotate button turns the window for viewing sideways on a laptop or hand held device.

The Zoom tools reduce and magnify with a single click.

The Single-Page View, Two-Page View and Fit Width buttons allow viewers to customize the page view.

The Hand allows a viewer to scroll when zoomed in on a page.

The Sharpen Text button allows you to adjust CoolType for legibility.

The Highlight and Annotate tools can be used to highlight text or add notes.

This menu gives you access to information about the books, preference settings, the dictionary, and permissions.

The Library offers a unique way of storing your titles. Books can be stored and organized in a number of ways, including by title or author, much like a physical library works. The benefit of the Library, of course, is that you don't have to physically move volumes around. You store information with a simple click of the mouse.

MENU

The menu allows you to access the title's publishing information, such as publisher, page count, and size (select a title and go to Menu> Info while in the library mode). It also gives you the permissions settings for a specified title, so you'll know if you are allowed to print, read aloud, or loan the book.

BOOKMARKS/ANNOTATIONS

Similar to the traditional method of dog-earing a page, electronic bookmarks can be added throughout an eBook. A bookmark can be added by simply clicking on the corner of a page. As bookmarks become numerous, they can be accessed and displayed through a list in the Menu.

As with a highlighter (either a physical one or an electronic one, such as the Acrobat Reader tool), text sections can be highlighted with notes attached.

In addition to the text highlighter, eBook Reader features a Note tool that lets you write in the margins of your book. The notes display can be turned on or off by clicking on the left corner of the box.

> **ⓘ OTHER FORMATS**
>
> *Strictly speaking an eBook is simply a book in an electronic form. PDF is not the only form of eBooks. Microsoft has created their own software, called Microsoft Reader, which allows you to read books saved in its electronic format. PDF documents can't be read in the Microsoft Reader. The Microsoft Reader is only available for Windows computers. eBooks can also be displayed on PDA devices or on dedicated eBook devices, such as the Franklin eBook-Man. At this time, it is unclear whether any specific format will become a standard for all eBooks.*

DICTIONARY/DOUBLE-CLICK

If you double-click a word anywhere in the text, the integrated dictionary will automatically open its definition for you.

READ ALOUD

The Read Aloud option is particularly helpful for people who are vision impaired. You must first check to see if the permissions have been set to allow the Read Aloud feature of a specific eBook. (We haven't figured out why a publisher would not allow this, but many books that we have downloaded have not included permission for this function.) eBook Reader pronunciation and cadence leaves something to be desired; it does take a little getting used to. It has potential to be used more widely for accessibility.

OTHER CONSIDERATIONS

When the Acrobat eBook Reader is installed, or a PDF eBook is downloaded, it is locked to the specific computer it is initially installed on. This is probably the biggest drawback in the adoption of eBooks. Remember to first back up the eBook Reader Data folder, in case you need to reinstall or upgrade your system software. If you do alter your system software, you'll have to call Adobe eBook Reader support in order to get an authentication certificate to gain access to your books. We've already read editorials complaining about these limitations.

As you create or download eBooks, remember that this technology is still in its infancy. You are bound to experience problems. We suggest that you experiment with using Acrobat eBook Reader by downloading some of the free eBooks on the Adobe website.

The Library has several methods for sorting and retrieving books. You can also create your own categories.

CoolType configuration and rotation direction can be found and modified in Menu>Preferences.

THE OLDEST MILITARY TREATISE IN THE WORLD

Our favorite feature—the double-click instant definition.

Menu>Info presents the title's publishing information and the access button that reveals the permissions.

The dictionary can also be found by selecting the Menu button on the tool bar.

The copying, printing, and read aloud permissions for Treasure Island.

The reader can make annotations with either a Highlight tool or a Note tool, which has a text function.

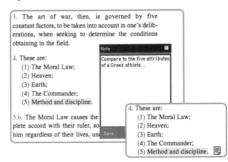

11.3 Translating Classics from Paper to Screen

Lisa Clark, a book designer for 13 years, had been working at Harvard University Press for ten years, when she stumbled into the new and exciting world of eBooks. In 1998, she met the two founders of the eBook company, Glassbook. Shortly after this meeting, they approached her to design a PDF eBook to give away with their GlassBook Reader software. She began designing for Glassbook. In August 2000, Adobe Systems acquired the Glassbook company. The Glassbook Reader became distributed as the Acrobat eBook Reader. Lisa Clark is now the eBook Publishing and Design Manager for Adobe Systems.

Lisa Clark had been trained in traditional printed book design. So when she was first offered the job to design eBooks, her mind was flooded with doubts and reservations about this new electronic format. Would people really want to read a book on screen? Who would give up the tactile relationship with a bound book?

Then she started thinking of all the possibilities of the new medium. "In fact," she thought, "it might just be fun to design an electronic book. It could be and do all the things a paper book couldn't. An eBook would have the ability to contain hyperlinks, sounds, movies, search capabilities, and would be able to cross-reference other sources."

Lisa liked the fact that the Glassbook Reader worked with the PDF file format, because the PDF format ensures the visual integrity of a design. Embedded fonts keep the text as set, lines do not reflow, and graphics do not become separated from their references. She wanted these first eBooks to counteract the notion of the sterile screen and lost aesthetics. She also wanted to translate elements of traditional book design, in order to maintain a sense of place, time, and visual heritage for these texts.

To achieve this effect she used traditional typographic elements, such as rules, dingbats, letter spacing, small caps, and color that evoked the design of classic letterpress books. She also used a combination of font families, such as Minion, Sabon, Bernard Modern, Perpetua, and Gill Sans in ways that exhibited the kind of high typographical standards that can't be reproduced in other eBook formats. Sensitivity to small details on a page made an enormous difference to the final book.

Like any other small start-up publishing company, Glassbook wanted to keep costs as low as possible on these first books. For this reason, they chose to publish classic texts that had entered the public domain. Lisa kept costs low by creating the interior illustrations entirely from public domain sources, enhanced with a few of her own embellishments. The beautifully appropriate and evocative cover illustrations were all images purchased inexpensively from PhotoDisc, then modified in Adobe Photoshop to suit Lisa's design needs.

500 YEARS OF KNOWLEDGE

Lisa's experience and expertise in book design is apparent in her final eBooks. The careful attention to detail in the typography, covers,

The cover of *This Side of Paradise*, as it appears in the Acrobat eBook Reader. Lisa used Bodoni Poster Compressed, Sabon, and Bernard Modern as the typefaces for the cover and the inside text.

The title page and the beginning of a chapter in the Acrobat eBook Reader, showing single page view and spread view.

and layout of the eBooks set them apart from most other eBooks. Lisa's designs illustrate our feelings that it would be foolish to discard 500 years of knowledge in book design just because the medium is electronic. Some traditional techniques translate quite well to the screen.

Some of the classic details that Clark employed include the addition of borders, rules, and dingbats on the title pages. She even created a tiny Raven dingbat for the Poe collection. The typefaces were chosen to reflect the time and mood of the content. The placement of the book title and page numbers on the interior pages of each book is deliberate and elegant.

The Acrobat eBook Reader lends itself to traditional notions of the book with consecutive pages and a beginning, a middle, and an end. Even though there is enormous potential to break new ground in the definition of what a book or eBook is and does, the current status of eBooks is transitional and the content available still falls into the traditional categories of what we normally think of as books.

When you go to design your first or next eBook, we advise you to pick a few tomes off of your bookshelf and thumb through them for inspiration.

CLASSICS TO EBOOK PROCESS

The techniques used to create an eBook are similar to those found in traditional book publishing. Lisa first creates sample pages which contain the different designs for her book. Unlike traditional publishing, she does not evaluate the designs on paper. Rather, she creates sample PDF files that she views in the Acrobat eBook Reader. Once the sample pages are approved, she creates the final PDF document.

① Build in Quark

Lisa designs and constructs the pages in QuarkXPress 4. Illustrations and embellishments are created and modified in Photoshop and Illustrator, then placed in the QuarkXPress document. The QuarkXPress document is then printed to a PostScript file with the fonts subset embedded.

② Distill

The eBook optimization settings in Distiller make this step quite simple. These settings provide a moderate amount of compression for graphics without sacrificing too much quality. (See the following subhead for modifications that Lisa Clark recommends.) The PostScript document was opened in Distiller with the eBook Job Options selected. It was then converted to a PDF document.

③ Link TOC with Chapters in Acrobat

Simple links were created for each chapter entry in the Table of Contents using the Link tool. (These links would be automatically created if InDesign or PageMaker was used to create the PDF document.)

⚡ EBOOKS PROCESS

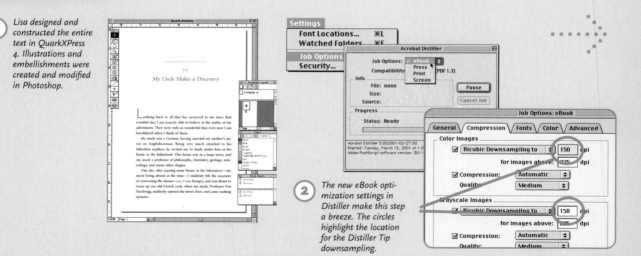

① Lisa designed and constructed the entire text in QuarkXPress 4. Illustrations and embellishments were created and modified in Photoshop.

② The new eBook optimization settings in Distiller make this step a breeze. The circles highlight the location for the Distiller Tip downsampling.

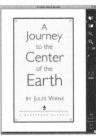

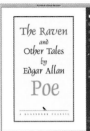

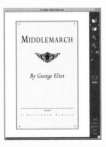

④ Acrobat to eBook Reader

The final step in the process is to upload the finished eBook PDF to Adobe's Content Server for distribution and sale. This is also where you apply the permissions to an eBook. For instance, you may allow an eBook to be read but not to be printed. You can prevent the book from being copied to another computer. You can also add security encryption that requires passwords to open the eBook or to change any of the permissions.

LISA CLARK'S DISTILLER TIP

Adobe added the eBook setting to Distiller as a convenience. This is a combination of Distiller options that produces quality graphics, but with a somewhat smaller file size than the Print Job Options. There is nothing special about this particular setting that is required for your document to be considered an eBook.

Lisa Clark found that sometimes the default eBook setting creates a PDF document that may be too large for convenient distribution. If your eBook PDF document is too large and you are willing to make some visual compromises, Lisa recommends that you modify the default Distiller 5 eBook settings—but only if your document does not contain critical graphic elements!

In Distiller 5, select Job Options>eBook. From the main menu, go to Settings>Job Options>Compression and change the Bicubic Downsampling from 150 DPI to 96 DPI (see step 2 below). This lowers the resolution of halftone images, such as files from Adobe Photoshop, but it does not change the quality of line art or graphics created in Adobe Illustrator.

COLLECTING THE CLASSICS

Most of the high quality, free eBooks that you find on the web are classic texts that have entered the public domain. All of the books you see in this section (and many more) can be downloaded at no cost from Adobe's eBook Central.

You can also find many eBooks for sale at a variety of websites, such as Fictionwise (www.fictionwise.com) and Barnes and Noble (www.bn.com).

The Adobe Systems website contains background papers, information on how to create and distribute eBooks, the eBook Reader for free download, and free eBooks at www.adobe.com. Another good resource, and forum on all aspects and formats of eBook publishing, is Planet eBook at www.planetebook.com.

③ *Simple page view links were created in Acrobat using the Link tool to connect the Table of Contents with the pages of the chapters. To link the Table of Contents to the appropriate page in a PDF file, select the Link tool and draw a rectangle around the chapter heading. This invokes the Link Properties dialog box, where you select Type>Invisible Rectangle and Highlight>Invert. Then you select Go to View from the Type menu, scroll to the page you wish to link and then click Set Link. The page number you link to will appear below the Edit Destination button.*

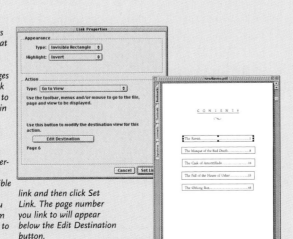

④ *The final step in the process is to upload the finished eBook PDF to Adobe's Content Server for encryption, permissions, distribution, and sale.*

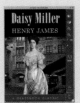

11.4 LiveReads: Integrating Form and Content

In the Spring of 2000, Neal Bascomb and Scott Waxman founded the innovative eBook publishing company, LiveReads. Bascomb and Waxman had both come from successful careers in the publishing industry as editors and agents. When some of the authors they represented began asking questions about eBooks and ePublishing, the duo realized the possibilities of creating a digital publishing company.

Bascomb and Waxman wanted their ebook venture to do more than simply translate printed works into electronic documents—they wanted to create original works for digital publishing. In addition, they wanted these works to be much more than just text on a screen. Their vision for LiveReads was to create eBooks that were portals or windows on a topic. These portals could then use cross-references and external links to connect the reader to other content, in addition to the traditional book text.

This vision culminated in the November 2000 inaugural publication of *Orpheus Emerged*, an unpublished novella written by Jack Kerouac when he was 23 years old. LiveReads achieved their goal of creating their portal on Jack Kerouac by interweaving an interactive Kerouac timeline, journal extracts, background on the Beats, and video and audio references into the novella itself. The publication consists of almost 400 pages of delicately orchestrated content.

CREATING AN EBOOK BESTSELLER

Research into eBook formats led LiveReads to decide that PDF offered the most possibilities in terms of design, media, interactivity, and external links. With PDF, there is no limit on what can be achieved with design or typography, and because there are no print production

costs, you can have color on every page. *Orpheus Emerged* is such a dynamic book because LiveReads approached the design as being part of the content. They were deliberate about using the design of the pages as a way to set the mood and reflect the time, place, and spirit of the 23-year-old Jack Kerouac. Bascomb and Waxman chose to work with Roger Gorman on the design of their first publication. Roger joined the team with a background as a highly successful designer for the music industry.

The team was especially concerned with creating the overall look and feel of the book, as well as with integrating all the sections of different content. It's odd to use the word "feel" when speaking of a digital book, but *Orpheus Emerged* is almost tangible as an object—almost tactile—because of its sensitive and innovative design. The plan was to create an experience that made the reader think differently about the text. One solution was to incorporate callouts as actual streams of the main text. Another was to use the typography as an expression or illustration of the text.

The main body of the novella was designed for two-page spreads, and this is the best way to read the book. The LiveReads consensus at the time was that there were many more possibilities when designing for spreads, as

The cover of the best-selling *Orpheus Emerged*, as viewed in the Acrobat eBook Reader.

The title page, as viewed in the eBook Reader's spread view.

opposed to single pages. This is evident in the juxtaposition of a text page with a full bleed photograph page; the gutter and margin-crossing of graphics and fields of color; and in the flow and rhythm of the typography used for the body of the text. The team followed the strategy of large type, loose leading, and plenty of white space, in order to make the overall experience easier on the eye.

The entire design of the novella was illustrated using only eight photographs. Each of these eight photographs was enlarged, manipulated, or repeated to create a feeling of photographic richness without the expected experience of redundancy. The book layout document was created using QuarkXPress, printed to a PostScript file, distilled to a PDF, and uploaded to the Adobe Content Server. There, permissions were assigned and the document was encrypted for distribution.

HYPERLINK AS NARRATIVE

Orpheus Emerged involves the integration of additional content through a thoughtful system of hyperlinking and navigation. A lot of time was spent on integrating and designing the additional material into the novella. Large sections of the book relate subject matter to background material that stacks consecutively. This includes excerpts from Kerouac's journals, a brief biography, an autobiography, a timeline, background on the Beat movement,

and much more. LiveReads incorporated this content in a way that enhanced the main text and was also easy to navigate.

DESIGN AS NAVIGATION

With so many elements in the eBook, it became important to let the viewer know which part of the book they were reading. For instance, the design of the novella itself keeps the look of a traditional printed page. However, the design of the interactive timeline is similar to the splash screen for a website. Another design look was applied to add footnote-type information to various elements within the text.

Step (1) Linking the Timeline

The Link tool was used to create vertical rectangles that defined the columns for each year of the timeline. In the Link Properties dialog box, the LiveReads design team selected Type> Go to View. They then clicked the Edit Destination button. They navigated manually to the page that corresponded to a specific point in the timeline. They also chose the fit View Magnification. None of the links needed any appearance settings, because the artwork within the timeline defined the link area for each year.

After the link was set, the LiveReads staff could make modifications to the link by switching to the Link tool and double-clicking the link rectangle.

⚡ HYPERLINKING

(1) The Link tool was used to create vertical rectangles encompassing each of the "year" columns.

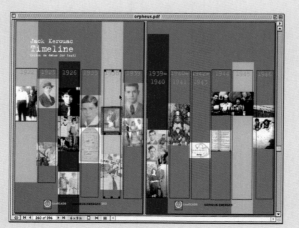

When the Link Properties dialog box appeared, the LiveReads team selected Type>Go to View and Edit Destination.

Step ② Timeline Navigation

After creating the timeline links, LiveReads needed to devise a navigation system to return the viewer back to the timeline from the hyperlink. Three links were created on each page using the Link tool and manually navigating to the correct pages. These links take the reader backward and forward through the hyperlinks, or back to the timeline.

As we discussed in Chapter 4, you can also use buttons to create navigation actions, such as Previous Page and Next Page menu commands. Buttons can easily be duplicated across many pages.

The benefit to working with links, as opposed to buttons, is that they add far less to the final file size. You can also use ARTS Link Tool to copy a link and then paste it onto multiple pages. This allows you to automate the process of creating links.

Step ③ Linking Text References

The novella contains internal text links that were created in the same way as the timeline, but function as a sort of footnote system for the text. The text for these references was colored within the page layout program. Invisible links were then added above the colored text.

Step ④ Text Link Navigation

These hyperlink pages required only one link to return the viewer to the page they were reading in the novella. Each text hyperlink was created individually and manually linked back to its reference page.

Step ⑤ Linking to Multi-Media Content

As we mentioned earlier, the eBook Reader is unable to display or play multimedia content, such as movies or sounds. So the LiveReads team needed to use external links to websites to play the books multimedia content.

The web links for the multimedia pages were created in much the same way as internal links. The Link tool was used to draw a link over the reference to the multimedia content. In the Link Properties dialog box, the designers chose Action Type>World Wide Web Link, and then selected Edit URL to insert the web address. When creating a web link, be sure to include the full address, including the http://.

The eBook also clearly explains that the link is to an external website. It also explains that certain web browser plug-ins are necessary for the multimedia content to be seen and heard. These are two very important nuances to consider when creating hyperlinks in eBooks. The explanation that the link goes to the web is helpful for those people who use a dial-up connection to access the web. This allows them to keep their modem from suddenly dialing the phone.

The notice about the required browser plug-ins gives the reader a chance to install

② These navigation links take the reader backward and forward through the hyperlinks or back to the timeline.

③ The novella contains internal text links that were created in the same way as the timeline, but function as a sort of footnote system for the text.

the plug-ins ahead of time. This type of convention shows thoughtfulness on the part of the LiveReads staff.

BEYOND ORPHEUS

Since the successful publication of *Orpheus Emerged*, LiveReads has added two more original eBook titles to their list. Both titles are excellent examples of the enhanced content that the eBook format provides.

Opening Day by Les Standiford, is a baseball novella that incorporates the history of the Negro Leagues. LiveReads has expressed its eBook vision in this publication by incorporating hundreds of hypertext and website links, streaming audio and video content, an interactive baseball trivia game, and rare photographs from National League Baseball Hall of Fame.

The 7 Steps to Perfect Health, by Gary Null, includes 100 original recipes, healing advice on a wide array of conditions, resource lists, and links. LiveReads added an online shopping component, which links directly to the products that are discussed in the book. *The 7 Steps to Perfect Health* is available as an eBook that can be downloaded immediately after online purchase, as a CD which is shipped to the reader, or as a traditional paperback book.

Bascomb and Waxman continue to experiment and innovate with their digital books. LiveReads has added a production division called The Studio. The Studio enables companies to take advantage of LiveReads' expertise and technical know-how, in order to create their own enhanced reading products. The production division is not limited to eBooks, but can work with any text, or any text and graphics document type. As LiveReads explains, "Anything that is now printed can be transformed into vibrant electronic works."

LiveReads eBooks can be purchased for download from the Barnes and Noble site (www.bn.com) or from the online eBook store, Fictionwise (www.fictionwise.com).

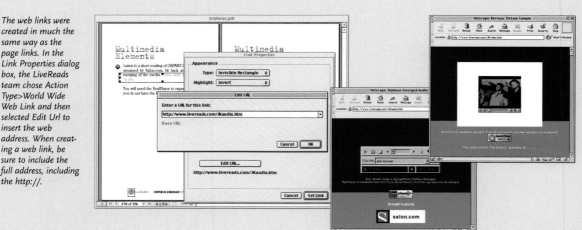

④ The web links were created in much the same way as the page links. In the Link Properties dialog box, the LiveReads team chose Action Type>World Wide Web Link and then selected Edit Url to insert the web address. When creating a web link, be sure to include the full address, including the http://.

These pages show how the design works across spreads, and shows the use of typography to tell the story. Notice that the eBook Reader's navigation system is down the right side and along the bottom of the application window.

The timeline, as viewed in Acrobat eBook Reader.

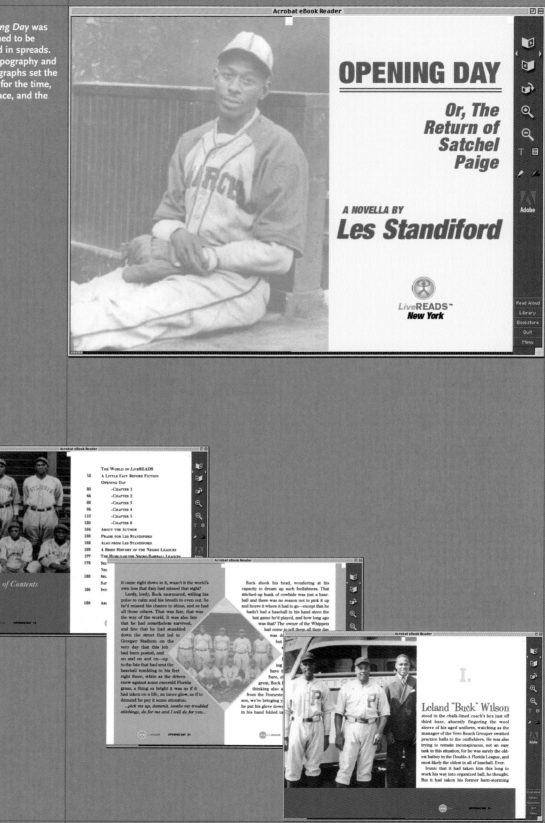

Opening Day was designed to be viewed in spreads. The typography and photographs set the mood for the time, the place, and the game.

Opening Day is hyper linked to background and reference material, as well as web links to rich media and other related sources on the web.

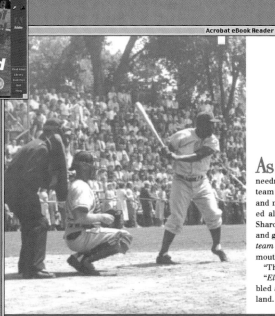

IV.

As it turned out, Wattles

needn't have worried. Hasslebrow called a team meeting before practice the next day and made the announcement. "I just wanted all you men...," here his eyes lit upon Sharon, who had just then crossed her slim and golden legs. "That is, I wanted all of you *team members* to hear it from the horse's mouth."

"The horse's what?" Wattles called.

"*El caballo es un pendejo*," Minoso mumbled absently, as his eyes drifted to another land.

The 7 Steps to Perfect Health adds an eCommerce element by linking directly to an online store and offering discounts for the health products described throughout the book.

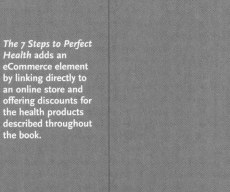

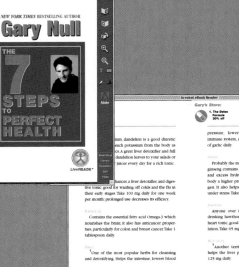

Gary's Store:
1. The Detox Formula 20% off

...ium, dandelion is a good diuretic ...each potassium from the body as ...ics. A great liver detoxifier and full ...dandelion leaves to your salads or ...juicer every day for a rich tonic.

...hancer, a liver detoxifier, and digestive tonic, good for warding off colds and the flu in their early stages. Take 100 mg daily for one week per month; prolonged use decreases its efficacy.

Contains the essential fatty acid Omega-3 which nourishes the brain; it also has anticancer properties, particularly for colon and breast cancer. Take 1 tablespoon daily.

One of the most popular herbs for cleansing and detoxifying. Helps the intestine, lowers blood pressure, lowers cholesterol, stimulates the immune system, and fights viruses. Take 1,000 mg of garlic daily.

Probably the most researched herb in the world, ginseng contains germanium which pulls mercury and excess hydrogen from the cells, giving the body a higher proportion of energy-boosting oxygen. It also helps the body stay in balance when under stress. Take 500 mg daily.

Anyone over the age of forty-five should be drinking hawthorn. Used throughout Europe as a heart tonic, good for arterial and peripheral stimulation. Take 65 mg daily.

Another terrific liver detoxifier, milk thistle helps the liver process toxins and poisons. Take 125 mg daily.

THE 7 STEPS TO PERFECT HEALTH 86

THE 7 STEPS TO PERFECT HEALTH 86

11.5 | ComicsOne

ComicsOne was the first website to offer Japanese comics (called Manga) in eBook form online. Providing comic books in digital format makes it possible for the company to sell eBooks for a fraction of what the printed versions cost. The average ComicsOne price range is $3–$5 for a 200–400 page series, while the printed counterpart is about $15 a copy.

After negotiating relationships with the original print publishing companies, ComicsOne had to go through a number of steps in order to create the eBook versions of Manga.

First, ComicsOne scanned the paper comic, and retouched the images in Photoshop and Illustrator. They then replaced the Japanese text balloons with English ones, and reversed the order of the pages (Japanese books, magazines, and comics read from right to left).

Then they converted the Photoshop files to PDF. The result was a digital version that looked exactly like the original.

The final step was to package the eBook versions for purchase, specify rights, and then encrypt the books using Adobe Content Server software. The ComicsOne website sells their eManga right alongside the printed versions.

You can find out more about ComicsOne and sample the Manga at www.comicsone.com.

ON THE CD

Look on the Acrobat Master Class CD-ROM *for a free Manga eBook from ComicsOne!*

Kazan is a boy warrior searching for his childhood companion on a desert planet. This is an example of the type of black and white comics available from ComicsOne.

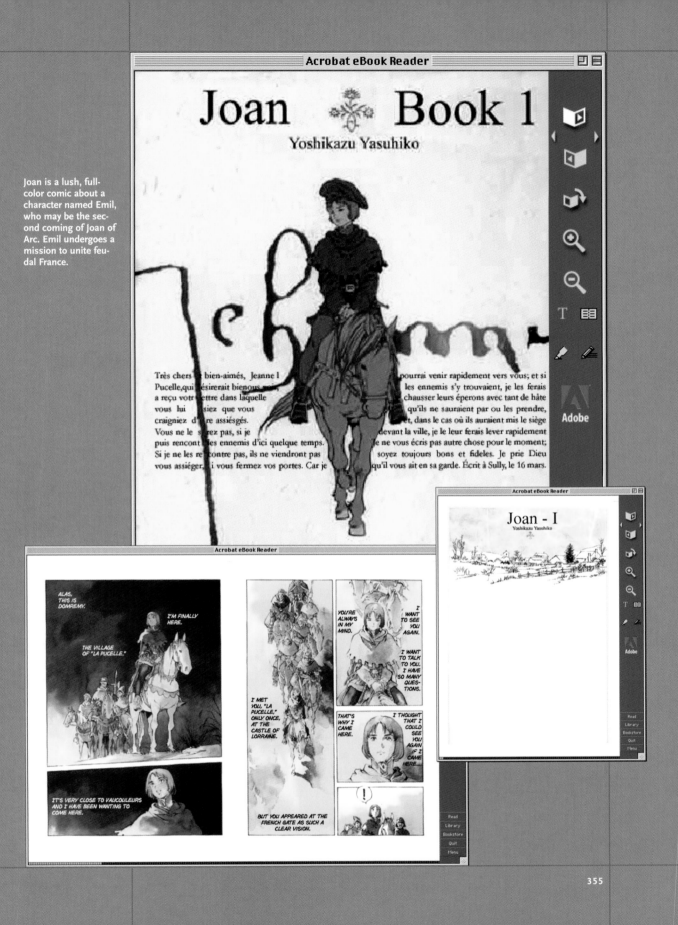

Joan is a lush, full-color comic about a character named Emil, who may be the second coming of Joan of Arc. Emil undergoes a mission to unite feudal France.

QuickGuide to Tools & Shortcuts

THE WORK AREA

MENU BAR

File   Edit   Document   Tools   View   Window   Help

⑧

Menu bar

TOOL BARS

①

File

②

Navigation

③

**View
History**   ④   **Viewing**

⑤

Basic Tools   ⑥

**Commenting
(Acrobat only)**   ⑦

Editing (Acrobat only)

STATUS BAR

1 of 21   8.5 × 11 in

⑨

Status bar

File   Edit   Document   Tools   View   Window   Help

74%

Creating Time

Thumbnail ▼

Bookmarks
Articles
Destinations
Thumbnails
Signatures
Fields
Comments

1

2

3

PART 1	PART 2	PART 3	ARTICLES
Exercise 1	Exercise 3	Energy 101	Value of Time
Exercise 2	Exercise 4	Exercise 7	Digital vs Analog
	Exercise 5		Eat, Drink & be Merry
	Exercise 6		

CREATING TIME

A Time Management Workshop for Creative People

Welcome to the eBook version of *Creating Time: a time management workshop for creative people*. This workshop is divided into three parts that interweave information and exercises on time management, mind management, creativity management, and energy management.

It has been designed with the underlying premise that helping people tap into happiness, health, and creativity translates directly into increased productivity, innovation, fewer absences and better bottom-lines.

Operating a business, organization, or life with efficiency and productivity requires daily innovation, creative ideas, resource allocation, and the ability to adapt to constant change. Learning to manage time and creativity can mean the difference between an individual or organization that operates with health and well-being or one that operates with burnout and high turnover.

1 of 44   9 × 6 in

NAVIGATION PANE
Select your navigation method here. The area is activated by clicking the file tabs (F6), or the Navigation Pane icon in the tool bar. Clicking a tab opens a corresponding navigation method. The navigation choices available depend on whether you use Acrobat or Reader, and what document open settings have been defined. It also depends on the user's choices in the Window menus, and whether the tabs have been dragged into the Tab palette.

STATUS BAR
The Status bar provides quick access to the screen display and the navigation throughout the document. It also displays buttons to show/hide the Navigation Pane, Document Window views, and display of page size and number.

DOCUMENT PANE
This is where the document is displayed. The settings for this area are specified in the document open options.

		M	W
Open *Opens file from directory/folder*		Cmd+O	Ctrl+O
Open Web Page *Makes capture of web pages possible*		Shift+Cmd+O	Shift+Ctrl+O
Save *Saves file to disk (use Save As to save space)*		Cmd+S	Ctrl+S
Print *Invokes print dialog box*		Cmd+P	Ctrl+P
E-Mail *Creates e-mail message and attaches current document*			
Create Adobe PDF Online *Accesses/creates PDF on Adobe's site*			
Paper Capture Online *Accesses/creates OCR on Adobe's site*			
Search Adobe PDF Online *Access/searches documents on Adobe's site*			
Find *Scans open document for word matches*		Cmd+F	Ctrl+F
Search *Searches indexes made with Catalog*		Shift+Cmd+F	Shift+Ctrl+F
Search Results *Displays PDF files by degree of relevance*		Shift+Cmd+G	Shift+Ctrl+G
Previous Highlight *Moves to highlights in previous view*			
Next Highlight *Moves to next highlight selection*			
Show/Hide Navigation Pane		F6	F6

	M	W
Previous Page button	Left Arrow	Left Arrow
Next Page button	Right Arrow	Right Arrow
First Page *Takes you to the first page of file*	Home	Home
Last Page *Takes you to the last page of file*	End	End

	M	W
Go To Next View *Takes you to the next document view*	Cmd+Right Arrow	Alt+Right Arrow
Go To Previous View *Takes you to the previous file view*	Cmd+Left Arrow	Alt+Left Arrow

4 VIEWING TOOL BAR

	M	W
Zoom out/Zoom in	Cmd+ +/–	Ctrl+ +/–
Actual Size *Displays document 100%*	Cmd+1	Ctrl+1
Fit in Window *Sizes document to maximum size in window*	Cmd+0	Ctrl+0
Fit Width *Sizes to fit width of document in window*	Cmd+2	Ctrl+2
Reflow *Reflows tagged PDFs to fit width of window*		
Rotate View Clockwise *Rotates orientation*	Shift+Cmd+ +	Shift+Ctrl+ +
Rotate View Counterclockwise *Rotates orientation*	Shift+Cmd+ –	Shift+Ctrl+ –

5 BASIC TOOLS BAR

	M	W
Hand tool *Moves through document freely*	H	H
Zoom In tool	Z	Z
Zoom Out tool	Shift+Z	Shift+Z
Text Select tool *Selects horizontally (across columns)*	V	V
Column Select tool *Selects one text column*	Shift+V	Shift+V
Graphics Select tool *Selects graphic objects*	G	G

6 COMMENTING TOOL BAR

	M	W
Note tool *Creates note comments in PDF*	S	S
Free Text tool *Creates visible text block*	Shift+S (cycle)*	Shift+S (cycle)*
Sound Comment tool *Attaches or records sound*	Shift+S (cycle)*	Shift+S (cycle)*
Stamp tool *Chooses between library of stamps/graphics*	Shift+S (cycle)*	Shift+S (cycle)*
File Attachment tool *Appends file to document*	Shift+S (cycle)*	Shift+S (cycle)*
Pencil tool *Draws free form lines*	N	N
Square tool	Shift+N (cycle)*	Shift+N (cycle)*
Circle tool	Shift+N (cycle)*	Shift+N (cycle)*
Line tool	Shift+N (cycle)*	Shift+N (cycle)*

		M	W
Highlight tool *Colors/highlights text passages*		U	U
Strike Out tool *Strikes out text*		Shift+U (cycle)*	Shift+U (cycle)*
Underline tool *Underlines text*		Shift+U (cycle)*	Shift+U (cycle)*
Spell Check Form Fields and Comments tool		F7	F7
Digital Signature tool		D	D

⑦ EDITING TOOL BAR

	M	W
Movie tool *Attaches movie clips to document*	M	M
Link tool *Creates internal/external links*	L	L
Article tool *Links text selections into article*	A	A
Crop tool *Crops page(s)*	C	C
Form tool *Creates form fields for interaction*	F	F
TouchUp Text tool *Fixes typos, etc.*	T	T
TouchUp Object tool *Alters mistakes in graphic*	O	O
TouchUp Order tool *Controls the order of graphic objects*	Shift+T (cycle)*	Shift+T (cycle)*

⑨ STATUS BAR

	M	W
First Page	Shift+Cmd+ Page Up	Shift+Ctrl+ Page Up
Last Page	Shift+Cmd+ Page Down	Shift+Ctrl+ Page Down
Previous Page	Left Arrow	Left Arrow
Next Page	Right Arrow	Right Arrow
Single Page document window layout		
Continuous document window layout		
Continuous-Facing document window layout		
Show/Hide Navigation Pane	F6	F6

NAVIGATION PANE

F6 toggles between Show and Hide Navigation Pane

Destinations
Named navigation targets are sorted according to your preferences.
No Properties. Only available in Acrobat.

Bookmarks
Commands list attached to document; mainly used for hyperlinks.
They can be customized according to a set of properties.   *F5*   *F5*

Signatures
Gives information on Digital Signatures pertaining to the
security given in Self-Sign.

Comments
A versatile group of items that can be sorted by different
properties. Comments have many tools/display options.

Thumbnails
Miniature representations of pages created automatically   *F4*   *F4*
that work like hyperlinks.

Articles
These are strings of content tied together. The viewer
clicks on the list and is transported to the content.

(8) MAIN MENU

File Edit Document Tools View Window Help	(M)	(W)
Open	*Cmd+O*	*Ctrl+O*
Open Web Page	*Shift+Cmd+O*	*Shift+Ctrl+O*
Close	*Cmd+W*	*Ctrl+W*
Save	*Cmd+S*	*Ctrl+S*
Save As	*Shift+Cmd+S*	*Shift+Ctrl+S*
Document Properties>Summary	*Cmd+D*	*Ctrl+D*
Document Properties>Fonts	*Option+Cmd+F*	*Option+Ctrl+F*
Document Security	*Option+Cmd+S*	*Option+Ctrl+S*
Page Set Up	*Shift+Cmd+P*	*Shift+Ctrl+P*
Print	*Cmd+P*	*Ctrl+P*
Quit	*Cmd+Q*	*Ctrl+Q*

Tabs (left margin): Bookmarks, Thumbnails, Comments, Signatures, Articles, Destinations

		M	W
Undo		*Cmd+Z*	*Ctrl+Z*
Redo		*Shift+Cmd+Z*	*Shift+Ctrl+Z*
Cut		*Cmd+X*	*Ctrl+X*
Copy		*Cmd+C*	*Ctrl+C*
Paste		*Cmd+V*	*Ctrl+V*
Select All		*Cmd+A*	*Ctrl+A*
Deselect All		*Shift+Cmd+A*	*Shift+Ctrl+A*
Find		*Cmd+F*	*Ctrl+F*
Find Again		*Cmd+G*	*Ctrl+G*
Search>Query		*Shift+Cmd+F*	*Shift+Ctrl+F*
Search>Select Indexes		*Shift+Cmd+X*	*Shift+Ctrl+X*
Search>Results		*Shift+Cmd+G*	*Shift+Ctrl+G*
Search>Word Assistant		*Shift+Cmd+W*	*Shift+Ctrl+W*
Search>Previous		*Cmd+[*	*Ctrl+[*
Search>Previous Document		*Shift+Cmd+[*	*Shift+Ctrl+[*
Search>Next		*Shift+Cmd+]*	*Shift+Ctrl+[*
Search>Next Document		*Cmd+]*	*Ctrl+]*
Properties		*Shift+Cmd+A*	*Shift+Ctrl+A*
Preferences>General		*Cmd+K*	*Ctrl+K*

		M	W
First Page		*Shift+Cmd+ Page Up*	*Shift+Ctrl+ Page Up*
Previous Page		*Left Arrow*	*Left Arrow*
Next Page		*Right Arrow*	*Right Arrow*
Last Page		*Shift+Cmd+ Page Down*	*Shift+Ctrl+ Page Down*

Go To Page	*Cmd+N*	*Ctrl+N*
Go To Previous Document	*Option+Shift+ Left Arrow*	*Alt+Shift+ Left Arrow*
Go To Previous View	*Shift+Cmd+ −*	*Alt+Left Arrow*
Go To Next View	*Cmd+O*	*Alt+Right Arrow*
Go To Next Document	*Option+Shift+ Right Arrow*	*Alt+Shift+ Right Arrow*
Insert Pages	*Shift+Cmd+I*	*Shift+Ctrl+I*
Delete Pages	*Shift+Cmd+D*	*Shift+Ctrl+D*
Crop Pages	*Cmd+T*	*Ctrl+T*
Rotate Pages	*Cmd+R*	*Ctrl+R*

File Edit Document Tools View Window Help   Ⓜ   Ⓦ

Comments>Summarize	*Shift+Cmd+T*	*Shift+Ctrl+T*
Spelling>Check Form Fields and Comments	*F7*	*F7*
Open Web Page	*Shift+Cmd+O*	*Shift+Ctrl+O*
JavaScript Console	*Ctrl+J*	*Ctrl+J*
TouchUp Text>Find First Suspect	*Cmd+H*	*Ctrl+H*

File Edit Document Tools View Window Help   Ⓜ   Ⓦ

Full Screen	*Cmd+L*	*Ctrl+L*
Zoom In	*Cmd+ +*	*Ctrl+ +*
Zoom Out	*Cmd+ −*	*Ctrl+ −*
Zoom To	*Cmd+M*	*Ctrl+M*
Fit in Window	*Cmd+0*	*Ctrl+0*
Actual Size	*Cmd+1*	*Ctrl+1*
Fit in Width	*Cmd+2*	*Ctrl+2*
Fit Visible	*Cmd+3*	*Ctrl+3*

Reflow	*Cmd+4*	*Ctrl+4*
Rotate Clockwise	*Shift+Cmd+ +*	*Shift+Ctrl+ +*
Rotate Counterclockwise	*Shift+Cmd+ −*	*Shift+Ctrl+ −*
Proof Colors	*Cmd+Y*	*Ctrl+Y*
Use Local Fonts	*Shift+Cmd+Y*	*Shift+Ctrl+Y*
Grid	*Cmd+U*	*Ctrl+U*
Snap To Grid	*Shift+Cmd+U*	*Shift+Ctrl+U*

File   Edit   Document   Tools   View   Window   Help   Ⓜ   Ⓦ

Cascade	*Shift+Cmd+J*	*Shift+Ctrl+J*
Tile: Horizontally	*Shift+Cmd+K*	*Shift+Ctrl+K*
Tile: Vertically	*Shift+Cmd+L*	*Shift+Ctrl+L*
Close All	*Option+Cmd+W*	*Alt+Ctrl+W*
Show/Hide Tool bars	*F8*	*F8*
Show/Hide Menu bar	*F9*	*F9*
Show/Hide Bookmarks	*F5*	*F5*
Show/Hide Thumbnails	*F4*	*F4*

File   Edit   Document   Tools   View   Window   Help   Ⓜ   Ⓦ

Acrobat Help	*F1*	*F1*

Contributors and Credits

CHRIS VON ACHEN
32 Union Avenue
Hawthorne, NY 10532
(914) 769-3262
chrisvonachen@earthlink.net
www.chrisvonachen.com
Credits:
Flash Book
© Chris Von Achen

J. KAYE BAUCOM
(704) 296-0232
jkbaucan@earthlink.com
Credits:
The Connected Classroom: Integrating Video
and the Internet in the Classroom (CD-ROM)
J. Kaye Baucom: Concept, design & construction
CD; Diana Radspinner, Director of Education,
KERA; Joan Fallis, Coordinator of Training
Services, KERA; Dorothy Embry, Curriculum
Consultant; Bob Perrenot, cover design.
Funding provided by a grant from Lucent
Technologies.

SANDEE COHEN
sandee@vectorbabe.com
www.vectorbabe.com

COMICSONE CORPORATION
Nicole Curry
48531 Warm Springs Blvd, Suite 408
Fremont, CA 94539
(510) 687-1388
nicole@comicsone.com
www.comicsone.com
Credits:
Kazan ©1997 Gaku Miyao
Joan ©1995 Yoshikazu Yasuhiko

JAMIE A. COSTA
25 Brian Road
Wappingers Falls, NY 12590
(845) 297-5477
jcosta1123@hotmail.com
Credits:
Interactive Portfolio
© Jami A. Costa

ICEHOUSE DESIGN
Bjørn Akselsen and Pattie Belle Hastings
www.icehousedesign.com

MICHAEL KING
KING DESIGN AS
Liaveien 11
Postboks 199, 1411 Kolbotn
Tel +47 66 80 30 66.
Fax +47 66 80 30 90.
mail@kingdesign.no
www.kingdesign.no

ADAM Z. LEIN
adamz@lein.com
www.adamlein.com

LIVEREADS
LiveReads ebooks can be purchased for
download from Barnes and Noble
(www.bn.com) or the online ebookstore,
Fictionwise (www.fictionwise.com).

LONN LORENZ
Adobe System, Inc.
345 Park Avenue, W13
San Jose, CA 95110
llorenz@adobe.com
Credits:
Craftman's Jeopardy
© Lonn Lorenz

PETER NEESE
Actino Software GmbH
Am Felde 132
22765 Hamburg, Germany
Tel +49 399 27 00
Fax +49 399 27 005
www.actino.de
Crossword Puzzle
© Peter Neese

MELISSA OLSEN
(718) 948-3665
moosebaby1@excite.com
Credits:
Coffee Chart
© Melissa Olsen

TED PADOVA
ted@west.net
www.west.net/~ted
Credits:
Acrobat eTips and Techniques Sampler
Acrobat Forms eTips and Techniques
Sampler
© Ted Padova

GLENN PAGE
GPM COMMUNICATIONS
20 Brookwood Drive
Vorhees, NJ 08043
(856) 783-5589
gpage@gpmconnect.com
www.gpmconnect.com
Credits:
GPM Brain, GPMC.pdf,
and Hudson & Felzer
© Glenn Page

JAMES MONACO
*Unet Corporation
80 East 11th Street
New York, NY 10003
(212) 777-5463 x313
jmonaco@unet.net
www.unet.net
www.readfilm.com
Credits:
How To Read film Multimedia Edition by
James Monaco. Published by harbor Electronic
Publishing; Art Director, David Lindroth;
Graphics, Nick Drjuchin; Editor Anne Sanow.
© James Monaco*

DEBORAH SHADOVITZ
*Author of the GoLive Bible
deb@shadovitz.com
www.shadovitz.com*

SHARON STEUER
www.zenofthepen.org

MELINDA VAN VLIET
*5 Orchard Trail
Monroe, NY 10950
Tel (845) 304-3853
melbip@yahoo.com
Credits:
Coffee Chart
© Melinda Van Vliet*

ANGUS WELLER
*Angus Weller Cartographic Services
2960 Cosgrove Crescent
Nanaimo, British Columbia,
Canada, V9S3P8
(250) 729-7292
weller@axion.net
www.mapmatrix.
Credits:
Cityscape: An Interactive Map
of the City of Nanaimo
© Weller Cartographic Services Limited
Interactive United States of America Map,
original base by the National Park Service
of America with additional cartographic
work by Weller Cartographic Services Ltd.
with permission obtained from the NPS.*

MAX WYSS
*PRODOK Engineering
Chapfstrasse 24,
CH-8906 Bonstetten, Switzerland
+41 1 700 29 21
max@prodok.com
www.prodok.com
Credits:
Swiss Holidays Planner: Illustration,
Design, Writing: Makiko Itoh
Concept, Programming: Max Wyss,
using the PRODOK Shopping Cart Toolkit
Photographs: Swiss Tourism
Pulley Designer: Client: René Baer AG,
Samstagern, Switzerland
Concept, Illustration, Design,
Programming: Max Wyss*

CHISA YAGI
*chisayagi@hotmail.com
Credits:
Rice Cooker & Interactive Portfolio
© Chisa Yagi*

YALE UNIVERSITY
*Graduate School of
Arts & Sciences
320 York Street
New Haven, CT 06520-8236
www.yale.edu/graduateschool*

PDF Resources

BOOKS/PERIODICALS

**Adobe Acrobat 5.0
Classroom in a Book**
*Adobe Creative Team
Adobe Press, 2001*

Adobe Acrobat 5.0 PDF Bible
*Ted Padova
Hungry Minds, Inc., 2001*

**Adobe Acrobat &
PDF Workflow**
*Incorporated Digital Media
CD-ROM
Digital Media Inc., 1998*

**Acrobat PDF and
Workflow in Detail**
*Frank Romano
Prentice Hall, 2000*

**Designing Interactive
Documents with
Adobe Acrobat Pro**
*John Deep and Peter Holfelder
John Wiley & Sons, 1996*

**Forms: Interactivity for
the World Wide Web**
*Malcolm Guthrie
Adobe Press, 1998*

**From Paper to Web:
How to Make Information
Instantly Accessible**
*Tony McKinley
Adobe Press, 1997*

Interactivity by Design
*Ray Kristof and Amy Satran
Adobe Press, 1995*

**Internet Publishing
With Acrobat:**
*A Comprehensive Reference
for Creating and Integrating
PDF Files With HTML on the
Internet or Intranets
Gordon Kent
Adobe Press, 1996*

PDF Printing and Workflow
*Frank Romano
Prentice Hall, 1998*

**PDF Reference, Second
Edition: Version 1.4**
*Adobe Systems, Inc.
Addison Wesley, 2001*

**PDF with Acrobat 5:
Visual QuickStart Guide**
*Jennifer Alspach
Peachpit Press, 2001*

**PDF Printing and Publishing:
The Next Revolution
After Gutenberg**
*Mattias Andersson, et al
Micro Pub Press, 1997*

**Postscript and
Acrobat/PDF Bible:**
*Applications, Troubleshooting
and Cross-Platform Publishing
Thomas Merz
Springer Verlag, 2002*

The Little Digital Video Book
*Michael Rubin
Peachpit Press, 2001*

**Web Publishing
with Acrobat/PDF**
*Thomas Merz
Springer Verlag, 1998*

**Web Publishing with
Adobe Acrobat and PDF**
*Bruce Page and Diana Holm
John Wiley & Sons, 1996*

Adobe
www.adobe.com/products/acrobat

PlanetPDF
www.planetpdf.com

PDFZone
www.pdfzone.com

Planet eBook
www.planetebook.com

Adobe
www.adobe.com/support/forums/main.html

PlanetPDF
www.planetpdf.com

PDFZone
www.pdfzone.com

Comp.Text.PDF Newsgroup
Google Groups:
Group: comp.text.pdf

There are hundreds of Acrobat and pdf related plug-ins and tools. We can't possibly list them all, but you'll find most of them at the ePublish store.

ePublish Store
www.epublishstore.com

Adobe
www.adobe.com/products/acrobat

PDF Zone
www.pdfzone.com

Lantana
www.lantanarips.com

ARTS
www.aroundtablesolution.com

Quite Software
www.quite.com

goBCL
www.gobcl.com

About the Authors

BJØRN AKSELSEN

Having moved to the U.S. from Norway at the age of 26, Bjørn continued a lifelong intellectual search, sheltering himself from reality in the halls of academia. This endeavour took him to places, such as Atlanta (where he met his wife and partner, Pattie Belle), Boston, New York, and finally, Yale University. After finishing his MFA in graphic design at Yale, Bjørn worked extensively with information architecture and visualization of complex information. Bjørn continues to lead Icehouse Design, specializing in education, arts, and the humanities, working with a variety of clients, including Yale University.

Bjørn's work has been published in international design books such as *Typographics 2 (London), New Logo/Trademark Design (Tokyo), Limited Color Graphics (Tokyo), Illustrator Wow Book (U.S.)*, and magazines such as *Visuelt (Norway)* and *Print's Regional Design Annual (U.S.)*. His work has been exhibited in Museum für Kunst und Gewerbe in Hamburg, Germany, and ArtSpace in New Haven, Connecticut.

Bjørn started collaborating with Pattie Belle in the early nineties at Icehouse Design. For over a decade, the studio has worked with a variety of clients, such as the Captain Planet Foundation of Turner Broadcasting Systems, High Museum of Art, IBM Atlanta Committee for the Olympic Games, and Yale University. Pattie Belle and Bjørn's collaborations also extend outside the design arena to arts projects, such as *Barrier Island,* and more recently, the authoring of this book.

PATTIE BELLE HASTINGS

PB (as we call her) was one of the early ones to got her hands on a Mac in the mid-eighties. Since then, not a day has gone by without serious computer brain.

Very early in life, PB established her own design practice. In addition to her design practice, PB has been teaching and has lectured across the country, such as at the AIGA.

Pattie Belle has been through most software at some point or other, but is often frustrated at either the low distribution of the programs and/or the steep learning curve involved. Enter Acrobat. While working on her MFA degree, she started experimenting with Acrobat as a means to quickly assemble multimedia elements and interaction as part of her thesis presentation. Since then, she has researched the program extensively, and has used it in cutting edge ways to create interactive experiences.

Her work with Acrobat has taken her on the road, from Seybold in Boston to a conference in Bergen, Norway. Years of using Acrobat for her art have also resulted in many articles, most notably a 10-page feature presentation in *Art Journal* Summer 2000 issue.

PB has always maintained a close connection to the more tactile and traditional art media, and has an extensive publishing and exhibition record as a book artist. Her titles, such as *If You Sleep on the Other Side, It Will go Away (Nexus Press, Atlanta), Alaska; Trail Tales and Eccentric Detours (Icehouse Press)* and *Elegy: An Intuitive Chronicle of War (Icehouse Press)*, have been distributed and collected in many institutions, such as the Museum of Modern Art

Library, NY, Harvard College Library, Yale University Library, and the New York Public Library, Special Collections. The duality between traditional methods and digital frontiers may seem odd to many, but to PB it is the essence of a career that refuses to be media specific.

Her artwork is frequently on the cusp of activist orientation, often garnering support and grants from institutions such as the NEA's regional awards (Southern Arts Federation). It is in this capacity that she has published books such as *Barrier Island*—a politically charged volume about a threatened natural ecologic system—with her husband, Bjørn, and collaborator Linda Armstrong.

In addition to her work, artist book career, and design practice, PB's teaching career spans over a decade. Pattie Belle is currently Associate Professor of Interactive Design at Quinnipiac University in Connecticut.

As if her other activities aren't enough, PB has been giving lectures in creative time management through a series of workshops called *Creating Time.*

SANDEE COHEN

Around 1987, Sandee was working at a New York advertising agency when a Macintosh II was set up for her creative group. Since she had a Macintosh SE at home, Sandee was constantly asked how to save a file, change kerning, or create colors. After a while, she realized that there was a market for someone who could teach "the machine" without using the geek-speak that most computer manuals were written in.

Sandee joyously left the world of Madison Avenue and has never looked back. Within a short period of time, she began teaching QuarkXPress and Illustrator classes for several private computer instruction schools in New York, as well as the New School Computer Instruction Center.

Around 1990, she began writing a monthly column on desktop publishing for the New York Macintosh Users Group. That monthly column has garnered writing assignments for magazines, such as *Step by Step Electronic Design*, *Design Graphics*, and *Macworld* magazine. Finally, she was asked by Peachpit Press to write some of their *Visual Quickstart Guide* books. She is also the co-author of *Non-Designer's Scan and Print Book*. Her most recent title is the *InDesign 2 Visual Quickstart Guide. Adobe Acrobat Master Class* is her tenth book for Peachpit Press.

Sandee is a frequent speaker for Seybold Seminars, Thunder Lizard conferences, and Macworld Expo. She started teaching Acrobat in 1997, with a special tutorial for Seybold Seminars on the use of Acrobat's multimedia presentation tools.

Sandee calls herself Vectorbabe and lives in New York City with her cat, Pixel.

Index

E